Praise for *The* Amistad *Rebellion*

"Gripping ... Superb ... As Marcus Rediker's new book reminds us, the place of the [*Amistad*] rebellion in popular memory hasn't always been secure."
—*The Nation*

"Vividly drawn ... This stunning book honors the achievement of the captive Africans who fought for—and won—their freedom."
—*The Philadelphia Tribune*

"The great strength of this work—aside from Rediker's vivid style as a writer and meticulous research—is that he brings the *Amistad* Africans back to center stage where they have often been pushed to the side."
—*Pittsburgh Post-Gazette*

"Rediker takes a fresh approach to the *Amistad* rebellion by focusing on the Africans who revolted rather than on the American political and judicial response, which takes the central place in most previous works."
—*Library Journal*

"A totally enthralling account of the *Amistad* rebellion and its place in the broader American story of revolt against a great threat to liberty."
—*Booklist* (starred review)

"A first-rate example of history told from the bottom up."
—*Kirkus Reviews* (starred review)

"Spectacularly researched and fluidly composed, this latest study offers some much needed perspective on a critical yet often overlooked event in America's history."
—*Publishers Weekly*

PENGUIN BOOKS

THE *AMISTAD* REBELLION

Marcus Rediker is Distinguished Professor of Atlantic History at the University of Pittsburgh. He has won numerous fellowships and book awards and lectured around the world. He is the author of five other books, including (with Peter Linebaugh) *The Many-Headed Hydra: Sailors, Slaves, Commoners, and the Hidden History of the Revolutionary Atlantic* and, most recently, *The Slave Ship: A Human History,* which won the George Washington Book Prize.

The *Amistad* Rebellion

AN ATLANTIC ODYSSEY OF SLAVERY AND FREEDOM

3 feet 3 in. high

Marcus Rediker

PENGUIN BOOKS

PENGUIN BOOKS
Published by the Penguin Group
Penguin Group (USA) LLC
375 Hudson Street
New York, New York 10014

USA | Canada | UK | Ireland | Australia | New Zealand | India | South Africa | China
penguin.com
A Penguin Random House Company

First published in the United States of America by Viking Penguin, a member of Penguin Group (USA) Inc., 2012
Published with a new preface and epilogue in Penguin Books 2013

Illustration credits appear on pages 287–88.

THE LIBRARY OF CONGRESS HAS CATALOGED THE HARDCOVER EDITION AS FOLLOWS:
Rediker, Marcus.
    The Amistad rebellion : an Atlantic odyssey of slavery and freedom / Marcus Rediker.
    p.   cm.
Includes bibliographical references and index.
ISBN 978-0-670-02504-6 (hc.)
ISBN 978-0-14-312398-9 (pbk.)
    1. Slave insurrections—United States.   2. Amistad (Schooner)   3. Antislavery movements—United States.   4. Slave trade—America—History.   5. Sierra Leoneans—United States—History—19th century. I. Title.
    E447.R44 2012
    326.0973—dc23
    2012014810

Printed in the United States of America
10 9 8 7 6 5 4 3 2 1

Designed by Carla Bolte • Set in Adobe Palatino LT Std. with Bodoni Ornaments ITC

For Wendy,

with love

CONTENTS

Two unusual developments have led to an expanded paperback edition of this book. In April 2013 a significant new body of archival sources concerning the *Amistad* case became available for study through the Connecticut Historical Society in Hartford. These were letters written by a twenty-one-year-old woman, Charlotte Cowles, a member of a prominent abolitionist family based in Farmington, Connecticut, where the *Amistad* Africans lived for eight months after the United States Supreme Court ruled in favor of their freedom in March 1841. The Cowles family was one of several that settled and helped to care for the Africans, which meant that Charlotte spent a great deal of time with them and got to know many of them personally. Indeed, one of the three little girls, Kagne, lived in the Cowles household and would subsequently take the name "Charlotte," suggesting her close relationship with the writer of the missives. The letters offer an extraordinarily intimate portrait, from an eyewitness, of many of the Africans in the months before their repatriation to Sierra Leone in November 1841.

In May 2013 I traveled to Sierra Leone in search of local memory of the *Amistad* rebellion in the place where the epic tale began. With three Sierra Leone specialists, Konrad Tuchscherer and Philip Misevich, both of St. John's University, and Taziff Koroma, of Fourah Bay College in Freetown, I visited ten villages and other sites associated with the case to talk to elders about oral traditions and their history. I found that parts of the story have been lost, but other parts preserved and retained, through the stories "my great-grandfather told me," as we heard again and again. I also found—with the help of local fishermen along the Kerefe River—the long-lost ruins of Lomboko, the slave-trading fortress from which the *Amistad* Africans and thousands of others were launched into the violent, lucrative Atlantic slave system. Like Charlotte Cowles, I too became something of an eyewitness, learning new truths about the nature of the rebellion and the people who made it.

Both developments serve the central purpose of this book: to tell the heretofore neglected African side of the *Amistad* tale—to show who the rebels were, how they thought and acted, and why they were able to capture a slave ship and gain their freedom, in a rare, profound, influential, and historic act. The new evidence deepens our knowledge of one of the most important events in the common history of Africa, America, and the Atlantic that connects them.

The *Amistad* Rebellion

Voices

During the moonless early hours of July 2, 1839, several captive Africans quietly slipped out of their fetters in the hold of the slave schooner *La Amistad*. One of them had managed to break a padlock, which made it possible to remove the chain that reeved them together and held them down in the hold below the main deck of the vessel. Forty-nine men and four children made up the human cargo of the *Amistad*. They had sailed from Havana, bound for the new plantations of Puerto Príncipe (Camagüey), Cuba. A few hours earlier, in cramped, airless quarters below deck, they had made a collective decision to seek a different fate.

A group of four men—Cinqué, Faquorna, Moru, and Kimbo—led the way as they climbed up and out of the hatchway onto the main deck. They moved with the grace and precision of warriors accustomed to daring midnight attacks. They picked up belaying pins and barrel staves and stole over to the ship's boat, where the mulatto cook and slave sailor Celestino lay sleeping. They bludgeoned him to death. As more men escaped their irons and swarmed up on deck, they opened a box of cane knives, tools they were meant to use in cutting sugar cane, but which would now serve the purpose of self-emancipation. The sight of flashing blades caused the two sailors who were supposed to guard against such uprisings to fly over the side of the vessel into the water. Captain Ramón Ferrer armed himself and fought back against the insurgents, killing one and mortally wounding another. Four or five of their comrades counterattacked, surrounding the captain and slashing him to death.

In a matter of minutes the *Amistad* rebels had turned the ship's wooden world upside down. They captured the two men who had considered themselves their owners, José Ruiz and Pedro Montes, clapped them in manacles, and sent them below deck as their prisoners. They took control of the ship and organized themselves to do the hard work of sailing it. But in their new-won freedom lay a dilemma: they wanted to return to their homes in southern Sierra Leone, but none of them knew how to navigate the schooner. After some debate they decided to keep the surviving Spaniards alive in order to help them sail the vessel eastward, toward the rising sun, which had been at their backs as they made the Middle Passage on a slave ship two weeks earlier.

Montes had been a merchant ship captain; he was experienced in the ways of the sea and shrewd in the ways of men. He used his specialized knowledge of the deep-sea sailing ship to deceive his new masters. During the day, he followed orders, sailing east, but he had the sails kept loose and flapping in the wind to slow the *Amistad*'s progress. By night he steered the vessel back to the west and the north, hoping to stay near the islands of the Caribbean and the coast of North America in order to be intercepted and saved. After eight weeks, he got his wish: a U.S. Navy survey ship captured the *Amistad* off Culloden Point, Long Island, and carried the Africans, the Spaniards, the cargo, and the schooner to New London, Connecticut.

What would happen to these African rebels now anchored in one of the world's leading slave societies? Would they be returned to Cuba to be tried—and certainly executed—for their crimes of mutiny, murder, and piracy, as the diplomats of Spain, and many American slaveholders, demanded? Or would they, as Lewis Tappan and other abolitionists on both sides of the Atlantic insisted, in the aftermath of the abolition of the slave trade, be allowed to go free? Had they not defended their own natural rights by killing the tyrant who enslaved them? These questions would engage people of all stations and several nations in fierce debate, propelling the *Amistad* rebels to the center of a massive controversy about slavery and the rights of unfree people to shape their own destiny. The rebellion became one of the most important events of its time.

An epic struggle ensued. Assisted in their legal battles by distinguished attorneys Roger S. Baldwin and former president John Quincy Adams, who made dramatic speeches before the United States Supreme Court in February and March 1841, the *Amistad* rebels won their freedom, to the joy of half the nation and the consternation of the other half. After a successful fund-raising tour organized by abolitionists, the rebels set sail for their African homelands in November of that year. The abolitionist movement claimed a great, historic, and altogether unlikely victory.

———

The popular memory of the *Amistad* rebellion has ebbed and flowed with the political tides. In its own day the event captured the popular imagination. A mere six days after the vessel had been towed into port, a drama troupe at New York's Bowery Theatre performed a play about its story of mutiny and piracy. Commercial artists converged on the jail where the *Amistad* Africans were incarcerated, drew images of Cinqué, the leader of the rebellion, reproduced them quickly and cheaply, and had them hawked by boys on the streets of eastern cities. Artist Amasa Hewins would paint a 135-foot panorama depicting the *Amistad* Africans as they surrounded and killed Captain Ferrer and seized their freedom by force of arms. Another artist, Sidney Moulthrop, would create twenty-nine life-size wax figures of the Africans and the *Amistad* crew, cast and arranged to dramatize the shipboard insurrection. Both artists would tour with their creations, charging admission to those eager to see a visual reenactment of the uprising. Meantime, thousands of people lined up daily to pay admission and walk through the jails of New Haven and Hartford to get a glimpse of the *Amistad* rebels, who were "political prisoners" before the phrase had been invented. When the case moved to law, citizens jammed the courtrooms to capacity and beyond, refusing to leave their seats during breaks for fear of losing them. Ministers delivered thundering sermons; correspondents wrote hundreds of highly opinionated newspaper articles; poets penned romantic verses; and those for and against slavery debated furiously, all about the *Amistad* rebels, what they had done, its morality and meaning, and what their fate should be. Discussed in public as never before, slave resistance became not only a main political issue of the day, but a commercial entertainment—a commodity that circulated in the ever-growing American marketplace, shaping public opinion and ultimately the outcome of the case.

The fascination would not last. After the Civil War the memory of the *Amistad* waned, barely kept alive by two related groups: abolitionists and African American writers and artists who wanted to glory in victory and remember the long, arduous struggle against slavery. In the dark times of Social Darwinism and scientific racism the *Amistad* uprising faded from public view. It disappeared from histories of the United States written in the late nineteenth and early twentieth centuries, and indeed it saw no major revival until new social movements exploded in the 1960s and 1970s. Especially important in this regard were the civil rights and black power movements with their demands for a new history of the United States that took seriously the long, bloody battle against slavery and racism. The Mississippi Freedom Summer Schools taught about the *Amistad* rebellion, while activists named their sons Cinqué after its heroic leader. "History from below" raised the consciousness of struggles past and present, and post-'60s historians made the *Amistad* story part of a new, more democratic and inclusive vision of the American past. Yet knowledge of the shipboard insurrection among the general public remained limited.[1]

A new phase in popular memory and culture began in 1997 with the appearance of Steven Spielberg's movie *Amistad*, which carried the history to millions of viewers, many of whom had never before known of it. Although not a commercial success, the film had a broad impact, creating a veritable cottage industry around the history of the event: school curricula incorporated the rebellion; children's coloring books depicted it; museums and art galleries celebrated it; novels, plays, and operas dramatized it. Independent efforts by organizers in

Connecticut to fund and re-create the vessel came to fruition after the appearance of Spielberg's film, resulting in a modern *Amistad* based in Mystic Seaport.[2]

The history and especially the movie gave the *Amistad* insurrection a renewed presence in American popular culture. The rebellion rapidly became one of the best-known events involving slavery in all of American history, and Cinqué joined Underground Railroad "conductor" Harriet Tubman and runaway slave-turned-eloquent-abolitionist Frederick Douglass as the most recognizable individuals of African descent associated with the histories of slavery and resistance in America.[3]

Yet the history and the movie have told only part of the story. The drama of the courtroom has eclipsed the original drama that transpired on the deck of the slave schooner. The American actors—abolitionists, attorneys, judges, and politicians—have elbowed aside the African ones whose daring actions set the train of events in motion. Curiously, the American legal system has emerged as the story's hero—the very system which, in 1839, held two and a half million African Americans in bondage. This triumphalism may be comforting to an American audience still haunted by the legacy of slavery, but it is deeply misleading.

This book tells the story of the *Amistad* in a different way. It begins in southern Sierra Leone, in West Africa, where those who would eventually find themselves aboard the *Amistad* were, by various means, captured and enslaved, inaugurating an odyssey of epic proportions. These multiethnic people—mostly Mende, but also Temne, Gbandi, Kono, Gola, and Loma—came from humble backgrounds. They were commoners and workers; a few had been slaves. Born of societies that shared commonalities of belief and culture, these West Africans began a long, slow process of social bonding and self-organization, first at the Lomboko slave-trading "factory" on the Gallinas Coast, where they were held for several weeks awaiting Atlantic transport on a slave ship called the *Teçora*. Under the extreme, terrifying conditions of the Middle Passage they bonded as "shipmates," cooperating for the sake of survival. The process continued in

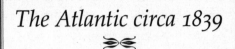

The Atlantic circa 1839

NORTH AMERICA

45°

Hartford
New Haven • Boston
New York
Philadelphia • New London
Washington, D.C. *Long Island*
VIRGINIA
Richmond — *Chesapeake Bay*

• Charleston

Atlantic

New Orleans
30°

Gulf of Mexico

BAHAMAS

Havana
CUBA **HAITI/SANTO DOMINGO**
Puerto Príncipe **PUERTO RICO**

JAMAICA

Caribbean Sea
15°

— **TRINIDAD**

Pacific Ocean

0°

SOUTH AMERICA

BRAZIL

© 2012 Jeffrey L. Ward

75° 60° 45°

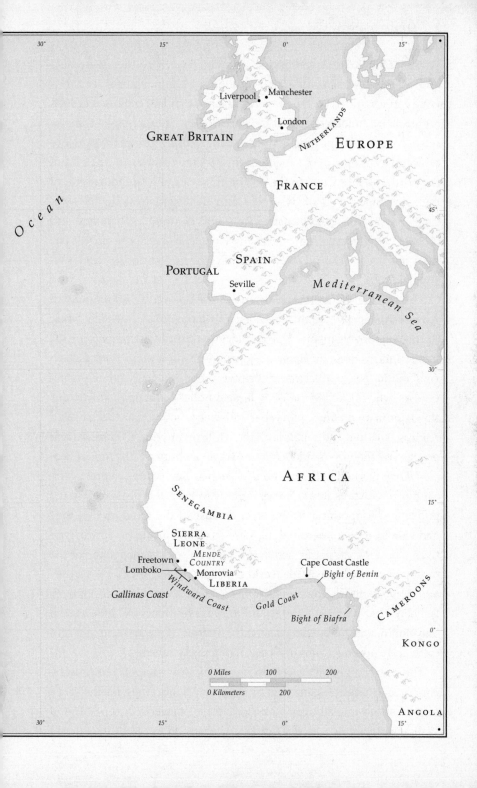

30° 15° 0° 15°

Ocean

GREAT BRITAIN

Liverpool Manchester

London

NETHERLANDS

EUROPE

FRANCE

45°

PORTUGAL

SPAIN

Seville

Mediterranean Sea

30°

AFRICA

15°

SENEGAMBIA

SIERRA
LEONE

MENDE
COUNTRY

Freetown
Lomboko

Monrovia

LIBERIA

Cape Coast Castle
Bight of Benin

CAMEROONS

Gallinas Coast

Windward Coast

Gold Coast

Bight of Biafra

0°

KONGO

0 Miles 100 200

0 Kilometers 200

ANGOLA

30° 15° 0° 15°

the barracoons, or slave barracks, of Havana, where they were held and, after two weeks, sold under humiliating circumstances, as if they were cattle. Guided by the practices of a powerful all-male secret society in their homelands called the Poro Society, they organized themselves to carry out the rebellion aboard the *Amistad*. Under the pressure of necessity they worked together to sail the vessel 1,400 miles from the north coast of Cuba to the northern tip of Long Island; several of their comrades died of dysentery and dehydration along the way. Captured by the United States Navy and charged with piracy and murder, they were incarcerated in New Haven, Connecticut. The maritime leg of the odyssey featured violence, suffering, and self-emancipation.

The rebels now took their drama of slavery and freedom onto an American stage. Once they reached the shores of Connecticut, their courageous revolt inspired profound popular interest among artists, playwrights, actors, theatergoers, journalists and writers, readers, lawyers and judges, politicians, and citizens, but especially among abolitionists, who flocked to the jail in large numbers. The *Amistad* Africans slowly built an alliance with other antislavery activists as they studied reading, writing, and religion, all the while organizing themselves and developing their own independent African identity as "the Mendi People." They worked with abolitionists such as Lewis Tappan and political figures such as John Quincy Adams to keep their case before the public and to mount a strong legal defense of the freedom that they had won by arms aboard the *Amistad*. The small group of African captives who took desperate action on the high seas caused some of the most powerful people in the world to debate the meaning of what they had done, including monarchs (Queen Victoria of Britain and Queen Isabella II of Spain), presidents and former presidents (Adams, Martin Van Buren, and John Tyler), statesmen, high-ranking government officials, and Supreme Court justices, among many others.

The meaning of the rebellion and trials was shaped not only by American political realities but by broader Atlantic ones, for the *Amistad* had sailed into a huge and historic wave of slave resistance. David Walker's *Appeal . . . to the Coloured Citizens of the World* (1829) had emphasized the continuing relevance to freedom struggles of Toussaint Louverture and the Haitian Revolution. Sailors black and white spread the revolutionary word by smuggling the pamphlet into slave societies. Nat Turner had led a bloody uprising in Southampton County, Virginia, in 1831, and Sam Sharpe had followed with his "Baptist War" in Jamaica in 1831–32. Other revolts, for example, in Brazil and Cuba, erupted against the backdrop of a growing abolitionist movement and indeed helped to make it possible. William Lloyd Garrison founded the *Liberator* in 1831 and Great Britain abolished slavery in its West Indian colonies in two stages, in 1834 and 1838.[4]

Wherever contemporaries debated the meaning of the *Amistad* rebellion, the ghosts of Walker, Toussaint Louverture, and Turner hovered above their heads. *Noticioso de Ambos Mundos*, a Spanish-language newspaper published in New York, posed a "delicate question" amid the debate about whether the *Amistad* rebels should go free: "Let us then see if the [American] Government establishes the principle that it is lawful for a slave to kill his master, because then they can with impunity rise up in Washington, and slay all masters and all members of the Government that allowed slavery." The broad Atlantic struggle against slavery generated the larger meaning of the *Amistad* controversy.[5]

The meeting of African insurrectionists and American reformers in the New Haven jail was an unprecedented and historic moment. The rebels had made a revolution in miniature aboard the ship, which inspired sympathetic coverage in the press, especially the *New York Sun*, and in turn generated intense fascination among the public. Tappan and other abolitionists responded, struggling to control and direct the enormous popular interest toward their own purposes, building in the process a determined, energetic, interracial defense campaign. Many who supported the *Amistad* struggle were not, strictly speaking, abolitionists; moreover, they celebrated the heroic insurrection in ways that made moderate abolitionists uneasy. The Africans themselves, through their actions on the vessel and their noble bearing in jail, continued to inspire an unprecedented interest in the fearsome subject of slave revolt. To many, especially African Americans enslaved and free, the *Amistad* rebels rekindled the radical egalitarian hope of the American Revolution.[6]

The insurrectionists and reformers who met in Connecticut jails represented the two main wings of a global movement against slavery. Black rebels had long played an important role in America's antislavery movement, especially by their audacious escapes from slavery, which inspired and mobilized abolitionists throughout the northern states. The *Amistad* case publicized a more controversial form of resistance—outright rebellion—and gave enslaved rebels and their resistance a more important place in an expanded, radicalized movement against slavery. This movement would help to establish the right of unfree people to seize freedom through armed self-defense and to claim their place as equals in society.[7]

Even though slave resistance was ubiquitous throughout the turbulent 1830s, revolts were infrequent, even rare, occurrences, especially in the United States. Slaveholders always enforced the consequences of a failed revolt with hangings, maimings, and violent repression of all kinds. Most slaves, like most other people, were reluctant to risk everything in a gamble few before them had won. But an example of success changed everything. This, of course, was part of the importance of the Haitian Revolution. The black men and women of Saint Domingue had demonstrated the bottom rail could be placed on top. Until 1839, slaves in mainland North America could find no similar example of success. Slave rebels had failed in New York in 1712 and 1741; in Richmond, Virginia, in 1800; in Louisiana in 1811; and in Charleston, South Carolina, in 1822. That record of failure changed in 1839, and with it changed the worlds of American slavery and abolition.

———

A history of the *Amistad* rebellion from below is supported by a collection of sources unique in the annals of New World slavery. Because the makers of the maritime insurrection spent twenty-seven months in Connecticut (nineteen of them in jail) and because their cause was both controversial and well publicized, they met thousands of people from all walks of life, both within the walls of the jails and without.

Journalists and ordinary citizens visited them, conversed with them through translators such as the Mende sailor James Covey, and transcribed their life stories, noting their work and nationality (hunter, Temne), where they lived in Africa ("two moons march to the coast"), and how they were enslaved (captured in war, kidnapped). Other visitors drew their portraits and silhouettes. Phrenologists measured the size of their skulls. Yale professors such as Josiah Gibbs compiled and published vocabularies of their languages. Many of these visitors published their findings in business newspapers such as the *New York Journal of Commerce*, in penny-press papers such as the *New York Sun* and *New York Morning Herald*, and in abolitionist periodicals such as the *Emancipator* and the *Pennsylvania Freeman*. As many as 2,500 articles were published altogether, many of them written by correspondents who had visited the African rebels in jail. No other makers of a modern slave revolt generated such a vast and deep body of evidence, which in turn makes it possible to know more about the *Amistad* Africans than perhaps any other group of once-enslaved rebels on record, and to get to know them, individually and collectively, in intimate, multidimensional ways, from their personalities and sense of humor to their specifically West African ways of thinking and acting during their ordeal.[8]

Throughout their odyssey the *Amistad* rebels struggled—sometimes alongside the American abolitionists, sometimes against them—for a voice of their own. As abolitionist Joshua Leavitt noted soon after they were brought ashore, "these unfortunate persons, who have been committed to prison and bound over to be tried for their lives" could not "say a word for themselves." Of course the rebels could and did say many words for themselves, but for weeks no one could understand them. Here enter a group of African sailors, most notably James Ferry, Charles Pratt, and James Covey, whose cosmopolitan knowledge of multiple languages finally allowed the rebels to tell their stories of origins, enslavement, and insurrection. Ferry had been liberated from slavery in Colombia at age twelve by Simón Bolívar, Pratt and Covey by the British naval anti-slave-trade patrols. They were

experienced in the struggle against slavery and they would be denounced by proslavery critics as "half-civilized, totally ignorant" sailors, who, like other men of color and low standing, were not to be
trusted or believed. The motley crews of ship and waterfront played a
critical role in the *Amistad* case.[9]

Leavitt's observation lingers. The *Amistad* rebels' struggle for voice
led them to learn English, to study American political culture and to
use it for their own ends, to tell both individual and collective stories
about what had happened to them and why. Even so, it was no easy
matter for them to be heard, in their own times, above or even alongside the voices of evangelical Christians; lawyers, politicians, and diplomats; middle-class antislavery reformers; and proslavery ideologues.
And it has proved no easy matter to hear them today. This is a history
of the *Amistad* rebellion from below. That, literally, is how and where
the *Amistad* case began, with the eruption of armed rebels from the
hold on to the main deck of the vessel. By viewing the courtroom
drama in relation to the shipboard revolt, or, put another way, the
actions taken from above in relation to those taken from below, the
entire event, from causes to consequences, appears in a new light. This
history puts the *Amistad* rebels back at the center of their own story
and the larger history they helped to make. Theirs was an epic quest
for freedom.[10]

CHAPTER ONE

Origins

On a May evening in 1841, an overflow crowd at the Presbyterian Church on Coates Street in Philadelphia listened as a Mende man named Fuli spoke about "man-stealing" in his native southern Sierra Leone: "If Spanish man want to steal man, he no steal him himself, but hire black man; he pay him I don't know how much." Fuli referred to the urbane, cigar-smoking Spanish slave trader Pedro Blanco and his ally, the African King Siaka, who dressed in gold lace garments, drank from silver bowls, and mobilized soldiers and kidnappers in the interior of the Gallinas Coast. "The man catchers live in villages," continued Fuli, "and honest people live in cities. If they come to the cities, the magistrate say you bad man, you go away." Some "honest people" took more direct action: they shot the man-stealers as they would other beasts of prey, "lions and tigers." Fuli and others sought to protect themselves against the slave traders, but they did not always succeed, as his own presence in Philadelphia attested. Fuli then demonstrated his knowledge of the Bible to the audience, interpreting his own experience and that of his comrades on the *Amistad*: "The man stealer, he walk crooked, he no walk straight, he get out of the high road. He walk by night, too, he no walk in the day time." He referred, in a single answer, to the books of Deuteronomy (24:7), Psalms (82:5), and Isaiah (59:8). He himself had been stolen around two and half years earlier by those who walked—and enslaved—in darkness.[1]

Until that fateful moment, Fuli, whose name meant "sun," had lived

Fuli

in Mano with his parents and five brothers, humble people who farmed rice and manufactured cloth. A portrait drawn by a young American artist, William H. Townsend, depicted him with a mustache, a broad face, prominent cheekbones, a full forehead with a slightly receding hairline, and distinctive, almond-shaped eyes. He was five feet three inches tall, apparently unmarried, and said to be "in middle life," which probably meant his late twenties. According to one who knew him, Fuli was a "noble-spirited" man and decidedly not someone who could be enslaved without resistance.[2]

One night, in darkness, a group of King Siaka's soldiers surrounded Mano and set it aflame. Fuli said that "some were killed, and he with the rest were taken prisoners." Apparently separated from his family (their fate is unknown), he began a monthlong march through Vai country and ended up at Fort Lomboko on the coast, where he was purchased by the notorious Pedro Blanco. He was a victim of "grand pillage," a brutal, plundering kind of warfare that had long helped to fill Atlantic slave ships with bodies.[3]

Margru, one of four children aboard the *Amistad*, took a different route to the slave ship. Born in Mendeland, she was about nine years old, a mere four feet three inches tall. Her name reflected parental love and affection. Townsend sketched her with a large, high forehead,

Margru

curly hair platted above each ear, and a slight smile at the corners of her mouth. Her manner was pleasant, quiet, reserved, and rather shy. She lived with her parents, four sisters, and two brothers. Her father was a trader, whose practices of credit and debt entangled him in some way with the slave trade. He pawned Margru, meaning that he left her in the possession of another trader for an agreed-upon period of time as a surety against commodities he had been advanced on credit—a practice common to many parts of West Africa. When he did not return in time to pay off his creditor—literally to redeem Margru—she was enslaved to satisfy the debt.[4]

Moru was a Gbandi man, born in Sanka. His life took a hard turn when, as a child, both of his parents died. Surviving evidence does not suggest how he grew up, or with whom, but it appears that at some point he became a warrior, and eventually a slave; perhaps he was captured in battle. His master, Margona, a member of what would become the ruling house of Barri Chiefdom in the Pujehun District of Gola, was a man of wealth with "ten wives and many houses." At some point, for reasons unknown, Margona sold Moru to a slave trader, who marched him twenty days (probably a couple of hundred miles) to Lomboko, where he was sold to Belewa, or "Great Whiskers," a Spaniard. Moru was described as "middle age, 5 ft. 8 ½ in. with full

Moru

negro features," and drawn by Townsend to have small eyes, full lips, high cheekbones, and a somewhat suspicious look.[5]

The webs of Atlantic slavery were broad and intricate, and many of the people who guided and shaped the destinies of Fuli, Margru, and Moru, as well as Siaka and his warriors and Blanco and his overseers, lived far from the societies where man-stealing took place. Decisions taken by kings and queens and presidents, imperial planners, merchants, and plantation owners profoundly influenced what happened to the two men and little girl who found themselves at Lomboko and eventually aboard a slave ship under sail to Havana. Intercontinental and transoceanic forces linked England and Spain to the Gallinas Coast, and, across the Atlantic, to the slave societies of the Americas, especially Cuba, Brazil, and the United States. The process and the logic that governed from afar the lives of captives at Lomboko, and indeed millions of others, were clearly explained a generation earlier in an unusual tract published in London.

The Voice of Blood

In 1792, at the peak of a broad popular agitation against the slave trade in Great Britain, an abolitionist published an anonymous pamphlet, in which Cushoo, an African who had been enslaved in Jamaica, engaged an English gentleman, aptly named Mr. English, in conversation. Cushoo had been owned by a friend of Mr. English. He begins by saying, "Ah! Massa Buckra, pity poor Negroman." Mr. English responds, "Why, Cushoo, what's the matter?" The matter, in short, was capitalism and slavery—more specifically, how a violent, exploitative global system hid its true nature in the benign form of commodities, especially slave labor–produced sugar and rum, the likes of which Mr. English and others around the world consumed, without understanding how they were produced and at what human cost.[6]

Mr. English does not understand, but the ever-patient and outwardly deferential Cushoo answers his questions and, in so doing, challenges the rationalizations that lie behind them. He explains in simple, vivid terms how the slave trade and slavery actually work. He shows that the pleasure Mr. English takes in eating sugar depends on the misery of the many. Those who produce his sugar are violently exploited in Jamaica and yet invisible in England. The material chains of slavery and the global chain of commodities are linked.

As the conversation unfolds, Cushoo gives the English gentleman what amounts to a lesson in the political economy of global capitalism. The message is that everything turns on commodities. The "poor Negro was bought and sold like cattle." The slave trade is fueled by "brandy, rum, guns, and gunpowder," which create wars throughout West Africa and in so doing help to manufacture the ultimate Atlantic commodity: the slave. By consuming the commodities rum and sugar, Mr. English supports the slave trade and the extreme violence on which it depends.

"In what manner?" asks the agitated gentleman.

"You pay for kidnap and murder of poor Negro," comes the quick retort.

> E. How? I don't understand you.
> C. O me soon make you understand, Massa—You pay de grocer—

E. Yes, or he wou'd not thank me for my custom.

C. Den de grocer pay de Merchant—de merchant de Sugar Planter—him pay de Slave Captain—de Slave Captain pay de Panyarer [kidnapper], de Cabosheer [village chief], or de Black King.

E. By this round-a-bout way you make us all thieves and murderers.

C. No round-about Massa, it come home straight line—only—

Cushoo thus invites Mr. English to follow the money involved in creating the commodity, from England, to Jamaica, to Africa, and back again. He wants Mr. English to join the abolitionist boycott of sugar that was then gaining strength throughout England. Cushoo had learned from previous struggles what might now be possible. His friend "Yalko say dat good while ago dey drink no tea in 'Merica—de Bostonian trow all in de sea. Ha! Ha! Dey made tea wid salt water." An Atlantic cycle of rebellion meant no tea then, hence the Boston Tea Party, and no sugar now. In the end, Cushoo's combination of historical knowledge, worldly experience, and pidgin eloquence persuades Mr. English to join the sugar boycott.

The pamphlet articulated what would eventually become one of the slogans of the antislavery movement: "sugar is made with blood." The point was announced in the title of the pamphlet: *No Rum! No Sugar! or, The Voice of Blood.* Cushoo would be the "voice of blood" in order to illustrate two passages from the Bible:

"What hast thou done? The Voice of thy Brother's Blood Crieth unto me from the ground." (Genesis 4: 10)

"My God forbid it!—shall I drink the blood of these men?" (I Chronicles 11: 19).

For perhaps the first time in history a member of a mass movement for fundamental social change had made a simultaneous popular critique of the exploitation of labor, the commodity form, and the capitalist world market. In this scenario, consumers were unconscious vampires.

Fuli, Margru, Moru, and indeed all of the *Amistad* Africans exemplified Cushoo's argument. The man-stealer may have walked crooked, as Fuli said, but the straight line of the Middle Passage, from expropriation in Africa to exploitation in the Americas, was an axis of modern capitalism. The profits to be made in a far-reaching system of sugar production shaped the enslavement of Mende, Gbandi, Temne, Kono, and others inland from the Gallinas Coast of West Africa, their transportation across the Atlantic aboard the Portuguese or Brazilian slave ship *Teçora*, their landing in Havana, Cuba, and their reshipment aboard the *Amistad* for Puerto Príncipe and its hinterland booming with the production of sugar. Cubans shared the early nineteenth-century aphorism: "Con sangre se hace azúcar"—Sugar is made with blood.[7]

The Atlantic in 1839

The Atlantic coordinates of the *Amistad* rebellion were London and Seville in Europe, the seats of the British and Spanish empires, whose monarchs, Queen Victoria and Queen Isabella, took an interest in the case; Cuba and the northern Caribbean, where the rebels were meant to work and where the revolt exploded; Connecticut and Washington, DC, where the trials took place and high-ranking American politicians, including presidents and ex-presidents, as well as middle-class reformers, got involved; and the Gallinas Coast of West Africa and its hinterlands, where Pedro Blanco, King Siaka, Fuli, Margru, and Moru lived. The growing capitalist economy linked these people, disparate of class and region, within a larger Atlantic economic transformation that combined bondage and industrialism.[8]

In 1839 Great Britain was the "workshop of the world." It was the first industrial nation and the preeminent imperial power, not least because of its Royal Navy. Manufacturing and maritime power went hand in hand. Merchant ships linked the markets of the world and naval ships protected Britain's interests therein. The island nation's role in the *Amistad* affair was indirect but important. Because the social movement that produced *The Voice of Blood* had successfully abolished the slave trade in 1807, and had pushed the state to conclude treaties with Spain and Portugal to end their slave trades, the British navy was deployed on the coast of West Africa to intercept illegal slave ships, waging a kind of war by sea against the trade. The Gallinas Coast was a major theater of battle, especially after the same movement abolished slavery throughout the British Empire in 1838. Pedro Blanco and his slave factories would be targets of special importance for the anti-slave-trade patrols.[9]

Spain had long dominated the Atlantic world, but was in decline in 1839, much of its vast empire destroyed by the Spanish–American wars of independence that took place between 1808 and 1829. Standing out amid the ruins, however, was the dynamic colony of Cuba, whose rise as a sugar-producing power owed everything to a successful revolution a generation earlier in neighboring St. Domingue, where 500,000 enslaved Africans had altered the course of world history. Until 1791 they had produced almost a third of the world's sugar, made with blood under the most horrific conditions. Their revolution, coupled with the decline of sugar production in British colonies after abolition, opened the global market for sugar planters in Cuba and Brazil, who became the world's hungriest consumers of transatlantic slave labor in the early nineteenth century. In 1839, enslaved people of African descent made up about 45 percent of Cuba's one million people. The illegal slave trade boomed and sugar production soared. In the half century between the beginning of the Haitian Revolution and the *Amistad* rebellion, Cuba's sugar production increased ninefold, making the Spanish colony the world's new leading source of the sweet commodity. The voice of blood was calling with full-throated urgency.[10]

The United States was a fledgling power, an increasingly massive continental empire in its own right, and one deeply riven by conflicts over the institution of slavery. With a highly productive agricultural hinterland based on family farms and free labor in the north and on plantations and slave labor in the south, and a growing class of industrial workers located primarily in the northeast, the United States was pursuing continental expansion—its "manifest destiny"—and Native American groups, one after another, suffered bloody expropriation. As slavery expanded westward, the abolitionist movement grew amid a logic of polarization between north and south. The arrival of the

Amistad rebels off the coast of Long Island in August 1839 was seen in some antislavery quarters as positively providential. It would rile the nation.[11]

When the *Amistad* Africans departed Lomboko in April 1839, they sailed head-on into a huge and historic wave of slave resistance that had been rippling around the Atlantic for a decade. From Toussaint Louverture to David Walker and Nat Turner, rebels throughout the Americas had struggled against a common plight. Resistance to slavery also convulsed the home region of the *Amistad* rebels in this period, as people captured by King Siaka and settled in "slave towns" rose up and waged a long, bitter, and partially successful struggle for freedom, the Zawo War, between 1825 and 1842. The *Amistad* rebellion may be seen as an oceanic extension of this struggle in West Africa and a linchpin that connected it to Brazil, Cuba, Haiti, Jamaica, and Virginia—an Atlantic geography of resistance. Taken together with the revolt led by former Virginia slave Madison Washington aboard the American slave ship *Creole* in November 1841, it capped a formative, decadelong wave of rebellion.[12]

Origins of the Amistad Africans

The slave trade tried to create a faceless, anonymous mass of laborers for the plantations, but the *Amistad* Africans can be known as individuals—who they were, where they were from, what nations and ethnic groups they were part of, what sorts of work they had done, what kinds of families they had lived in, how old and how tall they were, and finally, how they were enslaved and how they got to Fort Lomboko on the Gallinas Coast. Much can be known about the thirty-six men and children who were still alive in early 1840, considerably less about eight others who can be identified by name, bringing the total to forty-four of the fifty-three Africans who were aboard the schooner during the uprising. Little evidence has survived about the other nine. Everything the rebels did, from the moment of enslavement to the moment of repatriation and afterward, was based to a large extent on their experiences in Africa before capture.[13]

The *Amistad* Africans were multiethnic, or motley: the original fifty-three consisted of people from at least nine different groups. The dominant group were the Mende. Of the thirty-seven for whom a cultural identity can be recovered, at least twenty-five, and as many as twenty-eight, including Fuli and Margru, called themselves Mende. Four—Moru, Burna (the elder), Sessi, and Weluwa—were Gbandi. Bagna, Konoma, and Sa were Kono. Pugnwani was from the Kono chiefdom of Sando. Pie and his son Fuliwulu were Temne, while Gnakwoi was Loma, Beri was Gola, and Tua was Bullom. Burna suggested that among the ten men who died at sea after the rebellion were one Kissi and one from the multiethnic Kondo confederation. This represents most of the major culture groups of southern and eastern Sierra Leone in the first half of the nineteenth century. All except the Bullom were located in the interior, fifty to two hundred fifty miles inland.[14]

These groups had different histories and cosmologies, but they shared common cultural characteristics, practices, and beliefs, especially about kinship, family, ancestral spirits, and the afterlife. Most people lived in villages, towns, or cities that consisted of small conical houses, built of mud wattled around posts and sticks, with thatched roofs and compressed earth floors. Many settlements, especially among the Mende, were palisaded against the chronic threat of war. Town walls were twelve to fifteen feet high, three feet thick at the bottom, eighteen inches thick at the top, with sharpened sticks at the apex. Depending on the size of the population, the compound would have had four to six well-guarded gates and might encompass five to forty acres of land.[15]

Islam was spreading slowly through the region, largely among members of the upper classes, who converted, usually in superficial ways, grafting a thin layer of the new religion onto a long-held core of traditional spiritual beliefs. Muslim holy men, variously called *maribouts*, mori-men, or book-men, were growing in number on the Gallinas Coast and in its hinterlands, often as advisers to chiefs and kings such as Siaka. They also played a role in warfare by helping to create charms or amulets, locally called *greegree*, believed to have protective supernatural power for those going into battle. Arabic writing on a

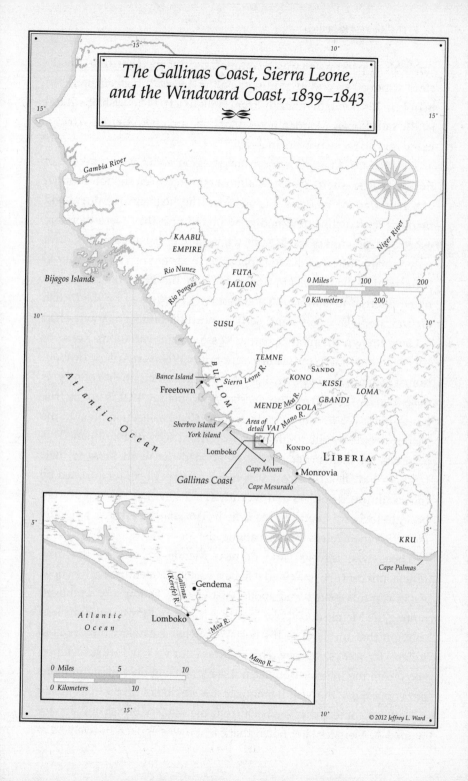

The Gallinas Coast, Sierra Leone, and the Windward Coast, 1839–1843

Gambia River

KAABU
EMPIRE

Rio Nunez

FUTA
JALLON

Rio Pongas

Bijagos Islands

SUSU

TEMNE

B
U
L
L
O
M

Bance Island

Sierra Leone R.

SANDO

KONO

KISSI

Freetown

LOMA

MENDE

Moa R.

GBANDI

Sherbro Island
York Island

GOLA

Area of
detail VAI

Mano R.

Lomboko

KONDO

LIBERIA

Gallinas Coast

Cape Mount

Cape Mesurado

Monrovia

KRU

Cape Palmas

0 Miles   100   200
0 Kilometers   200

Atlantic Ocean

Atlantic
Ocean

Gallinas
(Kerefe) R.

Gendema

Lomboko

Moa R.

Mano R.

0 Miles   5   10
0 Kilometers   10

© 2012 Jeffrey L. Ward

small bit of parchment was a common part of the charm or "medicine." Cinqué's second in command on the *Amistad*, Grabeau, had seen people in his hometown write "from right to left." The Irish abolitionist Richard Robert Madden noted that one unnamed *Amistad* African knew how to recite prayers in Arabic.[16]

The *Amistad* Africans came from a region about which people of European descent in 1839 knew almost nothing. Even though Europeans had traded in Sierra Leone since the sixteenth century, and mapped its coastline, few had gone inland and they were therefore especially ignorant of the Mende, whose name first appeared in print only in 1795. "Mende" did not appear on maps of West Africa prior to the arrival of the *Amistad* in Connecticut. By the 1830s, the people the name referred to—largely "Liberated Africans" taken by the British off captured slave ships and settled mostly around Freetown—had become known by another name: Kossa, or the variations Kosso or Kussoh. This added confusion to ignorance. When an American abolitionist explained that "we had a book in which their country is described as *Kossa*, they [the *Amistad* Africans] say, that is not its true name, but it is *a term of reproach*, a name that has been applied to the Mendi people by the English, and by those who dislike them! This accounts for their never having mentioned the word *Kossa* to their teachers and friends." Kossa was indeed a term of contempt, used by the acculturated settlers and recently freed slaves of African descent brought to Sierra Leone by the British. The *Amistad* Africans initially identified themselves by town and leader, not language group.[17]

Those who traveled into or near Mende country in the mid-nineteenth century imagined it to be a vast land, teeming with people. American missionary and abolitionist George Thompson, who lived among the Mende and spoke to both African and European travelers, thought that the land of his hosts "stretches eastward hundreds of miles—for weeks' journey. This we know, for we have often seen persons from the interior from such distances. Doubtless many millions of people speak the Mendi language, for we do not find it in its purity till we get some 200 miles back from the sea." A British missionary named A. Menzies later noted that Mende was spoken in twelve districts, only three of which had he been able to visit over an eighty-mile expanse. He too was sure that Mende country was immense. The *Amistad* Africans themselves told their teacher that Mende was "a very *great great* country." It was, in fact, less a country than a large agglomeration of localized societies loosely connected by a common, though regionally variable, language.[18]

Where had this numerous and expansive people come from? Some "old Mendians" told missionary John Brooks that "their forefathers came from the east," making war against western tribes, capturing large towns, settling and building farms along the way, intermarrying and forming alliances "with the people around them." The elders succinctly described what historians now call the "Mane Invasions," in which Mende warriors pushed south and west beginning in the middle of the sixteenth century, conquering and settling as they went, and permanently altering the political and cultural geography of southern Sierra Leone. Over the ensuing two centuries, the Mende shared a common language and culture over a wide geographic expanse, but they formed no large political state, had no sense of unity, and shared little sense of common identity. Victorious warriors gathered their families, friends, and soldiers to form farms and villages on newly conquered lands.[19]

Leadership among the Mende was, for the most part, earned rather than inherited. Kings, chiefs, and "big men" tended to be those who combined military and economic acumen and resources in what were predominantly small, decentralized societies. These leaders, usually in concert with a council of elders, ruled patrilocal and patrilineal societies, meaning that young families lived with or near the family of the husband and that the male line defined identity and property transmission. The Mende were also polygynous: a man could take two or more wives at the same time, if he had the necessary wealth. "Polygamy is common among the wealthier classes," explained the *Amistad* Africans. "Big men" in the region had "a plurality of wives, and if a king hundreds." Siaka's son, King Mana of the Vai, for example, was said to have five hundred wives. The accumulation of wives at the top often created a shortage of women for the poorer males, who found it difficult "to get even one." Bride-wealth costs could be prohibitive—four, five, or six bullocks and other goods. Wealth in Mende society was reckoned by the number of wives, children, slaves, and cattle a man had. Only thirteen of the *Amistad* Africans indicated that they had wives, which was a comment on their relative youth and class.[20]

Almost all of those held captive aboard the *Amistad* were commoners, people who worked the land or plied their craft. And the commons of Mende country was rich—decidedly not a place for the "starving savage" of imperial imagination. Wild bush yams and coco in particular made it easy to live with little work. "Blessings are scattered with a lavish hand," admitted the exasperated Thompson, who sought to discipline his Mende congregants to a Protestant work ethic. The lavishness included nuts, grapes, pineapple, orange trees, and fig trees. Learning to survive in the bush was an essential skill. The *Amistad* Africans explained to their teacher, "Their soil is very productive, and they are obliged to labor but a small part of the time to procure the comforts of life."[21]

Only four of the *Amistad* Africans claimed any kind of elite status. Gbatu explained that his father "is a gentleman and does no work." Fakinna's father, Bawnge, was a "chief or king" at Dzhopoahu, in Mende country. It was said that Cinqué's father was a "big man" in his own society. Several others, on the other hand, had been slaves. Yaboi had been captured when his village was surrounded by soldiers in an act of grand pillage and thereafter served a Mende master as a slave for ten years before he was sold to "Luiz, the Spaniard." Pugnwawni, a Sando man, was enslaved and forced to work for two years cultivating rice before he too was sold to the Spanish traders on the coast. Kimbo's experience encompassed both ends of the class structure: his father was a gentleman, he said, but after his death, Kinna was enslaved by his king (probably because his father was in debt) and given to a son who resided in Bullom country. He was then sold to another Bullom man, who sold him to a Spaniard at Lomboko.[22]

The Mende, like the Temne and many others from the Gallinas area, were traditionally rice farmers. Working the rice fields was a primary experience among the *Amistad* Africans. Cinqué, Grabeau, Ba, and Bagna described themselves as "planters of rice," while several others also mentioned the staple crop of the "Grain Coast." Rice lands were communally owned and labor was cooperative. Men and women tilled the plentiful rice fields as the young and the old fended off the small yellow ricebirds that could destroy a crop. In an upland system of rice production that depended on rainfall, they worked a given piece of land for two or three years, then let it lie fallow for five or six years before returning it to cultivation. Women had especially important roles in threshing rice, in ways that seemed to anthropologist Kenneth Little to have shaped their forms of dance: "There is a very close and striking similarity between the rhythm and movements of the Mende dancer and the rhythm and movements of a woman treading and threshing rice." They grew rice to eat and to sell, especially as the slave trade expanded and bondsmen had to be fed in the barracoons and on the ships. Some of the *Amistad* Africans may have been feeding the monster that would eventually devour them.[23]

Their communities were economically sophisticated, and several men engaged in more than one occupation. Burna the younger "was a blacksmith in his native village, and made hoes, axes, and knives; he also planted rice." Sessi, a Gbandi man, was also a blacksmith, a trade he had learned from his brother and one that carried prestige and spiritual power. Grabeau planted rice and worked as a merchant, traveling widely (and learning four regional languages) to sell ivory and camwood. Pie, on the other hand, was a hunter. He had killed five leopards in Temne country, "3 on the land, and 2 in the water," for which he may have earned royal distinction. One leopard skin he "hung up on his hut, to show that he was a hunter." His weapon of choice seems to have been the European musket. His hands had been "whitened by wounds received from the bursting of a gun barrel, which he had overloaded when showing his dexterity."[24]

The division of labor was sufficiently developed in Mende and other societies to make iron and cotton manufacture significant parts of their political economy. Iron ore was of especially high quality in the region, and metalworking artisans like Burna the younger and

Sessi were many. The tools they made of "true country iron" were valued above European imports. Cotton had been grown throughout the Gallinas region, especially in Mende country, since at least the seventeenth century. One of the *Amistad* Africans told his teacher, "Cotton make the hills *white*." George Thompson, who traveled extensively in Mende country, noted, "Everywhere I went, I observed many of the women spinning, and men weaving their country cloths." Weavers spun cotton and dyed it red (using camwood), yellow ("Bassel tree"), blue ("a green bush, called the Serang"), and green (camwood and "Bassel tree" together), then wove it into six-inch strips, which were sewn together, primarily to make clothing for personal use and for exchange. "Country cloth," as it was called, had a ready market, and a broad one. Several of the *Amistad* Africans were skilled weavers who practiced their craft while they were in jail to produce napkins in the "fringed African style," which, as skilled artisans, they proudly demonstrated at public meetings after their liberation from jail.[25]

The *Amistad* Africans were, by and large, urban people. Foone had lived in the "large town" of Bumbe, while Gnakwoi hailed from Tuma, "the largest town in the Balu country." Their home cities, they insisted, were roughly equal in size to New Haven, which in 1840 had a population of roughly twelve thousand, suggesting significant urbanization in Mende country. The urban past of many was illustrated by Fuli's comment about how man-stealers preyed on city dwellers, and perhaps even more dramatically by the way in which fully a dozen of the *Amistad* Africans were captured and enslaved while they were "on the road" traveling from one place to another, most often to "buy clothes." The leaders of the rebellion, Cinqué and Grabeau, were both caught while "traveling in the road." Burna was captured while "going to the next town," Kinna while on his way to Kongoli.[26]

They were living, clearly, within a vibrant system of regional trade. According to their teacher Sherman Booth, they "traffic principally in rice, clothes, and cattle, and these are the only currency of the country." There was also a ready trade in domestic items such as salt and fish, both from the coast, along with European goods of various kinds, especially the rum about which Cushoo spoke, as well as guns, gunpowder, textiles, and tools. Over time the main commodity exchanged for the European items was slaves, but there was "by-play" (secondary trade), as one merchant explained, in ivory and camwood, in addition to rice required by the slave trade.[27]

The *Amistad* Africans presented themselves as part of extended, usually multigenerational kin groups that lived under the same roof, as was common among the Mende and their neighbors. Sessi lived with his three brothers, two sisters, wife, and three children. Fabanna was the only person to mention that he had more than one wife; he had two, and one child. It was later discovered by missionaries that Burna, who, in detailing his kin mentioned no wife, actually had seven. Fuli lived with his mother, father, five brothers, and, for a time, with his grandmother. Family trumped everything else, in his world-view. When asked if he might wish to stay in the United States after gaining his freedom, he replied, "If America people would give him his hat full of gold, and plenty of houses and lands, to stay in this country, he would not, for gold was not like his father, nor his mother, nor his sister, nor his brother." Throughout their ordeal the *Amistad* Africans steadfastly insisted that they wanted to return to "their homes, their birth-place, the land of their fathers."[28]

It is difficult to know precisely how old the *Amistad* Africans were because they did not reckon age according to the European calendar. A visitor to the jail grouped them into four basic categories, probably based on appearance and whatever information he had been able to gain through interviews. The youngest group was the four children, each of whom (including Margru) was probably around nine years old in 1839. Then came five youths, very likely in their early to mid-teens. Another eleven were said to be "in middle age," which probably meant late twenties and early thirties. That left the largest group, six-teen, in early adulthood, late teens to mid-twenties. These numbers are consistent with the long-standing preferences of slave traders and American plantation owners, who always wanted to buy men between the ages of fifteen and thirty-five for plantation labor such as awaited the captives in Cuba. There was also a tendency, as the slave trade evolved and traders found fewer men in the prime of life, to buy younger men. Because age and experience were highly valued among the Mende and others of the Gallinas Coast, the eleven men of "middle age" exercised considerable authority within the group.[29]

The *Amistad* Africans were modest in size, although fit and athletic. In March 1841, John Pitkin Norton noted in his diary that they were "small men" but proud, unbowed by the experience of slavery. Ndzhagnwawni was the tallest adult at five feet nine inches, while Grabeau, an excellent acrobat, was the shortest at four feet eleven inches. The four children were all roughly four feet three inches tall. The average height of the *Amistad* men was a shade above five feet four inches at a time when the typical African American man was about the same size, and the American male of European descent was about two inches taller.[30]

Knowing and speaking multiple languages was common in Mende society, as George Thompson discovered in his own congregation: one man spoke Mende, Kissi, Bullom, Kittam (Krim), Vai, Kono, "Canaan," and English—eight languages altogether. Most people, he found, including children, could speak two, three, or four languages, as could many of the *Amistad* Africans. Mende and Gbandi, both historically part of the Mande language group, were mutually intelligible. Konoma knew Kono and Mandingo, both part of the Atlantic language group. The most versatile linguist in the group was Grabeau, who as a trader had traveled widely and added to his native Mende the ability to speak Vai, Kono, and Kissi. Burna the younger spoke Mende, Bullom, and Temne. Several men had facility in the Bullom language, probably through commerce—and a few had themselves been the commodity traded. Kimbo, Kinna, Fuliwulu, and Tsukama had slaved in "Bullom Country," where many merchants were allies of the Spanish. Fuliwulu had been to Freetown "a great many times," while others had met traders from the British settlement in their own villages, towns, and cities.[31]

Movement, free or forced, and contact with peoples and their languages throughout the region, created an unusual capacity for communication among the *Amistad* Africans. Unbeknownst to themselves, these experienced, mobile, sophisticated, multiethnic people had acquired tools that would serve them well in their Atlantic odyssey of slavery and freedom.

Poro Society

Central to the societies and identities of the *Amistad* Africans, and indeed to all peoples of the Gallinas region, was the Poro Society, an all-male secret society and fundamental governing social institution. All the adult men involved in the rebellion would have been members of the Poro in their native societies and therefore familiar with this type of self-government, even if the rules and rituals had varied from place to place and culture to culture. Everyone knew how the Poro worked, what it was supposed to do, and how to use it. They kept its secrets: there is no mention of the Poro Society in any contemporary records concerning the *Amistad* rebellion. Yet there can be no doubt that it played a significant role as *Amistad* rebels organized themselves throughout their long ordeal.[32]

First described in a book edited by Dutch physician Olfert Dapper in 1668, Poro in the Gallinas was shrouded in mystery because members took a "solemn oath" on pain of death not to reveal the society's lore. The Poro had a hierarchy of ranks, based on the degrees of sacred knowledge an individual possessed, and signified physically by ritual scarification. The greater the number of marks, the higher the authority of the Poro member. The heavily "tattooed" Grabeau's high standing in the Poro would have been visible to any and all of the *Amistad* Africans as soon as they laid eyes on him. Likewise Fabanna, "tattooed on the breast," and head man of his town. They read their bodies and honored their authority.[33]

In cultures in which ancestral spirits (*ndebla*) loomed large, the Poro derived much of its power from its claim to serve as intermediaries to past generations, to embody their spirit, and to reach, through them, the remote supreme deity, Ngewo, linking the people to spirits great and small and connecting past to present. The Poro Society therefore had supreme authority in making decisions on behalf of the corporate group. The Temne Poro, Major Alexander Laing remarked, "possess the general government of the country," a fact he considered "a most serious obstacle to its civilization," that is to say, to European control.[34]

The basic purpose of the Poro Society was to establish law and maintain social order—in a word, to govern—and its primary focus was settling disputes and policing the boundaries of behavior. Poro leaders adjudicated all of the normal disputes within and between communities, but a special concern was always witchcraft, the use of supernatural power for anticommunal ends. The elders of the Poro Society alone held the power of capital punishment and did not hesitate to use it against those they considered malevolent witches and sorcerers. In less extreme cases, the Poro used ostracism to move offenders "from communal grace to isolated individualism." According to anthropologist Kenneth Little, the main purpose of the Mende Poro throughout its history has been to create *ngo yela*—"one word" or "unity."[35]

The Poro Society also made decisions about war. This was done in tandem with kings and chiefs and "head war men" (who were Poro members themselves), but the Poro had the stronger hand because they had often helped to choose the political leaders in the first place. George Thompson noted that "even the greatest kings" in Mende country feared Tassaw, the mysterious and awful leader of the Poro. Laing saw the same power in Temne country and was moved to speculate that the Poro Society had originated among slaves who ran away to the bush to escape their African masters. In what would become the sacred space of the Poro, they "confederate[d] for mutual support." Because "the means of subsistence [was] easy to be procured" in the bush commons, and because the power of divided and quarreling local kings and chiefs "did not extend beyond the limits of their own town," such an organization from below may soon "have become too powerful for any probable combination against them." If true, Laing's theory might explain the limitations the Poro placed on slave masters, who were forbidden to do anything that would draw the blood of their bondsmen.[36]

Another important function of the Poro Society was to preside over the rites of passage in which boys became men. In the sacred bush, where the initiation took place, Poro members—all adult men—taught the skills of survival to the youth: how to hunt, how to fight, how to think about the material and spiritual worlds. They taught new disciplines of the body, such as acrobatics. They imparted knowledge about the values and beliefs by which the people lived. Each boy "died" in the bush and was reborn as a man and given a new name. The initiation into manhood also included scarification: "two parallel tattooed lines round the middle of the body, inclining upwards in front, towards the breast, and meeting in the pit of the stomach." When a young man emerged from the bush, he could proudly show the "teeth-marks" by which his juvenile self had been devoured. To conclude the initiation, the Poro elders, "dressed as demons and wild men," emerged from the bush, howling, torches in hand, to sow terror throughout the town, to impress upon one and all their arbitrary, absolute power. The ritual would be followed by all-night feasting and dancing.[37]

Crossing boundaries of territory, class, clan, and family, the Poro Society could create unity among disparate individuals and groups who did not know each other. The Poro was an instrument of "mutual assistance." F. Harrison Rankin could see this in the 1830s. He wrote that "the Purrah, or 'law' is a solemn bond uniting in brotherhood and purpose individuals scattered through immense districts." Arguing that the Poro Society was the main instrumentality through which the Mende (and Temne) organized the Hut Tax War against the British in 1898, the eminent Mende scholar Arthur Abraham has written that "the Poro, more than any other institution, gives continuity to Mende culture and a sense of unity to the Mende people."[38]

"Word Never Done"

The spoken word loomed large in all areas of life for the *Amistad* Africans, as theirs were oral, not written, cultures. Many European visitors commented on the eloquence of the people they encountered in and around Sierra Leone. In 1834 F. Harrison Rankin put the matter bluntly and broadly: "Negroes are eloquent by nature." Sigismund

Wilhelm Koelle, a German missionary and linguist who went to the Gallinas Coast in 1847 to prove the rational principles of African languages and the unity of mankind, heard with a linguist's ear "stirring extempore speeches, adorned with beautiful imagery and of half an hour's duration." George Thompson noted the many instances in which he heard "great native eloquence." Major Alexander Laing was impressed by Mandingo, Foulah, and Kuranko speakers, "who will talk for hours with the greatest fluency." Their eloquence lay in "familiar expressions, striking similies, and quaint remarks," punctuated by "vehement action and gesticulation."[39]

"Head war men" gave stirring speeches to warriors preparing for battle, reciting history and the transgressions against honor to be avenged. Spoken rites were critical to communication with ancestral spirits. Collective identity depended on the preservation of the history and cosmology of the village, town, and larger culture and their oral transmission from one generation to the next. Storytelling was an important art that used wit and drama not only to entertain but to impart knowledge and wisdom, all through an interactive, call-and-response communal style. Mende kings and chiefs often had a "speaker," or *lavale*, who communicated the ruler's wishes to lower-ranking officials and explained his goals and reasoning to society at large.[40]

Of special importance were the words spoken at the traditional West African palaver, adapted from the Portuguese *palavra*, or "word," which had a great many meanings. Among the Mende, a palaver could be a dispute or a problem that needed to be settled; a consultation ("peace palaver"); a religious meeting ("God-palaver"); a grudge ("a palaver live in my heart"); or simply a quest to learn. To read, for example, was called "book palaver." A palaver could concern an accidental killing of a villager's chicken or a deadly war that had gone on for years. A tremendous amount of cultural business was transacted through palavers at the *bari*, or public house, where the speaker learned his trade—how to combine intellectual rigor and dramatic flair to carry the day in argument. As the African interpreter of the German linguist Sigismund Koelle explained to him, "We can talk one thing in many ways ... word never done." Cinqué's training in the palavers of his native society would serve him well as an orator in America.[41]

Warfare

Chronic, bloody warfare wracked the homelands of *Amistad* Africans during the 1830s, and left them experienced in the ways of violence as both agents and victims. Signs of war were everywhere, even when the fighting could not be directly observed. George Thompson took a trip on which he passed the ruins of twenty towns, many of them burned and razed to the ground, "swept clean," as he put it. Here and there might be seen the skull of a head war man on a stick, a grisly public trophy by which conquerors announced their power. Piles of deliberately unburied bodies also littered the war-torn landscape as the vanquished were left to the disposal of wild animals. Wars closed roads and rivers and obstructed trade, as reflected in a comment Grabeau made about the extreme scarcity of salt in his village: it had become an expensive commodity that "none but the rich eat." War also transformed the routines of daily life. A Mende chief named Kambahway remarked that, in wartime, "if the people go to work farm, a part have to watch with guns, while the others work."[42]

Even the physical arrangements of Mende towns reflected ubiquitous warfare. At the center of each town was the "war village," where warriors and their weapons were always at the ready. Around this central place were built satellite villages, as many as eight to ten in number, with several thousand residents. Many towns had palisaded defense works with deep ditches; thick, oiled, slippery walls; spiked ditches on the inside; and an interior wall with gun holes and platforms from which town warriors might fire on invaders. Warriors worked as sentries on a town's perimeter to detect and warn against intruders, and towns had strategies of escape in case enemies should breach their walls. People fled with a few essentials into the forest, where they hid and lived for weeks at a time, commoning until the marauding army had moved on.[43]

Kissicummah, a "small, very old, smart, shrewd, kind" Mende king who had become a "Mahomedan," explained a fundamental cause of such warfare: "So many chiefs in the country is the cause of the difficulty. It is as if there were many Gods, each opposing the plans and desires of the other. One wants to send rain, another sunshine—one this, and the other that, so they would be all the time contending." He wished for a king powerful enough—himself, surely—to subordinate the others and thereby create peace, but he knew that "while there are so many kings, the country cannot come good." Competition over land, trade, and honor spurred endless bloody conflicts.[44]

By "many kings," Kissicummah also meant many nations: the Mende fought the Temne, the Vai, the Gola, the Kru, the Bullom, and they fought each other, furiously. The Mende were known at Freetown, where many landed as Liberated Africans taken off the slave ships by the British antislavery patrol, as "a wild savage people, continually at war amongst themselves and against their neighbours, the Timnehs particularly." One of the longest wars that wracked the region was fought between two rival Mende towns, Tikonko and Bumpe, whose warriors battled for almost twenty years. Reverend Thompson spent a great deal of time in peace palavers, trying to end the war between the two groups, repeatedly drawing attention to their cultural commonalities: "You are all in one country, of one color, speak one tongue, children of one Father, brothers of one family. Is it good for such persons to fight? Is it right?" Struggles for resources among localized polities pitted warriors of similar cultures against each other.[45]

A second and related cause of war was the aggressive expansion of the slave trade, led by the Vai King Siaka, who, for the coastal region at least, became the kind of dominant leader Kissicummah had called for. Koelle noted that until around 1830 the Vai had controlled the area fifteen to twenty miles inland from the coast. At the instigation of the Spanish slave traders, they drove another twenty-five to thirty miles into the interior. War and slave-raiding slowly depopulated the coastal region, driving people inland to escape capture. Those who remained gained protection, but they suffered deskilling as they came to depend on European traders for useful items they had once made themselves.

Most of all they depended on weapons—the guns and powder provided by Blanco and other traders that armed Siaka's warriors and enabled their work of expropriation.[46]

Because the Vai were not numerous and did not have enough warriors to carry out Siaka's territorial and slave-raiding designs, the king hired mercenaries, sending messengers to villages near and far to "buy war"—that is, to make deals with head men for warriors who would be rewarded for their labors with plunder of various sorts: money, commodities, slaves, and land. Many of the mercenaries hired were Mende, whose warrior traditions served Siaka's ambitions. Indeed, scholars agree that the movement of the Mende toward the coast in the late eighteenth and early nineteenth centuries owed much to successful mercenary fighting, after which leading warriors were awarded land upon which they built new towns of their own. During the prolonged war of the 1830s between Siaka and Amara Lalu, Mende warriors fought on both sides. It seems that at least two of the *Amistad* captives, Cinqué and Bau, fought for Amara Lalu, against Siaka, in a losing cause.[47]

At least one of the *Amistad* Africans, and probably several more, had experience as a mercenary "war boy." Gnakwoi, a Loma, had served under the famous warrior Goterah, a "well-built, muscular man" who growled like a leopard, the magnificent creature from which he took his name. Goterah once announced to Thomas Buchanan, the American governor of Liberia, that "he makes war and carries it wherever he pleases." As one of his instruments of war, Gnakwoi served the Vai against the Gola. He may have served in other campaigns in which Goterah and his men fought on behalf of Kondo and Mende kings against various enemies. But Gnakwoi's service against the Gola came back to haunt him, for after the war, as he traveled through Gola country on his way to market, he was recognized as an enemy warrior, captured, and promptly sold into slavery, eventually to the very people—the Vai—on whose behalf he had once fought against his new masters. A Vai merchant in turn sold him to a Spaniard named Peli, which is how he ended up at Lomboko, then aboard the *Teçora* and finally the *Amistad*.[48]

The main style of warfare in the region, which the Mende shared, was one of guerilla action—surprise, small-scale attacks, almost always at night, often when "the moon was dead," the heavens dark. Goterah promised to attack a local mission at the "death of the moon," and made good on the pledge. Some African soldiers used muskets and pistols, as these had been "scattered all over the country" by slave traders. The Temne and the Susu preferred the bow and arrow, while the Mende went into battle with the cutlass as their weapon of choice. Mende warriors uttered "horrible war shouts" as they breached the walls of a fortified town, rushing about, once inside, "in a frantic manner from one side to the other, and cutting anyone whom they encounter." Slashing away right and left, they sowed "panic amongst the enemy," forcing them to abandon the stockade. They sought to terrify and force flight, rather than to kill, partly because they wanted plunder, which included the capture of slaves for both domestic and Atlantic purposes.[49]

Domestic Slavery

The *Amistad* Africans knew domestic slavery in their own societies. Grabeau's wealthy uncle owned slaves, and several of the rebels had slaved for African masters—Yaboi, for instance, for ten years. Adam Jones notes that slavery existed by the early seventeenth century, its extent was unknown, and that throughout the region the free and the enslaved were easily distinguished one from another. Yet "slavery" covered a broad array of power relations. West African varieties differed fundamentally from plantation slavery across the Atlantic, where people were brutally exploited as they produced commodities such as sugar for the world market. To be sure, labor could be harsh for slaves who labored in the Gallinas salt pans, and it could be deadly for those forced into armies and battle. Most slaves, however, probably cultivated rice, under material conditions that sometimes made it hard for European observers to tell who was the master and who was the slave. Authority over domestic slaves was paternal and familial, and many over time were absorbed into their host families and cultures.

Pugnwawni noted that during his two years of slavery at the hands of an African man named Gardoba, he cultivated rice: "His master's wives and children were employed in the same manner, and no distinction made in regard to labor."[50]

Domestic slavery was increasing in the Gallinas region in the early nineteenth century; transatlantic slavery was one of the main reasons why. As Walter Rodney noted, African rulers who engaged in the slave trade with Europeans accumulated more slaves of their own, often vastly more, and this was certainly true of King Siaka, whose rise to power on the Gallinas Coast was based not only on sending thousands to the barracoons of Lomboko, but on settling thousands of others in towns, where they could be governed and kept ready for European demand. Many such towns existed throughout the region. During his travels in Temne country Major Alexander Laing mentioned several times Konkodoogore, a slave town of three to four thousand people.[51]

Even though most of the *Amistad* Africans had never seen European ships or people, they had, perhaps without knowing it, felt their impact as the global market sunk its tentacles ever more deeply into the Gallinas and its hinterlands. Commodities such as guns, alcohol, and tobacco—all brought to the coast by slave traders—were mentioned frequently as the captives described their homelands and their paths to the coast. Some had been trained in the use of firearms, part of the guns-for-slaves trading cycle that sustained the commerce in human beings. Grabeau mentioned that "smoking tobacco is a common practice" in his hometown of Fulu. Almost all of the *Amistad* men smoked, with relish. Several had pipes in their mouths when their portraits were sketched by William Townsend.[52]

As domestic slavery expanded throughout the Gallinas and its hinterlands, so did its antithesis, antislavery. The enslaved resisted, on African soil, in a wide variety of ways: they committed suicide, they ran away, and they formed fugitive (maroon) villages in inaccessible places, just as the enslaved were doing simultaneously on the other side of the Atlantic. The greatest antislavery event was the Zawo War, in which thousands of slaves, beginning in 1825–1826 and lasting into the early 1840s, fought back against King Siaka and his supporters. During this time, entire towns of insurgent slaves not only served as magnets for runaways and other fugitives, they waged war against the Vai king and won major concessions, including, for some, their freedom. The *Amistad* Africans knew the struggle against slavery in the 1830s and would carry their knowledge into a wider Atlantic world.[53]

Slave Trade

The *Amistad* Africans were unwilling actors in an Atlantic slave trade that began with Portuguese traders in the early sixteenth century and evolved slowly to connect the four continents around the Atlantic. Traders such as the Englishman Zachary Rogers arrived in the Gallinas region in the 1670s; he married an African woman and produced a multigenerational dynasty of slave merchants. By 1700, human cargo was a minor, though increasingly significant, part of European trade, alongside ivory, camwood, and *melagueta* pepper. In 1712, when the monopoly of the Royal African Company of England ended, "free traders" sent more slaving vessels to the Gallinas Coast, and by 1750 the trade in slaves had become a dominant part of the trade. The region became more important in the 1790s and then crucial following the abolition of the slave trade by the British and American governments in 1807 and 1808, when Cuban and Brazilian demand for slaves skyrocketed in the aftermath of the Haitian Revolution. Another turning point was the rise to power of Pedro Blanco and King Siaka in the 1820s. Whereas in the eighteenth century slave ship captains had "coasted" from one minor shipping point to another, buying a few slaves at a time, post-abolition they had to load large numbers quickly from a centralized location, which required a concentration of capital and labor. As "fleets of prison ships" plied the coast in the 1830s, slaving was "the universal business of the country and, by far the most profitable."[54]

The slave trade at Gallinas was lucrative, but it was also a desperate gamble for all involved. In an 1841 report to Parliament about the

Sierra Leone region, the knowledgeable British diplomat Richard Robert Madden estimated a 180 percent return on investment in slave trading. Yet high profits for merchants, high salaries for captains, and high wages for sailors all were shadowed by death and disaster. Slave-trade merchants lost money when British officials confiscated their vessels, as they did with increasing regularity as the government expanded the anti-slave-trade patrols after 1822, but Royal Navy Captain Frederick Forbes thought that one successful voyage out of four made the full investment profitable. Captains and seamen lost their pay, and often lost their lives, in the area long considered to be the "sepulchre of the Europeans." The enslaved may have suffered most of all in this war, because of an irony on which naval officers, antislavery activists, and slave traders could agree: the abolition of the slave trade and the subsequent policing of the seas by the British navy, in the face of surging demand for slaves from Brazil and Cuba, fomented social conditions at the factories and on the slave ships that were more violent, more degraded, and generally more horrifying than ever. This would be the experience of the *Amistad* Africans as they were enslaved and transported to Lomboko and then across the Atlantic to Havana.[55]

Slavers used the tried-and-true methods of the Atlantic slave trade to capture the *Amistad* Africans. Local leaders sentenced Kwong, Shule, Yaboi, and Burna the younger to bondage, the first three for adultery, the last for a reason unknown. Soldiers took another six in one of two ways: like Fuli, in grand pillage, or perhaps like Moru, in battle, in which the vanquished were seized as the spoils of war and sold to traders. King Siaka's men captured Beri and sold him to a Spaniard at Lomboko. Debt landed three of the *Amistad* Africans in slavery. Grabeau explained that his uncle "had bought two slaves in Bandi, and gave them as a payment" for a debt of his own. When one of them ran away, Grabeau was seized by the man to whom his uncle owed the debt, as satisfaction of it. Kagne's father left her as a pawn, a deposit against goods or credits extended by slave traders, then never redeemed her. Pugnwawni had a hard and distinctive fate within the group: "His mother's brother sold him for a coat." The largest number of *Amistad* Africans were essentially kidnapped—that is, captured unexpectedly as they went about their daily business, often, as mentioned earlier, in traveling from one place to another. A few were apparently tricked—promised by traders a view of the Spaniards' "big canoe," the slave ship, then promptly enslaved as soon as they went aboard.[56]

The slave trade was so pervasive in the Gallinas region that almost everyone would have had a brush with it. Several knew others who had been shipped overseas before them. Cinqué's own "closest brother" Kindi had been captured in 1835 or 1836, sold to the Spaniards, and loaded aboard an Atlantic slaver. The vessel was soon captured by the British and taken to Freetown, where it was condemned as a prize, and he was liberated. He eventually returned to his family in 1838, with harrowing tales to tell. Cinqué knew the African side of trade and he knew that a war involving the British surrounded it, but neither he nor others seem to have known much about slavery in the Americas.[57]

The geographic origins of the *Amistad* Africans illustrate the catchment area for Pedro Blanco and King Siaka. The enslaved came from near and far, and from many ecological zones. Cinqué and Shule came from "the open country," that is, the riverain grasslands east of Lomboko. Gbatu, Ba, Ndzhagnwawni, and Burna came from a more mountainous region farther east. Others had lived in rich forested lands, where Pie, for example, had hunted leopards and other big game. The rivers and lakes common to the region were home to several others: Gnakwoi grew up on a large river where "fish are caught . . . as large a man's body—they are caught in nets and sometimes shot with guns." Ndamma lived on the Ma-le River; Bau and Shule both on the long, meandering Moa, "which runs from Gissi, passes through Mendi, and runs south into the Konno country." Growing up amid streams, rivers, and lakes, many of the Africans were expert swimmers and knew the use of watercraft.[58]

The *Amistad* Africans reckoned the time in getting from their homes to Lomboko in suns and moons, roughly equivalent to days and months. The one who traveled the shortest distance was Burna the younger, who was in transit only four days to Lomboko from nearby Bullom country. Several said they traveled "two moons" in getting to the coast. It took Shuma twice as long, four moons, to reach the factory. Yet all of the time may not have been spent in travel. It was common for traders to take a slave a certain distance, then sell him or her to another trader, who might put the person to work for a month or two before selling him or her to someone else closer to the coast. Cinqué's path illustrated the process: he was captured by four men, who tied his right hand behind his neck to limit his ability to resist. The original captor, Mayagilalo, sold him to the son of King Siaka, Bamadzha, who carried him from Vai country to Lomboko, where he sold him to a Spaniard. The slaving zone for Lomboko ranged up to 250 miles into the interior, which is why many of the *Amistad* Africans had seen neither the sea and European sailing ships, nor white people, until they arrived at Lomboko, operated by the man most appropriately named Blanco.[59]

Lomboko

Slave traders marched the *Amistad* Africans overland and ferried them by canoe around and through a hydrographic system made up of four rivers—the Kerefe, Moa, Mano, and Waanje—and large coastal lagoons. Surrounding Lomboko were thick forests of mangrove trees, whose ropy roots stood ten to fifteen feet above the waterline, fringing riverbanks and a swampy shore. Looming high above were majestic cottonwood trees, each as tall as one hundred thirty feet, with a root system that might cover five acres. Croaking frogs, grating crickets, and buzzing cockroaches created what European ears heard as a loud and disturbing cacophony. Rattling rain and flooding were the order of the day on the Gallinas Coast during the rainy season, from May to November, when the fast currents of swollen rivers caused ship captains to use two anchors when they visited the coast to trade. The Atlantic surf was so heavy that it could sometimes be heard two miles inland. The region was also given to heavy reddish fogs, which the local residents called "smokes," and to sudden, violent tornadoes with "vivid flashes of forked lightning" and thunder that sounded like the collision of "great metallic bodies." By the time the *Amistad* Africans arrived in February and March of 1839, things had begun to dry out. The famous Harmattan winds swirled off the Sahara Desert, blowing sand far and wide and causing the leaves of trees to droop.[60]

The slave-trading Gallinas Coast lay between imperial outposts of Britain and America, formed by declared opponents to slavery. North of Lomboko lay the British settlement of Freetown, established in 1788, a bustling port of 42,000 people, the overwhelming majority of them Liberated Africans taken off the slave ships by the British anti-slave-trade patrol. People who spoke fifty different languages animated a sprawling public market where one might buy a fishhook, a dried rat, or a leopard's tooth. The ninety-nine whites, mostly British officials, who lived in Freetown were rarely to be seen during the day, unless at the promenade or the racetrack. To the south and east along the coast lay Monrovia, a fledgling center for the American Colonization Society, which carried former American slaves back to the continent of an ancestor's birth.[61]

When Fuli, Margru, Moru, and the others finally reached Lomboko, the slave traders put each of them through a careful—and demeaning—physical examination, to be sure that all were likely to survive the Middle Passage and bring a good price in the slave markets of Havana. A trader named Theophilus Conneau, who worked for Blanco for a time and soon became the second most notorious slave trader on the Gallinas Coast in the late 1830s, was an old hand in the examination and purchase of human beings; he knew the routine intimately. He left a detailed record of what those bound for the *Teçora* would have gone through.[62]

As the various small traders—Vai, Bullom, Temne, and Mende—arrived with their human coffles at Blanco's place of business, they stripped every man, woman, and child "perfectly naked." All were closely inspected "from head to foot"; no part was spared, recalled Conneau. The soundness of limbs for would-be plantation workers was crucial, so arms and legs were squeezed, tugged, flexed, and rotated. "Every joint was made to crack; hips, armpits, and groins were also examined." Buyers looked carefully into each person's mouth; missing teeth would mean a reduced payment to the seller. Likewise with eyesight: a squint—or a cast in the eye such as Burna had—decreased the purchase price. Buyers even demanded that the captives speak in order to evaluate voice. They scrutinized every finger and toe, knowing that the struggle against enslavement included self-mutilation: "in order to unfit himself for service," a man might "cut off his first finger." Women, even little girls like Margru, were subjected to a special set of indignities. Rejects might be killed, or be sold to local masters.

Big merchants like Blanco and Conneau were wary of the tricks and treachery of the petty traders. When he was first learning the trade, Conneau was shocked to see an experienced merchant, John Ormond, known as "Mongo John," pass on a man so big and strong he had to be double-pinioned. John's searching eye had seen that the man was "medicated," probably with "powder and lemon juice," by the petty trader to disguise sickness. This was one of the "jockey-tricks practiced by a sharper to sell off a sick slave." Men like Blanco and Conneau thus kept a close lookout for a "yellowish eye," "swollen tongue," or "feverish skin" and for marks of a rebellious temperament, seen in scars that might indicate previous resistance. All of the Africans who ended up on the *Amistad* somehow passed this "rigid muster," and became residents of Lomboko while they awaited their slave ship to Havana. In Lomboko they met people of many ages, nations, and descriptions, "from the grey-haired man to the merry sportive child," all of whom had arrived "with ropes around their necks & irons on their feet."[63]

Lomboko was actually a complex of slave-trading factories, all owned by Blanco and located at the mouth of the Gallinas (Kerefe) River and on a cluster of seven small islands. A British Admiralty chart of 1839 labeled the three largest islands Kamasoun, Kambatin, and Taro, all with small rectangular marks that represent buildings. Across a channel from Kambatin, on the north coast of the Gallinas River, lay Lomboko (here called Dumbacora)—two buildings in a clearing surrounded by coastal forest. Nearby are three more buildings and a larger rectangle denoted as the "Castle," which was the fortified centerpiece of the slaving operation. On the south side of the Gallinas, at the mouth, is another cleared area with three buildings labeled "Pedro Blanco's House."[64] Because Blanco worked for the infamous Havana-based House of Martinez, one of the biggest slave trading operations in the world in 1839, above the factory buildings he flew white flags emblazoned with the letter M. Blanco's chain of forts stretched 150 miles over the Windward Coast, which enabled him to shift slaves from one place to another according to the policing practices of the British Royal Navy. His international network was even larger: he had connections in London, Liverpool, Manchester, Havana, Puerto Rico, Trinidad, Texas, New Orleans, and Freetown (to buy back condemned vessels).[65]

Pedro Blanco—tall and slender, clean-shaven, "with small, black, piercing eyes," a dark complexion, and "an easy gentlemanly deportment"—had arrived in Africa as a bankrupt, it was rumored, in 1824 or 1825 and began to build business operations and create local alliances that would soon make him the most powerful man on the coast. Determined to rebuild his "shattered fortunes," he initially organized a slaving voyage from the area and accompanied the ship to Cuba. Success allowed him to return to the Gallinas, settle, and expand operations. He "opened an extensive correspondence, received consignments of vessels and cargoes, and loaded and despatched cargoes." His run of good fortune continued, and he slowly built a small empire that linked African kings (notably Siaka) and a cadre of European adventurers much like himself, to the House of Martinez. Gallinas "soon became, not only the centre of an extensive and lucrative traffic, but the theatre of a new order of society and a novel form of government, of all of which his excellency, Don Pedro Blanco, was the head, the autocrat." By the early 1830s, "his authority was absolute, acquired and maintained, not by his wealth alone, but by his will, energy, ability and address; for Pedro Blanco was no common man. He was a well-born, high-bred, Spanish gentleman, and in all save his profession, a man of honor—yea, of strict integrity, whose word was his bond."[66]

Living, as one visitor said, as a combination of European gentleman and African king, with a "seraglio of wives" for each part, Blanco became the stuff of legend. A story that circulated along the coast concerned a trip he made to Sherbro, where he was, at that time, unknown. He "approached the hut of a native with a view of taking rest and refreshment," and soon asked for fire with which to light his Cuban cigar. When the man "bluntly refused," Blanco took a gun from one of his attendants "and shot him dead upon the spot." This man of "strict integrity"—and extreme violence—would not tolerate such an insult to his aristocratic sense of honor.[67]

The illegality of the slave trade, and the British patrol vessels that scoured the coast trying to enforce the law, made Blanco's business secretive, dangerous, and urgent. Blanco had his own African (Kru) canoemen paddling up and down the coast, and as far as forty miles out to sea, to gather intelligence. "Watch-boxes," or lookout posts, were built into the towering cottonwood trees. Here his employees, shielded from the sun and rain, scanned the ocean with telescopes to discern the comings and goings of slave ships and anti-slave-trade patrols. Captains who wanted to bring their vessels ashore to load signaled with lights to the lookouts, who responded in kind. One light meant the coast was clear. Two lights conveyed, proceed with caution. Three lights, flashing, indicated danger. The ultimate signal to stay away was a bonfire, into which were thrown bags of gunpowder, producing explosions that could be seen twenty miles offshore.[68]

When a ship came to the bar at the mouth of the river to receive its human cargo, a fleet of canoes and boats burst into action, for the slaves and their food had to be transported and loaded quickly, before British vessels could arrive and turn the voyage into a catastrophe for any and all merchants—European, American, Brazilian, Cuban, or African. Dr. Thomas Hall, a Maryland colonizationist who visited all ten of Blanco's factories in 1837, believed that as many as "1,000 slaves could be shipped in four hours, all things favorable." A ship the size of the *Teçora* might therefore have been filled in a mere two hours. Loading was a dangerous time for both the canoemen and the people being shipped. The rivers, lagoons, and waterways surrounding the islands teemed with sharks, schools of which were aptly called "shivers." They followed the watercraft in great numbers and preyed on any that overset in the rough surf. In this way, "many a boat load of poor wretches becomes food for sharks."[69]

Chained bondspeople, as well as baskets of rice, casks of water, and livestock, would be loaded and stowed as quickly as possible, the canoemen and ship's sailors working rapidly in concert. As soon as the men loaded everything the delivery craft could carry, back they went to shore for a second load of freight as the receiving vessel sometimes sailed back out to sea, in order not to be seen—or worse, caught—at the slaving factory. Half-loaded vessels would not head out to the main sea-lanes, but would stick close to the coast, hiding in lagoons and estuaries where the British vessels could not easily patrol.

The canoes and other small craft that swarmed around the slave factories were manned by the men of an ethnic group called the Kru, or "Fishmen," because they oscillated between slave trading and fishing as the seasons and economic demand dictated. They lived along the coast of Liberia and were known for their maritime skills. Drumming and singing, the Kru deftly handled their canoes through "surge and breakers" others could not navigate. Their strength and stamina were legendary: they made two-hundred-mile journeys and could paddle fast enough to overtake vessels under sail. When they reached arriving vessels, they scrambled up the chains and got to work. They wore colored handkerchiefs around their loins and large carved bone or ivory rings around their wrists and ankles. Distinguished by their "country marks"—a line from the forehead along the ridge of the nose, with similar short horizontal lines at the outer angle of each eye—they also sported tattoos on their forearms, "in imitation of the English seamen with whom they associate." These "universally great watermen" sported newly given names, such as Bottle of Beer, Frying Pan, and Duke of Wellington as they did the work of the slave trade and, indeed, almost all trades from Freetown to Monrovia.[70]

British, Dutch, French, Portuguese, and American vessels called at Lomboko, most of them in defiance of their own nation's laws. The British government negotiated numerous treaties in which their trading competitors agreed to abolish the commerce in human beings, but the trade thrived illegally, much of it in the 1830s beneath the American stars and stripes. This was because the United States, unlike the other nations, refused to sign an agreement that allowed British naval captains to inspect their vessels. Francis Bacon, who was shipwrecked on the Gallinas Coast and spent two and a half years enjoying the hospitality of Blanco and other traders, noted that "the American flag is a complete shelter; no man of war dares to capture an American vessel." The colors of the United States were often flown even when the owner of the vessel, the merchant, and the captain were not American, in order to disguise and protect their illegal activities. The proslavery American consul in Cuba, Nicholas Trist, supported these unlawful activities.[71]

Each factory along the coast "consisted of a business room, with warehouse attached, filled with merchandize and provisions, and a barracoon for the slaves." The buildings were constructed in the common regional style: workers drove stakes into the ground and wattled them together with tough, willowy vines and topped them with thatch. According to Frederick Forbes, a naval officer who had visited the factories of the Gallinas region in the 1840s, the barracoon was "a shed made of heavy piles, driven deep into the earth, and lashed together with bamboos, thatched with palm leaves," equipped with chains, neck-rings, and padlocks. The walls of the structure were "four to six feet high, and between them and the roof is an opening about four feet, for the circulation of air." The floor had planks, "not from any regard to comfort to the slave, but because a small insect, being in the soil, might deteriorate the merchandise, by causing a cutaneous disease." Connected to each barracoon was a yard, where the enslaved were required to exercise daily. Dr. Hall noted that most enclosures contained "from 100 to 500 slaves," the largest "near 1,000." The *Amistad* Africans were held here for several weeks awaiting

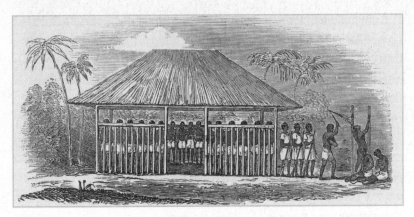

Barracoon

transit to a slaver. Sessi noted that he was incarcerated at Lomboko for a month, Cinqué for two months. Burna stayed at the fortress for "three and a half moons," during which time he did something to earn a flogging from no less a person than Pedro Blanco himself. His future as a rebel aboard the *Amistad* was foretold.[72]

Two to four white men, usually Spanish or Portuguese, tended each barracoon. "A more pitiable looking set of men we never met with," reported Dr. Hall. Blanco employed seventeen fellow European adventurers, who were variously feverish, suffering from malaria, emaciated, swollen, and dirty. They had dared to come to the "White Man's Grave," where, survivors said darkly, premature death was "*la fortuna de guerra*." Many died under ignominious circumstances, far from home, chasing the wealth that could be accumulated rapidly in the slave trade on the Gallinas Coast.[73]

During the 1830s the barracoons of Lomboko were often filled with children. Dr. Hall recalled visiting an enclosure that contained "some 300 boys, all apparently between ten and fifteen years of age, linked together in squads of twenty or thirty." Children, he thought, were popular among traders because larger numbers of them could be jammed aboard the slave ships and, once there, more easily controlled. Hall was haunted by the thought of "these bright-eyed little fellows" who were "doomed to the horrors of a middle latitude passage, probably in a three and a half feet between decks." Grabeau recalled that there were about two hundred children on board the *Teçora* during their voyage, which commenced in April 1839. Some of these children had been branded like cattle at Lomboko. Kagne, who would end up aboard the *Amistad*, "was burnt upon her shoulder with a red-hot pipe." Ever after she bore a scar "exactly the size of a pipe bowl."[74]

The condition of the enslaved held in the barracoons varied over time. Blanco was known for what some considered "humane" treatment—reasonable amounts of food, and limited violence on the part of the barracoon overseers. The regional system for the delivery of provisions did not always work well, and famine-like conditions could arise, whereupon, under extreme circumstances, "whole barracoons of slaves have been let loose for want of food." Those who escaped of their own initiative would be hunted down by overseers using dogs, and sometimes killed.[75]

The social routine at Lomboko was similar to what the enslaved would encounter at sea; indeed, it was in many ways a preparation for it. Forbes noted that "night and day these barracoons are guarded by armed men: the slightest insubordination is immediately punished." Those who resisted their enslavement would not be allowed out of the barracoon for meals, washing, and dancing. Overseers fed captives fish and rice twice a day. Grabeau recalled that men were "chained together by the legs." Any man the guards considered strong and dangerous was singled out for special treatment: he might be "beaten half to death to ensure his being quiet," then heavily fettered and locked in place between two others to limit his movements. Any man who dared to resist his captors would be given vicious exemplary punishments in order to terrorize everyone else. The most rebellious might be flogged to death.[76]

The horror stories of Lomboko spread far and wide. Brazilian, Portuguese, and Spanish seamen told Captain Forbes "fearful tales" of fever, famine, and mass death at the factories. George Thompson heard that because of rough waters and the "bad bar" at the mouth of the Gallinas River, "hundreds of poor natives" had been lost to "swarms of sharks" when canoes overset. On one occasion, the sea for miles around was "red with their blood." The *Amistad* Africans would carry horror stories of their own as they left Lomboko and boarded the slave ship *Teçora.*[77]

A Brazilian Slaver

As it happened, George Thompson went aboard a Brazilian slave ship of roughly the same size as the *Teçora* soon after he arrived in Free-town, Sierra Leone, in May 1848. The vessel had been captured by the British antislavery squadron. The five hundred enslaved on board would be liberated and the ship itself would be condemned and later sold at auction. Thompson, it must be noted, was no stranger to slavery. He was a committed abolitionist who had spent five years in a Missouri prison for his efforts to free the enslaved and ferry them to freedom. Still, he was profoundly shocked by what he saw.[78]

The first thing he noticed about the slaver was the extreme, promiscuous crowding: the "deck was literally covered with men, women and children *in a state of nudity*—many young girls and boys, and many *mothers* also!" Another two to three hundred people of all ages sat packed below on the lower deck, *"crowded between each other's legs"* in a space of thirty to thirty-six inches headroom, "not sufficient for a person to sit up straight!" As he paced the main deck, everywhere Thompson looked, "a *dense mass* of human beings" stared back at him mutely. "It was a soul-sickening sight." Will not the Lord awake? he wondered.

Thompson included an image of the ship he visited, drawing, literally, on the abolitionist tradition of rendering the slave ship in order to make its horrors visible and real to a reading public. He provides three views of vessel. The main one, at the top, diagrams the "form, divisions, arrangement and cargo" of the ship, with its main deck, lower (slave) deck, and hold, along with gun rooms for the ship's thirteen cannon, and the captain's cabin. In the hold are "leaguers," the huge water casks required to sustain hundreds as they crossed the ocean in the tropics, as well as smaller casks for food, and ship stores. At the bottom of the page is an aerial view of the ship's main deck, showing the two small gratings that were likely the only sources of air to those locked below.

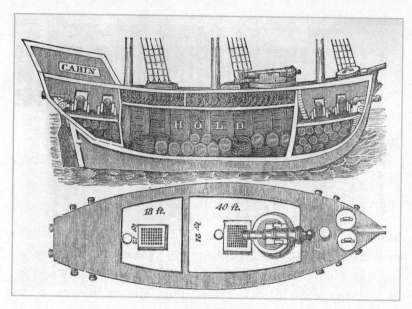

View of a slave ship

At the left is a depiction of the enslaved stowed on the lower deck, "crowded very thickly together." Thompson wrote that they were "shackled and handcuffed together, two and two (the right leg of one to the left leg of the next, and also the arms) to prevent their rising on the captors." In this dark and miserable place "deadly fevers" erupted, causing many bodies to be thrown overboard each morning to "the monsters of the deep." Such was the grim reality for several weeks as such vessels carried four hundred to six hundred people to the slave markets of Brazil and Cuba.

Thompson concluded that his efforts, in word and image, must be a failure: "No one can get a realizing sense of the horrors of a slave ship from any oral or written description—it must be *seen* or *felt*." His final words on the subject were, "It certainly was the most awful and shocking sight that I ever beheld." And yet whatever success he had describing these horrors owed something significant to the *Amistad* rebels. Not only was Thompson in Sierra Leone because his own American Missionary Association had been founded to accompany the *Amistad* captives in their repatriation, his very visualization of the slave ship

Lower deck, Middle Passage

had been shaped by the successful rebellion nine years earlier. For in drawing the lower deck full of the enslaved, Thompson drew upon an image that had been engraved by John Warner Barber and published in *A History of the Amistad Captives* (1840). The original image was based on conversations the artist had with the rebels themselves in the New Haven jail. The distance between decks in both images is listed as "3 feet 3 in." One of the faces on the lower deck appears to be that of Cinqué.[79]

The Middle Passage

Because the *Teçora* was an illegal slaver, very little documentation about it has survived. Yet the experience of the *Amistad* Africans can be reconstructed by drawing on evidence about other, similar slave ships and voyages from the same era, and by analyzing carefully what nine of the Africans—Bau, Burna, Cinqué, Fabanna, Grabeau, Kale, Kinna, Margru, and Teme—said about the ship and its Middle Passage. Within an ordeal of violence, suffering, and death lay a bonding experience that would prove crucial to their resistance and survival.[80]

The vessel was said to have been Portuguese, but it may have been Brazilian. Its name may not have been *Teçora* at all, but rather *Tesoura* (scissors) or, more likely, *Tesouro* (treasure), a not uncommon way to refer to the black gold it carried. Cinqué and Bau explained that the vessel was "crowded with slaves," five or six hundred in all, with "plenty of children." It was a brig, a two-masted vessel, and it was middling in size as slave ships went, probably between a hundred fifty and two hundred tons carrying capacity. It was therefore significantly more crowded than British slave ships as regulated by the Dolben Act of 1788—and those vessels were certainly crowded enough, as the infamous depiction of the Liverpool slave ship *Brooks* made chillingly clear. Like all other slavers in the post-abolition era, the vessel would have been designed for speed: it had to be able to outrun the vessels of the British anti-slave-trade patrol.[81]

The *Teçora* possessed the standard equipment of a slave ship. It had hundreds of sets of irons—shackles for the ankles, manacles for the wrists, and rings for the neck—as well as numerous chains and padlocks. Bau testified that they were "two and two chained together by hands and feet, night and day, until near Havana, when the chains were taken off." On the main deck was a huge copper pot, used to prepare the victuals of the enslaved (and the crew) for a passage that took "two moons," roughly eight weeks. In the hold, below the slave deck, sat the huge water casks, on top of which were piled wood for cooking, naval stores, and provisions, especially the rice that most peoples of the Gallinas region were accustomed to eat.[82]

The *Teçora* had a main deck, and below it a "slave deck," where the *Amistad* Africans and the hundreds of others would spend sixteen hours a day, more in bad weather. Men and women were stowed separately, the former forward, the latter aft. The lower deck itself featured platforms, built by the ship's carpenter in order to squeeze another hundred or more people into the vessel. According to Captain Forbes, who had sailed aboard a slave ship captured off the Gallinas Coast in 1838 and had seen many others, the usual distance between the lower deck and the main deck above was between thirty-six and forty-eight inches. He had seen one lower deck with a height of only eighteen inches. This claustrophobic nightmare had been specially designed to ship children, perhaps like another vessel Forbes saw that carried boys and girls between the ages of four and nine.[83]

Grabeau estimated that on the *Teçora*, the distance from the deck below them to the underside of the deck above was about four feet.

Those who were stowed on or below the platforms would therefore have had about twenty-two inches head space—not enough to sit up straight, as Thompson had noted. Even those with maximum head-room could not stand up, but were forced, as Grabeau and Kimbo explained, always "to keep a crouching posture." So tight was the typical stowage, remarked Forbes, that "when one moves, the mass must." The sea of bodies below deck rippled like the ocean waves outside.[84]

These bodies forced into small spaces were often left contorted and disfigured. This was evident in Freetown where some Liberated Africans—many of whom had probably spent less time on the lower deck of a slaver than the *Amistad* Africans because they had usually been captured *before* the Middle Passage—came off the slave ships in frozen deformity. F. Harrison Rankin saw "liberated slaves" on the streets of Freetown "in every conceivable state of distortion." Many would "never resume the upright posture." Some fit the bill described by an African constable: "He no good. He go for die."[85]

The men and women aboard the *Teçora* came from a broad array of culture groups in southern Sierra Leone. Probably the largest group were the Mende, as on the *Amistad*. And since people of Gbandi, Kono, Temne, Bullom, Gola, Loma, Kissi, and Kondo backgrounds were later aboard the *Amistad* and all had crossed the Atlantic on the same vessel, they must have been aboard the *Teçora* as well. Burna also mentioned the Mandingo, who were probably present along with several other groups, perhaps including some Vai who had fallen afoul of the law and been sold to Pedro Blanco. The *Teçora* thus contained a multiplicity of nations and ethnicities, some of whom, it must be emphasized, had been at war with each other. Had mercenary warboy Gnakwoi fought the Gola man Beri? Former enemies might find themselves sold to the same merchant and placed aboard the same ship. Each blamed the other for the horrific situation in which he now found himself, and vicious fights broke out regularly. "Warlike habits" filled the ship, and would eventually find their way onto the *Amistad*.[86]

The Transatlantic Slave Trade Database provides a statistical portrait based on 531 voyages of Portuguese or Brazilian slave ships between

1835 and 1840. They shipped 223,790 Africans and delivered 201,063 to the New World, with an average mortality rate of 13.8 percent (data for 496 voyages). The vessels averaged 169.2 tons and carried 451 slaves, 70.5 percent of whom were male and 49.8 percent children. These ships carried 2.67 slaves per ton on a Middle Passage that lasted 46.9 days. The database also contains evidence on fifty-four voyages that originated in Sierra Leone or the Windward Coast between 1835 and 1840. These vessels were considerably smaller at 89.4 tons, and more crowded: they carried an average of 323 slaves, 3.61 slaves per ton, shipping 17,442 and delivering alive 15,403. They made faster voyages—the Middle Passage was 42.6 days—and they relatedly suffered lower mortality: 9.6 percent. They had fewer males (68.2 percent) and more children (55.1 percent). In comparative terms, the *Teçora* appears to be a fairly typical ship of its time, similar to other Portuguese or Brazilian vessels in size, number of slaves carried, and the slave/ton ratio or degree of crowding. Its less common characteristics were its longer voyage and its higher incidence of mortality.[87]

The Middle Passage of the Africans was vexed and deadly from the beginning. After Kru canoemen had loaded the five to six hundred slaves, a British anti-slave-trade warship was spotted, which necessitated a frantic unloading and the hiding of the captives in a large, hot, airless cave, where several died. That vessel of unknown name, empty but equipped as a slaver, was captured by the British, taken to Freetown, and condemned. A short time later, when the coast was again clear, another vessel appeared and everyone was reloaded. Once aboard, the hardware of bondage was attached, said Grabeau: "They were fastened together in couples by the wrists and legs, and kept in that situation day and night." Women and children were not shackled; the latter had the free run of the ship except in bad weather when the hatches were battened down with everyone stowed beneath. It was common for the captain and crew to enlist the help of a few Africans to help control the others. The largest males were often made "head men" to oversee groups of ten to twenty. Once the voyage began, the captain spotted another British patrol vessel off the coast, hid the ship in a nearby inlet, and delayed the passage.[88]

The daily routine of the slave ship under sail was standard: two meals a day, taken on the main deck, with singing and dancing afterward, organized by the captain to preserve health and protect investment. Grabeau recalled that "they had rice enough to eat, but had very little to drink. If they left any of the rice that was given to them uneaten, either from sickness or any other cause, they were whipped. It was a common thing for them to be forced to eat so much as to vomit." Kale confirmed the dismal picture: "When we eat rice white man no give us to drink." Worse, he whipped "all who no eat fast." Kinna added that he "was sick & was forced to eat." He also recalled that "on their way to Cuba, they had scarcely any water & were sometimes brought upon deck to take the fresh air & chained down in the full blaze of a tropical sun, this was so intolerable that they often begged to go below again." That they wished to return to a lower deck where they would face seasickness, disease, overcrowding, and the pungent "smell of bondage" among the prisoners—the stench for which slave ships were infamous—is remarkable. In Brazil, slavers were sometimes burned after the voyage because it was impossible to eradicate the odor. Perhaps this was the fate of the *Teçora*.[89]

On the wide Atlantic, Cinqué exercised what may have been his first act of leadership: he "tried various ways to animate & keep up the depressed spirits of his countrymen." He exhorted his comrades to get rid of the "sad faces" and to make the best of the situation. "Is not ours a bold warlike nation?" he demanded to know. He reminded all that they were freeborn and that "who knows but we may be freemen yet!" He had plans of rebellion already in mind.[90]

It is powerfully suggestive that the Mende way of describing death was "crossing the waters," that is, crossing from the human to the spirit world. Whether the slave ship crossing the "great waters" was experienced as a kind of living death, one can only wonder. But actual, not merely metaphorical, death aboard the *Teçora* was certainly real and pervasive. All of the *Amistad* witnesses commented on the number who died. Bau explained in court that there were a "good many in the vessel, and many died." Burna noted the many who "died on the passage from Africa to Havana—signifying by gestures that they were thrown into the sea," as indeed happened each morning, when dead bodies were brought up from the lower deck. Some may still have been alive when thrown overboard by the illegal slavers as they sought to lighten ship when being chased by British vessels: the captain cynically wagered that their pursuer would stop to rescue those thrown overboard rather than continue the chase.[91]

Several of the *Amistad* captives resorted to a kind of guerilla theater to represent their experience of the Middle Passage. In order to make real the horrors of life below deck for those in a federal courtroom in January 1840, Cinqué sat on the floor, acting out how they had been manacled and shackled, their heads stooped low because there was so little headroom. On another occasion, in jail, he "got down on the floor, to show us [visitors] how they were stowed on board, then moved about on his knees, and as he rose put his hand of the top of his head, to indicate how low the deck was." Grabeau and Kinna did likewise: they "lay down upon the floor, to show the painful position in which they were obliged to sleep" aboard the slaver.[92]

Throughout these demonstrations, Cinqué emphasized the common experience of the Middle Passage. Speaking of the forty-nine men aboard the *Amistad*, he recalled, "We all came to Havana in same vessel." They were, in short, shipmates, or "ship-friends" as the relationship was sometimes called in Freetown in the 1830s: theirs were "the bonds of fellowship, bound in days of misery." The Mende word was *ndehun*, which means brotherhood. Fellow inductees of the Poro called each other "mates." It was noted of Burna that he "manifests much feeling when reference is made to his companions who have died," those people of many nations aboard both the *Teçora* and the *Amistad*. The social bonding—what anthropologists call "fictive kinship"—began in Lomboko, continued aboard the *Teçora* and in the barracoons of Havana, and reached a kind of apotheosis in action aboard the *Amistad*. It would continue in the New Haven jail and emerge finally as ethnogenesis, the formation of a new group called "the Mendi People."

Conquering warriors had been assimilating people from other cultures for centuries. As Arthur Abraham has noted, to this day Mende people "with no degree of consanguinity" routinely call each other father, mother, brother, and sister. Indeed, this seems to have been a regional phenomenon in Sierra Leone. Surgeon Robert Clarke noted that the multiethnic Liberated Africans in Freetown commonly used the terms "mammy," "daddee," "broder," and "sissa" as forms of address. The "additive" nature of Mende and other West African cultures served the *Amistad* Africans well when they were far from home. Life itself depended on *ndehun*.[93]

The Barracoons of Havana

In the middle of June 1839, after an eight-week voyage from Pedro Blanco's factory, the *Teçora* encountered another British antislave frigate as it neared Havana. Foone and Kimbo testified that they were landed "by night." Slavery was legal in Cuba, but the slave trade was not, for Spain had signed a treaty outlawing the trade, and the British meant to enforce it. Security was tight during disembarkation and afterward: Cinqué and Bau recalled that they were "ironed hand and foot." In addition, "every two were chained together at the waist and by the neck." The vessel was one of many slave ships arriving in the dynamic slave society of Cuba at the time: British Superintendent of Liberated Africans Richard Robert Madden claimed in November 1839 that some eighty vessels, bearing twenty-five thousand enslaved Africans, had already arrived in Havana during the year. It was customary for the slavers to allow a couple of weeks for their human cargo to recover their health before final sale.[94]

After five days the captives were moved to a new set of barracoons, named La Misericordia, located "nearly in front of the governor's country house, situated outside the walls of Havana, on the Paseo Militar, or public promenade." They took their place alongside sheep, oxen, and cattle for sale. According to Madden, who made it a point to find and visit these barracoons in order to learn more about the experience of the *Amistad* Africans while they were in Cuba, the keeper was the same Riera who had worked for Pedro Blanco/Pedro Martinez in Gallinas. When told of the revolt and the escape to freedom,

Riera said to Madden, "Que lástima" ("What a pity"). He referred to "the loss of so many valuable Bozals, or newly imported Africans." He regretted "that so much property should be lost to the owners."[95]

Cinqué and Grabeau recalled the time at La Misericordia and the moment of their purchase by José Ruiz. Cinqué saw Ruiz (nicknamed "Pepe") for the first time at the place he recollected as the "prison house." His future "owner" was conferring with the "man that brought us from Lomboko," the captain of the *Teçora*. Cinqué specifically remembered the humiliating medical examination: "Pepe feel of me— said 'Fine' 'fine.'" Grabeau went into more detail: Ruiz picked a number of them from the larger mass of the enslaved in the barracoon and "made them stand in a row." He then went up and down the row and "felt each of them in every part of the body; made them open their mouths to see if their teeth were sound." Abolitionist George Day, who took down Grabeau's account, added that Ruiz "carried the examination to a degree of minuteness of which only a slave dealer would be guilty."[96]

After Ruiz had selected the "prime slaves" he wanted, he prepared to remove them to another barracoon. This occasioned great turmoil, as the deep, painfully acquired social and emotional bonds of shipmates were now being torn apart. As "they were separated from their companions who had come with them from Africa," many wept, Grabeau recalled, especially women and children. Cinqué joined in, shedding tears of his own, but Grabeau did not, "because he is a man," he explained. Kimbo noted that at that moment "he thought of his home in Africa, and of friends left there whom he should never see again."[97]

Ruiz, on the other hand, recalled a routine business transaction when he testified about the purchase. He told a correspondent of the *New York Morning Herald* that "he first met these negroes in the fields close to Havana." He took his time in deciding who to buy: "He saw them and examined them for two or three days before he made his purchases." He was not concerned about their ethnicity or nationality. He did not bother to "inquire whether they were Congo negroes, or Mandangoes, or where they came from." He simply saw that "they were stout bodied men and he bought them." Ruiz purchased the forty-nine men "on account of his uncle, Don Saturnino Carrias, a merchant of Puerto Príncipe, not for any property of his [own] but for sale at that place." Pedro Montes bought the four children separately, in a different place, "the house of a tobacconist in Machandas street, in Havana," from petty traders named Xiques and Azpilaca. Ruiz and Montes stressed that the buying and selling of slaves was a normal part of life in Havana in 1839.[98]

It is impossible to appreciate the full experience of the *Amistad* Africans while they were held in the barracoons of Cuba's major city, but evidence suggests that it was a profound one, in which old bonds were broken and new ones formed amid dreadful uncertainty. The Africans would have been incarcerated along with large numbers of others who came from a much broader expanse of West Africa, from not only the Gallinas Coast, but also, moving from west to east, from Senegambia; the Gold Coast; Lagos and Onim in the Bight of Benin; Bonny in the Bight of Biafra; Princes and São Tomé in the Guinea Islands; Cabinda, Loango, and the Congo River in West Central Africa; even Mozambique in southeast Africa. They also would have interacted with some enslaved Africans already present, acculturated, and working in Havana. What kinds of discussions took place in the barracoons of Havana about urgent matters of common interest, and through what means of communication? Where are we? What kind of place is Havana? Where are we going? What will happen to us after we get there? Is there a place to which we might escape?[99]

Something happened in Havana to create terror among the *Amistad* Africans. Clues may be found in commentary by Madden, who lived in Havana and was roundly despised there for his abolitionist principles. He said repeatedly after the rebellion that

> these unfortunate persons, if they are returned to Cuba, will every man of them be put to death. This was understood as a matter of course by every body at Havana; and the feeling of every one there is that they deserve such a fate. Their act in boldly rising against their oppressors and striking a blow for freedom is looked upon as a deed of peculiar atrocity, and as demanding signal punishment.

The Spanish ambassador to the United States, Angel Calderón de la Barca, had stated in his first letter about the case, dated September 6, 1839, that the "internal tranquility" of Cuba depended on proper punishment "to prevent the commission of similar offenses" on the island. The *Amistad* rebels themselves shared the view that they would be executed if they were returned to Havana. The most likely speculation is that sometime during their stay in Havana, while they awaited sale and transport to another part of the island, they witnessed the execution of rebellious slaves, perhaps their very own shipmates from the *Teçora*, at "El Horcón" (place of the gallows), near the harbor. The *Amistad* Africans would tremble at the very mention of the city's name ever after.[100]

CHAPTER TWO

Rebellion

Night had fallen, and Havana's streetlamps cast a golden glow on the prisoners, now dressed as sailors, as they trudged toward the waterfront. None of them had a clear idea about where they were going nor why they were clothed in mariners' slops. Their captors herded them along, speaking quietly, even furtively, to them in the Spanish language not a single one of them could understand. After ten days in the city's infamous barracoons, they were, on this Friday evening, June 28, 1839, entering a new phase in their transatlantic ordeal.[1]

The white men guiding their way were nervous. The prisoners did not know why. Later they would learn that their captors feared the British vessel *Romney*, a large fourth-rate man-of-war (1,227 tons) anchored in the harbor and to be avoided at all costs, lest its soldiers and sailors seize the enslaved and liberate them, which a recent treaty between Britain and Spain had allowed them to do. The Afro-Cuban sailor Antonio recalled, "There were Spanish and Yankee men of war in the port, and English too. There were many vessels there in pursuit of slavers." This is why they were boarded in disguise and under cover of darkness.[2]

When they arrived at the dock they could barely make out their intended vessel, which was anchored several hundred yards off shore, "about a musket shot" away. José Ruiz helped to load his recently purchased adult male prisoners into lighters to carry them to a vessel with a rather cruel name: *La Amistad*, Spanish for "Friendship." Sailors rowed one boatload of disoriented captives after another out to the schooner, driving them up a rope ladder and over the rail to the main deck. Fifteen minutes after the last group of men came aboard, the sailors brought aboard three little girls and a boy, who arrived with their master, fifty-eight year-old Don Pedro Montes.

As they went aboard, the Africans would have noted how everything about the *Amistad* was smaller than the *Teçora*, on which they had made the Middle Passage. The vessel was modest in size—the schooner possessed a seventy-ton carrying capacity compared to one hundred fifty to two hundred tons for the brig. So too were their own numbers smaller: now only fifty-three compared to the five hundred to six hundred men, women, and children who had boarded the original slaver. The *Amistad*'s crew was tiny, too. Captain Ramón Ferrer commanded only four others, including the sailor and cook Celestino, a twenty-six-year-old mulatto from Puerto Rico, and the teenage Afro-Cuban sailor/cabin boy Antonio, both of whom Ferrer called his slaves. Two sailors, Manuel Padilla of Catalonia, Spain, and Jacinto Verdaque of Santo Domingo, would work the sails, steer the vessel, and keep an armed guard over the prisoners.

The well-educated young gentleman Ruiz and the older, less genteel Montes were not part of the crew, but they were unmistakably men of power in the larger scheme of things. Having bought the forty-nine adult male captives directly from the captain of the *Teçora*, Ruiz planned to take them to a burgeoning region called Puerto Príncipe and sell them to local sugar planters. Montes had purchased the children: Margru, Kagne, Teme, and Kale. Ruiz and Montes seemed so powerful, the captives could not easily tell who was actually in charge of the vessel.[3]

La Amistad

The *Amistad* was a long, low schooner, a popular type of two-masted craft the captives may have seen on the Gallinas Coast or indeed most anywhere around the Atlantic in the early nineteenth century. "La Amistad" was written on its square stern. The bottom was painted green, above which was a white streak. The upper works were black. The vessel was sixty-four feet long, nineteen feet nine inches wide, with a golden eagle on its prow and gilt stars on both sides. Built in Cuba of high-quality "West Indian hard wood"—the deck and hull bottom were made of red Spanish cedar, the sides of mahogany—this "sharp clipper" also had copper sheathing, with iron fastenings, to protect the hull against the shipworms and mollusks that routinely destroyed sailing ships in tropical waters. Captain Ferrer had ordered an awning to be built over the deck to protect the crew and human cargo from the blazing sun until the time for sailing came.[4]

The *Amistad* was essentially a coastal trader, but it had made longer voyages to Jamaica, and the coppered hull suggests the possibility of a transatlantic slaving voyage or two, as such protection was expensive and not common among vessels built solely for local and regional commerce. Better known for speed than carrying capacity, the schooner could outrun most British ships policing the slave trade and hence became a preferred vessel after the commerce in bodies had been outlawed in 1807 in Great Britain and 1808 in the United States. As the sailor Antonio testified in U.S. District Court in January 1840, "The Sch. Amistad had carried slaves before—every two months made trip." The temporary awning was common to slave ships.[5]

Because Captain Ferrer had run an advertisement in *Noticioso y Lucera* seeking passengers and cargo a week before the voyage, the hold of roughly 6,600 cubic feet contained a big, well-sorted cargo. Manufactured goods made up a large part, many of them destined for use on sugar plantations: "6 mill rollers, 8 cogg wheels, 6 piece of iron, one box of iron wedges," as well as iron castings, and a "mill for grinding sugar cane." Boxes and bales of fabrics and clothes were also abundant: silks, crepes, calicoes, ginghams, gauze, German and Silesian linens, muslins, and "50 pairs of shirts and pantaloons." Other items were for everyday use: soap, glass knobs, crockery, toys, needles, iron pots, "48 rolls of wire," and leather goods of several kinds: saddles, bridles, and holsters. The *Amistad* was a floating general store of plantation life. As on any vessel involved in nefarious activities, the captain made sure to have an assortment of national flags, "half a dozen" of them, to be used as the occasion demanded. Another especially important part of the cargo was "1 box containing 4 percussion guns." These weapons, probably produced in Britain, represented a new and recent improvement over previous models in that they allowed quick firing and were not damaged by water and dampness—two features that would have made them very useful on a vessel like the *Amistad*. The sailors carried muskets to overawe the enslaved.

The hold also held a huge amount of food: six hundred pounds of rice, the main staple of life to Mende people and others who lived on what was sometimes called the "Grain Coast" of West Africa, as well as substantial quantities of bread, fruit, olives, Spanish beans, sweet potatoes, sausages, and "fresh beef." Ten barrels of biscuit, 480 bunches of bananas, five hundred pounds of jerked beef, and three dozen fowl stored in hen coops rounded out the extensive edible holdings. There was much less available on board to drink: fourteen demijohns of wine, not to be consumed on the voyage but rather sold at its end, and only six casks of water. As it happened, in the days leading up to the voyage, ship captains in Havana were having "great difficulty of finding a sufficient quantity of water casks," as one of them put it, a shortage that would have consequences.[6]

Unlike the *Teçora*, the *Amistad* did not have a lower deck, where the enslaved would be jammed together overnight and in bad weather. It was a single-deck vessel with a hold, which measured six feet six inches from the top of the keel to the underside of the main deck above, with headroom diminishing on both sides as the hull curved upward to meet the outer edges. The bulky cargo already stored in the hold left limited room for the human freight, which was jumbled in with, and on top of, the hogsheads, casks, and boxes. The enslaved, crammed below deck, had very little headroom.

Indeed, the hold was so crowded that half of the captives would have to be quartered on the main deck and forced to sleep in the open, overnight, in chains for the three-day voyage. The rest were fettered and kept below. Because the *Amistad* had made numerous voyages in the coastal slave trade, its timbers retained the smell of previous terrified passengers, a condition made worse by the lack of ventilation. The prisoners would sit in the dark, stuffy, cramped hold for long hours at a time, in a painful crouch, enveloped by, and themselves exuding, the sharp odor of bondage.

The deck of the *Amistad* was crowded, especially during the day when all sixty people (fifty-three Africans, five crew members, and two passengers) inhabited its 1,200 square feet, much of which was devoted to the masts, the longboat, the hatchway, and other shipboard fixtures. The *Amistad* lacked not only the size of the *Teçora*, but several features of larger slave ships, notably a barricado on the main deck, a defensive bulwark behind which the crew could retreat in the event of an uprising and from which they could fire their muskets and pistols down on the insurgents. It also lacked a gun room for the secure stowage of weapons. The *Amistad* did have a galley with a brick oven for the preparation of the captives' food—a telltale sign of its slave-trading purpose. It also had a large hatchway amidships for the easier movement of bodies from above and below during the voyage. It had ten sweeps (oars) for self-locomotion and easier maneuvering along the treacherous shoals and inlets of the north coast of Cuba.[7]

Because the schooner carried a lot of sail on its tall, light spars—more sail than most other vessels its size—and because the crew was small for the intended three-day voyage, sailors based in port would have helped to prepare the ship to sail. Once at sea, the *Amistad* was a "great sailer," that is to say, very fast and maneuverable by the standards of the day. One knowledgeable observer pointed out that it would outsail most United States Navy revenue cutters, which also were designed for speed in order to catch quick and evasive smugglers.[8]

A New Middle Passage

The sailors hoisted the anchor and the vessel slipped quietly past the British antislavery vessel, sailing by Fort Moro at the mouth of the harbor around midnight, just as the evening gun fired. The intended voyage was fairly routine, one hundred ten leagues (three hundred miles) eastward from Havana to Guanaja in Puerto Príncipe (now called Camagüey), a thriving new region for sugar production. Landowners bellowed for slaves as they sought to hew plantations from the verdant forest. Captain Ferrer himself had made the trip many times, as had his bondmen, Antonio and Celestino, and likely too his sailors, Manuel and Jacinto. The regional slave trade was crucial to local, colony-wide, and imperial economic development.[9]

The voyage began well, with a good wind. Yet Captain Ferrer, who had made the passage many times, knew that the winds could shift and that the usual three-day voyage could stretch to two weeks, or longer. He immediately put the enslaved on short allowance, conserving food and especially the understocked water for the additional time they might be at sea. On the second day out, the small vessel ran into a storm, no doubt terrifying all of the Africans on board, but probably not the experienced sailors who would have known harder weather. Turbulence without was soon matched by turbulence within.

The first sign of trouble came early, when on the night immediately following departure "one of the sailors observed that the slaves were coming up from the hold of the forecastle, and that they made some noise, on which account the sailor reprimanded them and told them to be quiet and go down into the hold." This seemed innocent enough; "murmurings" and commotion were common on slave ships. Crowded conditions produced anger, frustration, and fights among the captives and with the crew. Currents of tension and violence coursed through all slaving vessels, including the *Amistad*.[10]

The hardware of bondage was part of the charge. Grabeau and Kimbo, both leaders in the resistance, remembered that "during the night they were kept in irons, placed about the hands, feet, and neck. They were treated during the day in a somewhat milder manner, though all the irons were never taken off at once." The captain and crew slapped manacles, shackles, and neck-rings on the captives, especially overnight because some of the prisoners slept near them, on the main deck. Kinna remembered the neck-rings as a special humiliation: "Chain on neck—you know dey chain ox." Fetters turned human beings into property, but not without a struggle.[11]

Casual violence was commonplace on slaving vessels and the *Amistad* was no exception. Captain and crew alike used whips, clubs, and fists to terrorize and control the captives. On the deck of any deep-sea sailing ship could be found many tools and other items that handily became instruments of violent discipline. Cinqué and Bau recalled, "The captain of the schooner was very cruel; he beat them on the head very hard with any thing he could catch." Cinqué remembered with fierce anger a time when Celestino slapped him on the head with a plantain. The cook would pay dearly for this mistake.[12]

The *Amistad* Africans also complained that they were given too little to eat and drink on the voyage—"half eat half drink" was how Fuli described short allowance. In concrete terms this meant two potatoes and one plantain twice a day, in the morning and evening. The fare may have been enough for the children on board, but it was too little for the men. Kinna recalled that the captain "gives us but little eat." Cinqué and Bau added that they were kept "almost starved"—this on a vessel that was full of food.[13]

Water was a greater source of strife. Grabeau and Kimbo recalled that "their allowance of food was very scant, and of water still more so. They were very hungry, and suffered much in the hot days and nights from thirst." The allotment of water was half a teacupful in the morning and half a teacupful in the evening. As the prisoners suffered, they watched the crew wash their clothes in fresh water. To make matters worse, Celestino taunted them by taking long drafts in front of them. Kinna recalled, "he drink plenty, long." On a craft sailing through the tropics in midsummer, the Africans simply were not given enough water to support nature.[14]

At least some of the captives seem to have been able to move around the vessel during the daytime, and they took matters into their own hands. They searched for water and they found it belowdecks. To satisfy their burning thirst, they tapped and drank it, without permission. When they were caught, Captain Ferrer decided to teach everyone a lesson. At least five men—Fuli, Kimbo, Pie, Moru, and Foone—and perhaps as many as seven (Sessi, Burna)—were each, by turn, restrained and flogged.[15] "[F]or stealing water which had been refused him," Fuli "was held down by four sailors and beaten on the back many times by another sailor, with a whip having several lashes."

He referred to the lacerating cat-o'-nine-tails, the primary instrument of power aboard a slave ship. The sailors then flogged the other four, then repeated the entire cycle of punishment four times on each person. In order to maximize the torture, the seamen, with Ruiz's permission, mixed together "salt, rum, and [gun] powder" and applied the burning compound to Fuli's wounds. Not surprisingly—for gunpowder was often used by sailors in tattooing—the marks of the wounds on Fuli's back were still visible months later. Kinna later pointed out another use of the compound: "Rum, salt, powder—put togedder, make eat dis I tell you." In October, one of the Africans was still "lame, so as hardly able to walk, as he declares from blows received on board the Amistad." Tensions aboard the schooner escalated amid the hunger, thirst, violence, torture, and blood. As the Africans later announced, "They would not take it."[16]

Who Is for War?

Shortly after the morning meal of Sunday, June 30, Cinqué and Celestino squared off in a fateful encounter on the main deck of the Amistad. Tension had been rising between the two. Celestino had cuffed Cinqué and had likely been greeted in return by fiery eyes of resistance. He expanded his campaign by taunting the proud prisoner, of whom it could have been said, "Dat man ha big heart too much."[17]

Because the two men shared no common language, Celestino communicated by signs and gestures—"talking with his fingers," as one African recalled—and the menacing cook's knife he held in his hand. In order to answer the questions that were on every captive's mind—where are we going and what will become of us at the end of the voyage?—Celestino drew his blade's edge across his throat: they were going to a place where they would all be killed. The cook then made a chopping motion with his knife to show that their bodies would then be hacked to bits by the white men. He took the imagined bits of flesh to his mouth: they would be eaten. He gestured to a cask of salt beef, implying that it was filled with the bodies of Africans from a previous voyage; he gestured again to an empty cask indicating that therein lay their fate. As Cinqué noted, "The cook told us they carry us to some place and kill and eat us." Kinna added that Celestino "with his knife, made signs of throat-cutting. &c., and pointed to the barrels of beef, and thus hinted to Cinquez, that himself and his companions were to be cut up and salted down for food like beef." He pointed to "an Island ahead where the fatal deed was to be perpetrated." His words had direct impact, although they did not terrorize and pacify, as he had intended they should. Instead, they galvanized the Africans to action. Every account of the uprising told by any of the *Amistad* Africans emphasized the decisive importance of Celestino's threat as a catalyst of rebellion.[18]

The slave-sailor's taunt resonated with a potent set of beliefs held by the *Amistad* Africans. In their African homelands, people had long believed that the strange white men who showed up on the coast in "floating houses" were cannibals. Those forced aboard slave ships often thought that the casks of beef they saw held the flesh of previous captives and that puncheons of "red wine" held their blood. Slave-holders in many parts of West Africa had tried to strengthen discipline in their own societies by threatening to sell slaves to the white men, who would, they explained, carry them across the "great waters" and eat them. Since many of the *Amistad* captives came from deep inland and had never seen white men, their ships, or even the sea, Celestino's threat of cannibalism was believable.[19]

Strengthening that grim prospect was another belief, common among the Mende, the Temne, and other groups that cultural power was often wielded through the control and manipulation of body parts, which provided access to the world of malevolent spirits. Witches and sorcerers made special efforts to secure the hair, teeth, and bones of famous warriors, which might be used to create potent "medicine." Was Celestino a sorcerer, a *honei*, who used his powers on behalf of the white men? Did Cinqué the warrior feel threatened by the taunt? One of the main functions of the Poro Society was to punish, and at times to execute, witches and sorcerers who worked against the common good.[20]

That night, after the vexed encounter between Cinqué and Celestino, as the Amistad sailed past Bahia de Cadiz a little before midnight, a storm arose from the shore. Rain poured from a dark, cloudy, moonless sky. Ruiz remembered it as a "black night." High winds prompted Captain Ferrer to order all hands aloft to take in the topsails to reduce the power of the wind to buffet the vessel. In a couple of hours, the rain stopped and the storm abated. All of the crew and passengers, except the helmsman, retired and were soon "sunk in sleep."[21]

A bigger storm was brewing in the hold of the vessel. Celestino's murderous sign language had created a crisis among the captives. As Grabeau stated and Kimbo affirmed, his sinister threat of death and cannibalism "made their hearts burn." Kinna remembered, "We very unhappy all dat night—we fraid we be kill—we consider." Soon, "We break off our chains and consider what we should do." Crowded together in the hold of the ship, where their broad capacity to communicate allowed them to "consider," they held a palaver and urgently debated what to do in the face of an unspeakably horrible mass death.[22]

An "old man" named Lubos had earlier reminded everyone that "no one ever conquered our nation, & even now we are not taken by fair means." They were warriors, after all, and someone, perhaps Cinqué, soon asked, "Who is for War?" Everyone was, except a few Bullom men, who did not want to "make war on the owners of the vessel." Lubos responded to their reluctance by asking whether they would rather be "slaughtered for Cannibals" or "die fighting for life." The latter was at least an honorable death.

These warriors would not be transformed into slaves easily. The Amistad Africans had actually begun to organize themselves much earlier, at Lomboko, where Cinqué and Grabeau met. The former was a warrior, perhaps a head war man; the latter was apparently a high-ranking member of the Poro, as suggested by his extensive scarification and a comment by someone who knew him in Mende country before his enslavement, that he was "connected with a high family, though poor himself." Cinqué and Grabeau used their combination of military, spiritual, and political authority to expand the core group that would lead the rebellion: Burna, the third leading figure, and

Moru, both Gbandi; Shule ("fourth in command, when on board the schooner") and Kimbo, both Mende; and Fa and Faquorna, nationality unknown, but likely Mende. All had probably been warriors of reputation in their native societies. Their knowledge, experience, and mindset of combat would now be crucial components of self-defense and emancipation. Other experienced warriors included Gnakwoi, who had fought with Goterah's mercenary army, and Grabeau, who had battled "insurgent slaves" not far from the American colony of Liberia. Cinqué, Bau, and no doubt many others "had been in battles, in their own country" and were trained in the use of muskets, likely as members of the army of King Amara Lalu, who fought the aggressive expansion of King Siaka, the aging, almost blind but still paramount king allied with the Spanish.[23]

The rebels had even more recent and relevant experience in warfare: they had engaged in an uprising aboard the slave ship *Teçora*. Their reputation had followed them ashore into the barracoons of Havana, where Captain Ferrer of the *Amistad* was "warned, previous to sailing, to keep a look out for the negroes, as they had attempted to rise and take the vessel in which they were brought from Africa." That rebellion failed. Some of its makers may have been executed at El Horcón; others would get another chance to seize a vessel and free themselves. They studied the ship and whispered their findings to each other in the hold. They wanted to know how the vessel worked (some had probably worked on the *Teçora*), how many were the crew, what were their habits, what were their arms. (The crew was small; they kept no regular watch; they had muskets, pistols, and whips.) The warriors saw that the prospects for rebellion aboard the *Amistad* were much greater than they had been on the *Teçora*.[24]

Their hearts aflame over Celestino's threat, the Africans met as a kind of displaced but reconstituted floating Poro Society, far from its normal meeting places inland in West Africa, to "consider" the situation. United by the "fictive kinship" that grew ever stronger out of their common ordeal at Lomboko, on the *Teçora*, in the Havana barracoons, and now on the *Amistad*, they made a fateful collective life-and-death decision: together they would rise up, throw off their slavery, regain their freedom, seize the vessel, and try to sail it home to Sierra Leone. At the end of the palaver, everyone had "one word WAR!! and war immediately." The Poro had created *ngo yela*—"one word" or "unity".[25]

The decision made, the Africans now faced a literally iron dilemma. How would they get out of the manacles, shackles, neck-rings, chains, and padlocks that rendered them unable to move about the ship? Cinqué later remarked that "the chain which connected the iron collars about their necks, was fastened at the end by a padlock, and that this was first broken and afterwards the other irons." Kinna also stated, "We break off our chains," but he added a second, somewhat different description of what they did: Cinqué found a loose nail on deck and used it to pick the central padlock. Whether the locks were broken or picked, it was significant that two of the forty-nine enslaved men were blacksmiths, who knew the properties of iron intimately from their work. Sessi was described as "a blacksmith, having learnt that trade of his brother; he made axes, hoes, and knives from iron obtained in the Mendi country." When speed was crucial to avoiding detection, getting so many people out of irons was necessarily a communal undertaking. Soon a substantial number of men were free of their chains and ready to fly into action, awaiting Cinqué's "signal for them to rise upon their vile masters and the crew."[26]

Facing the prospect of a horrific death at the hands of the white flesh-eaters, they would risk a different kind of death to escape their captors' bloody clutches. At four a.m. the ship was in almost total darkness. Everyone was asleep except the sailor at the helm. Cinqué, Faquorna, Moru, and Kimbo climbed up from the hold through the hatchway and onto the main deck. It is not clear whether they had to break open the grating or whether it had been left unlocked by mistake. They snuck quietly toward Celestino—not Captain Ferrer—as the first and primary object of their wrath. He was sleeping in the ship's longboat, which lay in the waist, on the larboard side, near the cabin. Along the way Cinqué picked up a belaying pin, or handspike, used to turn the ship's windlass, and his mates did likewise, quietly gathering weapons from the main deck. They surrounded Celestino and clubbed him repeatedly with hard, crushing blows. Fuli later recalled, "The cook was killed first—was killed by Jingua [Cinqué] with a stick, while lying in the boat." Burna agreed: "He saw Cinguez strike the cook with a club, probably a handspike." During the beating, Celestino did not cry out, did not groan, did not make any sound at all, according to Antonio. The only sounds to be heard in the damp night air above the rolling of the sea and the creaking of the ship were the thuds of wood on flesh and bone.[27]

Now began "the whooh," as Burna called the chaos of open rebellion that engulfed the small main deck. The commotion woke up the captain, who was sleeping on a mattress not far away, as well as the rest of the crew and the two passengers, Ruiz and Montes, who were in the cabin. Ferrer called out, "Attack them, for they have killed the cook." Amid the "confusion and uproar," as Ruiz remembered it, they scrambled frantically in the dark for arms, grabbing whatever was close at hand; there was no time to load pistols or muskets. Captain Ferrer seized a dagger and a club and fought furiously to defend his vessel from capture. The two sailors, Manuel and Jacinto, who were supposed to be the armed guard to prevent what was now happening before their very eyes, threw themselves into the battle, one with a club, the other with no weapon at all. Montes armed himself with a knife and a pump handle, screaming all the while at the Africans to stop, to be still. The unarmed sailor yelled to Montes to get the dead cook's knife and give it to him. Ruiz grabbed an oar as he scrambled from his passenger's quarters, shouting "No! No!" as he came on deck. Ruiz then "stood before the caboose and halloed to the slaves to be quiet and to go down into the hold." They ignored the command of the (now former) master; indeed, more Africans escaped their chains and joined the fray, wielding fearsome machetes that had been found by the little girls, who had had free range of the vessel. Seeing that the situation was far beyond exhortation, Ruiz called to Montes to kill some of the rebels in order to frighten the rest and to restore order. He believed, wrongly, that the Africans were all "great cowards."[28]

At first the crew and passengers were able to drive the rebels from amidships beyond the foremast, and at this point Captain Ferrer, who desperately hoped that this was a rebellion of the belly, commanded

Antonio to fetch some sea biscuit and throw it among the rebels in the hope of distracting them. He knew they were hungry—hunger had been a complaint since the voyage began. Antonio did as his master commanded, but the insurgents, he explained, "would not touch it." Antonio himself opted for neutrality: he climbed up the mainstays, where he would watch the struggle unfold, safely from above.[29]

Several of the Africans were reluctant to attack the captain until Cinqué exhorted them to do so. A small group formed a "phalanx" to surround him, machetes in hand. As the battle raged, Captain Ferrer killed a man named Duevi and mortally wounded a second, unnamed rebel, which infuriated the other Africans and made them fight harder. He also wounded others, as Kale recalled: "Then captain kill one man with knife and cut Mendi people plenty." Two of the rebels attacked Montes with an oar, which he grabbed and used to hold them off. Montes wrestled with the men until one of the sailors cried out that he should let it go or they would kill him. At this point, a blow to his arm caused Montes to drop his knife. He groped desperately around the deck in an effort to find it. Ruiz continued to scream at the rebels to stop fighting and go below, but they ignored him, soon disarming him of his own makeshift weapon.[30]

Suddenly the tide of battle turned—red. An insurgent wielding one of the machetes slashed one of the sailors, who cried out "Murder!" He and his crewmate saw not only defeat but certain death in the ever-larger mob, now armed with machetes, so they threw a canoe overboard—they would not have had time to lower the longboat, which was in any case heavy with the battered corpse of Celestino. They jumped into the water, leaving the remaining five to battle ten times their number. Of one of the sailors, Kinna recalled: "He swim— swim long time—may be swim more—we not know." The two sailors, cut and bleeding, eventually crawled into the canoe and began paddling for land. They had about eighteen miles to cover and it was by no means certain they would make it.[31]

Someone now gave Montes "a powerful blow on the head with a cane knife, and he fell senseless on the deck." Stunned, with another deep wound on his arm and "faint from the loss of blood," he roused himself, staggered from the battle scene, and fell headlong down the hatchway. Once below, he remained conscious enough to crawl into a space between two barrels and hide beneath a canvas sail. It was a frail hope against death.[32]

On the main deck, Cinqué and the other leaders of the rebellion now surrounded Captain Ferrer in a fury of flashing blades. Faquorna apparently struck the first two blows; Cinqué struck the last one. Antonio testified, "Sinqua killed Capt with cane knife—see it with my eyes."[33] When the time for the death blow came, one of the brave combatants, Kimbo, proved to be squeamish: "When the Captain of the schooner was killed, he could not see it done, but looked another way." Slashed several times on his face and body, the captain collapsed on the deck, bloody, crumpled, and lifeless. The warriors danced, yelled, and beheaded the captain in their customary rituals of war called *kootoo*.[34]

The rebels now went in search of Montes, whose ragged, heavy breathing gave away his hiding place below deck. An enraged Cinqué found him and swung at him twice with his cane knife, narrowly missing. Montes begged for his life, to no avail as Cinqué prepared to swing again, until Burna stayed his arm. Cinqué and Burna then carried Montes up to the main deck, where he saw Ruiz, "seated upon the hen coop with both hands tied." He, too, was pleading for his life. The rebels laced the two Spaniards together, "making at the same time horrible gestures" and threatening to kill them. Someone dragged young Antonio down from the stays and tied him to the two other prisoners. After a little while, Ruiz recalled, the insurgents "made signs that they would not hurt me." The new masters of the vessel then locked their prisoners below as they went through the captain's cabin and also familiarized themselves with the cargo.[35]

With two dead, two overboard, and three disarmed, bound, and begging for their lives, an eerie silence came over the bloodstained deck. The rebellion was over. The Mende way of war had carried the day. Mende warriors always used knives—the cutlass at home, the very similar cane knife aboard the *Amistad*. They used typical Mende military tactics: encouraged by a moonless night they launched a surprise guerilla attack, using war shouts and swinging their blades wildly in a successful effort to make their enemies abandon position. The goal of warfare was not death, but rather capture of people and place, and both were quickly achieved aboard the vessel. The social world of the *Amistad* had been turned upside down. The captain and cook had been killed, the sailors had been forced to jump overboard, and the slaveholders were now prisoners. Those who had once been slaves had won their freedom in a desperate armed gamble.

A New Order

Cinqué the warrior apparently remained in something of a rage for a time after the rebellion had formally ended. Antonio testified that Cinqúe threatened to kill him, Ruiz, and Montes. He even threatened to kill Burna for defending Ruiz and Montes, partly, it seems, because he feared Burna was conspiring with them to return the vessel to Havana. Ruiz noted that Antonio had a special skill that kept him alive: "They would have killed him, but he acted as interpreter between us, as he understood both languages." It also helped that Antonio had become good friends with one of the teenage captives, the "stout built youth" Ndamma, who protected him. Montes was forced "to fall on his knees and kiss the feet of the ring leader before he would spare his life."[36]

Burna gave his own account of the clash with Cinqué: "I say where whitey man? where old man? (meaning Montez) where sailor man? Cinguez say he will kill 'em; Cinguez want me tie old man; I say no—you cut off my head first—Cinguez give me money in cloth; I no take it; I tell him he no hurt young massa, (Ruiz) he say no, he kill old man; I say no, I take him off." Burna won this heated debate, as Ruiz and Montes lived to tell the tale of the uprising. The warriors did not annihilate all of their enemies.[37]

The following morning, the rebels were in a state of jubilation. Montes recalled, "They were all glad, the next day, at what had happened." Neither he nor Ruiz, however, were sure what had actually transpired amid the chaos. They saw that the captain, cook, and two sailors were missing and they supposed all had been killed. Antonio, who had seen everything, told them that the first two had been killed, but the others had escaped in a canoe.[38]

The rebels, led by Cinqué, Grabeau, and Burna, locked Ruiz and Montes in irons, many unused sets of which they suddenly had at their disposal. When the slaveholders complained of their chains, Cinqué howled in righteous fury: "You say irons good enough for nigger slave; and if they good enough for slave, they are good enough for Spaniards, too." Ruiz and Montes were likewise allowed little to drink, likely the same half teacupful of water twice a day that not long ago had been the portion of the Africans. Again they complained of their treatment and again Cinqué pointed out the contradictions: "You say water enough for nigger slave; so water enough for Spaniards." The object lesson continued for two days, in order to give Ruiz and Montes "a taste of their own cruelty toward the slaves," said Kinna. Thereafter the chains were removed and they were given food and water in the same proportions as everyone else. They were threatened many times, but never again beaten or harmed, as Ruiz and Montes themselves admitted.[39]

The morning after the rebellion Cinqué and Faquorna threw the headless body of Captain Ferrer overboard and washed the deck of his blood. The rebels released Ruiz and Montes from their irons, stripping the latter of his clothes, which were badly stained by the blood from his wounds. They then "took from him the key of his trunk and brought him clean clothes, which they made him put on." A new phase of life aboard the *Amistad* had begun.[40]

Toward a Free Country

The final, and in many ways the biggest, questions about the revolt aboard the *Amistad* remained: Could the rebels sail the ship? Could they set and manage the sails, operate the windlass, raise and lower the anchor, handle the longboat, and steer the ship? Could they navigate the treacherous shoals of the Caribbean and survive violent tropical storms at sea? Could they, in the end, get themselves to a place where their desperate rebellion would result in true emancipation? Could they work their way to freedom?

Cuban authorities, as soon as they learned of the revolt from the sailors who jumped overboard and made it to shore, assumed that the answer to all these questions was no. They dispatched a ship of war, the *Cubano*, to search for the *Amistad*, thinking that the Africans would run the vessel aground on the north coast of Cuba and go ashore as maroons. They would not, or could not, remain at sea. Yet this is precisely what the *Amistad* rebels decided to do, outthinking the government of the slaveholders and wagering that they could provide affirmative answers to the big questions facing them. For a disparate group of people who had grown up in non-seafaring societies and had had nothing to do with deep-sea sailing vessels until they were engulfed in the twin catastrophe of enslavement and Atlantic shipment, it was a bold and daring decision.[41]

Even though the *Amistad* rebels had established their leadership roles before and during the uprising, the collective continued to meet and act together as the situation unfolded. As Ruiz noted, a few days after the rebellion, the group met and officially chose Cinqué as their leader, as the Poro Society might. He had earned the position in the customary Mende way, through action. Other positions also were established: Sessi, who apparently possessed some seafaring knowledge (probably acquired aboard the *Teçora*), would steer and "make sail." Foone would be delegated as the group's cook.[42]

As the new masters of the *Amistad*, the rebels gave their most important order to Montes, who had once been a sea captain and therefore knew navigation, to take them home—to sail back across the "great waters" to Sierra Leone. Using Antonio as interpreter, they made it clear that they wanted to reverse the Middle Passage. Montes protested that he did not know the way, but the rebels refused to accept this as an answer. Cinqué told Montes that he should "steer toward the rising of the sun." It had been behind them as they came westward on the *Teçora* and would now be ahead of them on the return voyage. The sun would guide the way.[43]

Montes had no choice but to do as he was told, for the demand was made with cane knives hovering above his head. "Every moment my life was threatened," Montes recalled. Yet he bravely and cleverly developed a plan to thwart his new masters and to save his and Ruiz's lives. During the daylight hours he would sail, as instructed, toward the rising sun. He would do so slowly, with sails loose, beating in the wind, to limit headway. But at night he would tack back to the west and north, to stay in coastal waters, where he was more likely to encounter other vessels. The man who had done all he could to evade the British antislavery patrols in Cuban waters now hoped against hope that one of them might find him. Naval officers who once would have confiscated his property might now save his life.[44]

The Africans did not trust Montes, and rightly so. Fear and stress roiled the vessel. The first time Montes reversed course, they sensed something was wrong and worried that he was secretly taking the *Amistad* back to Havana. They held a "consultation"—another Poro meeting—and decided to kill both him and Ruiz. It would be better to go it alone than risk the treachery of the white men. When the time came for the killing, Montes fell upon his knees and begged again for his life, pleading for his children and family. The influential Burna probably supported him. A majority of the rebels relented again, and let Montes live.

Ruiz and Montes also wrote a letter and explained to Cinqué that if he would give it to the captain of any vessel they should encounter at sea, the recipient would take them to Sierra Leone. Cinqué took the letter, pretending to agree to the proposal, but afterwards discussed the matter with his brethren and expressed his suspicion. Unfamiliar with written language because they had none in Mende, and unable to read what the Spaniards had written, Cinqué and his comrades decided that it was impossible for them to know what was in the letter. The leader concluded, "There may be death in it." Indeed there may have been, for Ruiz and Montes were undoubtedly trying to send a message that would result in the recapture of the vessel, their own liberation, and the reenslavement of the Africans. The Africans attached a piece of iron to the letter with a string and sent it "to the bottom of the sea."[45]

On another occasion, Cinqué perceived what he thought was decep-tion and demanded that the anchor be dropped so that progress in the wrong direction might be halted. When Montes told him the waters were too deep to anchor at that location, Cinqué, an adept swimmer and diver, "jumped overboard and was under so long they thought he would never rise." Finally he emerged from the water to say that "there was no bottom to be found." Montes was right: the ocean was too deep for anchoring. Westward they drifted—not by accident and not for the last time.[46]

Uncertainty about where they were going was soon compounded by another, more immediate problem, one that would plague them for the entire voyage and severely limit what they could do: they did not have enough water. Because water puncheons and casks had been scarce in Havana when the *Amistad* set sail, they not only lacked water, they lacked enough *containers* for water, so they had to stop every few days, under dangerous circumstances, to refill the vessels they had. They caught all the rainwater they could, squeezing the sails for each lifesaving drop. Every time they went ashore for water, on one iso-lated cay after another across the Bahamas, they did so with dire fear of being discovered and recaptured. Even when they could fill their demijohns, pots, and bottles, "it was soon drunk up" and the search began all over again. They spent more than a month sailing around a relatively small geographic area in the Bahamas in search of water.[47]

The rebels were plagued by another big problem: they simply did not know where they were. They had no maps, no navigational knowl-edge, and few visual markers at sea by which to judge the ship's loca-tion or progress. To make matters worse, they did not know where they could get reliable information or who they could trust in the per-ilous Caribbean world of bondage. They did not realize, for example, that in the very Bahama Islands around which they were now sailing, the British government had freed all slaves less than a year before, on August 1, 1838, and that they might have found refuge there, as other self-emancipated people had done and would continue to do. They went ashore to look for water in one place because Montes told them "there were only negroes in that part and no slaves." The rebels proceeded cautiously, and upon seeing two white men they jumped back into their boat, rowed back to the schooner, hastily weighed anchor, and sailed back out to sea.[48]

Encounters with other vessels at sea were fairly common and always terrifying. Small fishing smacks, pilot boats, schooners, brigs, and big ships—all sailed nearby, especially since Montes tried to keep the *Amistad* in busy sea-lanes. Several vessels approached, whereupon the Africans immediately sent Ruiz and Montes below. The strangers wondered if the schooner was in distress or needed a pilot to navigate the dangerous waters, but they rarely got close enough to ask their questions. When they saw forty-odd men armed with cane knives, they usually backed away in fear. They must have known that something dramatic had happened on the vessel. Ruiz and Montes hoped they would inform local authorities, who might in turn dispatch a warship to investigate, but the prisoners were repeatedly disappointed in this hope. Meanwhile, the Africans regarded every vessel they encountered with suspicion and hostility, a threat to their hard-won freedom. Sometimes they slept with cane knives in their hands.

Meanwhile, the Africans worked the ship, but the sailing was not easy. Lacking a pilot and having no local knowledge, on several occasions they got into dangerously shallow waters, hitting the bottom or, worse, rock formations invisible beneath the surface, which damaged the hull. Accidents tore away pieces of the hull that gave protection, strength, and lateral resistance to the keel. Another time they lost an anchor. Montes recalled a moment when they repeatedly struck rocks; "it was next to a miracle that [the vessel] was not wrecked." This being summer in the Caribbean, they also experienced several tropical storms. They were forced to weather "violent gales" under "bare poles"— that is, without sails, to reduce resistance to the winds and prevent capsizing. They rocked and rolled with the winds and waves, thinking all the while that everyone aboard was going to die.[49]

The Africans did their best not only to sail the vessel, but to appease the apparently angry water spirits (*jina*) who governed their way. The two went hand in hand, as the peoples of southern Sierra Leone, especially those who lived on or near riverine systems, as many of the rebels did, saw supernatural beings associated with the water as important figures. Such spirits, they believed, could help the waterborne traveler or, if they were unhappy and not properly placated, could create utter disaster. When the *Amistad* was once run aground, Montes recalled, "the negroes began to perform superstitious ceremonies; they threw their shirts over board, the pots and other utensils." Some of these "utensils" were apparently the manacles, shackles, neck-rings, and chains from which they had liberated themselves, now thrown into the angry seas. The rebels then brought to Montes "a piece of plate, a pistol and other articles [so] that he might throw them overboard." They then explained to him and Ruiz that "the object of these ceremonies was to break the charm in which they supposed they were; they said the plate, which was white, was to please God, and that the dirty and black articles were to please the Devil"—or so the matter seemed to Montes as he translated it into Christian categories. On another occasion, everyone took off their clothes and cast them into the sea, donning new, clean ones immediately thereafter. The old clothes were likely meant as gifts to appease Mami Wata, the female water spirit worshiped by peoples from Senegal to Angola and around the Black Atlantic. Her name grew from the pidgin language of trade on the African coast and she was thought to mediate relationships between Africans and foreigners. The *Amistad* Africans desperately needed her help.[50]

They also needed fresh water, and often the only available source was other vessels. Thirst compelled communication. One such encounter was with the *Kingston*, whose sailors were at first afraid to come alongside the *Amistad*, but eventually did so. In broken English Burna "asked those on board of the schooner if they were very far from Africa, and if they would sell them water, rice, and rum." At the end of a halting, confused conversation, he exchanged a doubloon and a few shillings for a quarter cask of water, sweet potatoes, and sea biscuit, but he got no information about proximity to their native land.[51]

After about six weeks Montes grew discouraged. He thought that he, and indeed everyone on the ship, was doomed. He "made up his mind to die." By this time they had only one cask of water on board and no prospect of getting more anytime soon; they were heading east with no land in sight and no other vessels nearby. As Burna noted, "hard wind—broke the sails" and of course they had no instruments of navigation. In desperation, Montes asked Ruiz if they should propose going to the United States. It seemed their only hope. Ruiz agreed that they should try it.[52]

Montes then "asked the negroes if they wished to go to a free country where there were no slaves." In terrible need of water and knowing that a long voyage was at this point out of the question, they answered yes, they were "willing to go." To the long-term goal of "going home to Mendi" was now added another, necessary short-term goal: to find a place that was not "slavery country." Was the United States such a place? Montes lied, saying that it was, adding that it was not far away, only an eight- to ten-day voyage "if the weather was good." Montes "intended to go to the southern part of the United States," because it was nearest and no doubt because officials there were most likely to be sympathetic and turn the world right side up— that is, free the white Cubans and restore the Africans to bondage. In any case, the rebels now had an immediate, achievable objective. They tacked west and north, riding the North Equatorial Current, moving into the powerful Gulf Stream that would carry them more than a thousand miles up the North American coast.[53]

This would be the most difficult part of the voyage. Some of the Africans had already grown weak, some with dysentery, more with dehydration. Several would die; survivors would be reduced to drinking and cooking with sea water, which of course only made the dehydration worse, leading to muscle spasms, bloated limbs, seizures, kidney failure, and death. Some lost so much weight that they were "emaciated to mere skeletons."[54]

Under such circumstances, suspicions continued to run high against Montes and Ruiz, who were thought still to be plotting to take them back to Havana. Another Poro meeting resulted in yet another death sentence for Montes. Cinqué came up on the main deck with a dagger and a sword, and he and the rest of the men "sung the death song round him; all joined in the song and in the threats." This ritual song and dance of Mende warriors again reverberated around the *Amistad*. Making "the most horrible contortions with his eyes" as he engaged in Mende war ritual, Cinqué prepared to kill Montes, but once again he was restrained, this time by two or three of his comrades, one of whom was surely Burna, who remained the Spaniards' steadfast protector. Burna even promised to "sleep near them" so that they would not be killed in the middle of the night.[55]

As they neared the American coast after seven weeks of sailing, they encountered more vessels, many of which they would now ask their main question: were they near Africa? On several other occasions, as approaching captains eyed the *Amistad* with the intention of taking it into port and claiming it—and its people—as salvaged property, the Africans grew suspicious, armed themselves, and drove their would-be captors away. Sailing up the coast off Fire Island and Long Island, they spotted Montauk Point Lighthouse, the oldest in North America. Some of the Africans, according to Montes, initially mistook this for the coast of Africa. They told Montes to steer towards it, which he did. They anchored that evening about a mile offshore and sent four or five men in the boat to search for water, which they found. Had they arrived in a place that was not "slavery country"? Montes had suggested that "the slaves friends lived there."[56]

They spent the entire next day loading water and in the end delegated a man named Fa, who probably had the skills of a warrior and scout, to explore what lay beyond the beach. Fa ended up staying out overnight, which worried his shipmates, who berated Ruiz and Montes, saying with sarcasm that the "country must be very free indeed" to have captured and "bound their comrade." When they went ashore early the next morning, they found a piece of rope, which they thought had been used to capture their brother. Their worst fears were confirmed.[57]

Later that morning, around ten a.m., after the rebels had returned to the *Amistad*, they saw a white man standing with Fa on the shore. The body language and other signals of their comrade indicated that all was well. They rejoiced and dispatched a small group to meet them. In half an hour they returned with "a bottle of gin and some sweet potatoes." Around two o' clock several more white men appeared on the beach, on horseback, with wagons. Captain Henry Green, Captain Peletiah Fordham, Schuyler Conklin, and Seymour G. Sherman had been out hunting with their muskets and dogs when they encountered Fa and the other white man. They made "a great noise" and summoned the Africans on the vessel to come ashore to meet them. Two boatloads, about twenty in all, rowed over to Culloden Point.[58]

When the Africans disembarked, they approached the white men, Burna stepping forward to ask fateful questions: "What country is this?" he asked. Green replied, this is America. Burna continued, with urgency, "Is this slavery country?" No, came the answer, there is no slavery here; and indeed there was not: New York had abolished slavery in 1827. "Any Spanish here?" No: "It is a free country." As soon as Cinqué understood the answers, he let loose with a joyous whistle and yell, signaling the rest of the Africans, who "all ran from the sand and shouted." They burst into rapture, whooping and hollering, dancing and celebrating. Their exuberant actions surprised and scared the white men. Green explained, "We were alarmed and ran to our wagons for our guns." The fear could not compromise the victory. After a journey that began in West Africa four and half months earlier, and a storm-filled, deadly voyage of 1,400 miles over the previous eight weeks, the *Amistad* Africans had at long last arrived in a place that was not "slavery country."[59]

Danger and Deception

Having found in a free land white men who were apparently willing to help them, the *Amistad* Africans tried to make the most of a big opportunity. Yet they proceeded cautiously, understanding the divergence of interests in the encounter at Culloden Point. They desperately wanted to sail to Sierra Leone and needed the help of the white men to do so. But could the white men actually help them? Somehow the

Amistad Africans figured out that Green and Fordham were ship captains who had maritime knowledge and experience. Burna cleverly chose two places the white men were most likely to have heard of—Sierra Leone and Gambia—to describe where they wanted to go. He pointed east and said, "Make sail and go."[60]

The white men, however, did not want to go to West Africa, and the last thing they wanted to do was actually to help the rebels. They wanted to get their hands on any money the Africans might have on board the *Amistad*, and to get possession of the ship itself. They already had some understanding of the situation, for they had read about the mysterious "long, low black schooner," said to be flush with gold, in the newspapers.[61]

The most immediate task of the *Amistad* Africans was now to calm the fears aroused by their boisterous celebration of freedom. They initiated a ritual of peacemaking, what they would have called a "peace palaver." They gathered around the white men in as friendly and unthreatening a way as they could, shaking their hands and offering gifts, a hat and a handkerchief at first, then more importantly, their weapons: they handed over a loaded musket and, crucially for the Mende warriors, a cane knife. As Cinqué explained, at this moment the "black men gave up the knife." He referred to the ritual of symbolic surrender among the Mende, when warriors acknowledged defeat and placed their fates in the hands of a stronger force. Thus they surrendered themselves, their weapons, and their vessel, but all with a condition attached: the white men must help them sail over the "great waters" to get home.[62]

The *Amistad* Africans knew that surrender might not be enough and that the white men wanted money. They too were capable of deception, and having little money to offer, they contrived a ruse. First they showed that they had some money by buying two hunting dogs from the white men for a doubloon each. Then they returned to the vessel and filled two chests with the metal parts of plantation sugar machinery, locked them, and rowed ashore with them. They hoisted the heavy chests and shook them to suggest to the white men the reward for taking them to Sierra Leone. Burna said to them, "money," held up four fingers and added, "400 doubloons." Of the "two trunks [that] were brought on shore by the blacks," Fordham recalled that he and Cinqué "lifted one trunk, and I heard the money rattle. Me and another nigger lifted the other trunk, and then I heard some more money." At that point, Fordham explained, "we determined to have the vessel at all hazards—forcibly if we can, peaceably if we must." Green also heard the clanking of what he thought was coin and asked if he could go on board the *Amistad*. He admitted, "It was my object to take possession of the vessel." The answer, however, was no, not yet. Tomorrow the *Amistad* Africans would take the white men on board, probably after a meeting of the collective, perhaps with the intention of kidnapping them if they could not otherwise persuade them to sail the vessel to Africa. Fordham worried that they might encounter trouble if they went on board.[63]

The excitement of the *Amistad* Africans in discovering a "free country" was tempered by disorientation and fear. Their lack of geographical knowledge continued to plague them. Having spent much time on the "trackless ocean," with no landmarks in sight, and finding themselves now in a strange land, they had little idea how far they were from Africa. They had some notion that it was still distant, as they later stated they had not been able to get as much water as they wanted for the long voyage home. They also knew, of course, that their dealings with the white men might not work out. So they developed a secondary strategy to guarantee their hard-won freedom. Having sailed for many miles along uninhabited parts of Fire Island and Long Island on their way to Culloden Point, they saw land they might have considered suitable for building a runaway community (marronage), which was a well-known practice of resistance against slavery in Sierra Leone, Cuba, and the southern United States. Indeed, they had probably anchored and rowed a small boat ashore several times along the way and would have found resources, from fresh water to edible plant life to wild game, especially deer. Hence they bought the hunting dogs in case they should need to settle in a remote, uninhabited area. Pie would use the dogs and his skills as a hunter to provide food for the group.[64]

A disturbingly familiar vessel suddenly appeared on the horizon. Looking out to sea, everyone on shore "saw a brig standing to the eastward." Burna asked, "Where that came from?" It was the United States brig *Washington*, a navy survey vessel, and it was sailing directly for the *Amistad*, anchored a few hundred yards offshore. The Africans instantly grew agitated. It was, after all, a brig, the same kind of ship as the *Teçora*, on which they had made the Middle Passage from the Gallinas Coast to Havana. In short, it looked like a slave ship. They urgently turned to the white men to ask if that vessel "made slaves." Green and his colleagues, wanting the *Amistad* Africans to stay on shore, said yes, it did, but their answer had the opposite effect of what they had hoped for, causing the Africans to jump into their boats and row hard toward the *Amistad*.[65]

If the Africans thought the *Washington* was a slave ship, Lieutenant Thomas Gedney aboard the naval vessel thought the *Amistad* was a pirate, or a smuggler, as suggested by the "men and carts" involved in trade ashore. Gedney dispatched a boat with Lieutenant Richard Meade and several armed sailors to board the *Amistad*. As Meade later testified, they arrived at the vessel, "jumped on deck, and drove the Africans below." As they took charge of the *Amistad* they encountered the grateful Pedro Montes and José Ruiz, who tearfully proclaimed the sailors their saviors, as indeed they were. Montes hugged Meade so hard the officer had to threaten to shoot him to make him relax his grip. Meade then offered Montes and Ruiz the tender embrace of white-skin privilege. He freed them as he locked the Africans in the hold, the very place where they had originally hatched their plot for freedom.[66]

Meade and company encountered only fifteen Africans on the vessel, four of them children, and most of the rest probably sick, emaciated, and otherwise weak, as the strongest and fittest would have been rowing to shore, filling water casks, and negotiating with the white men. It is impossible to be sure what would have happened if the full body of healthier warriors had made it back to the *Amistad* before the naval detachment arrived, but it seems likely that they would have fought back and attempted to escape. Gedney certainly thought so. Cinqué had apparently long maintained that, if attacked, they would kill Montes and Ruiz, and that they would themselves consider it better to die fighting than to be enslaved again.[67]

Meantime the *Amistad* Africans in the boat witnessed the capture of their vessel. They reversed course and now rowed with all their might back toward shore. With the *Amistad* under control, Meade dispatched a group of sailors to follow the remaining Africans. When they caught up to them, Midshipman David Porter "fired a pistol with a ball over their heads, and took a musket and pointed at them with it and made motions to them to go on board the Schooner." They submitted, rowed back, and went aboard.[68]

Cinqué made one last bid for freedom. Trusting his skill as a swimmer and diver, he "jumped up the hatch way—and sprang over board" into the water. Meade sent yet another boat after him, and the chase was on. An eyewitness noted that at one point Cinqué stayed under water for "at least five minutes." Whenever and wherever he came up for air, the sailors rowed after him in hot pursuit, only to watch him go under and pop up somewhere else a little later. This aquatic game of hide and seek went on for forty exhausting minutes until Porter pointed a gun at Cinqué again, then commanded the sailors to bring him aboard the boat by slipping a boat hook under his wet clothes. Pulled up into the boat, Cinqué "smiled and putting his hands to his throat, intimated that he was going to be hanged."[69]

Events off Long Island had not gone unnoticed, as newspapers published lurid accounts of the mysterious "long, low black schooner." On August 31, 1839, the *New York Sun* reported, in a widely circulated and influential account, that Cinqué gave two speeches on the *Amistad* after he and his comrades had been captured by Meade and his crew. In the first, which was said to have been remembered and translated by Antonio, Cinqué told his countrymen,

You had better be killed than live many moons in misery. I shall be hanged, I think, every day. But this does not pain me. I could die happy, if by dying I could save so many of my brothers from the bondage of the white man.

The rhetoric sounds artificial and stilted, more like an academic exercise for the sons of Harvard and Yale than the actual speech of an African warrior, but the use of "moons" to reckon time is realistic, as is the language of "brethren," fictive kinship. Moreover, the speech sounds similar to others made by Cinqué and memorized by his comrades as part of their own account of their adventure. In the second speech, the *Sun* reported, the leader tried to rally his mates to resist the American occupation of their vessel:

I came to tell you that you have only one chance for death, and none for liberty. I am sure you prefer death, as I do. You can by killing the white man now on board, and I will help you, make the people here kill you. It is better for you to do this, and then you will not only avert bondage yourselves, but prevent the entailment of unnumbered wrongs on your children. Come—come with me then—

The warrior was essentially proposing a collective suicide pact to resist reenslavement—not uncommon among warriors in southern Sierra Leone when they realized that their military situation was hopeless, since captured warriors were frequently executed anyway.[70]

A week later, Lt. Meade vehemently denied that Cinqué ever gave the speeches, but he himself provided evidence of them in an article he wrote about the capture of the *Amistad*, published in the *New London Gazette* on September 4, 1839: "Cinquez had declared that in case they were likely to be taken, he should kill the passengers, and that he would die rather than be taken, and he enjoined upon his comrades to take his knife and avenge his death—that they had better die in self-defense than be hung, as they would be if taken." It seems likely that the writer for the *New York Sun* had heard this story, perhaps from Meade or Antonio, and rendered it in a sensational way for the penny-press newspaper; and it is also likely that the sentiment and the actual event behind it were real. Cinqué had perhaps unwittingly echoed the words of Patrick Henry, "Give me liberty or give me death," or, more appropriately, those of the enslaved rebel Gabriel, whose conspiracy in Richmond, Virginia, in 1800 had been guided by the phrase "Death or Liberty."[71]

Meade's account of the capture was strongly shaped by his own material interest in the case. He and his commanding officer, Thomas Gedney, would apply to the court for salvage rights, that is, for payment of a portion of the value of the ship and its cargo that they had "saved" for the owners, which might include the immensely valuable human commodities, the former slaves. Indeed, they may have chosen to tow the vessel to Connecticut, rather than New York, because slavery was still legal there. Such matters were clearly on Meade's mind from the beginning of the encounter. In another article he apparently wrote for the *New London Gazette*, he observed that Cinqué was a strong, "well built" man "who would command, in New Orleans, under the hammer, at least $1,500." The auction block was on his mind.[72]

Cinqué's comrades cheered his words of resistance after capture and "leapt about and seemed like creatures under some talismanic power." Fearing an uprising, Meade ordered the sailors to put Cinqué in manacles, separate him from his countrymen, and transport him to the *Washington*. On his way there, "the hero moved not a muscle, but kept his eye fixed on the schooner." Aboard the brig, the leader sat belowdecks, manacled and incarcerated for a third time in recent months, expecting reenslavement or death. At that moment it must not have seemed that he had arrived in a "free country."[73]

In any case, the planning and execution of the rebellion—and no less the long, dangerous, even tortuous voyage afterward—were historic achievements. Based on shared African experiences of work, culture, and self-organization, and on the fictive kinship that grew out of their common struggles in slave factory, barracoon, and ship, the fifty-three rebels aboard the *Amistad* did what few of the millions before them had done: they carried out a successful uprising aboard a slave ship, then sailed the vessel to a place where they might secure the freedom they had fought for and won. They did not choose their way into the dilemma that confronted them aboard the *Amistad*, but they did, collectively, choose their way out. Their movement from below, onto the main deck of the slaver, where they would wage and win an armed struggle for emancipation, would now trigger a larger historic social movement ashore.

CHAPTER THREE

Movement

Locked belowdecks in the hold of the *Amistad*, with armed white men standing guard above them, the Africans felt the tug of forward motion as the *Washington* began to tow their vessel across Long Island Sound toward New London, Connecticut. The hold was once again a place of abject misery: many were sick and emaciated, some had bloated limbs, a few were dying. Their American captors had, without hesitation and without question, taken the side of the slaveholders José Ruiz and Pedro Montes when they boarded the vessel, freeing the white Cubans and incarcerating the Africans. Separated from their leader Cinqué, who lay manacled and chained on the brig ahead of them, the Africans once again had no idea where they were going or what would become of them. For all practical purposes, they had been reenslaved, or so it must have seemed.

When the *Washington* and the *Amistad* arrived at New London on August 27, the naval vessel docked at Lawrence Wharf, while what was now effectively a prison ship was anchored several hundred yards off shore, "in the bay near the fort," for the sake of security. Federal Marshal Norris Wilcox took formal possession of the captives, while Lt. Gedney went ashore to send an express message to Judge Andrew Judson of the district court in New Haven, notifying him of the crimes of piracy and murder that had, in his view, been committed. Word of the arrival of the *Amistad* rebels began to buzz around the waterfront, spreading rapidly, locally and throughout Connecticut, north to Boston, and south to New York and Washington. Spectators flocked to the docks in the thousands to see the so-called pirate ship and its fearsome black crew.[1]

What they saw offshore was a ghost ship, with torn, tattered sails and a foul hull, covered with barnacles and sea-grass. One of the first to go aboard saw "a sight as we never saw before and never wish to see again." The vessel's "Ethiop crew" were "decked in the most fantastic manner in the silks and finery pilfered from the cargo, while others in a state of nudity, emaciated to mere skeletons, lay coiled upon the decks." Cargo lay scattered around "in the most wanton and disorderly profusion." The visitor at one point rested his hand "on a cold object," only to discover that it was the naked corpse of a man who had died the night before, his face frozen and mouth open in "the ghastly expression of his last struggle." Nearby sat Konoma, described by the visitor as "the most horrible creature we ever saw in human shape." His teeth projected from his mouth at right angles and his eyes held a savage look. He was surely a cannibal. At last the visitor eagerly disembarked because of "the exhalations from her hold and deck"—the characteristic stench of a slave ship.[2]

Judge Judson arrived in New London the morning of August 29 to conduct a judicial investigation and to determine if the *Amistad* Africans should be charged with piracy and murder. Judson was a former congressman known for his racist opposition to schoolteacher Prudence Crandall's efforts to educate African American children in Canterbury, Connecticut, in 1833. President Andrew Jackson had appointed this member of the American Colonization Society and determined opponent of racial "amalgamation" to the federal bench in 1836. Judson decided to hold his hearings on the vessels, first on the *Washington*, where Ruiz and Montes gave their testimony about the rebellion, subsequent voyage, and capture by the navy, then on the *Amistad*. Lt. Meade, who spoke Spanish fluently, translated for the Spaniards, and added his own testimony about the encounter at Culloden Point. Judson apparently solicited no testimony from any of the Africans, perhaps because he himself could not communicate with them directly, perhaps because he felt he could learn all he needed to know from the white men. He did, however, order Cinqué to be brought, in chains, to the commanding officer's cabin aboard the *Washington*.³

Cinque's appearance gave a clue as to how he saw the legal proceeding. Wearing a red flannel shirt and white duck pantaloons he had found in the hold of the vessel, he also had "a cord round his neck, to which a snuff box was suspended." The witness who offered the description did not understand what he was looking at, nor did any of the American officials at the hearing. The "snuff box" was actually a *"greegree* bag"—a container of sacred objects, charms or amulets charged with spiritual power, designed in Mende country to protect the person who wore it. Sometimes called "medicine," these objects were believed to ward off bad fortune—"sickness, trouble, death." Small bags or boxes containing objects such as cloth, graveyard dirt, a bit of iron, leopard skin, and perhaps a Quranic inscription on parchment, were important to warriors in southern Sierra Leone as they entered battle, especially what they called "big war." Unable to understand the English and Spanish in which the white men spoke, Cinqué, according to an eyewitness, gazed at his accusers with fearless intensity, maintaining a "hero-like expression." He knew his life was at stake. The warrior hoped the powerful objects in his greegree bag might help him in the "big war" against slavery.⁴

At the first hearing Judson listened to the testimony and inspected the *Amistad*'s papers: a license for carrying slaves from Captain-General Joaquín de Ezpleta of Havana; certificates for the working sailors aboard the vessel; and a customs house clearance, which listed the Spanish names for the Africans, to make it appear that they were acculturated "ladinos" rather than "bozales" recently, and therefore illegally, imported from Africa. The main issues before Judge Judson were piracy and murder, but Ruiz and Montes had petitioned to recover what they considered to be their slave property. Charles Ingersoll represented the United States District Attorney, supporting the Cuban masters and expressing the hope that the former slaves would be returned to them.

Judson then moved to the *Amistad* for a second hearing, not to get testimony from the Africans, but so that Antonio, the cabin boy, who saw the entire rebellion (when Ruiz and Montes did not) might specifically point out, during his testimony, precisely who had killed his master, Captain Ramón Ferrer, and the slave-sailor Celestino. With Meade serving as translator, Antonio described the uprising and pointed out three as the murderers: Cinqué and two others the correspondent did not name, probably Moru and Kimbo. At the end of the day Judson ruled that the Africans would be tried for "murder and piracy on board the Spanish schooner *Amistad*" in the Circuit Court of Hartford on September 17, 1839. He issued an order that they be held in the New Haven jail, to which they would be transported on August 30.[5]

Government officials, naval officers, the Cubans, and the Africans were not the only people aboard the *Washington* and the *Amistad* during the hearings. Of special importance were an artist, J. Sketchley, an unnamed newspaper correspondent, and a local abolitionist named Dwight Janes. Drawn to the slave ship revolt that had taken place eight weeks earlier by the popular interest in it, these three visitors would strongly shape the evolution of the *Amistad* case in the aftermath of the hearing, in ways neither the Africans nor anyone else could have foreseen.

Birth of a Hero

Sketchley produced for popular consumption the first graphic image of the *Amistad* Rebellion, dated August 30, 1839: Cinqué stands on the deck of the vessel in a sailor's frock (what is today called a buccaneer's shirt) and a pair of duck pantaloons, striking a gallant pose, with his cane knife at the ready. Below the image of the swashbuckling hero is a caption: "Joseph Cinquez, Leader of the Piratical Gang of Negroes, who killed Captain Ramon Ferris and the Cook, on board the Spanish Schooner Amistad, taken by Lieut. Gedney, commanding the U.S. Brig Washington at Culloden Point, Long Island, 24th Augt 1839." Beneath the caption was a speech delivered by Cinqué in which he exhorted his mates to fight back against slavery. The leader acts, talks, and looks like a Roman hero.[6]

An arresting color lithograph was produced from this image soon

"Joseph Cinquez,
Leader of the Piratical
Gang of Negroes"

thereafter: Cinqué appears in the red flannel shirt and the white duck pantaloons he actually wore to the judicial investigation. He is not a fearsome cannibal or "primitive" savage, but a handsome dark-skinned man in European garb. A man who was soon to stand trial for piracy and murder is depicted at the scene of the crime with the deadly weapon in his hand, as transcendently good and noble in his cause. Indeed, he appears as an executioner of justice, a slayer of tyrants. His history of resistance is simultaneously celebrated and commodified in the form of an image to be bought and sold.[7]

A related image, drawn by another New London artist named Sheffield, appeared as a broadside the following day, August 31, 1839, four days after the *Amistad* came into port. It contained another sympathetic image of Cinqué, dressed in the same frock, but this time with more explicit antislavery commentary: "JOSEPH CINQUEZ, the brave Congolese Chief, who prefers death to Slavery, and who now lies in Jail in Irons in New Haven Conn. awaiting his trial for daring for freedom." Below the caption appeared another stirring speech

"Joseph Cinquez, the brave Congolese Chief"

Cinqué gave to his comrades. The image and text, in broadside form, were hawked in the streets of the cities, spreading the sensational news of heroic revolt.[8]

A fourth image produced about the same time represented the rebellion and its aftermath by depicting not only Cinqué, but all of the Africans: "Joseph Cinquez Addressing his Compatriots on board the Spanish Schooner AMISTAD 26th Augt 1839." The engraving chronicled a specific moment: the officers and sailors of the U.S. brig *Washington* have captured the vessel, and Cinqué, who had been separated from the others, has returned to give a speech designed to inspire collective resistance against their American captors. He strikes a classic orator's pose, his right hand and eyes raised to the heavens. He explains to all that it would be better to "be killed than live many moons in misery."[9]

The main deck of the *Amistad* appears as a theatrical stage from which Cinqué delivers his lines. Standing by from right to left are the cast: "Señor Montes" smoking a cigar; Lt. Meade, his sword at the ready; the young Don José Ruiz; and Antonio the cabin boy. At the far left are three armed sailors, two with cutlasses drawn, all with pistols in their belts. They are at ease and one is smoking a short pipe. In the foreground are the "three children slaves of Montes" and beyond

"Joseph Cinquez Addressing his Compatriots on board the . . . AMISTAD"

them, the *Amistad* men, in motley attire. They look at Cinqué with eager eyes and rapt attention. Although he speaks about resistance, the scene has a peaceful, even transcendent, communal feel. The original artist was likely Sketchley, who drew Cinqué in the same style, and in the same clothes, in the second portrait above.[10]

These glorifications of armed struggle were not, as they might appear, the work of an underground group of militant abolitionists. They were, rather, commissioned by, advertised in, and distributed by the penny paper the *New York Sun*. Moses Yale Beach, editor of the *Sun*, sensationalized the case and appealed to the popular appetite for heroic sea-robbers to sell newspapers and prints to a mass public. He succeeded beyond his wildest dreams. He and his fellow editors of the *Sun* were shocked by how popular the images became. After publishing portraits of Cinqué on Saturday, August 31, 1839, they noted the following Monday that the supply of prints had been exhausted immediately and that they had been unable to meet the clamor for more. They announced to their readers that they would, "by an early hour this morning, have another and a very large edition printed, and shall be prepared, on the opening of our office, to supply demands for any number." They explained that they had printed enough on Saturday to satisfy "any *ordinary* demand," but encountered a "tremendous run for them" for which they were not ready. This "was as unexpected to us as it was astonishing in itself." They printed the image on "thick, fine paper, in a style of excellence," suitable for framing. They also noted that the print had been republished in the Sunday editions of other newspapers. They were clearly proud of what they had done.[11]

The *New York Sun's* correspondent, who was also present at the judicial investigation in New London, created the textual equivalent of these images in what was probably the single most influential article published the first week the *Amistad* Africans were brought ashore, entitled "The Long, Low, Black Schooner." Republished in the *New York Journal of Commerce* and several other newspapers, including an edited version as far south as the *Charleston Courier*, the long article (5,700 words) initiated a process that would continue for the next two years, with great historical effect: it created and disseminated widely a heroic and romantic image of Cinqué and hence of the entire rebellion.[12]

The article begins by noting the intense public excitement caused by the arrival of the schooner in New London, then mentions the availability of the "splendidly lithographed" image of Cinqué. Early in a long summary of the rebellion, the voyage, and the capture, the article sketches the history and character of the leader of the revolt, identified as "the son of an African chief." He is no ordinary man. He is, rather, "one of those spirits which appear but seldom." Possessed of "sagacity and courage," he is physically strong, able to endure privation; he has "a full chest, large joints and muscles, and built for strength and agility." He has thick lips, beautiful teeth, and nostrils that flare with anger. His eyes convey "the cool contempt of a haughty chieftain" or "the high resolve which would be sustained through martyrdom," as he wished. In repose his countenance "looks heavy, but under excitement it assumes an expression of great intelligence." His bearing is free of levity, and "many white men might take a lesson in dignity and forbearance from the African Chieftain, who although in bondage, appears to have been the Ozeola of his race." Compared to Osceola, a recently killed leader of the Second Seminole War being fought in Florida at that very moment, Cinqué was, in short, the perfect man to "become the leader in such an event as that which has thrown him on our shores." By the time he had stepped off the *Washington*, he was, courtesy of the *New York Sun*, on his way to celebrity, soon to be embraced by an incipient social movement.[13]

The Abolitionist Movement in 1839

Another person who came aboard the *Washington* and the *Amistad* on August 27, 1839, was not a journalist, a lawyer, or a law enforcer, but a rank-and-file political activist, Dwight Janes. He was a grocer who knew the docks and the coming and going of ships. He went aboard the vessels, where he saw Ruiz, Montes, and the sickly Africans. He quickly gathered the essential facts: the name of the ship and its slave-holders; the variety and value of the cargo; and what had happened in the rebellion. He talked to Ruiz and Antonio, from whom he garnered important evidence. He learned that the Africans had not been in Havana long enough to become subjects of Spain and that "none of them can speak any thing but their native language." He understood that finding Africans in America who could communicate with those of the *Amistad* would be crucial to the case. He realized that the ship's papers had been fabricated. Perhaps most importantly, he knew that Spain's slave trade was now illegal and argued, presciently, that "the blacks had a perfect right to get their liberty by killing the crew and taking possession of the vessel." This was a natural opportunity for a national campaign. Humanity and justice, thought Janes, would move many to defend these "Citizens of Africa."[14]

Janes wrote a flurry of urgent letters in which he conveyed both critical information and strategic perspective to leading abolitionists, soliciting their involvement in a case he immediately recognized as extremely important. He wrote to Joshua Leavitt, a minister and editor of the *Emancipator*, Lewis Tappan, a wealthy silk merchant and New York businessman, and Roger S. Baldwin, a distinguished Connecticut attorney. In a short time, when time was of the essence, Janes anticipated the entire abolitionist strategy for the case and quickly activated the movement. He embodied and expressed the strength of abolitionism from below.[15]

Janes and his antislavery comrades flew into action, along the waterfront and up and down the eastern seaboard, causing a correspondent for the *New York Morning Herald* to write of the *Amistad* captives on September 2, "the Abolitionists are moving heaven and earth to effect their release; several members of the society have left town for Connecticut to see them, to employ the most able counsel in their behalf, and to contest every point inch by inch; and, judging from appearances, we should say that there are general preparations making in all quarters for a grand explosion in this matter of slavery and the slave trade." The powder would be mixed in jail.[16]

Janes was part of a movement that was growing dramatically in the 1830s, around the world and in the United States, in opposition to a dynamic American and Atlantic slave system. The global movement was strongest in Great Britain, where it already boasted two major victories: the abolition of the slave trade in 1807 and the abolition of slavery in all British colonies in two stages, in 1834 and 1838. At the same time, a national polarization on the issue of slavery was taking shape in the United States, pitting firebrands in the South, who increasingly saw slavery as a "positive good," against abolitionists who saw it as pure evil. Janes saw the main chance presented by the *Amistad* rebellion and he seized it.[17]

The two primary antislavery organizations of the day were the New England Anti-Slavery Society, formed in 1831, and the larger national group, the American Anti-Slavery Society, founded in 1833. Inspired by the moral perfectionism of the Second Great Awakening and based largely in northern churches, both were to some extent interracial and committed to nonviolent "moral suasion"—seeking to convince the nation that slavery was a sin and that it must, for moral reasons, be abolished. In 1837 the American Anti-Slavery Society had 145 local societies in Massachusetts, 274 in New York, and 213 in Ohio. In 1838 it had 1,350 affiliates and a membership of 250,000. In a nation of seventeen million people, the abolitionists were modest in number, but they were committed, outspoken, and growing.[18]

By 1839 abolitionist societies had created a strong, durable network of communication and material support. They had their own newspapers and journals such as the *Emancipator* (New York), the *Liberator* (Boston), and the *Pennsylvania Freeman* (Philadelphia), which they published, along with other antislavery pamphlets and books, using their own printing presses. In 1835 they had organized a postal campaign in which they mailed a huge volume of antislavery literature to a hostile, defensive South. They organized massive petition campaigns, delivering hundreds of thousands of signatures opposing slavery to Congress and prompting southern politicians to effect a "gag rule" in 1836 to evade them. The abolitionists had their own lecture circuits, their own means of publicity and fund-raising, their own lawyers to employ on behalf of the *Amistad* prisoners.[19]

The abolitionist movement crossed lines of race and class, and its full variety was reflected by those who gravitated to the *Amistad* case. They were black and white, male and female, middle-class and working-class, enslaved and free. They included businessmen such as Tappan, whose home had been trashed by an anti-abolition mob in 1834. They included ministers such as Simeon Jocelyn, who preached to an interracial congregation in New Haven; "enlightened" figures such as Professor Josiah Gibbs, a scholar of oriental languages at Yale University; artisan-artists such as John Warner Barber and Nathaniel Jocelyn; black sailors such as James Covey; Lydia Maria Child, an eminent writer and feminist; and former slaves such as James Pennington, the runaway "fugitive blacksmith" who became a leading black minister in Hartford, and Isabella Baumfree, who would become known as Sojourner Truth, a leading figure in the women's movement who asked, "Ain't I a Woman?"[20]

Slave rebels themselves played a crucial part in the abolitionist movement, on the *Amistad* and elsewhere. Their actions throughout the Western Hemisphere shaped the battle against slavery on plantations, in cities, and even in rural areas where no slavery existed. The *Amistad* struggle took its place alongside contemporaneous slave conspiracies, revolts, and mass escapes in Mobile, Alabama; Lafayette and St. Martinsdale, Louisiana; Anne Arundel and Charles County, Maryland; and Purrysburg, South Carolina. Slave incendiaries were said to be active in Charleston, New Orleans, Mobile, and Natchez, Mississippi. Many of the uprisings took place in sugar-producing regions in the United States, Jamaica, Cuba, and Brazil. Meanwhile, the fires of resistance raged in Florida, where many self-emancipated slaves fought in the Second Seminole War.[21]

Running away from slavery was an ever-brighter flashpoint in the struggle. Indeed, the year 1839 was the very moment when the reality and the name of the Underground Railroad came into existence. Most people of African descent who escaped slavery, it should be noted, did so on their own, without the assistance of organized middle-class abolitionists. A large portion of them got away by sea, as stowaways on ships, with the assistance of proletarian dockworkers and sailors. The Underground Railroad for the movement of former bondspeople remained important, as sources of hope among the enslaved and as provocations to southern slaveholders, who railed fiercely against it. Three main routes had begun to evolve by 1839: from Missouri to Illinois; from Kentucky to Cincinnati and Oberlin College in Ohio; and from Virginia and points south to Washington, DC, Baltimore, Philadelphia, and New York. All three went on to Canada by various routes.[22]

Crucial to the early formation of the Underground Railroad was another antislavery organization called the Vigilance Committee, formed in New York in 1835, Philadelphia in 1837, Boston in 1841, and in numerous other places thereafter. Given to direct action, and made up to a large extent of African American men such as former sailor David Ruggles, leader of the New York group, the committees worked, often along the waterfront, to assist free people of color who had been kidnapped or "blackbirded" into slavery as well as runaways trying to escape it. Vigilance Committees tended to attract militant abolitionists, sometimes called "ultras," who believed that uncompromising direct action would bring slavery to an end. This group was small but growing in importance in 1839.

The waterfront had long been an important and dangerous zone of conspiracy and subversion. Throughout the age of revolution, sailors, slaves, and freedpeople played key roles in uprisings in America, Haiti, and on ships of the Atlantic where mutiny exploded on a massive scale in the 1790s. Lawmakers continued to fear the circulation of subversion on the waterfront in the 1820s, passing the infamous Negro Seamen Acts beginning in 1822, following former sailor Denmark Vesey's conspiracy in Charleston, South Carolina. All black seamen coming into South Carolina ports would be taken off their vessels and held in prison, at the captain's expense, until departure. This was a policy of revolutionary quarantine: those "whose organization of mind, habits, and associations, render them peculiarly calculated to disturb the peace and tranquility of the State," would be treated "in the same manner as . . . those afflicted with infectious diseases." Over the next twenty years Georgia, North Carolina, Florida, Alabama, and Louisiana would follow South Carolina's lead. In 1829, waterfront slopseller and political thinker David Walker gave slaveholders more to worry about when he published his famous *Appeal . . . to the Coloured Citizens of the World* and then sewed it into the clothing of sailors, black and white, who in turn smuggled the incendiary document into Southern ports. Walker appealed to the minds, habits, and associations of enslaved and oppressed people all around the Atlantic. It was no accident that abolitionist Dwight Janes met the insurrectionists of the *Amistad* aboard ships anchored on the waterfront of New London, making a connection that would grow into a powerful alliance.[23]

The New Haven Jail

On the orders of Judge Judson, Marshal Wilcox arranged for transportation of the *Amistad* Africans from New London to New Haven and its jail of six large rooms. Because several arrived in poor physical health, suffering from the "white flux" (dysentery) and prolonged dehydration, Wilcox and his assistant, local jailer Stanton Pendleton, set up one room as a hospital under the supervision of Dr. Edward Hooker. A visitor noted that several of the Africans were almost as thin as Calvin Edson, the curious "living skeleton" who had made a circus-like tour some years earlier. Several of the *Amistad* veterans would not recover: Faquorna, Fa, Tua, Weluwa, Kapeli, Yammoni, Kaba, and one or two others whose names are unknown, died between late

August and mid-December 1839. Several of them were buried in New Haven's Grove Street Cemetery, located at the corner of Grove and Prospect streets.[24]

Special arrangements were also made for the four children—Kale, Margru, Kagne, and Teme—and for Cinqué. The four youths were given a room to themselves, until Pendleton removed the three girls and essentially made them domestic servants in his own household. Fear of Cinqué's militant influence caused the jailer to isolate him from his comrades: he was placed in a special secure cell, the "strong hold," with "several savage looking fellows, black and white, who are in jail on various charges." The jailer worried that these desperate prisoners would try to escape, so the door to that part of the jail was rarely opened and visitors were not permitted inside. Those who wanted to speak with Cinqué had to do so through the "aperture of the door." The remaining *Amistad* Africans, a majority, were confined together in three rooms, in "gangs." During the day, they had access "to a very large airy front chamber," where they could sit by an open window. One of their first priorities would be to engage the jailer in a struggle for the "open air."[25]

Even though the *Amistad* Africans had much experience of incarceration by the time they arrived in the New Haven jail, they must have found the place disorienting and nervewracking. No one understood their languages and they still had no clear idea of where they were, nor of what the future held. The threat of execution hung heavily over their heads. Cinqué "drew his hand across his throat, as his room mates said he had done frequently before, and asked whether the people here intended to kill him." Decapitation was a common fate for a captured warrior in his native society.[26]

To make matters worse, the jail shared features of the slave ship beyond the brute fact of incarceration. Not the least of these was the pungent smell of bondage. A visitor wrote that "the rooms occupied by the Africans are infected with the odor peculiar to jails that are badly ventilated, or not ventilated at all." The stench was "almost insupportable." A main reason why were the "necessary tubs," which were public and located "in the eating and sleeping rooms." The four children were jammed into a single bed, the men slept on straw, amid vermin, and the food was poor in quality.[27]

Among the curiosities of their new life in the New Haven jail were the clothes the *Amistad* Africans were expected to wear. Accustomed to dressing in a single, light piece of cotton "country made" African cloth, which they wrapped around the body and hung over the shoulder, they were now presented with something different, though not entirely unfamiliar, for they had found, and some, like Cinqué, had worn, European-style clothing on board the *Amistad*. Still, when the jailer brought striped cotton shirts and trousers called "hard times" (prison "fatigues"), woolen stockings, and caps, they had to laugh at the preposterous clothing of white people. According to Lewis Tappan, "The prisoners eyed the clothes some time, and laughed a good deal among themselves before they put them on." Cinqué in particular did not like them; he thought them too tight and confining. Meanwhile Margru, Kagne, and Teme turned some of their clothing to a purpose all their own: they "made the little shawls that were given them into turbans." The thing the entire group may have appreciated more than anything else about their attire in the New Haven jail was that it did not include manacles, shackles, or neck-rings.[28]

During the confinement of the *Amistad* Africans, the New Haven jail became an extraordinary meetinghouse for all kinds of people, ranging from African slaves of many nationalities to rowdy young boys, to sailors from the waterfront, to respectable middle-class abolitionists, to the rich and high-born. Many came because of the publicity that surrounded the case and to see the insurrectionists who had, with high drama, made a successful revolution, turning the wooden world of the *Amistad* upside down. Others came to indulge their curiosity about Africa and Africans. Some appeared at the jail because they supported the abolitionist movement, others because they opposed it. The jail—a much more open institution in 1839 than it would be later—was "filled with men, women, and children of all ages, colors, and sizes."[29]

No matter why they came in the first place, most of the visitors, claimed Lewis Tappan, who had spent much time in the jail and was therefore in a position to know, "express much sympathy with these much abused strangers, and utter sentiments of strong indignation against those who have torn them from their native land, or meditated their enslavement." Many of those who filed through the jail brought gifts. Some came with food, such as confections and "dainty cakes"; some brought the always welcome "baccar" (tobacco); and others gave "coppers," money, or "trinkets" to the prisoners.[30]

In early September 1839 the Amistad case was the talk of the town, if not the entire nation. It was "the only topic touched upon in conversation, in the streets, the bar room, the ball room, the boudoir, the bed room, the kitchen, the parlor, and the pulpit." People came in huge numbers, jamming the New Haven jail to capacity and beyond. On August 31, the first full day the Amistad Africans spent in the New Haven jail, two thousand people paid their "York shilling" (twelve and a half cents) to visit. In their first four days, jailer Pendleton took in $500 ($12,000 in 2012 dollars), paid by some four thousand visitors who had come from "New York, Vermont, Massachusetts, Philadelphia, and all parts of Connecticut." The prisoners, reported one newspaper, represented "a golden harvest to the Jailor." Meantime, another two thousand people were visiting the Amistad in New London. Some came out of carnival curiosity, others out of a commitment to antislavery ideals.[31]

The correspondents of the proslavery New York Morning Herald beheld the crowded, tumultuous, enthusiastic scenes in jail and they were appalled. One of them wrote:

These blacks have created a greater excitement in Connecticut than any event that has occurred there since the close of the last century. Every kind of engine is set in motion to create a feeling of sympathy and an excitement in their favor; the parsons preach about them, the men talk about them, the ladies give tea parties and discuss their chivalry, heroism, sufferings, thews and sinews, over their souchong; pious young women get up in prayer meetings and pray for them; scouts are sent round the country to hunt up all the negroes that can speak any kind of African dialect; interpreters by dozens arrive daily

at Hartford; grammars and spelling books and primers without number, in all sorts of unknown tongues, are sought for and secured.

The jail had become, in their view, a circus, a world turned upside
down, a place the *Amistad* Africans truly enjoyed: "The ingress and
egress of visitors furnish abundance of opportunities for them to
escape, but so far from wishing to do so, it would be difficult to drive
them out of jail." The place of confinement had become "a sort of fool's
paradise, filled with gaping curiosity, silly men, infatuated women,
and happy negroes."[32]

What did the *Amistad* Africans make of all this? They must have
experienced no small amount of sheer bewilderment, as suggested by
the *New York Morning Herald*: "The poor blacks themselves are utterly
astonished at the prodigious sensation they have created." Beneath it
all lay a deep, nagging fear, as suggested when several of the prisoners, "under much apprehension," asked a sympathetic visitor "if they
were to have their throats cut, passing their hands across their necks
when they made the inquiry." Getting a negative answer, one of the
Africans then asked, "If they don't mean to kill us . . . why are so many
people here to see us?"[33]

Townsend's Sketches

One of the early visitors to the New Haven jail was a seventeen-
year-old artist named William H. Townsend, who drew a series of
twenty-two portraits of the incarcerated Africans. These included
Grabeau and Burna, two of the leaders of the rebellion, though not
Cinqué (probably because he was segregated in a different cell), and
two of the four children, Kale and Margru, a boy and a girl who were
each about nine years old. Townsend also drew the portrait of Faquorna, who with Cinqué led the attack on Captain Ferrer and had
been indicted by the courts for murder. Since Faquorna died in early
September, only a few days after the *Amistad* rebels were brought
ashore, it appears that Townsend was in the New Haven jail soon
after the prisoners arrived there. Faquorna has dark circles under his

eyes and looks like he might have been sick when the portrait was sketched.[34]

Very little is known about Townsend, not least because he, like Faquorna, died young. Born in 1822, he lived in New Haven and died in 1851. The young aspiring artist likely got swept up in the excitement when the *Amistad* Africans arrived in town. He visited the jail and decided to try his hand with them. Family lore confirmed that Townsend visited the captives in jail, and suggested that he had some trouble in getting them to pose for his drawings. It was said that he resorted to bribes of candy. "The Amistad Negroes," as he called them, were finally "drawn from life." The sketches were modest in size, as small as two by three inches and as large as five by seven inches; most were in between, roughly four inches square.[35]

Townsend was not interested in the rebellion, per se, but rather in the individuals who made it. This guiding preoccupation resulted in portraits that were astonishing for their variety, intimacy, depth, and complexity. He depicted Burna with his unusually shaped head, curly eyelashes, and stylish mustache; Shuma, with a long, thin face, a mustache, a beard, and a look of gravity. Little Kale sported a spry look in his eye and a striped stocking hat on his head, ears tucked up under it, hair creeping out below. Townsend's drawings conveyed a range of moods, from relaxed and bemused (Burna), to tired and stern (Ba), to solemn and dignified (Faginna), to uncertain and a bit overwhelmed (Fuliwulu). The Africans appeared, for the most part, in white shirts and dark jackets, their standard jail dress, it would seem. Some wore hats and a few smoked pipes.

Townsend drew especially evocative portraits of Grabeau and Kimbo. The former appears as a round, friendly face with three or four wrinkles toward the hairline. He had almost no neck, his head sitting on (as known from other sources) a compact, athletic body. His hair was short, his mustache and beard full. His slightly hooded eyes were rather too widely open, suggesting perhaps vulnerability and certainly the playfulness for which he was known. Kimbo was one of the four Africans who attacked and killed Captain Ferrer on the *Amistad*, a fact made quite believable by a portrait that conveys a direct, uncompromising gaze, psychological intensity, and inner strength framed in a handsome, youthful face. By paying close attention to the individual characteristics and psychology of so many of the *Amistad* captives, Townsend accomplished in his small sketches what the abolitionist movement would try to do over the next two and a half years in American society at large: he humanized the rebels of the *Amistad*.

The Long, Low Black Schooner

On September 2, 1839, three days after the *Amistad* Africans arrived at the New Haven jail and thousands of people had already filed through to see them, the Bowery Theatre of New York began its performance of *The Black Schooner, or, The Pirate Slaver Armistead*; or *The Long, Low Black Schooner*, as it was more commonly called. An advertisement announced "an entire new and deeply interesting Nautical Melo-Drama, in 2 acts, written expressly for this Theatre, by a popular author," almost certainly Jonas B. Phillips, the Bowery Theatre's "house playwright" during the 1830s.[36] Based on "the late extraordinary Piracy! Mutiny! & Murder!" aboard the *Amistad* and the sensational newspaper reports of "black pirates" that had appeared in the press before their capture, the play demonstrated how quickly the news of the rebellion spread, and with what cultural resonance. The title of the play came from the title of the *New York Sun* article about the *Amistad* rebellion published on August 31, 1839, which in turn had drawn on the recent descriptions of a pirate ship captained by a man named Mitchell, who had been marauding in the Gulf of Mexico.[37]

In 1839 the Bowery Theatre was notorious for its rowdy, raucous working-class audiences: youthful Bowery b'hoys and g'hals (slang for young working-class men and women of Lower Manhattan) and dandies, as well as sailors, soldiers, journeymen, laborers, apprentices, street urchins, and gang members. Prostitutes plied their trade in the theater's third tier. The audience cheered, hissed, drank, fought, cracked peanuts, threw eggs, and squirted tobacco juice everywhere. During an especially popular performance, the overflow crowd might sit on the stage amid the actors and props, or they might simply invade

"La Amistad," ca. 1839

The schooner *Amistad* after the rebellion, off Culloden Point, Long Island, just before capture by a U.S. naval vessel, the brig *Washington*, approaching at left. The Africans had sailed fourteen hundred miles to a "free country." They negotiated with several white men, handed over a musket to signify peaceful intentions, and bought a hunting dog for future subsistence (detail below). They sought help to return to Africa.

Throughout the 1830s the homelands of the *Amistad* Africans were wracked by war-fare, much of it caused by the slave trade. Men were trained as warriors to protect their village, town, or city. This early-nineteenth-century warrior, probably Temne, went into battle wearing around his neck a greegree bag filled with spiritually charged sacred objects to protect him. Cinqué the warrior wore the same as he fought a life-and-death battle in American courts.

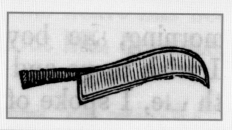

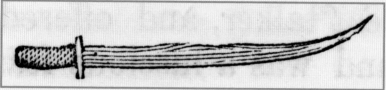

Knives played a central role in Mende culture, for clearing land (the "booker," at top) and, more important, in combat, as the warrior's weapon of choice. Missionary George Thompson wrote that the Mende used the pictured cutlass "to cut limbs and brush, to hew (instead of a hatchet), and also to fight with."

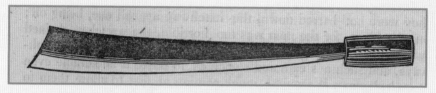

The discovery of a box of cane knives aboard the *Amistad* by the three little girls, Margru, Teme, and Kagne, must have seemed a gift from ancestral spirits to the warriors. The weapon they used in making war against enemies in Africa would now be used against enemies aboard the slave schooner.

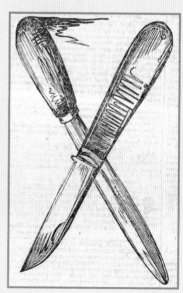

The *Amistad* Africans created a scandal when they rearmed themselves soon after they were incarcerated in the New Haven jail, affirming their right to self-defense. These knives, brought to them by sympathetic visitors and the African sailors who served as their translators, made local abolitionists nervous.

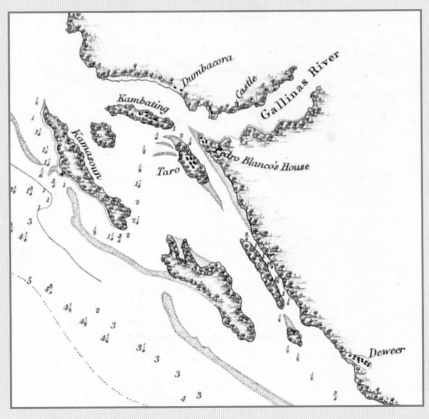

After enslavement in the interior of southern Sierra Leone, the *Amistad* Africans were marched or canoed to the Gallinas Coast, pictured here on a map drawn in the late 1830s. The Africans were held at the slave trading factory Lomboko, labeled "Dumbacora" on the map, awaiting the slave ship and the Middle Passage. Spanish merchant Pedro Blanco, whose house also appears on the map, allied with local African kings, especially Siaka, leader of the Vai, to build a vast slaving empire in the region.

The abolition of the slave trade by Great Britain in 1807 and the signing of treaties with Portugal and Spain made the commerce in human bodies on the Gallinas Coast illegal and more violent and dangerous than ever. Blanco and other traders employed Kru sailors to man large canoes to load the enslaved and to transport them to the slave ships as quickly as possible, in order to escape the British anti–slave trade patrols.

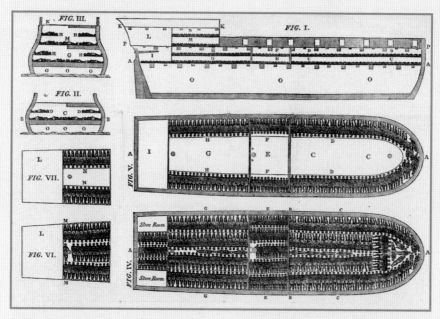

The slave ship *Teçora*, on which the Africans made the Middle Passage from Lomboko to Havana, Cuba, carried roughly the same number of enslaved people as the infamous slave ship *Brooks*, which sailed out of Liverpool between 1783 and 1804. Grabeau recalled that the distance between decks, where the enslaved were held, was 48 inches and that conditions there were horrific.

The *Diligenté*, a Portuguese slave brig captured by the British in 1838 and painted by naval lieutenant Henry Samuel Hawker, was the same kind of vessel and roughly the same size as the *Teçora*. The *Amistad* Africans recalled their own Middle Passage as deadly: many of their shipmates died and were thrown overboard in the manner shown by a sailor and marine at midship (detail below).

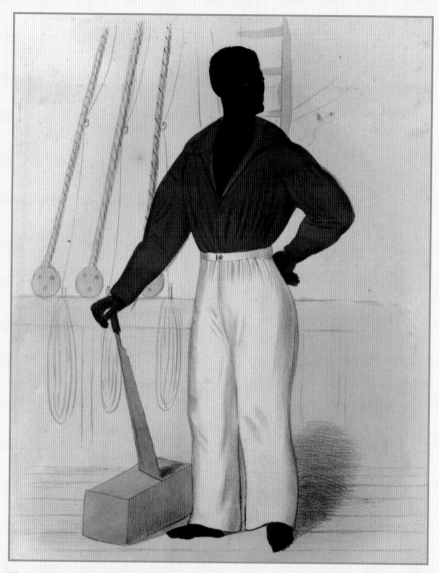

The penny paper the *New York Sun* played a crucial role in depicting Cinqué and the rebellion in a positive, even romantic, light, inspiring broad popular interest in the case. Here the leader appears in a heroic pose, having slain the tyrant and won his freedom. Below the image appeared a speech Cinqué was said to have given to his comrades after the rebellion, insisting that death was preferable to slavery.

Kale was one of four children on the *Amistad*. When abolitionists organized the New Haven jail as a school, teaching the prisoners to read, write, and study the Bible, Kale was the star student. With the assistance of his elders he wrote an important letter to John Quincy Adams, boldly instructing the seventy-three-year-old former president what to say as he represented "the Mendi People" before the United States Supreme Court.

Grabeau was, by all accounts, the most important leader of the *Amistad* Africans after Cinqué. In his homeland he was a traveling trader, a poor member of a wealthy and powerful family, and apparently a high-ranking member of the Poro Society, an all-male secret society that wielded great power among the Mende and most of the other cultures of southern Sierra Leone. The Poro played a key role in the self-organization of the rebels during the uprising and incarceration.

The young Mende man Kimbo was one of the warriors who led the attack on Captain Ferrer, but at the moment of the coup de grâce, he proved squeamish and had to turn his face away. His direct, uncompromising gaze in the portrait conveys a strong personality.

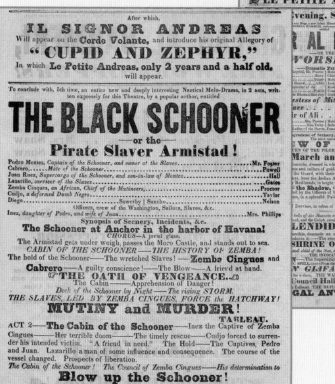

One of the many expressions of public fascination in the *Amistad* rebellion was a play performed at the Bowery Theatre in New York, which opened a mere six days after the rebels were brought ashore in New London, Connecticut. The play was seen by thousands of New Yorkers, many of them workers, and was called one of the hits of the season.

A popular pamphlet published in October 1839 depicted Cinqué as a Barbary corsair, with a *keffiyah* (head dress), a *shemagh* (a traditional Muslim scarf), and a *kaif* (a curved Arabian sword), facing a rising sun with a spyglass in his hand. Influenced by the recent Barbary Wars, the author of the pamphlet was under the mistaken assumption that Cinqué and the other Africans were Mandingo, and hence likely Muslim, rather than Mende.

 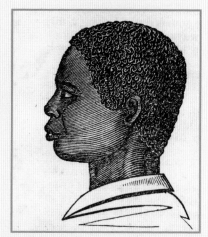

A portrait of Cinqué (top right) and a silhouette of Konoma (bottom left) show how John Warner Barber used his meetings with the *Amistad* Africans in the New Haven jail to individualize their portraits as shown in these corresponding details from his famous engraving of the rebellion entitled "The Death of Capt. Ferrer."

The images of the *Amistad* rebellion created by artists John Warner Barber and Amasa Hewins drew on this famous painting of frontier violence, *The Murder of Jane McCrea* (1804) by John Vanderlyn, in which two Native Americans kill a white settler. Even though the artists sympathized with the *Amistad* rebels and supported their bid for freedom, they nonetheless drew on racial tropes in depicting the rebellion.

HORRID MASSACRE IN VIRGINIA·

The Scenes which the above Plate is designed to represent, are—Fig 1. a Mother intreating for the lives of her children.—2. Mr. Travis, cruelly murdered by his own Slaves.—3. Mr. Barrow, who bravely defended himself until his wife escaped.—4. A comp. of mounted Dragoons in pursuit of the Blacks

The generally positive and sympathetic depictions of the *Amistad* rebellion stood in stark contrast to the only other image of slave revolt created in the United States before the Civil War—this representation of Nat Turner's rebellion, which took place in Southampton County, Virginia, in 1831.

A wealthy silk merchant and the founder, in 1841, of the Mercantile Agency, which would evolve into Dun and Bradstreet, Lewis Tappan was an evangelical Christian and a zealous abolitionist. His commitment of money, time, and energy to the *Amistad* rebels was extraordinary from the first moment he heard of the uprising through the long freedom struggle in the United States to the establishment of the Mende Mission in Sierra Leone.

"Old Man Eloquent," as the former president and still member of Congress John Quincy Adams was called, gave a stirring speech on behalf of the *Amistad* Africans before the Supreme Court, helping them to win their freedom and go home. Before the hearing Adams had remarked, "if he should be in any way instrumental in rescuing these people, he should consider it *the greatest event of his life.*"

Descended from a powerful Connecticut political family, Roger S. Baldwin used his social position, legal learning, and abolitionist commitments to play a critical role in the *Amistad* case. In his successful argument before the Supreme Court he emphasized that the rebels arrived in the United States in "the actual condition of freedom," which they had legitimately won under arms.

The African American abolitionist Robert Purvis of Philadelphia played an active part in the Vigilance Committee, a precursor of, and contributor to, the Underground Railroad. Purvis took a strong interest in the *Amistad* cause, contributed money to it, hosted the rebels in his home, and commissioned Nathaniel Jocelyn to paint a soon-to-be famous portrait of Cinqué.

Artist and committed abolitionist Nathaniel Jocelyn imagined and painted the hero of the *Amistad* rebellion back home in Africa, anticipating the victory that finally came in November 1841, when Cinqué and the other thirty-four survivors boarded the *Gentleman* to reverse the Middle Passage and return to their homelands. Meantime, Jocelyn's portrait helped to inspire a man named Madison Washington to organize and lead a successful slave revolt on the American slave ship *Creole*.

it and become part of the performance. The owner and manager of the theatre, Thomas Hamblin, employed a pack of constables to prevent riots, which on several occasions exploded anyway. That the Bowery Theatre was associated with a big, violent anti-abolitionist riot in 1834 makes its staging of *The Long, Low Black Schooner* all the more remarkable.[38]

Paired with *Giafar al Barmeki, or, The Fire Worshippers*, an orientalist fantasy set in Baghdad, the play attracted "multitudes" to the nation's largest theater. If performed every other day for two weeks (it may have run longer) at only two-thirds capacity of the theater's thirty-five hundred seats (it may have been greater), the play would have been seen by roughly fifteen thousand people, about one in twenty of the city's population. Another way of estimating the number in attendance is to divide the production's gross earnings of $5,250 by prevailing ticket prices (most were twenty-five cents, some were fifty and seventy-five cents), which also suggests roughly fifteen thousand viewers. The play therefore played a major role not only in interpreting the *Amistad* rebellion, but in spreading the news of it soon after it happened. It was not uncommon for playwrights to work with timely and controversial events in order to draw larger audiences to their theaters.[39]

No script survives, but a detailed playbill provides a "Synopsis of Scenery, Incidents, &c." Set on the main deck of the *Amistad*, the play featured the actual people who were involved in the uprising. The leading character was "Zemba Cinques, an African, Chief of the Mutineers," based on Cinqué and played by Joseph Proctor, a "young American tragedian," perhaps in burnt-cork blackface, as was common at the Bowery.[40] The "Captain of the Schooner, and owner of the Slaves" was Pedro Montes, the actual owner of four of the enslaved who sailed the vessel after the rebellion. The supercargo was Juan Ruez, based on José Ruiz, owner of forty-nine slaves on board. Cudjo, "a deformed Dumb Negro," who resembles the "savage and deformed slave" Caliban in Shakespeare's play *The Tempest*, was apparently based on the "savage" Konoma, who was ridiculed for his tusk-like teeth and decried as a cannibal. Lazarillo, the "overseer of the slaves," probably drew on the slave-sailor Celestino. Other characters included Cabrero the mate, sailors, and the wholly invented damsel soon to be in distress, Inez, the daughter of Montes and the wife of Ruez.[41]

Act 1 begins as the vessel sets sail from Havana, passing Moro Castle and heading out to sea. The history of Zemba Cingues, the hero of the story, is recounted as a prelude to entry into the "hold of the schooner," where lay the "wretched slaves!" The bondsmen plot and soon take an "Oath of vengeance." In a rising storm, also noted in the accounts of the rebellion, "The Slaves, led by Zemba Cingues" force open the hatchway, which results in "MUTINY and MURDER!" The rebels seize the vessel and reset its course, heading eastward across the Atlantic to their native Sierra Leone. "Prospects of liberation" are at hand.[42]

Act 2 shifts to the captain's cabin, now occupied, after the rebellion, by Zemba Cingues, as Montes and Rues sit, as prisoners, in the dark hold of the vessel (as their counterparts actually did). The world has been turned upside down: those who were below are now above, and vice versa. The reversal poses great danger to Inez, who has apparently fallen into the clutches of Cudjo and now faces "terrible doom." Someone, probably Zemba Cingues, rescues her, forcing Cudjo to "surrender his intended victim." Did the audience see a black hero rescue a white woman from the hands of a black villain? This is a theme of no small significance, given prevailing popular fears of racial "amalgamation," which had ignited anti-abolition riots.

Zemba Cingues then sees a vessel (the U.S. brig *Washington*) sailing toward them, and holds a council among his fellow mutineers to decide what to do. They choose death over slavery—a sentiment repeatedly ascribed to Cinqué in the popular press—and decide to "Blow up the Schooner!" (The *Amistad* rebels made no such decision, as many of them were off the vessel at Long Island when the sailors of the *Washington* captured their vessel.) Alas, it is too late as the "Gallant Tars" of the *Washington* drop into the cabin from its skylight and take control of the *Amistad*.

The end of the play is left uncertain, much like the fate of the *Amistad* captives, who were sitting in the New Haven jail not far away, awaiting trial on charges of piracy and murder. The playbill states: "Denoument—Fate of Cingues!" What indeed will be his fate? Did the play enact his execution, an ending that many, including Cinqué himself, expected? Or did it dramatize his liberation along with all of his comrades?[43]

The Long, Low Black Schooner was not an unusual play for its time. Slave revolt and piracy were common themes in early American theater. Rebellious slaves appeared in Obi, or, Three-Finger'd Jack, a play about a Jamaican runaway slave turned bandit, which was a staple after its American premiere in 1801; and in The Slave, an opera by Thomas Morton about a revolt in Surinam, first acted in 1817 and many times thereafter, into the 1840s. The Gladiator dramatized the famous slave revolt led by Spartacus in ancient Greece. It premiered in 1831, starred working-class hero Edwin Forrest, and may have been the most popular play of the decade. Pirates headlined popular nautical melodramas of the 1830s, such as Captain Kyd, or, The Wizard of the Sea, performed first in 1830 and numerous times thereafter, then published as a novel by J. H. Ingraham in 1839. John Glover Drew adapted Byron's The Corsair for performance at Brook Farm in the early 1840s. The great African American actor Ira Aldridge would soon act the lead in The Bold Buccaneer. Slave rebels and pirates sometimes appeared in the same plays, as they did in The Long, Low Black Schooner: "Three-Finger'd Jack" was something of a pirate on land, and indeed had been called "that daring freebooter." Pirates also played a significant role in The Gladiator.[44]

Like other melodramas of the times, The Long, Low Black Schooner featured virtuous common people, usually laborers, battling villainous aristocrats—in this case, enslaved Africans striking back against the Spanish slaveholders Montes and Ruez. "Low" characters like Zemba Cingues spoke poetic lines in honorable resistance. They were routinely celebrated for their heroism, encouraging some degree of popular identification with the outlaw who dared to strike for freedom. As Peter Reed has noted, audiences "could both applaud and fear low revolts, both mourn and celebrate their defeats."[45]

The theater shaped the news of the Amistad rebellion as it spread it.

A sympathetic, even romantic view softened the violence of the original event. Cinqué's poised and dramatic personal bearing during the legal proceedings earned him comparison to Shakespeare's Othello.[46] He was also likened to "a colored dandy in Broadway." He clearly had the "outlaw charisma" so common to the "rogue performances" of the era. Having captured the attention of the theater world and the public at large, it was fitting that *The Long, Low Black Schooner* should be followed, in December 1839, by a production of *Jack Sheppard, or, The Life of a Robber!*, also written by Jonas B. Phillips. Like Sheppard, whose jailbreaks became "the common discourse of the whole nation" in Britain in the 1720s, and to whom the public flocked, paying admission to see him in his cell, the "black pirates" of the *Amistad* were winning in their own bid to take the good ship *Popular Imagination*. A "Nautical Melo-Drama," based on real people and dramatic current events, was playing out in American society as a whole.[47]

The Struggle to Communicate

Amid the explosion of images and newspaper articles, and the enormous number of visitors to both jail and theater, the *Amistad* Africans struggled to tell their own story to their American captors and allies. Yet they could communicate only through sign language and Burna's few words of English. The Africans spoke at least fifteen languages, but none of these could be understood by the people in whose hands their collective fate now rested, especially after Antonio, who had translated during the freedom voyage, had been separated from them. The Reverend Joshua Leavitt noted with sadness that these unfortunate persons, facing trial for their lives, could not speak for themselves. As noted earlier, they could and did say plenty for themselves; the problem was, no one could understand them.[48]

Leavitt and others quickly grasped the necessity of communicating with these strangers who had made it to their shores as well as the larger significance of allowing the rebels to tell their own stories about how they got there. Dwight Janes and other antislavery activists on the scene in New London had written Leavitt and Lewis Tappan, asking that they "find some old Africans in your vicinity, who can speak the native language, so that you may learn the facts from them." When Leavitt visited the *Amistad* Africans in the New Haven jail on September 6, 1839, he took with him "an old African man," a sailor who spoke the Congo language, but the captives "all say they are not Congoes." The correspondent of the *New York Sun* had reported in error that they were Congo, probably because he misunderstood when a few described themselves as "Kono." Leavitt added, "Many of them say Manding, whence it is supposed they are Mandingoes," but this too reflected confusion, for what they had said was "Mende." He did grasp, correctly, that "it is not unlikely there are persons of several tribes among them."[49]

The same day, Tappan brought three more Africans, who spoke different languages, into the jail, hoping that they could communicate with the prisoners. He found to his disappointment that they could not. Undeterred, the next day he brought two more. So zealous were his efforts that the *New York Morning Herald* resorted to racist ridicule, noting that every time Tappan came into the jail, he did so with a "black tail"—"a great number of negroes of all ages and sizes, and colors, and speaking all languages from the Monshee down to the Mandingo."[50]

Success appeared in the form of James Ferry, a Kissi man about thirty years of age whose own dramatic international odyssey of slavery and freedom began when he was kidnapped in southern Sierra Leone as a child and ended when he was "liberated in Colombia, by Bolivar," probably around 1821. The path Ferry took to the New Haven jail eighteen years later is unknown, but when he arrived, new understandings of the *Amistad* case became possible, even though there were no Kissi people among the prisoners. It turned out that Ferry also knew Vai, called Gallinao (after Gallinas) by Tappan, as did the Mende man Bau. Tappan wrote, "You may imagine the joy manifested by these poor Africans, when they heard one of their own color address them in a friendly manner, and in a language they could comprehend!"

Ferry thus made possible a formal interview, the first full account any of the *Amistad* Africans had offered about what had happened to them. Antonio was also on hand to help out with translation, because both he and Ferry spoke Spanish. Lawyers, professors, law enforcement officials, ministers, and activists all gathered round to get the story. Communication remained difficult, however, as Ferry translated Tappan's questions into Vai, which was his and Bau's second (or third) language, and Bau then translated them into Mende so that Cinqué and others could answer by the same circuitous linguistic route.[51]

Amid the search for better means of communication, and at the end of a week of wildly popular fascination with the case, abolitionists formed the Amistad Committee on September 4, 1839. Tappan, Jocelyn, and Leavitt made an appeal to the "Friends of Liberty" to rally around "thirty-eight fellow-men from Africa," who, "piratically kidnapped from their native land," were "transported across the seas, and subjected to atrocious cruelties" before being "thrown upon our shores, and are now incarcerated in jail to await their trial for crimes alleged by their oppressors to have been committed by them." They added that "they are ignorant of our language, of the usages of civilized society, and the obligations of Christianity," thereby setting an abolitionist cultural agenda for the future. The committee announced several immediate tasks for itself: to acquire and distribute clothing among "these unfortunate men"; to find and employ interpreters in order to understand them; and to hire attorneys who would help to "secure the rights of the accused."[52]

The *Amistad* rebellion detonated a bomb in American popular culture, inspiring prints, drawings, newspaper articles, a play, and long lines of admission-paying visitors to the jail, all during the first week the rebels were ashore, all *before* the abolitionists organized their campaign. The Amistad Committee would now work with the rebels to enhance, direct, and control the popular interest in the case. Radical action taken by the Africans would inspire a new movement against their enslavement, which would in turn strengthen an older, larger movement against slavery in general. What had been, for many people, an abstract issue would now become concrete as the *Amistad* Africans and their allies waged a war for freedom. The struggle against slavery had suddenly acquired a human face: a dignified, heroic warrior named Cinqué, who was being transformed by writers and artists into a revolutionary symbol before he ever stepped onto American soil.

CHAPTER FOUR

Jail

The *Amistad* Africans arrived at the New Haven jail on August 30, 1839, the latest link in a transatlantic chain of incarceration. The first link was the slave factory at Lomboko; the second, the lower deck of the *Teçora*; the third, the barracoons of Havana; the fourth, the hold of the *Amistad*. Following their successful rebellion, freedom voyage, and capture by the United States Navy, they were forced belowdecks again on the vessel they had seized, and now they had arrived at another place of confinement. The material reality of unfreedom in the *Amistad* case was Atlantic: a slave factory in Africa, a ship on the Atlantic, a slave pen in Cuba, a schooner in the Caribbean, and a jail on the shores of North America.

The *Amistad* Africans had exercised their political will in the rebellion and in sailing their vessel from the "slave country" of Cuba to the "free country" of New York and Connecticut, capturing the popular imagination and mobilizing abolitionists along the way. Now that they were incarcerated again, their agency would be circumscribed, its setting reduced from the wide Atlantic to several small rooms in a jail. They were, in essence, political prisoners before the term had been invented. (It would be coined a few years later, in 1860, by Charles Dickens in a short story called "The Italian Prisoner.") From the moment the sailors of the U.S. brig *Washington* captured the *Amistad* rebels off Culloden Point, Cinqué and his comrades expected death. Now, charged by the federal government with piracy and murder, both punishable by execution, they had good reason. The closest African parallel to the latest captivity would have been "prisoner of war," a pervasive reality in their conflict-riven homelands. Enclosed in a small space and shadowed by death, they would search for new ways to shape their destiny.[1]

How the African insurrectionists would relate to American abolitionists amid a burst of popular interest would be a key to achieving their ultimate goal of free return to their native lands. The two groups that met in the New Haven jail represented the main wings of the antislavery movement in the United States and around the world. The parties would discover how to communicate, learn from and influence each other, and cooperate toward common ends, legal and political. Trust would develop slowly, as would an antislavery alliance. What happened in jail would shape what happened in the courtroom and the case more broadly. If the abolitionists wanted to make "political capital" of the *Amistad* case, the Africans would be the labor to make it possible.[2]

The meeting of slave rebels and abolitionists in jail had a history, and indeed had already produced an idea central to the movement. "Immediatism," a personal commitment to end slavery immediately, not gradually, and with no compensation to slaveholders, had emerged from an experience of incarceration earlier in the decade. In 1830, William Lloyd Garrison, a fiery young abolitionist born of a Boston sailor, attacked merchant Francis Todd in print for a connection to the illegal slave trade. Todd in turn filed a libel suit and got Garrison locked up in the Baltimore jail. There the budding activist had his first close encounter with slavery: he met captured runaways as well as enslaved Africans awaiting sale. He talked with them. They made the horrors of slavery real to him and deepened his opposition to the "peculiar institution." Arthur Tappan (brother of Lewis) read the young editor's defiant account of his jailing and immediately bailed him out. Garrison then toured New England to spread the gospel of immediatism, which he now, thanks to the jail experience, linked to the issue of black equality. The same political issues would be raised anew in the New Haven jail.[3]

The African Story

On the morning of Tuesday, September 10, Lewis Tappan and a host of associates arrived at the home of Marshal Norris Wilcox for an important meeting. The most crucial member of Tappan's entourage was James Ferry, the recently discovered Kissi man who spoke Vai and was therefore able to communicate with the *Amistad* Africans through Bau. Five other men arrived with Tappan and Ferry: two professors from Yale University, Josiah Gibbs, a linguist, and Denison Olmsted, a physicist and astronomer; two Congregationalist ministers, Leonard Bacon of New Haven and Henry G. Ludlow of New York; and Roger S. Baldwin, an eminent attorney from a powerful New Haven political family. They were committed abolitionists and fellow travelers. The homes of Tappan and Ludlow had been trashed by anti-abolition mobs.[4]

The purpose of the meeting was a formal interview with Cinqué and Bau, who would now, with Ferry's assistance, begin the all-important process of telling the African story of the *Amistad* rebellion. Up to this moment, public accounts of the uprising had been based primarily on the testimony of the white Cuban slaveholders José Ruiz and Pedro Montes. Ruiz's ability to speak English (it was said that he had been educated in Connecticut) and Lt. Richard W. Meade's ability to speak Spanish, coupled with the inability of anyone to understand the many languages of the Africans (until the discovery of Ferry), had assured that only one side of the tale of rebellion was being told at a time when everyone was fascinated by the case and determined to know what had happened.[5]

When Wilcox brought Cinqué and Bau into the room, probably in manacles and shackles, the prisoners were filled with uncertainty, for they still expected to be executed. They had met Tappan, Gibbs, and Baldwin the previous Sunday evening in the New Haven jail, but they did not know the others, nor did they know why they had been summoned to a strange place for a meeting. Cinqué was "under some apprehension," but still he moved with confidence and dignity, filling the room with his magnetic presence.[6]

Speaking through Ferry, Tappan tried to put the men at ease: "We endeavored to impress upon their minds, in the first place, that we were their friends, and that they must speak the truth." The latter concern produced what may have been the first "God palaver," or religious discussion, between the *Amistad* Africans and the American abolitionists. Tappan noted that "both of them appeared to have some idea of a good Spirit, and also of an evil Spirit." Through Ferry they explained that "if they told lies, the evil Spirit would take them somewhere, they did not know where." Tappan asked Cinqué if he knew that God would punish him if he did not speak the truth. The *Amistad* leader answered yes, and "added in his own language—'me tell no lie; me tell the truth.'" Asked where God lived, "he pointed upward," no doubt to nods of approval from the onlooking Christians. This would be a "private examination," but Tappan clearly wanted it to have public credibility and perhaps legal force, hence his emphasis on truthfulness.

Cinqué and Bau then began to unfold their personal histories to the gentlemen through John Ferry. A master storyteller in the Mende tradition, Cinqué warmed to the occasion and relished the opportunity. Sensing that the persons in the room were "friendly to him," he began to tell "his story" in an animated manner. He relayed the details of his life and the calamity that had brought him to New Haven. Occasionally he "would shake hands with the interpreter, and laugh very heartily," building into his narrative human connection and humor.[7]

Cinqué and Bau began with the free lives they led in southern Sierra Leone, establishing their identities first and foremost through their families, which was the traditional way in their homelands. Cinqué "left his father, mother, wife and three children" in Mani, where his father was "a leading man." Two of his children were "a little larger than the African girls who are prisoners, and the other about as large," which would have put him in his early thirties. He was kidnapped and marched to Gendema, the capital of King Siaka's slaving empire, about fifteen miles from the coast. Siaka in turn sold him to "a great man" named Fulekower, who sold him to the Spaniards at Lomboko.[8]

Bau—"sober, intelligent looking, and rather slightly built"—left a wife and three children in the Mende country. Four men captured him as he was on his way to the rice fields, tied his left hand to his neck, and marched him for ten long days to Lomboko, where he probably met Cinqué and many others who would be his shipmates. Both men had the skills of warriors: "They had been in battles, in their own country, using muskets."[9]

From their arrival at Lomboko, Cinqué and Bau shared a common history of incarceration, shipment, and resistance. Brought to the coast, they "were chained when put on board the slaver, which was a brig. It was crowded with slaves—200 men, 300 women, and 'plenty of children.'" At this point Cinqué "sat down on the floor, walked about on his knees, and bent his head beneath the imaginary deck above, all to dramatize the cramped conditions he and his comrades experienced on the lower deck." Their sufferings on the eight-week Middle Passage were great; many of their shipmates died.

Cinqué and Bau were put ashore in Havana "in the night." They were "ironed hand and foot" and "chained together at the waist and by the neck." Ten days later they boarded the *Amistad* in the evening and sailed around midnight. Once at sea, their irons were taken off, although the two seamen kept watch with muskets. Some of the Africans slept below, the rest on deck. Captain Ferrer, they emphasized, was "very cruel," beating them routinely and keeping them "almost starved." They decided that they "would not take it, to use their own expression, and therefore turned to and fought for it." Once they had captured the vessel, they told the Spaniards to take them to Sierra Leone, but, according to Cinqué, "They made fools of us." Because Cinqué officially faced execution for murder, he and Bau discreetly stated that "they were down in the hold, and did not see the fight." So much for the spirits and their punishments.

Despite Ferry's translation, confusion remained. Tappan and his colleagues continued to think that Cinqué and most of the others were Mandingo, from Senegambia, rather than Mende, and that a few were Congo rather than Kono. Tappan understood that the quality of communication left something to be desired and therefore, at the end of his published account of the interviews, he made an appeal to "native Africans in this city, or elsewhere in this country, who were born near the sources of the river Niger, or in Mandingo, or who can converse readily in the Susoo, Kissi, Mandingo, or Gallinas dialects" to call on the Amistad Committee at 143 Nassau Street in New York. He also made a request for books and pamphlets that might illuminate the history and cultures of that part of Africa from which the prisoners came.

The African story of the rebellion thus emerged, through John Ferry, in an interaction that featured abolitionist questions and prisoner answers, shaped by native traditions of storytelling. The narrative of the uprising began with freedom in Africa, where families were torn asunder, the storytellers violently enslaved and forced into a gruesome Middle Passage, incarcerated in the barracoons of Havana, and mistreated on the *Amistad*, where they finally launched a rebellion in order to achieve their ultimate objective: to go home to the freedom where their tale began. The Africans offered a narrative of freedom to slavery to freedom—a coherent, compelling story that would captivate people throughout the United States and beyond.

Romance Denied

As the *Amistad* Africans spent their second week in jail, and as they began to tell their story to the abolitionists who would represent them in court, the public uproar over the case and their presence in New Haven, continued unabated. Those who visited the prisoners included a cross-section of mid-Atlantic and New England society. In addition to Tappan, Gibbs, Olmsted, Bacon, Ludlow, and Baldwin, other visiting luminaries in coming months would include the Reverend George E. Day (divinity) and Benjamin Silliman (chemistry and natural history), both from Yale. Day and several others—Robert C. Learned and Benjamin Griswold of the Theological Seminary, S. W. Magill, and, of special importance, Sherman Booth, a senior at Yale University—instructed the captives in jail. The Irish abolitionist/British diplomat Richard Robert Madden came all the way from Havana, speaking to several of the *Amistad* Africans in Arabic and estimating the ages of several others. Former president, current member of Congress, and future attorney for the *Amistad* Africans John Quincy Adams made what he described as a pleasurable visit, remarking afterwards that the "clothing, bedding &c of the Africans are not what they ought to be." Even United States District Court judge Andrew Judson visited the *Amistad* Africans in jail, twice. Phrenologists such as L. N. Fowler were busy studying and measuring the heads of the Africans, to deduce their temperaments and characters. Artists entered the place of confinement with pencils and brushes to sketch and paint portraits. Among the throngs in jail a newspaper correspondent saw "the finest looking women there that ever God made." Some of these women were determined abolitionists.[10]

As the *New York Sun* and other newspapers reported favorably, even romantically, on the *Amistad* Africans and their struggles, James Gordon Bennett and his colleagues at the proslavery *New York Morning Herald* took a dissenting view. They howled in protest against the sympathetic depictions of Cinqué and his mates and declared the *Sun* to be "the New York penny nigger paper." During a time of polarization on the issue of slavery, the correspondents for the *Morning Herald* angrily sought "to destroy the romance which has been thrown around [Cinqué's] character." They roundly denied that he had the dignified, graceful bearing of Othello. Rather, he was a "blubber-lipped, sullen looking negro, not half as intelligent or striking in appearance as every third black you meet on the docks of New York." The entire lot of the *Amistad* Africans represented nothing so much as "hopeless stupidity and beastly degradation"—they were likened to baboons. Back in Africa, they had been "slothful and thievish," and were "sunk in a state of ignorance, debasement and barbarism, of which no adequate conception can be formed." They were in no way equal to whites. They were "a distinct and totally different race, and the God of nature never intended that they should live together in any other relation than that of master and slave."[11]

The writers for the *Morning Herald* considered the depictions of the Africans in the *New York Sun* to be not only dead wrong, but dangerously egalitarian and subversive. In response they spewed racist invective against the *Amistad* Africans and viciously lampooned those who visited and supported them while they were in jail: "Parsons go to preach to them, philosophers to experiment on them, professors to pick up a knowledge of their language, phrenologists to feel their heads, and young ladies to look and laugh at them." These depictions, more extreme than anything that appeared in Southern newspapers, were the textual equivalent of the demeaning "bobalition" prints of the day.[12]

To Hartford

When Wilcox the marshal and Pendleton the jailer arrived at the New Haven jail Saturday morning, September 14, to take the *Amistad* Africans to Hartford for their second legal hearing, the little girls, Kagne, Teme, and Margru, began to weep bitterly. They did not want go. Neither did the men, one of whom hid in a remote room and could not be discovered for some time. Others tried to escape the jail altogether. Cinqué listened to the upheaval from his isolated cell, for the plan was to take this dangerous prisoner separately, two days later. Burna cocked an ear from the sick room, with Weluwa, who lay near death. They were too ill to travel. None of the others seemed to know where they were going, nor why. Having been in New Haven barely two weeks and assuming that a change could only be for the worse, perhaps their own execution, they were "filled with awful forebodings."[13]

The authorities eventually got everyone into a canal boat, bound for Farmington, an "abolition town," where farmer Roderick Stanley saw them, as he noted in his journal: "38 Afrecans passed here on their way to Hartford to be tryed on an Indightment for Piracy and Murder, they were lately from Afreca—3 small girls, the rest males." Word had already begun to circulate in abolitionist circles that they were "lately from Afreca" and hence had been illegally enslaved, a positive sign, but unknown to the anxious travelers. In Farmington they shifted to wagons for the final ten miles to Connecticut's capital city, their mood brightening along the way.[14]

They found in Hartford the same tumultuous, agitated scene they had come to know in New Haven: the city was suddenly "crowded with strangers," convinced advocates of abolition, equally determined opponents, and those who had no opinion on the great debate of the times. All had heard of the dramatic rebellion and wanted to get a look at the prisoners. Into the jail strode "many distinguished members of the bar" who had come from all over Connecticut and as far away as New York and Boston. The U.S. Hotel and various other public houses were "full to overflowing" with "politicians, lawyers, judges, sheriffs, reporters, editors, &c., all visiting Hartford to be present at this trial." Indeed, the most commonly heard question around town at the time was, "Which way is the jail?" Correspondents both hostile and sympathetic to the *Amistad* Africans agreed: the "rush to prison has been immense"; "not less than four thousand have visited them so far this week."[15]

The appalled editors of the *New York Morning Herald* not only sent a correspondent to Hartford, they commissioned artist Peter Quaint to depict what was going on inside Hartford jail. The correspondent described what the engraving illustrated:

On the left hand is Lewis Tappan, with his white hat, attended by another abolitionist, looking at Cinguez kissing a pretty young girl, who was handed up to him by her sympathetic mother. Near the mother is the celebrated phrenologist, Mr. Pierce, who has been forming a vocabulary of their language, hereunto annexed. In the centre of the prison group is Garrah, turning a somerset before the Africans and white company—and below, in the foreground, are two negroes scratching themselves, for it is well known that many of them have the itch. Away to the right is the fashionable, pious, learned, and gay people of Connecticut, precisely as they appeared during these amusing scenes in Hartford prison, receiving lectures and instructions in African philosophy and civilization.[16]

The interest of women in the case (and in the abolitionist movement more broadly) was especially disturbing to the writers of the *Morning Herald*: theirs was "a species of hallucination." The *Amistad* affair had taken on "all the romance of an eastern fairy tale, and they [women]

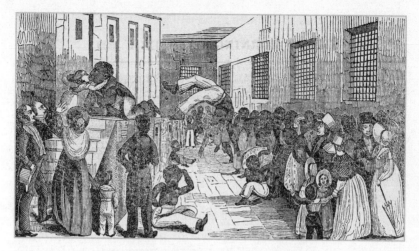

"The Captured Africans of the *Amistad*:
Teaching Philosophy to Lewis Tappen & Co."

consider the black fellows as worthy of as much honor as the colored
Moorish Knights of old." The staunchest and most vocal opponents of
the *Amistad* Africans and their abolitionist allies fanned the flaming
fears of amalgamation, but their anger and agitation suggested that
the heroic images were winning the day.[17]

The legal hearing was supposed to begin on Tuesday, September 17,
but was delayed for two days until federal circuit court judge Smith
Thompson arrived to join district court judge Andrew Judson. Once
he did, the courtroom filled every day, "crowded to suffocation." On
the final day of the hearing, Monday, September 23, the court was
"thronged to overflowing" by eight a.m. Even a correspondent for the
proslavery *Richmond Enquirer* was moved to observe, "A more interested audience—judging from the earnest attention of those present,
were never assembled together."[18]

The judges had a complex welter of issues to adjudicate, first and
foremost whether the Africans were to be tried as pirates and murderers. Then came salvage claims by Lt. Gedney and other naval officers;
salvage claims by the Long Island hunters Henry Green and Peletiah
Fordham; claims by Ruiz and Montes for their slave property; claims
by the Spanish consul on behalf of the family of Ferrer for the schooner

and enslaved cabin boy Antonio; and a request by the federal government that all property, both vessel and slaves, be returned to Spain. On a related issue, abolitionist attorney Theodore Sedgwick argued a habeas corpus brief for the three little girls, to remove them from the case altogether, because they were clearly too young to have been in Cuba long enough to predate the treaty that made the slave trade illegal in 1820.[19]

Over four days many gave testimony: Ruiz, Montes, and Meade about the *Amistad*'s voyage, rebellion, and recapture. Ferry translated as Bau (called "Bahoo" by the court) testified about the three little girls. Roger S. Baldwin spoke for two and half hours on behalf of the *Amistad* Africans, making what one of his abolitionist colleagues called a "forcible and ingenious argument" in which he ridiculed the salvage claim of Gedney and asked, with a sneer, of United States District Attorney Charles Ingersoll whether "the offices of the executive were to become slave catchers for the Spanish government."[20] Thompson acknowledged that "the feelings of the community are deeply involved" in the case, but he denied the habeas writ for the little girls. He and Andrew Judson of the U.S. District Court dropped the charges of piracy and murder, whereupon the claims of property became the key issue. They responded to questions about the jurisdiction of the courts by ordering an investigation of precisely where the *Amistad* had been captured by the *Washington*. They ruled that the case resume in Hartford on November 19, 1839. The *Amistad* Africans remained in the Hartford jail, which continued to teem with visitors, until September 28, when they were returned to New Haven. What they made of the intense engagement with their cause, in the courtroom and in the jail, is unknown.[21]

Warrior Moves

When the *Amistad* Africans returned to the New Haven jail, their daily regimen changed. First and perhaps most importantly, because the judges had ruled that they had not broken any laws of the United States, the rationale for keeping Cinqué separate from his comrades was no longer legally valid. He was therefore moved out of the strong-hold and into the rooms where the rest of the *Amistad* Africans were kept. The collective was happily reunited. Second, all of the prisoners were now freer to talk about what had happened in the rebellion, deepening the drama of their story and expanding the public interest in it. Third, the prisoners were now allowed to go outside, under supervision, to New Haven Green for fresh air and exercise.[22]

When the *Amistad* Africans went to the green, they contributed—perhaps wittingly, perhaps not—to the circus atmosphere surrounding their case. They performed acrobatics, gymnastics, and tumbling before the buzzing crowds that assembled to see them. The Reverend Alonzo Lewis, who saw the *Amistad* Africans through the wonder-filled eyes of a seven-year-old boy, recalled:

> The negroes were splendid specimens of manly strength and vigor. No circus athlete could excel them in "ground and lofty tumbling." They would stand still, leap into the air, and turn a double (or treble) somersault before reaching the ground. They would extend their arms and leap and revolve along the ground like a wagon-wheel without its tire. There was nothing in the acrobatic line they could not do.[23]

The group as a whole was graceful and talented, but two stood (or leapt) out for their extraordinary skills. Cinqué, who was "muscular, athletic, and extremely active," performed "astonishing feats of agility." Grabeau, short, burly, and strong, executed moves one observer had "never before seen attempted." In Hartford he had balanced "himself on his hands," then "tumbled wheelbarrow fashion, without touching his feet" the entire fifty-yard length of the jail.[24]

Given the excitement, debate, and publicity that surrounded the case, these performances became public spectacles. The massive crowds that filed through the jail assembled to watch the bodies fly through the air across the green, then followed them back to their cells for another look. At the moment when flamboyant popular com-mercial entertainments were on the rise in America—circuses being a prime example—the *Amistad* Africans made a curious and unexpected discovery: their acrobatic skills could earn them money. This made many people, on both sides of the *Amistad* debate, profoundly uneasy. Writers for the proslavery *New York Morning Herald* complained about how the "spectators shell out the sixpences freely" to the performers when watching the tumbling "exhibition." The abolitionist *Emancipator* expressed disdain for the displays of "astonishing bodily activity" by saying, "The Marshal who has them in charge, will, we think, do a service to them and to good morals, by forbidding any more exhibitions of the kind." As it happened, the Marshal made money as the performers dazzled the multitude of visitors, so the show went on.[25]

What the good folk on New Haven Green saw as circus-like had a very different genesis and meaning in Africa. The *Amistad* Africans had learned these "wonderful feats of strength and agility" not in a commercial marketplace of entertainment and leisure activity, but rather as part of their initiation into the Poro Society back in West Africa, where athleticism was linked to the rituals and communal traditions of the warrior. As anthropologist Kenneth Little wrote of the young Mende men engaged in Poro rites of passage, "They practice somersaults and acrobatics, and altogether their experiences produce a strong sense of comradeship." The higher the level of initiation into the Poro, the higher the level of gymnastic skill one might possess. This is a main reason why the two Africans repeatedly described as the most astonishing acrobats and tumblers—Cinqué and Grabeau— were also the two primary leaders of the rebellion, and the group as a whole, while they were in jail. Probably none of the American spectators who watched them had any idea that they were actually demonstrating their own lofty standing in the Poro Society, the basis of their authority within Mende culture. Probably none of the expropriated warriors who left jail and gathered on New Haven Green to tumble, leap, turn, and somersault understood how they would appear as "showmen" and "circus athletes," nor how their Poro training would help them to capture the American imagination and make their freedom struggle more popular.[26]

People Will Talk

Even though the first steps had been taken to get the African story of the rebellion into the courts and the public sphere, the search for better means of communication continued. Next to try his hand, or rather hands, in late September 1839, was the pioneer in education for the deaf, the Reverend Thomas Hopkins Gallaudet. He had heard of the difficulties of communication and wanted to apply his own theories and methods. He spent hours each day for several days in the Hartford jail "conversing with the Africans by signs, and endeavoring to make up a vocabulary of their own language." Like many other Christian visitors, Gallaudet was deeply interested in the religious ideas of the *Amistad* Africans, so he tried to discover "whether they had any distinct idea of a Supreme Being." He asked, by signs, "whether they knew of anything higher than the sun, moon, stars &c.; and several of them answered in succession that they did—that Gooly [their name for God] was above all these things." He wanted to know if they believed that Gooly would punish people for wrongdoing, such as murder, the idea of which he conveyed by the motion of cutting the throat. As soon as the *Amistad* Africans read the sign language, "they cast down their eyes and were silent," refusing to carry on the conversation. Gallaudet soon realized that he had signed his way into their fear of execution in the aftermath of the rebellion. Fortunately, James Ferry came into the jail at that very moment and was able to clear up the misunderstanding.[27]

Professor Josiah Gibbs took an avid interest in the case and worked "day and night" to facilitate mutual understanding. He talked with the *Amistad* Africans in jail, noting the meanings of their words, constructing vocabularies, and trying to understand the nature of their languages. Among the many things he learned was how to count from one to ten in Mende, "1, eta; 2, fili; 3, kiau-wa; 4, naeni." How did he learn it and from whom?[28]

A clue may lie in an encounter that took place in jail on September 6, 1839. A correspondent to the *New York Commercial Advertiser* observed that "several young gentlemen" visiting the jail were "under the tuition of the little girls, studying the Mandingoe tongue." Margru, Kagne, and Teme, he noted, were "familiar with mathematics" and were able to "count ten—and to give the name of each numeral." They taught the gentlemen how to count, not in Mandingo but Mende. They also taught them other words, "the names in their language of such things as they are acquainted with, such as ear [*gu-li*], mouth [*nda*], &c." The correspondent was sure that the agency of the little girls would be long lasting and that the jail would remain a place of learning: "Should these people stay here long some of the Yankees will become adept scholars in the Mandingoe tongue, I have no doubt."29

What the little girls taught, Gibbs took to the waterfront of New York. He walked up and down amid the hustle and bustle of the docks, counting loudly from one to ten in Mende until two curious sailors, Charles Pratt and James Covey, approached him and spoke to him in the language he was hoping to hear. One or both may have said, "*gna gi-hi-ya Men-di*" (I come from Mende). The professor probably did not understand what they said, but since they both also spoke English, he knew immediately that he had found his interpreters. The mostly Mende-speaking *Amistad* Africans would now be able to deliver a full, detailed version of what happened aboard the "long, low black schooner."

Gibbs used the methods of the little girls to link the struggle against slavery inside the New Haven jail to the struggle against slavery on the Atlantic waterfront. Pratt and Covey were both working sailors aboard the British brig of war *Buzzard*, a vessel in the West African antislavery patrol. Pratt, who was about twenty-five years old and illiterate, was the cook for Captain James Fitzgerald. Born in Sierra Leone, he knew both the Mende and Gbandi languages, having traveled as a child with his father, a merchant, to both lands. He testified that "he knew at Lonboko [*sic*] on the coast of Africa a man called Petro Blanco who was a Spanish slave trader." He did not say whether he knew him because his father traded with him or because he, like the *Amistad* Africans, had passed through the factory as a slave on the way to the New World.30

James Covey was even better equipped to play a central role in the case. Born of a Kono father and Kissi mother, the twenty-year-old young man grew up in Mende country and could therefore speak several languages. Covey explained, "I was stolen by a black man who stole 10 of us." He was twelve years old at the time. He was sold, first, to a Bullom merchant, for whom he worked as a slave for three years cultivating rice, then to Pedro Blanco at Gallinas, who placed him on board a Portuguese slave ship bound for Havana, which was soon captured by the British anti-slave-trade patrol. Covey and his shipmates were taken to Freetown, where he was educated by representatives of the Church Missionary Society. He could therefore speak and write English. He had enlisted aboard the *Buzzard* in November 1838. Captain Fitzgerald apparently held strong antislavery beliefs himself and was happy to lend the young sailor to the abolitionist cause when asked to do so by Lewis Tappan. Covey thus possessed not only a personal background of Kono and Mende language and culture, he had experienced enslavement, Lomboko, the slave ship, and liberation, and he had practical antislavery experience aboard the *Buzzard*, which was in New York in October 1839 because it had captured a slaver and brought it to the American port for adjudication.[31]

The moment Pratt and Covey walked into the jail and began to address the *Amistad* Africans in Mende, everyone knew that a breakthrough had been made. A gentleman who was present at the time described the entry of Covey during breakfast, which caused Marshal Wilcox to object. One of the prisoners, "finding a countryman who could talk in their own language, took hold of him, and literally dragged him in. Such a scene ensued as you may better conceive than I describe. Breakfast was forgotten; all crowded around the two men, and all talking as fast as possible. The children hugged one another with transport." Another eyewitness added, "As soon as one of the new comers addressed them in their native tongue, there was an instant explosion of feeling—they leaped and shouted and clapped their hands, and their joy seemed absolutely uncontrollable." At last the words they would say for themselves could be understood by all.[32]

The Story Continued

The Mende-speaking sailors Pratt and Covey were the strategic link between the African insurrectionists and the American abolitionists. Their translations made possible an immediate escalation of the struggle on two fronts. First, the full, detailed life-and-death histories of the *Amistad* rebellion and of those who made it could now be told fully. Tappan and his colleagues immediately interviewed all of the Africans, highlighting and publishing the vivid first-person accounts of Grabeau and Kimbo, two dynamic leaders of the group. With each life story collected and published, the *Amistad* case grew in human stature. The *New York Journal of Commerce* announced the arrival of the "Narrative of the Africans" on October 10, 1839.[33]

A second escalation was more confrontational. Lewis Tappan and attorney Theodore Sedgwick used the translations of Pratt and Covey to bring lawsuits, on behalf of Cinqué and Fuli, then Foone and Kimbo, against José Ruiz and Pedro Montes for "assault and battery, and false imprisonment" during their time aboard the *Amistad*. On October 17, Tappan accompanied a police officer to 65 Fulton Street in New York to have Ruiz and Montes arrested. The outraged *New York Morning Herald* reported that Tappan, wearing a "half-benevolent, half-malignant smile," asked, "How do you do, Mr. Ruiz?" He then turned to the officer and said, "This is your man—take him." The officer took both men before Judge Inglis of the Court of Common Pleas and Judge Samuel Jones of the Superior Court. The plaintiffs sought damages of $2,000 (almost $50,000 in 2012 dollars) for "the brutal scourging, &c., they received on board the Amistad, by order of Ruiz."[34]

Judge Inglis imposed a hefty bail of $1,000 each on Ruiz and Montes. The wealthy Ruiz claimed that he could not pay it and went to jail—in a bid for public sympathy, the abolitionists thought. Inglis eventually ruled that Montes was not liable in the suit and released him. Rattled by the aggressive tactics of the Africans and the abolitionists, Montes immediately left the city, taking passage on the brig *Texas* to Neuvitas, Cuba. Inglis eventually reduced Ruiz's bail to $250, which the young gentleman paid, and left the jail.[35]

In affidavits dated October 7, 1839, each of the Africans told a similar story, like those Cinqué and Bau had told Tappan and others in the first interviews a month earlier. The narrative began at home, in freedom in Africa, then progressed through enslavement, the Middle Passage on the *Teçora*, the barracoons of Havana, and violent mistreatment aboard the *Amistad*. They all emphasized the grim realities of the slave ship: the use of irons, the short allowance of food and water, the beatings and floggings. Foone and Kimbo alleged that they had been tortured: "powder salt and rum were applied to the wounds" left by the whip and "the marks are still visible."[36]

The lawsuits against Ruiz and Montes provoked a howl of protest from the *Richmond Enquirer* and the *Southern Patriot*, published in Charleston, South Carolina. The former condemned this "worse than savage conduct towards the unfortunate strangers who were brought upon our shores by the mischances of the sea." The latter decried the fact that Ruiz was cruelly imprisoned in "Egyptian catacombs." Both expressed the worry of every southern master who traveled northward: "Before long, a citizen from the South will be arrested here and thrown into prison, on the oath of his servant, procured by the abolitionist." Might his case then be "sent before a prejudiced and fanatical Jury? Is this the point to which these Abolitionists are aiming?" Indeed it was. Tappan wrote of the provocative arrest, "I doubt not it will exasperate the tyrants & their abettors throughout the country." The abolitionist newspaper, the *Pennsylvania Freeman*, crowed: the arrest and imprisonment of slaveholders represented a "Great Point Gained." Tappan had wanted "to test the civil rights of the free born and illegally enslaved Africans in this free community" and to bring more of the African story before the public. He succeeded, but at the cost of great personal vilification. He was accustomed to it, and in any case was sure that God would protect him.[37]

Education and Self-Defense

Pratt and Covey also made possible a new approach to teaching and learning, which was announced in the *New York Journal of Commerce* on October 9, 1839. Because the interpreters "can communicate very freely with all of them and have acquitted themselves to perfect satisfaction," giving their labors to the cause "with great cheerfulness," the abolitionists developed "Plans to Educate the Amistad Africans in English." Professor George Day, a theologian at Yale, stepped forward to take charge. He planned to use a blackboard and slates, "Gallaudet's Elementary work for Deaf and Dumb, which seem well adapted to the first lessons," and several Yale students to assist him. Cinqué assured Day and the other abolitionists that he and his comrades were eager to learn and would apply themselves. They were ready for the book palaver with the white men.[38]

Meantime, life in the dangerous place called jail continued for Cinqué and his comrades. Incarcerated alongside the *Amistad* Africans were other prisoners, some of them desperate and no doubt eager to escape, perhaps by any means necessary. The Africans were still deeply uncertain about who to trust and what their fate might be. They therefore took steps to arm themselves, which was of course against the law, but nonetheless crucial to their sense of self-organization, safety, and survival. Since many if not most had been Mende warriors, their preferred weapon was what they had used in combat in their native land, and what they had used to procure their freedom aboard the *Amistad*: they wanted knives, and they got them.

A correspondent for the *New York Morning Herald* was the first to break the story about their illegal possession of knives, on October 23, 1839, a mere seven weeks after the *Amistad* Africans entered the jail. He wrote:

It seems that Jinqua and his associates have been furnished secretly with knives. Who did this? Who would do this? Is it not likely that those weapons were conveyed to the savages by the same fanatics who would suborne them to perjury, in order to incarcerate Messrs. Ruiz and Montez? Is not this the most probable supposition? And if so, for what intent were they furnished with the weapons of murder? Was it to make the prison of New Haven as red with the blood of the white man as the decks of the Amistad?

To the defenders of slavery, the presence of the knives proved that the *Amistad* Africans were murderers, making fresh plans for "blood and massacre." In the eyes of the *Morning Herald* reporter, they were already clearly guilty of "the cold blooded murder of the captain and cook of the Amistad, and the aggravated cruelties practiced on Messrs. Ruiz and Montez." The knives also proved that their abolitionist allies were dangerous fanatics who aided and abetted horrific new crimes to come. The *Morning Herald* correspondent shrieked in outrage: "Humanity must shudder at such doings! religion hang her head! and justice cry aloud for vengeance!" He concluded that the *Amistad* "savages" did not deserve the protection of the American legal system.[39]

The uproar began when jailer Stanton Pendleton found a "large knife" in the possession of one of the *Amistad* Africans. Taken aback, he immediately ordered a thorough and careful search of the entire jail, whereupon he found eight more knives and yet "another deadly weapon" a little later. Cinqué had two of them. Each was about eight inches long, and both were drawn by an artist and included as a telling illustration in the *Morning Herald*. In his first interview with Tappan (assisted by Ferry), Cinqué had stated, "I would never take any advantage of any one, . . . but would always defend myself." The largest of the recovered blades was a pruning knife, with a blade of three to four inches, "very sharp at the point." The correspondent assumed that the purpose of the knives was "regaining their liberty, of which they are said to be unjustly restrained." The *Amistad* Africans apparently considered the knives to be important possessions, for when the jailer tried to confiscate them, they resisted. He had to take them away "by force."[40]

The exposé by the *Morning Herald* created a scandal. The abolitionists were clearly embarrassed: the illegal possession of weapons made the *Amistad* Africans appear to be something other than the meek and peaceable Christians the abolitionists hoped they were becoming as a result of their ministry in the New Haven jail. The abolitionists comforted themselves that the Africans "wanted the knives to amuse themselves with, like children and savages generally." They finally felt compelled to answer the charges through the newspaper, and in so doing they revealed more about what the *Amistad* Africans had been doing and how they had done it. They explained that the so-called dangerous weapons that had elicited such "alarm and suspicion" were in fact "nothing but common jack-knives." They had been smuggled into the jail and given to them by visitors. The abolitionists singled out "boys" for blame; such were among the thousands who filed through the jail to get a look at the famous insurrectionists. More of the knives, it seems, had been secretly "brought them by the interpreters," the sailors John Pratt and James Covey. This is not surprising. The knife was a common weapon of choice on the waterfront. It was easy to carry and conceal, and it could be useful in many situations. Knife fights among seafarers were commonplace. Yet respectable middle-class abolitionists did not approve of this rough and dangerous milieu, nor did they approve of the knives in jail. They stated that it was proper that the *Amistad* Africans be disarmed, insisting all the while that the knives were wanted for no "other purpose than their own amusement and convenience." They were "perfectly harmless, peaceable and good tempered" people after all.[41]

Pirates and Law Again

When a handful of the *Amistad* Africans—Cinqué, Grabeau, Burna, Fuli, Ndamma, and Fabanna—returned to Hartford for the continuation of their legal hearing (the rest remained in New Haven), they may have encountered a strange publication about themselves. *A True History of the African Chief Jingua and his Comrades* was anonymously written by someone who hoped to capitalize on, and contribute to, the swell of popular interest in the rebels and their now widely known leader. The twenty-eight-page pamphlet was published in October 1839 and based to a large extent on early newspaper coverage of the rebellion and its aftermath.[42] The title page indicates that it was published simultaneously in Hartford, Boston, and New York, but this may have expressed a hope for sales rather than a fact of publication. It was most likely published in Hartford in anticipation of a crowd for the November hearings. The author of the pamphlet fleshed out the newspaper reports with a variety of plagiarized sources, in large part narratives of travelers to Africa. Most of them had not been to Sierra Leone, nor to the Gallinas coast, and least of all to the inland areas where the *Amistad* Africans had lived before they were enslaved.[43]

The pamphlet was based, in its central assumption, on a misunderstanding. The author wrote *A True History* in September 1839, before Pratt and Covey had been found on the docks of New York, and so proceeded on the basis of erroneous reports that the Africans were, not Mende, but Mandingo, Senegambians now better known as the Mandinka. He therefore included "a Description of the Kingdom of Mandingo, and of the Manners and Customs of the Inhabitants." Because the Mandinka had to a considerable extent converted to Islam, the author assumed, wrongly, that the *Amistad* captives were Muslims.[44]

The popular pamphlet reflected the early newspaper reporting that the *Amistad* Africans were "black pirates," even though the official charges of piracy had been dropped at the September hearings. Cinqué was depicted as a Barbary corsair, with a *keffiyah* (headdress), a *shemagh* (a traditional Muslim scarf), and a *kaif* (a curved Arabian sword), facing a rising sun with a spyglass in his hand. The *Amistad*'s rigging, a block, and a mast are visible in the background. Another engraving featured "The Sugar Knife, with which the Captain of the Amistad was killed," thereby dramatizing the rebellion itself. The author also expressed an odd sort of abolitionism, calling Cuba a "receptacle of the buccaneers," by which he meant slave traders. Since Cuba was like the "piratical state of Barbary," the United States should take possession of it, and bring it to heel, as France had recently done with Algiers.[45]

The centrality of James Covey to the legal and political defense of the *Amistad* Africans was made clear when, after a brief discussion in court of the issue of jurisdiction—did it belong to New York, because the Africans were brought ashore on Long Island, or to Connecticut, where the naval officers brought the *Amistad*?—it became clear that the proceedings could not continue "on account of the sickness of the interpreter." Judge Judson postponed the hearing again, until January 7, 1840. The *Amistad* Africans returned to New Haven.[46]

Soon thereafter the Africans enacted a legal hearing of their own. One evening as the jailer was closing cell doors for the night, he discovered that an unnamed African was missing. He found him hiding in the provision room in the cellar, "snugly stowed away between two casks, and locked up so that he could not get out." Returned to "his brethren," he faced a palaver, with Cinqué presiding, to consider allegations of theft. Found guilty under "African law 'for tiefy,'" he was to suffer "30 stripes" upon the "naked body" with a "common riding whip." Someone was deputed to administer the "African mode of punishment": the culprit was "ordered to stand in a bending posture, with his arms folded," apparently after refusing to have his hands tied. He bore his punishment with "the stoicism of an old offender." The jailer apparently tried to intervene, without success. The offender's fellows "then seated him on the floor, in the middle of the room, and passed round him, pointing and crying 'tiefy, tiefy,'" in an act of ritual humiliation. This, they explained to the jailer, was "Mendi law," designed to enforce moral norms and maintain social discipline as decided by the group. The traditions of the Poro Society commanded the *Amistad* Africans to discipline and govern themselves while in jail.[47]

By now New England's snow and cold were coming on. The *Amistad* Africans had never known such weather. Some had seen ice and snow on mountaintops, but it was a novelty to experience them firsthand. They laughed in astonishment as they held ice in their hands and likened snow to "fresh salt." The raw, persistent cold was another matter, especially because New Haven's jail, like most others, was damp, drafty, and poorly heated. Abolitionists were quick to demand warmer garments for the prisoners for winter, and when the Africans complained of the cold, the jailer (who had made plenty of money on admissions) finally installed stoves in four of their rooms, which made it warm enough for some of them to dress in their lighter, more traditional garments. The gnawing, numbing cold would continue to be "much dreaded by Cinque and the rest."[48]

January Hearings

Tensions rose as the next round of hearings neared. All interested parties—and there were many—prepared their arguments as debates about the fate of the *Amistad* captives intensified in newspapers across the nation. Even though the charges of piracy and murder had been dropped, the issue of whether they were the lawful slaves of Ruiz and Montes remained, and the Africans continued, with good reason, to think that the big palaver might end in death. When the Havana-based Richard Robert Madden visited New Haven in November, he noted that if the Africans were returned to their so-called owners, Ruiz and Montes, in Havana, their likelihood of suffering execution as rebellious slaves was great. The gallows continued to shadow the case.[49]

This was made clear one day in jail when one of the teachers, probably Benjamin Griswold, asked his *Amistad* students "if they would like to go to Havana." "Havana," each one repeated deliberately, making sure they understood the question. "Yes," replied the teacher, "Havana." Suddenly, "'No, No,' burst from every tongue, accompanied with a most decided shake of the head," their faces "assuming an expression of the deepest anxiety." One of them then "drew his hand across his throat, indicating the fate they feared." A second "laid his arms across each other at the wrists," rehearsing the recent bondage of manacles. A third "declared, by signs, that their legs were secured as well as their hands." A fourth "extended his arm violently, and by bringing his thumb and finger together, imitated the snapping of a whip." Answering his question with a dramatic reenactment of their previous experience, the Africans made it clear that they associated Havana with slavery, violence, and death.[50]

On another occasion, several of the *Amistad* Africans watched through the jail window as the local militia gathered, reviewed, and paraded on New Haven Green. According to an eyewitness, "They all shrunk back, and directly inquired if preparations were making to cut their throats." Their fears grew worse when some curious members of the militia—wearing their swords—stopped by the jail to visit them. As warriors who understood the material and symbolic powers of the bladed weapon, especially in beheading captured fighters, they believed that "they were about to be put to death."[51]

It may have been a comfort that the hearings beginning January 7 would be held in New Haven. The location held an advantage for the *Amistad* Africans and their allies as the city had been the epicenter of the struggle over the last four months. As in Hartford in November, only a few of the *Amistad* Africans were allowed to attend the hearing, even though it would have been much easier to get them to Judge Judson's courtroom this time: Cinqué and "half a dozen of his countrymen were in court, comfortably clad." They watched as "hundreds," many of whom had visited them in jail and some of whom had gotten to know them quite well, crowded into the courtroom. The officers, professors, and students of Yale University turned out in force. Lewis Tappan noted that "the principal inhabitants of New Haven" attended the hearing, as did working people such as the artisan-artist John Warner Barber. People from all walks of life "thronged the courtroom." In this moment of "thrilling interest," the "sympathy of the community" was clearly with the Africans.[52]

One of the most important witnesses was the rank-and-file abolitionist Dwight Janes, who had gone aboard the *Amistad* soon after it was towed into New London harbor. He recounted his conversation with Ruiz, whom he had asked, "Can they speak English?" The reply was, "A few words." "Can they speak Spanish?" "Oh no, *they are just from Africa.*"[53] Another was James Covey, who also testified on the first day, apparently with great effect: "The prisoners speak the Mendi language, have Mendi names, and are from Mendi, the country of which he himself is a native."[54] Charles Pratt, who was recalled by Captain Fitzgerald to resume service aboard the *Buzzard*, left a deposition that was admitted as evidence. Pratt spoke Gbandi with Moru and testified that his countryman, and indeed all of the others, had recently come from Africa, and could not have been longtime residents of Cuba, as Ruiz and Montes maintained.[55]

Cinqué, Grabeau, and Fuli—three of the most powerful personalities among the rebels—gave testimony, continuing the trend they had established: they cited their origins in Africa, their enslavement, shipment, confinement in Havana, and abuse aboard the *Amistad*. Cinqué once again acted out the trials of the Middle Passage: he sat down on the courtroom floor and "held his hands together and showed how they were manacled." The Africans said more about the rebellion than ever before: "Sinqua killed cook because cook said he was going to kill them and eat them. Killed Captain after he killed African." They also added considerable information about what had happened on Long Island before their capture by the Navy.[56]

When on the second day (January 8) Professor Josiah Gibbs began his testimony, giving his "decided opinion" that "they are native Africans and recently from Africa," Judson interrupted him, saying "he was fully convinced that the men were recently from Africa, and that it was unnecessary to take up time in establishing that fact." This was an astonishing development, as it went to the heart of the case and signaled that the judge had decided it in favor of the *Amistad* Africans. It is likely that the combined testimony of Janes, Covey, Pratt, Cinqué, Grabeau, and Fuli had persuaded him.[57]

At various points in the hearing Judson had trouble controlling the crowd, which pulsed with sympathy for the Africans and vocally expressed pleasure on points in their favor. Lewis Tappan observed that the assembled actually cheered Baldwin as he vigorously demanded that his clients go free. Baldwin got another rise when he turned to—and turned on—United States District Attorney W. S. Holabird: "By what right does the U.S. Attorney appear here at all?" Whenever the eloquent lawyer or one of his associates (Theodore Sedgwick and Seth Staples) spoke, the crowd "hung upon their lips spell bound."[58]

After five long days of hearings, Judson issued several rulings. The district court did have jurisdiction because the *Amistad* had been found on the "high seas." Lieutenant Thomas Gedney and his fellow officers were entitled to salvage, on the vessel but not on the Africans, who under Connecticut law could not be considered property. The Long Island hunters Green and Fordham were not entitled to salvage. The court would send the cabin boy Antonio back to the heirs of the deceased Captain Ferrer in Cuba.[59]

In the ruling that everyone had been waiting for, Judson declared that the Africans were in fact "each of them Natives of Africa and were born free and ever since have been and still of right are free and not slaves." It was a stunning vindication of the African and abolitionist argument; indeed, Judson repeated verbatim what Baldwin and Staples had submitted to the court in their opening plea. Moreover, the words had been spoken by a member of the American Colonization Society, whose attitudes and legal record on race had caused many to expect a contrary ruling. The *Amistad* Africans would therefore be turned over to President Martin Van Buren for repatriation to their native land.[60]

Tappan concluded that "the Judge felt the pressure of public sentiment." Judson lived in New Haven, ground zero in the struggle, and witnessed the widespread support for the Africans. He visited the prisoners in jail on two occasions, which meant that the issues before him were concrete and human. Some pressure he felt came directly from the Africans themselves, for when he visited them, they made it a point to tell him how much they wanted to go home.[61]

When the Reverend Day arrived with James Covey at the jail and relayed the news of Judson's ruling to the Africans who had not been in the courtroom, their "hearts overflow[ed] with gratitude." "Words cannot express the joy they felt," Day wrote. All but one understood the Mende translation of the news. The one who did not (the Temne man Pie) "sat still, not knowing what was meant" until one who spoke both Mende and his language "communicated the decision to him." He began to clap his hands for gladness of heart, and expressed his thanks to Day. The Congregational minister seized the moment to pray with the Africans, to direct "their thoughts to the Lord Jesus Christ as their Deliverer. They knelt, and followed the interpreter audibly, and with apparent devoutness." Day also noted that "They long to go back to their Father-land."

Other Plans

So unsure were the Africans about the outcome of the legal hearing, and so convinced were the abolitionists that President Van Buren wanted to resolve the issue by returning the *Amistad* Africans to deadly Havana, the anti-slavery coalition strategized about what to do in case the verdict should go against them. Prior to the early hearings it was by no means certain that the judges would rule in favor of the rebels. In fact, it seemed more likely that they would not.

The USS *Grampus*, a schooner like the *Amistad*, sailed into New Haven harbor under mysterious circumstances on Friday, January 8, the very day on which Cinqué, Grabeau, and Fuli testified before the district court about their enslavement, Middle Passage, and rebellion. The vessel was to many a "strange and sudden apparition," as John Quincy Adams later described it. Why would sailors be dispatched from the Brooklyn Navy Yard to a New England port in the dead of winter? When a local pilot asked an officer of the *Grampus* about the vessel's destination, the man said he did not know: "She had sealed orders." Well supplied "with provision, &c. for twenty months," that is, a long voyage, the *Grampus* provoked heated speculation. One rumor had it that the vessel was meant to join the small American squadron fighting the slave trade in West Africa, and that the *Amistad* Africans might be picked up in New Haven and taken to their native lands. Yet most abolitionists were convinced that the purpose of the vessel was the opposite: Van Buren and Secretary of State John Forsyth, a Georgia slaveholder, had sent the *Grampus* to New Haven to seize the *Amistad* Africans as soon as the court ruled that they were indeed "merchandize." In fact, the sealed orders instructed Captain John S. Paine to take them to Cuba immediately, before an appeal could be made, and to restore them to their so-called owners, Ruiz and Montes, thereby honoring the demands of Spain. Abolitionists howled that the United States government was now acting as slave catcher and trader: the goal intended for the *Amistad* Africans was to "hurry them to death or to a bondage that shall end only with death!"[62]

The activists did not stand idly by. Fearing a negative verdict, they began to organize their own vessel that would carry the *Amistad* Africans, not to a living hell or actual death in Cuba, but rather in the other direction—to freedom in Canada. The work likely involved African American sailors based in Connecticut ports, from which David

Ruggles had emerged. The plot remained a closely guarded secret for many years, although Lewis Tappan alluded to it in a letter he published in the *Emancipator* soon after the *Grampus* arrived in port: if Captain Paine and his crew expected to secure the Africans and deliver them to the Spanish authorities, they would be in for a surprise. He wrote, "as the quaker lady said to the agent of a fugitive slave, 'thy prey hath escaped thee.'" [63]

Evidence appeared years later to confirm that the rebels and the abolitionists had planned a jailbreak if the legal ruling had gone against them. The obituary of Nathaniel Jocelyn (brother of Simeon, member of the Amistad Committee) disclosed in 1881 that the artist was part of a group of abolitionists who plotted, in service of "higher law," to break the Africans "out of jail by force" and put them aboard a vessel "in which they were to sail away." Simeon Eben Baldwin, the son of Roger S. Baldwin, also noted, in 1886, that the Amistad Committee, "had another vessel here [New Haven] ready to receive the Africans in case of an adverse decision, and run them off to some more friendly shore." The Reverend Alonzo Lewis likewise confirmed the existence of a direct-action plot, in a reminiscence of the *Amistad* case published in 1907. He wrote, "It will do no harm, at this late day, to reveal a secret which has been carefully guarded, viz., that there was a plot to rescue the captives if the case went against them." Lewis learned of the intended action from the Reverend Day, who was deeply involved in the struggle. Lewis himself was only seven years old in 1840, so he must have learned of the plot years later. The abolitionists may have hoped that the provocative act would cause a war with Spain that might lead to the "liberation of Cuba" and the ending of slavery in one of its strongholds. [64]

Many abolitionists had long since concluded that the *Amistad* Africans had not committed any crime and therefore should not be held as "criminals in loathsome dungeons." As early as October 1839 a writer using the pen name "Common Sense" appealed to the memory of both the American and French revolutions in asking, ominously, "Is a Connecticut jail to be converted into a Bastille, and shall its doors not fly open?" Many involved in the case, from Jocelyn to

African-American abolitionist Robert Purvis, had worked on the Underground Railroad; experienced direct-actionists, inspired by the rebellion, gravitated to the case. Determined not to let the *Amistad* Africans be hanged as pirates, murderers, or slave rebels, nor even to see them slave in Cuba, making sugar with blood, antislavery activists exhibited their antinomian disdain for unjust laws. One direct action aboard a small vessel in the Caribbean had helped to inspire another, made ready on the New Haven waterfront. Such militance pointed toward the future.[65]

CHAPTER FIVE

"Mendi"

The victory in Connecticut was quickly negated, or at least stalemated, by a national politics in which slaveholders held great influence. They were not known to abolitionists as the "Slave Power" for nothing. Martin Van Buren supported the Spanish crown, and at bottom, both Cuban and southern masters, by appealing the rulings Judson and Thompson had made on January 23. The verdict declaring the *Amistad* Africans free was cruelly reversed when the federal government appealed it to the Supreme Court. The Africans would remain incarcerated as the case ran its long, slow course through the American legal system.

The news of the appeal was crushing and incomprehensible to the rebels. "[T]hey seemed much grieved," noted someone who conveyed the news to them and tried to explain it. "Their hopes had been raised; their hearts were set upon Africa; and it is a sore disappointment to them to have their hopes deferred, with the possibility of their never being realized." The visitor tried to console them, saying that the delay would give them more time to study, which would ultimately be to their benefit. They replied that the gallows still looming over their heads discouraged their efforts: "They say it will be of no use for them to try to learn, if in a few months they are to be hanged."[1]

Abolitionists were outraged by the appeal, quick to see and denounce "executive interference" in the judicial process. The *Emancipator* wondered of the president: "Why should this democratic functionary be so aggrieved at a decision in favor of liberty?" The *Oberlin Evangelist* stated, "The Africans cannot to this day understand the justice of his proceedings, nor do we think white men can understand it as just." It was time for opponents of slavery to "buckle their armor again in the defence of righteousness." Would the public continue to support the cause, was the question.[2]

Slowly the Africans pulled out of their despair, resetting their sights on their long-term goal of going home. They were able to use their undiminished popularity to strengthen their alliance with the abolitionists and to participate in activities that would keep their case before the public eye. The doors of the jail continued to revolve as people from all walks of life paid their shilling to visit, some to propose projects of their own that would connect the prisoners to the American people in one way or another. Artists such as John Warner Barber, Sidney Moulthrop, and Amasa Hewins went into the jail to create images of the rebels through engraving, wax-casting, and painting. Over the long term of incarceration, the most faithful and purposeful visitors to the jail were the abolitionists, who came to teach and proselytize. The Africans and the American antislavery reformers in particular would develop a complex, sometimes vexed relationship—what might be called a working misunderstanding. It would allow both sides to navigate a broad cultural divide, work together, build trust, and maintain independence of perspective and objective. During the next year in jail, the Africans would emerge as a new cultural and political entity: the "Mendi People."[3]

Teaching and Learning

The agendas of the rebels and their allies converged on the issue of education. At the heart of the jailhouse encounter lay a reciprocal, mutually influential process: Africans and Americans, neither of whom knew much about their counterparts, learned from and about each other—about America, Africa, politics, culture, and a host of other subjects. Both sought the practical knowledge of how to understand and work with the other in the common project of abolishing slavery. The "book palaver" was central to the jail experience for both groups.

The reciprocity had its limits. The abolitionists and the *Amistad* Africans approached education in jail with different assumptions and goals. The former saw it as a civilizing process, a means to turn pagan savages into sober, orderly, disciplined, virtuous Christians. In January 1840 Lewis Tappan reported with pleasure, "most of their savage habits have been relinquished, and habits of civilized life acquired." A writer for the newspaper *Farmer's Cabinet* agreed: "They are also acquiring ideas of order and moral duty, and gradually conforming to the habits of civilized life; readily assembling at stated hours, when summoned by a bell; recognizing the Sabbath, and giving regular attendance upon their religious exercises, &c."[4]

The Africans took a less imperial view. They were uninterested in reforming—or being reformed. They did not try to make their abolitionist visitors into new people, nor could they have done so, in any case. They were more or less content to try to understand them and work with them toward common goals of survival and freedom, but bafflement sometimes prevailed. Translator James Covey related a story about the reception of time-discipline among the Africans. In the New Haven jail on a Sunday morning, he and Cinqué heard a church bell ring. The leader asked (no doubt in Mende, which Covey later translated into pidgin English), "What for bell ring?" Covey explained, "When 'Meriky people go pray to God, they ring bell." Cinqué was perplexed. He said, "These people be fool. When want to pray to God, what for ring bell?" It was a real question for someone unaccustomed to social life organized by the clock. Missionary George Thompson noted that the Mende in Africa were both fascinated and puzzled by his watch, which they called "the living man," probably because it seemed to give instructions to the one who wore it. Cinqué and his comrades would have to come to terms with "the living man" and much else, no matter how strange it all may have seemed.[5]

The brute geographic and political facts of being incarcerated and subjected to an alien legal process demanded certain responses from the Africans. With simple eloquence Cinqué took his abolitionist teachers to the heart of the matter, stressing the equality and the political necessity of the jailhouse encounter: "If you were in my country and could not talk with any body, you would want to learn our language; I want to learn yours." He assured the abolitionists that his comrades "will apply themselves to learning." From beginning to end, education in jail entailed a struggle to communicate. Even after translators had been found, teacher Benjamin Griswold had "great difficulties in making them [the *Amistad* Africans] understand his instructions."[6]

Everyone agreed that the captives approached their studies with abiding enthusiasm and commitment. As Covey put it in a letter to Lewis Tappan, "Our African friends love to read." They had a special interest in geography, as expropriated and displaced people might. They expressed curiosity about the "countries beside Mendi and America," even as these two no doubt loomed in equal importance above all others. Other interests included almanacs, grammar, and the Bible. Covey requested a "big dictionary" for himself and his fellow Africans, in order to "look out hard words." Visitors to the jail saw many men "intently engaged with books and slates." Their teacher summarized their attitude to learning: "Their whole souls are absorbed in their studies, to which they give their undivided attention. They are the most attentive pupils I have ever saw and never get tired of learning. They are very inquisitive, and manifest great joy when they gain a new idea.—They are affectionate, grateful, and warm in their attachment."[7]

The commitment of the *Amistad* Africans to education was more than a matter of good attitude. Studying became something they could do among and for themselves, for the purpose of emancipation. They realized early on that learning, and demonstrating what they had learned, would be a key to cementing the alliance with the abolitionists, who had organized the jailhouse as a school. The Africans then made the project their own, as they made clear by their actions on numerous occasions. They used their own money, given as gifts by visitors to the jail or earned through acrobatics, to buy Bibles and other books. One stormy morning when their teacher did not show up for class, Cinqué gathered the group for self-instruction and study. Commitment to education eventually enabled the *Amistad* Africans to contribute to the legal strategy of their case and to express in English their own political ideas.[8]

Informal teaching and learning in the jail began immediately. The first steps were the teaching and learning of primary numbers, one through ten, and the use of body parts to create vocabulary—eyes, nose, ears, mouth—as the little girls taught the "gentlemen" soon after they arrived in the New Haven jail. The presence of Yale professors added a systematic component to the process of learning. Josiah Gibbs took down Kissi, Vai, and Mende words to create vocabularies he published in leading scientific journals. George Day brought images to teach vocabulary, so that the *Amistad* Africans might "pronounce the name upon seeing either the picture or the printed word." Some of the pictures reflected the abolitionist imagination of exotic Africa—wild beasts such as lions, tigers, and elephants, which the rebels sometimes recognized as creatures of their native lands. Other images included tools and implements. By these means they were "acquiring a good stock of English words." The learning proceeded so quickly that Professor Day soon ran out of pictures.[9]

Initial instruction in reading and writing began in October 1839, and became more intensive and systematic after the January 1840 court hearings. Teacher Sherman Booth eventually organized his students into three groups of ten to twelve each, based on what he perceived as ability. The top class (which included Cinqué, Kinna, and Fuli) read the Gospels, concentrating on the Book of Luke; studied a spelling book; and did exercises in arithmetic. The youthful Kale was the star pupil of this group, which was, by late 1840, "using pen and paper, and expressing their own thoughts, in our language, quite intelligibly." At the same time a second class studied spelling and had covered seventy pages of Lowell's "first class book." A third class, still working on the alphabet and the discipline of writing letters and words, were showing "some weariness" in their studies. Abolitionist teachers were especially pleased when books and slates replaced "native games," as they apparently did after a few months of study.[10]

Because most abolitionists were religious, and some, like Lewis Tappan, were evangelical, devotional services were a significant part of jailhouse education. Ministers as well as laymen preached and commented on a huge array of Biblical passages and subjects. Tappan wrote a fellow abolitionist: "Every Sabbath divine service has been held at the prison, and the Africans had the prayers and instructions interpreted to them by Covey. They behaved quite orderly and apparently took much intent at the services." Professor Gibbs gave an example of Covey's translation of a prayer:

> O Ge-waw wa, bi-a-bi yan-din-go; bi-a-bi ha-ni gbe-le ba-te-ni; bi-a-bi fu-li ba-te-ni; bi-a-bi nga-li ba-te-ni; bi-a-bi tûm-bi-le-gai ba-te-ni; bi-a-bi ngi-yi ba-te-ni; ke ndzha wa; bi-a-bi dzha-te ba-te-ni, ke ngu-li, ke gnwaw-ni, ke nwu-a, ke nûn-ga wu-lo-a.

One of the abolitionists wrote, "We have preaching, or a palaver, tomorrow, with the Africans, on the subject of the religion of the white men." It was one of many.[11]

Eventually the *Amistad* Africans learned to speak the language of Christianity, which is evident in each and every surviving letter they wrote. In writing a letter to Miss Juliana Chamberlain, who had contributed $5 to the Amistad Committee fund, Kale managed, in a single paragraph, to rehearse his entire recent study of Christianity. He mentioned the love of "Great God," who "sent his beloved son into the world to save sinners who were lost" and "sent the Bible into the world to save us from going down to hell." He noted that Jesus had "made the sick well he made the lame walk he made the dumb speak and deaf hear." He expressed the hope that God would help and bless the benevolent Miss Chamberlain, give her a "new Soul," and "take her up to Heaven when she dies." He concluded, "All Mendi people thank you for your kindness and hope to meet you in heaven," but he was quick to add to his godliness a political demand: "I want you to pray to the Great God make us free and go our home and see our friends in African Country."[12]

It is difficult to know what the *Amistad* Africans heard, found significant, and remembered from the "God palavers," but one passage of the Bible seems to have had a special resonance: Psalm 124:7, which the rebels themselves used to explain their ordeal of enslavement and emancipation. Cinqué, Kale, and Kinna wrote, "We read in this Holy Book, 'If it had not been the Lord who was on our side, when men rose up against us, then they had swallowed us up quick, when their wrath was kindled up against us. Blessed be the Lord, who hath not given us a prey to their teeth. Our soul is escaped as a bird out of the snare of the fowler; the snare is broken and we are escaped. Our help is in the name of the Lord, who made Heaven and Earth.'" As people whose skill at catching birds on New Haven Green amazed onlookers, they drew a metaphor directly from their own experience. The "men who rose up against us" were the slave catchers and traders. Slavery itself was likened to being eaten alive, preserving memory of the threat of cannibalism through a Biblical parable.[13]

"Speaking Christian" reflected how the *Amistad* Africans understood their allies and acted to secure their long-term cooperation and commitment. But it was only one means among many. They also understood, and quickly, how much the abolitionists detested the slave trade and slavery. Shortly after coming ashore, Cinqué and others "performed slavery" in acts of guerilla theater, in courtrooms and in jail. After translator James Ferry made it possible for them to tell their own stories, Cinqué and his fellow rebels emphasized the violence of enslavement, their separation from wives and children, and the destruction of their families, all of which tapped into central, highly emotional messages of the abolitionist movement, and indeed into one of its greatest propaganda victories, the successful broad popular agitation against the slave trade as epitomized by the nightmarish Middle Passage.

The *Amistad* Africans were, in the words of Charlotte Cowles, "extremely observing of the manners of white people," which included abolitionists. They went out of their way not to offend the people whose help they needed. They somehow grasped the Christian hostility to the polygyny that was widely practiced in their own societies. Burna told the abolitionists that he lived with his mother, and did not mention that he was married, least of all to seven different women. Several other men probably had more than one wife as well, but only one of the *Amistad* Africans admitted as much: Fabanna said he had two. Another example of sensitivity to cultural difference occurred when Tua died on September 11, 1839. The Africans remained in the background while abolitionist minister Leonard Bacon performed the service. After he had finished his eulogy, Shule stepped forward, stood at the head of the corpse, and "muttered a sort of prayer of address," which took "four or five minutes." As he spoke, "his companions responded in short ejaculations," in the communal African style, with great feeling. The *Amistad* Africans later explained to their teacher that the ceremony "was not a Mendian burial rite, as was published at the time in the papers, but an imitation of American customs."[14]

The civilizing study of the Bible changed everything about the *Amistad* Africans, thought abolitionist Charlotte Cowles, even their complexion! When she first saw them at Hartford Jail, in September 1839, they "looked then a dusky yellow, like some of our mulattoes, and very disagreeable, but now they are so black and some of them so handsome that I can hardly believe I ever saw them before." Indeed, so handsome did she consider a young man named Bagna, she developed quite a crush on him. She wrote her brother that the eighteen-year-old was "the most splendid specimen of African beauty I ever saw." She then criticized her own racial attitudes, saying that even though she had read of African beauty in books, she never thought she would regard an African as handsome. Yet Bagna's "beaming face and sparkling eyes" unmasked all prejudice. Were he to play Shakespeare's Othello, "the whole *beau monde* would be delighted." She also loved his "dashing elegance of manner, . . . which is indeed the rarest accomplishment in the most polished society." She was so smitten, and so carried away, that she wondered, in her next letter to her brother, whether it sounded foolish for "an American young lady" to admire "a half-wild African boy."[15]

Among the *Amistad* Africans themselves it is impossible to tell to what extent their use of Christian language was a matter of belief and to what extent it was a matter of strategy. It was undoubtedly a combination of both. By March 1841, Lewis Tappan hoped that three or four might have been converted to Christianity and seemed relieved that the rest were still willing to be instructed in the faith. All that can be said with certainty is that the *Amistad* Africans understood the importance of Christianity within the worldview of the abolitionists and acted to accommodate it, within the larger context of their own main objective: to go home.[16]

The Art of Rebellion

As the *Amistad* Africans studied reading, writing, and religion, they met artists who wanted to connect their cause to people beyond the jailhouse. The artists were interested most of all in the rebellion, assuming, correctly, it seems, that it was what fascinated the public about the case above all else. The artists John Warner Barber, Sidney Moulthrop, and Amasa Hewins all visited the *Amistad* Africans in the New Haven jail during the first few months of 1840. Barber produced an engraving and a pamphlet, Moulthrop a set of wax figures, and Hewins a massive painting, all depicting and interpreting the rebellion. Barber wrote, "The capture of the Amistad with her cargo of native Africans, and the peculiar circumstances of the case, have excited an unusual degree of interest in this country, and in Europe." The artists sought to capitalize on the public captivation, which was bound to intensify as the case made its way toward the Supreme Court. All three artists would use their direct contact with the Africans in jail to establish their credentials to represent the rebellion. The artists would give "accurate," "factual," and "real life" images to a hungry public.[17]

By 1840 Barber was well known as an engraver of New England's historic buildings and landscapes. A native of New Haven, he got caught up in the local excitement surrounding the *Amistad* case. He noted in his diary that he attended the court hearings of January 7–13, 1840, and was present when Judge Andrew Judson ruled that the Africans were recently, and therefore illegally, imported to Cuba, and hence not to be returned to their so-called owners, Ruiz and Montes. On April 1, Barber began to visit the *Amistad* Africans in jail. Over the next two months he would create drawings and engravings of them to illustrate a thirty-two-page pamphlet, *A History of the Amistad Captives: Being a Circumstantial Account of the Capture of the Spanish Schooner Amistad, by the Africans on Board; Their Voyage, and Capture Near Long*

Island, New York; with Biographical Sketches of Each of the Surviving Africans; Also, an Account of the Trials had on Their case, Before the District and
Circuit Courts of the United States, for the District of Connecticut, self-
published in June 1840 by E. L. and J. W. Barber, in New Haven. The
popular pamphlet cost twenty-five cents.[18]

Compiled from "authentic sources," A History of the Amistad Captives reproduced newspaper articles from the New London Gazette and
the New York Journal of Commerce; court records, including depositions
by Ruiz, Montes, Richard Robert Madden, and Francis Bacon, a traveler to the Gallinas Coast; African narratives of the Middle Passage; an
account of the culture of the Mendi people; diplomatic correspondence; and most importantly a section of Barber's own original creation: illustrated biographical sketches of the Africans, based on
"personal conversation with them, by means of James Covey, the
Interpreter." During his visits to the jail, Barber drew portraits, from
which he would engrave silhouettes of the Africans, including Covey.[19]

Barber added several other illustrations to the portraits: a map of
"Mendi country, with regard to other portions of Africa," on which the
Gallinas River and Fort Lomboko were located, between Sierra Leone
and Liberia; a depiction of nine of the Amistad Africans as they sat
cramped and huddled together on the lower deck of the slave ship that
carried them from Lomboko to Havana; and a representation of a
Mende village, adapted from a similar illustration by African "explorer"
Richard Lander and "recognized by the Africans as giving a correct
representation of the appearance of villages in their native country."[20]

Barber stressed his impartiality in presenting a "correct statement of
the facts of this extraordinary case," but he himself opposed slavery.
Yet the pamphlet was not an abolitionist tract. Although Barber made
use of the work of Josiah Gibbs, George Day, and Benjamin Griswold,
who worked closely with the captives and the Amistad Committee,
there is no evidence that the leaders of the defense campaign (Tappan,
Joshua Leavitt, and Simeon Jocelyn) played any role in making the pamphlet. Indeed, they would not have approved of the central image, The
Death of Capt. Ferrer, which depicted the insurrection. Nonetheless it
became the most famous representation of the rebellion. The engraving

"Death of Capt. Ferrer, the Captain of the *Amistad*"

circulated widely with the pamphlet and as a broadside, some copies
of which were hand-colored, presumably by Barber himself.[21]

Barber's image featured nine of the *Amistad* Africans, five of them
armed with cane knives; Captain Ferrer, who is cut, bleeding, and
dying; a worried Ruiz; and Antonio, watching as he climbs up the
shrouds. The corpse of Celestino lies on the deck in the background.
Because Barber drew the portraits of the *Amistad* Africans "from life"
in jail and sought to represent them accurately, it is possible to identify
specific individuals in the image. With a cane knife at left is Cinqué,
preparing to strike the killing blow, as he and three others surround
the captain. The other three are probably meant to be Moru, Kimbo,
and Faquorna, who were known to have carried out the attack with
Cinqué—although Warner would not have known what Faquorna
looked like, as he had died before the engraver entered the jail. At the
far right is Burna, who is not armed and was known in the story of the
uprising for his merciful defense of the Spaniards. He raises his hand
as if to try to stop the violence of the armed Konoma, who rushes
toward the Spaniards and is identifiable by his so-called tusk-like teeth.

Barber may have had antislavery sympathies, but he used racial-
ized tropes of savagery in representing the *Amistad* Africans. In composition and title, he seems to have drawn upon *The Murder of Jane
McCrea*, a painting and print widely circulated at the time. In this set
piece of frontier hostility two cruel, demonic Native American warriors armed with tomahawks slay a young white woman. Like McCrea,
Captain Ferrer is the central figure, commanding the sympathetic

Cinqué and three fellow warriors surround Captain Ramón Ferrer (above), as Konoma joins, and Burna tries to limit, the attack (right).

attention of the viewer. In a diary entry for April 27, 1840, Barber described the image using clipped, racially charged language: "Drawing Massacre Amistad." A gang of black men slaughter a single defenseless white man. In the hand-colored versions of the image, blood pours from the wounds on Ferrer's head.[22]

Despite the graphic violence, Barber's engraving projects an oddly peaceful, almost tranquil mood. The Africans are not possessed by rage as were the Native Americans as they killed Jane McCrea. Barber softened the faces of the rebels, making them reflect not fury, but calm determination. They stand in contrast to the gruesome image of the only other slave rebels to be graphically represented in the United States before the Civil War, in the *Horrid Massacre in Virginia*, which depicted Nat Turner's uprising in Virginia in 1831. Barber's image of the rebellion reflected necessity—what the *Amistad* rebels had to do "in order to gain their freedom," as the artist described their purpose in the engraving's caption.[23]

Slavery Waxed

"The thrilling and unprecedented events connected with the capture of the Amistad, which have excited so much public attention, not only in this country, but throughout the civilized countries of Europe, furnishes a subject of uncommon interest." So began an advertisement by Peale's Museum and Portrait Gallery, located opposite city hall on Broadway in New York, inviting the public to see "the accurate likeness of 29 of the Africans" in life-size wax figures. Artist Sidney Moulthrop repeated the rationale of John Warner Barber as he explained the public value of his art. Like Warner, he cast and arranged the figures at the peak moment of rebellion, when Cinqué and others surrounded and killed Captain Ferrer. He too thought this was what the people wanted to see.[24]

Moulthrop thought right. Beginning June 16, 1840, the exhibition was originally slated to run for a week, but the crowd that flocked to see it, and "the urgent desire for its continuance by several who have not yet had an opportunity," caused the manager to hold it over. Newspaper advertisements appeared in the column "Amusements," and the wax figures shared gallery space with live performers: the magician Signor Antonio Blitz, the pianist S. W. Bassford, and the fancy glassmaker Mr. Owens. The show would circulate to Armory Hall in Boston, Town Hall in Norwich, Connecticut, and finally, several years later, to Phineas T. Barnum's American Museum. Barnum, himself an opponent of slavery, included the wax figures in a show with a live orangutan and a performance by black men in blackface, the "Ethiopian Serenaders," whom Frederick Douglass thought "may yet be instrumental in removing the prejudice against our race." The price of admission to see the rebellion in wax was usually twenty-five cents.[25]

Like Barber, Moulthrop lived in New Haven and visited the *Amistad* Africans in jail. He somehow managed to convince them to allow him to take molds of their faces and even to give him some of their hair, which he used to enhance the realism of his sculptures. Perhaps he paid them, or perhaps the Africans were simply interested in his project and freely supported it. The museum announced, "By means of this process, a perfect exhibition of the form of each face, embracing every wrinkle, &c., is given." Each wax figure was constructed to "exact height and form." The display also featured painted portraits of all of the "surviving Africans, drawn from life, to each of which is attached their history." The "history" was in all likelihood based on the biographical sketches collected in Barber's *A History of the Amistad Captives*, copies of which were on sale at the exhibition. Indeed, Barber and Moulthrop had worked together in making their images of rebellion. Barber had drawn his profiles using a pantograph, a mechanical copying machine, on the busts made by the wax artist.[26]

Moulthrop's centerpiece was "a sinking representation of the death of Captain Ramón Ferrer, the Spanish Captain of the Amistad." Cinqué and several others, armed with knives, rush up on the captain, "who is seen falling mortally wounded." Again, the corpse of Celestino, the slave sailor, lies in the background. "A correct likeness of the boy Antonio, the slave of Captain Ferrer, is given," as Burna appears "saving the lives of Ruiz and Montez." Moulthrop added a wax figure of James Covey, the sailor-translator, who had not been aboard the *Amistad* but was playing a large part in the contemporary drama, and hence was of interest to the public. Covey had probably translated for Moulthrop as he had done for Barber.[27]

A correspondent for the African American newspaper the *Colored American*, who had not been able to visit the jail in New Haven to see "the great originals" of the *Amistad* drama, had been told that the "counterfeits, done in wax" are "perfect likenesses: every muscle, every lineament of countenance is portrayed with all the appearance of life." He urged readers to go to Peale's Museum to witness the wax figures that "possess a fidelity to nature which is truly astonishing." The *Workingman's Friend* also gave the exhibit a warm reception, encouraging its readers, "Go and see them and take a friend or two with you." A writer for the *Norwich Aurora* thought, "No pen can do justice to this exhibition. Nothing of the kind has ever come near it." It appears that even the *Amistad* Africans got to see the life-size reproductions of themselves, because, as one correspondent noted, "When the real and the representative figures have been placed together, persons could not distinguish the one from the other." What the real figures made of the wax ones is not known. It must have seemed to them that *ta-mo ko-lin-go* (the white man) was clever but strange.[28]

Rebellion Magnificently Painted

Boston artist Amasa Hewins created the most monumental work of art inspired by the *Amistad* Rebellion—a 135-foot panorama, more than twice as long as the *Amistad* itself. He took a crooked path to the jail. Born in Sharon, Massachusetts, in 1795, he tried his hand at West Indian commerce, failed, then turned to painting portraits in the 1820s. In 1830 he toured Europe during dramatic times: he was in Italy and France during the revolutions of that year, and he kept a journal of his travels. Hewins was a committed republican, hence his sympathies were with the people in struggle against the aristocracy and the church, although the "rabble" in various towns in Italy seem to have made him nervous. In 1839–1840 he had no studio and apparently made a living as an itinerant artist, working in Boston, in various towns in Connecticut, and as far south as Baltimore and Washington, DC, no doubt painting portraits. He modestly entitled his grandest work *The Magnificent Painting of the Massacre on board the schooner Amistad!!* It circulated to various venues, including Denslowe Hall in Hartford and the Phoenix Building in New Haven, where the artist installed the gigantic canvas and charged admission to those eager to see the uprising on a human scale.[29]

Alas, the painting has been lost. Simeon Eben Baldwin, son of *Amistad* attorney Roger S. Baldwin, noted in an article published in 1886 that it was at that time in the possession of the New Haven Colony Historical Society. How something so huge could have been lost is an interesting question to ponder. In any case, efforts in recent years to find it have failed, but fortunately numerous written descriptions of the painting, some by the artist himself, survive and permit its reconstruction as both image and interpretation of the rebellion.[30]

Because Hewins had visited the jail and painted individual portraits of the *Amistad* Africans, he could claim that the larger work, "strikes the beholder as real life." Some reviewers of the work had also been in the jail and agreed: "The likenesses of many of the blacks will be readily recognized." A writer for the *New Haven Herald* noted that the painting offered "a view of the vessel and every person on board, many of which are portraits, particularly those of Cinquez, and Grabeau." Hewins apparently showed the painting to the *Amistad* Africans themselves at some point, for he used their approval in a broadside he prepared and distributed far and wide in order to publicize the display of his painting: "Its faithfulness to the original [event] has been attested by those who participated in the awful tragedy."[31]

Following Barber and Moulthrop, Hewins dramatized the moment at which Cinqué and his comrades killed Captain Ferrer. He described the content of the painting: "The Scene represents the rise and struggle of the Africans, in which Capt. Ferrer and the cook lost their lives, and Don Pedro Montez, one of the owners of the Slaves, was dangerously wounded." Hewins depicted the Cubans and about twenty of the Africans, most of whom were armed, and, according to another viewer, dressed in "cloth or skins fastened round the waist & extending to the knees." At the center of the huge canvas was Captain Ferrer, surrounded by Cinqué, Grabeau, Konoma, and several others. Celestino's corpse lies in the background. Pedro Montes, blood streaming from a wound to his temple and a look of "Terror . . . in his countenance," surveys the scene and "seems to say, this catching and carrying negroes is bad business—not a very comfortable situation." He looks for a "hiding place." Ruiz stands nearby, in fear and misery. Antonio has climbed up the shrouds, and looks down on the uprising.[32]

At the center of the tumult stood Cinqué, in the group amidships, armed with a cane knife, his eye on the Spaniards. He attacks Captain Ferrer, who "has one cut upon his head & another upon his breast" and "has fallen partially, rests upon one knee, his head drooping, his left arm hanging powerless." As Cinqué prepares to strike the killing blow, two or three of his comrades attempt "to check his hand & restrain him." Possessed by "the wildest rages," with a desperate, even demonic, expression on his face, he struggles to escape them.

Ferrer is beset on other sides by Konoma "the cannibal," who grips his right wrist and "points a dagger at his bosom," and Grabeau, whose "right hand is elevated, firmly grasping a cane-knife, with which he appears about to strike." Like Cinqué, Grabeau is "transported with anger." In the background, Fuli looks upon the scene "with hellish satisfaction" and a "countenance expressive of deep malignity." The youth Ndamma stands back from the rebellion, "his hand upon his breast, his eyes raised to heaven," with much "veneration . . . in his countenance." His was the only "commendatory representation" in the entire group.[33]

The similarities to Barber's engraving are clear, in both form and content. Hewins also depicted the *Amistad* Africans as "savages": Konoma was a "cannibal," Cinqué appeared demonic, all but one of the Africans were represented as outraged and brutal; the entire scene was a "massacre." Hewins also drew on *The Murder of Jane McCrea*. Like McCrea, whose wrist is gripped by one of the barbarous warriors, the vulnerable Captain Ferrer, clutched by Konoma, stood at the center of the canvas.

Savage or not, the painting also contained a message of antislavery, as the artist himself was quick to explain to abolitionist Benjamin Griswold, divinity student at Yale University and one of the main teachers of the *Amistad* captives in the New Haven jail. Griswold wrote to Lewis Tappan that Hewins "seems to feel an interest in these men [&] to sympathize with them, & their friends, to hope that they will be suffered to return to their own country, if they wish." Indeed, Hewins went further, arguing that their cause was, in American terms, both honorable and revolutionary: "He compares the act of Cinque in liberating himself & companions to the efforts of the man who led the armies of the U.S. in her struggle for independence, & thinks that he has shown as much of the hero, considering the sphere in which he has acted." By depicting what he described as "the rise and struggle of the Africans" and by comparing its leader to George Washington, Hewins produced a painting that might be seen—could we but see it—as a contradictory American equivalent of Eugene Delacroix's *Liberty Leading the People*, the greatest work of art to come out of the revolutions of 1830.

The Abolitionist Dilemma

Hewins may have held antislavery beliefs, but his decision to depict the most violent moment of rebellion upset abolitionists close to the case. At a time when they increasingly described the *Amistad* Africans as "hapless victims" who had been miraculously "cast upon our shores"—as if they had made neither the rebellion nor the freedom voyage to Long Island—Hewins reasserted a militant, indeed revolutionary view of the case. Griswold, who had extensive, direct, personal knowledge of the individual prisoners, wrote a long, detailed letter to Lewis Tappan describing the painting and offering his own thoughts about it. More than any other document produced in the era of the *Amistad* case, Griswold's letter revealed the liberal abolitionist dilemma in the representation of slave revolt.[34]

Griswold's complaints about the painting were many. The artist got the character of several of the individual Africans all wrong (the "kind-hearted" Fuli appeared in the painting with a malignant look); he did a poor job in rendering physical appearance ("none with the exception of Konomo & possibly Grabeau bear the most distant resemblance to the men in the New Haven jail"); his depiction of the uprising contained several factual mistakes (Ndamma appears angelic, removed from the fray, but he bore a scar on his head that suggested an active role in the attack).

The biggest worry, however, was the emphasis on violence, the killing of Captain Ferrer, and the effect this might have on the public. In short, Griswold believed Hewins to be dangerously misguided. The artist may have hoped that the *Amistad* Africans would be freed, but his painting would not help the struggle. Griswold wrote, "I have no reason to doubt his sincerity—the soundness of his judgment I may be permitted to question. The moral effect of the painting, so far as it has any, I do think will be bad—perhaps I err." So worried was Griswold about the painting that he hesitated to publish his critique of it, fearing that it would draw attention to the violent representation and thereby do "injury" to "the cause of humanity," that is, to the sacred struggle against slavery. He wrote Tappan, "I do not know whether it is best to broach anything about it in public or not." He left the matter up to Tappan, who apparently decided against it.

Abolitionists fretted about the popular depictions of the *Amistad* rebellion, but in truth they themselves had originally done much to encourage them. As soon as the rebels were brought ashore, Dwight Janes had proclaimed that "the blacks had a perfect right to get their liberty by killing the crew and taking possession of the vessel." He added, uncertainly, "I mean a legal right," referring to Spain's agreement with Great Britain to end the slave trade. Janes was thus the first to address the dilemma: how would abolitionists, many of them committed to nonviolence, depict and defend a violent slave revolt in a society where there was a broad fear of such events and where they themselves were considered by many to be dangerous, fanatical extremists in their opposition to slavery?[35]

Abolitionists flocked to the *Amistad* case and defended the rebels and their actions as if nonviolence had never crossed their minds. If they were to use the case to attack the institution of slavery—and the opportunity seemed to them nothing less than providential—they would have to come up with arguments to justify the rebellion. Following the lead of Janes, they did so: the *Amistad* rebels, they would proclaim repeatedly over the next two and a half years, had the fundamental right, shared by all people, to resist tyranny and to seize their own liberty, by force if necessary. If this meant killing a tyrant—a slave ship captain—so be it. That act would not constitute murder, no matter how loudly slaveholders in Cuba or the United States might howl in protest. This radical argument would become a big part of the public debate on the *Amistad* rebellion and a centerpiece of the abolitionist defense.[36]

The argument possessed a deep ambiguity. What *kind of right* allowed the Africans to kill their oppressor and seize their freedom? Here the abolitionist movement was of two minds. The more conservative approach was to insist that the right was, narrowly, a legal right. Because the Spanish slave trade had been made illegal by treaty, the Africans aboard the *Amistad* had a right to rise up, kill Captain Ferrer, and seize the vessel. This was the argument of attorneys as they represented the *Amistad* Africans in court, and a persuasive argument it was. Other abolitionists took a more radical approach. They reached back to an argument that originated with Tacky's rebellion in Jamaica in 1760, after which a man in London known as J. Philmore defended the rebels and articulated the "higher law" doctrine that would become central to the antislavery cause. Enslaved rebels had a "natural right" to their freedom, no matter what man-made law said on the matter. In contrast (and contradiction) to the legal approach stood what might be called an antinomian argument: rebels who took radical, direct action were right to take the law into their own hands as long as it served the noble cause of freedom.[37]

Some abolitionists took the idea further than others, African American opponents of slavery leading the way. Their preferred image of the *Amistad* Africans was not that they were citizens doing what was proper and legal, but that they were free people doing what was glorious and right. Like Amasa Hewins, they repeatedly likened Cinqué to George Washington, and endlessly compared the *Amistad* rebellion to the American Revolution. The actions of the rebels were "in the highest degree noble," as the *Colored American* explained:

The spirit that prompted Patrick Henry to exclaim on a memorable occasion, 'Give me liberty, or give me death,' that same spirit fired the bosom and nerved the arm of this daring yet generous African. Joseph Cinquez is more than a hero. He is, emphatically, one of God's noblemen. And by all the reasons and principles on which we eulogize George Washington and his brave compeers, for resisting unto blood the attempts of Great Britain to subdue our people to political slavery, by all those principles and reasons, and by many others superadded, are we bound to laud Joseph Cinquez and his comrades, for resisting unto blood the miscreants that would doom them to personal slavery.

This radical statement makes clear that not all abolitionists worried about the popular depictions of rebellion; some applauded them. Still, those conducting the defense campaign, who were uncomfortable with depictions of the rebellion, had to decide how to translate their own political commitments into images that would shape the public debate and affect the judgment in court.[38]

Jocelyn's Portrait

The abolitionist dilemma of representation was finally resolved by Nathaniel Jocelyn, the best known of the artists who went into the New Haven jail, and the one most firmly connected to the movement. Born in 1796 in New Haven into an artisanal family (his father was a clockmaker and engraver), Jocelyn was apprenticed to a watchmaker but soon took up drawing, engraving, and painting. His sensibilities about slavery were affected by the two years (1820–1822) he spent in Savannah, where he worked as a portrait painter for the Georgia aristocracy. He made his view of the world clear in 1833, when he painted a sympathetic portrait of William Lloyd Garrison, about which, the controversial abolitionist noted, its accuracy would be doubted as it had "no horns about the head."[39]

By 1840 Jocelyn had become an active abolitionist, working in the nascent Underground Railroad in Connecticut. His brother Simeon was also a committed abolitionist: he had been the pastor at the predominantly African American church on Temple Street in New Haven, a victim of attack by an anti-abolition mob in 1837, and one of three founding members (with Joshua Leavitt and Lewis Tappan) of the Amistad Committee. Living and working in New Haven, Nathaniel Jocelyn was, like the other artists, close to the epicenter of the struggle. His antislavery views and activism, expressed in his commitment to break the *Amistad* Africans out of jail by force in January 1840, connected him to the man who commissioned the painting. The African American abolitionist Robert Purvis was a leading member of the Philadelphia Vigilance Committee in 1840 and likewise involved in assisting runaways as they made their way toward freedom. The

Based on Nathaniel Jocelyn's painting, John Sartain produced a mezzotint engraving, "Cinque: The Chief of the Amistad Captives."

skilled, radical, and activist Jocelyn was just the man to paint the "official," soon to become iconic, abolitionist portrait of Cinqué.[40]

Jocelyn's painting could hardly have been more different from the images produced by Barber, Moulthrop, and Hewins. Painted during the winter of 1840–1841, the leader is composed, at rest, not on the ship or in jail, but at home in an idealized African environment. The moment appears to be sunset, with gentle clouds and a reddish sky above majestic mountains. Cinqué is not fighting for freedom in an act of slave rebellion; he is free, and has always been free. The artist imagines him in the happy home to which the abolitionists wanted him to return. The entire portrait radiates serenity. The eyes of the leader are not demonic, but rather soft, intelligent, compassionate, liquid. The left hand is relaxed and almost aristocratic in appearance. Jocelyn manages to represent the famous leader of a violent revolt in a way that suggests no violence at all. He presents the abolitionist movement and its goals to the public in a profoundly peaceful way, embodied in a single individual rather than an armed collective.

The painting features Cinqué in traditional Mende dress, a white cotton cloth thrown over his left shoulder, holding a staff, a symbol of leadership among his people. Jocelyn probably got the ideas for both symbols directly from Cinqué, as he would not have known about Mende culture. But Jocelyn cleverly built double meanings into both: viewers of the painting might see the African leader as wearing a toga, like a virtuous Roman republican citizen, or as Moses, staff in hand, having led his compatriots back to the Promised Land. A direct-action abolitionist such as Robert Purvis might imagine the staff as a spear, a weapon of self-defense.

Jocelyn's portrait of Cinqué was a commercial transaction, between patron and artist, but unlike the artwork of Hewins, Moulthrop, and Barber, it was not meant to make money—until Purvis had John Sartain of Philadelphia make an engraving and lithograph of the same image, which would then be sold for $2 per copy, the proceeds to go to the Pennsylvania Antislavery Association. This gave the image a much broader, even transatlantic circulation, as copies of it ended up in Bristol, England, among other places, through abolitionist circuits. One copy came to the hands of the *Amistad* Africans, who were "delighted" by the likeness of Cinqué and by his "imposing" attitude in the portrait. When shown his own image, the leader himself exclaimed, "oh, good, good."[41]

The art of Barber, Moulthrop, Hewins, and Jocelyn served a common vital purpose, keeping the *Amistad* struggle before the public during an otherwise quiet time of incarceration. These artists had met the prisoners and heard their stories of the rebellion. Through their art they helped not only to publicize the struggle, but to project antislavery ideas to people inside and outside the movement. The biographical element that all artists included, by text or portraiture, gave a human face to the struggle for freedom, for the "Mendi People," and indeed all enslaved people.

The Collective

The abolitionists who went to the New Haven jail sought to turn those who had engaged in communal armed struggle into peaceable, disciplined Christian individuals. The *Amistad* Africans cooperated in this work, but their own project was in a fundamental way the very opposite: to create and preserve a disciplined sense of the collective, to hold everyone together for the sake of survival and the accomplishment of what remained the primary goal from the beginning of the ordeal to the end: to return to Africa. The fictive kinship that began to grow at Lomboko expanded on the *Teçora*, in the barracoons of Havana, aboard the *Amistad*, and came to full fruition in the jail of New Haven. The bonding eventually took a novel collective form called "the Mendi People."

The original power of the collective took the form of successful rebellion. A second achievement was a 1,400-mile voyage aboard the *Amistad*. The collective reared its head again on board the *Washington*, where Cinqué tried to inspire his comrades to another round of resistance. American authorities recognized the threat of solidarity and sought to weaken it by segregating the leader from his mates. The power of the collective was once again made clear by the laughing, screaming, weeping, and rejoicing that was audible and visible to all every time he was reunited with his shipmates.[42]

Burna also played an important role in knitting and keeping the group together. Unable to go to Hartford for the first hearing because he was sick, Burna was upset to be separated from his shipmates, "the more so," one observer noted, "because two of the three little girls are his sisters." They were not, of course, his biological sisters, but they were sisters within his own idiom. He manifested the same sensibility months later in Farmington, in an exchange with abolitionist A. F. Williams, who sought the help of the *Amistad* Africans when a "Mr. Chamberlain, a young gentleman of intelligence and worth," disappeared into the river; it was feared that he had drowned. Burna replied, "Me think me hear you say your brother in water, me no sleep, we come find." Williams did not understand the system of fictive kinship, so he felt compelled to correct Burna: "You are mistaken, said I, not my brother, my friend." Burna answered, "Well, we look, we find." At great peril to themselves as they dove into "the loaming water below the dam," Burna and his shipmates recovered the lifeless body of Williams' "brother" and returned it to him for a funeral and burial. Burna was also known to manifest strong feeling when discussing his multiethnic shipmates who had died, especially the Bullom man Tua who passed away in New Haven after the freedom voyage.[43]

The *Amistad* Africans came from societies in which the common good of the group almost always came before individual preference, advantage, and advancement. Charlotte Cowles thought the *Amistad* Africans had "less of the spirit of *meum et tuum* about them than any people I have ever heard of." Though they had few material possessions, they "always find something to give each other," taking "no pleasure in keeping, but all in giving" and treating each other with affection and generosity. Because their survival in jail, and indeed throughout their entire Atlantic ordeal, depended on group solidarity, they organized themselves accordingly, on the model of the Poro Society. As the Rev. James Steele, one of the missionaries who accompanied the *Amistad* Africans back to Sierra Leone, noted, they "were under great restraints, especially in America; they thought if one did anything evil it would be charged upon the whole, and this with a desire to secure friends in a strange land, made them very watchful over each other."[44]

Tensions

The emphasis on maintaining a united front did not mean that there were no tensions within the group. The relationship between Cinqué and Burna, for example, was fraught with stress. They had clashed during and after the rebellion. According to several reports, Cinqué apparently wanted to kill Ruiz, Montes, or both, and on more than one occasion Burna stayed his machete-wielding hand. Cinqué seems not to have trusted Burna, and he may have been right in not doing so: Burna was the only *Amistad* African who criticized Cinqué for his treatment of Ruiz and Montes. It was rumored that Burna was afraid of Cinqué.[45]

Why Cinqué and Burna clashed is not easy to discern. They may have had cultural differences: Cinqué was Mende; Burna was Gbandi. They had strong personalities and may have had differing approaches to their common dilemma. Part of it was surely that Burna was the only person among the rebels who knew some English and could therefore communicate with Ruiz, who spoke fluent English, and through him with Montes. Was Cinqué insecure that he could not understand what the three men were talking about? He seems to have been worried that Burna was cooperating in a plan to return the vessel to Havana. As Antonio testified before the district court in January 1840, "Sinqua thought when Burnah talked with Pedro they take Sch[ooner] back to Havana. He wanted to go to Africa."⁴⁶

A disturbing possibility fueled the mistrust and insecurity. Had Burna learned to speak English while working in the slave trade in Sierra Leone? There is no direct evidence that he had, but there are hints. As the correspondent of the *New York Morning Herald* noted after interviewing Burna, his "language is an odd melange of English and Spanish, with an occasional French word, and a slight sprinkling of some African lingo." This was a pidgin language, designed to facilitate trade between Europeans and Africans on the coast, suggesting the circumstances in which Burna acquired his language skills. It would have been difficult to have been involved with Spanish, French, and English traders on the Gallinas Coast in the 1830s without having been involved in the slave trade. Moreover, it turned out that Burna was quite a rich man in his native land. He had seven wives, a sure sign of wealth. If Cinqué knew or suspected any of these things, he may have had good reason to worry about the conversations between Burna and the Spaniards, and about Burna's commitment to their collective freedom.⁴⁷

More important than any tension within the group was the long, formative struggle between the Africans and jailer Stanton Pendleton. He diminished the collective when he moved Margru, Kagne, and Teme from the jail to his household, then tried to keep them there after the rest of the *Amistad* Africans were moved from New Haven to Westville in September 1840. This aggravated tensions that had been roiling between the jailer and his charges for months over issues of labor, discipline, and racism. Abolitionists may have held a favorable opinion of Pendleton, but the *Amistad* Africans took a decidedly different view, leading to explosive confrontations in February 1841.

One of the first hints of conflict was reported in the *Hartford Courant* and the *Boston Courier* in early September 1840: "One of them [the *Amistad* Africans] was put in irons the other day, for an attempt to assault his keeper, who restrained some of his 'largest liberty.'" The source of the conflict was not disclosed, though perhaps a clue can be

178 | The *Amistad* Rebellion

found in reference to some of the African attitudes: "Their notions of property are entirely Agrarian: 'What's yours is mine, and what's mine is my own.'" The conflict may have spurred the abolitionists to make arrangements to move the captives to a jail in Westville, which happened less than a week later.[48]

When, a few months later, one of the proslavery newspapers resorted to racist stereotypes to suggest that the *Amistad* Africans were lazy and shiftless and refused to work, Cinqué, in a conversation with his teacher, Sherman Booth, revealed a previous history of conflict over labor issues: "My people work for Pendleton plenty and he never pay." They worked on the roads, in taverns, and elsewhere around New Haven. So valuable was their labor that Pendleton told Tsukama to wash his clothes on his own time, on Sunday, so that he would be available for other work on weekdays. Tsukama objected to "working on the Sabbath" (Christianity had material advantages), to which Pendleton replied, "What does a 'nigger' care for Sunday?" Pendleton also required the *Amistad* Africans to do their own cooking and woodcutting. Cinqué indignantly asked, "We no work?! Man no work, he no eat—he die, he no work." Reflecting his rising knowledge of the gospel of "free labor" and the labor theory of value, he stated: "We all work, if men pay; but no pay, we no work." He and his comrades insisted on choice in the labor market: "We no work any more for Mr. Pendleton [even] if he pay." Still, Cinqué would not reduce all to an economic logic: "We work for [abolitionists] Mr. Tappan and Mr. Townsend without pay, because they good friends."[49]

James Covey also clashed with Pendleton, partly because his translations had made possible the arrest of Ruiz and Montes, with whom Pendleton apparently sympathized. Covey also refused to treat Pendleton "with the Defference and respect [to] which his station entitles him." The jailer retaliated by limiting Covey's access to the Africans until the abolitionists could smooth the matter over.[50]

A big confrontation with Pendleton occurred in early February 1841, after the move to the less populous Westville, just northwest of New Haven, which would have limited the income the jailer received in New Haven for admission to see the popular prisoners. The *Amistad*

Africans and their abolitionist allies had begun their efforts to remove Margru, Kagne, and Teme from the jailer's household, and to reattach them to the group, which made him furious. Pendleton spread what Cinqué called a "bad rumor," which was the subject of much "jail talk" among the "Mendi People." Pendleton claimed that the abolitionists were not telling the truth about their plans for the *Amistad* Africans: "they tell you lie: Mendi people not go to Mendi." They would go to Havana. Worse, Pendleton said of Tappan, for whom he had a special dislike, "he all destroy you." Cinqué responded to Pendleton's allegation with Christian patience, saying, "Mr. Tappan in New York, he was very good man and Mr. Townsend, and God will bless them."[51]

Lurking behind the "bad rumor" was a history of antagonism that had been building during a yearlong term in the New Haven jail. Cinqué alleged, "When we in New Haven, he whip Mendi people too hard." Now the angry jailer had arrived in Westville cursing, with chains in his hands, and he was threatening to do so again. At this moment Cinqué the warrior seemed to be having trouble with the Christian command to "love thy enemies." But in a letter to Baldwin in which he explained the confrontation, he said dutifully, "We forgive him and he curse us and he whip us and all he do that is not better for us." He wanted Baldwin's assurance that Pendleton would not do this again.

The Africans also wrote a group letter to Tappan, alleging frankly that Pendleton was a violent, racist, exploitative, ungodly man. He had whipped Fuli and Kinna and he had threatened to "kill the Mendi People," all of them. He said "all black people no good"; they "stink." He sought "to make all black people work for him." He was, in short, a "wicked man," the very kind denounced in the Bible. He and his entire family were "all bad—do not love God." It was clearly time to remove the girls from his household.[52]

The Mendi People

During the winter of 1840–1841, almost two years after their initial enslavement in Africa and about seventeen months after they had been confined in American jails, the *Amistad* Africans began to think of themselves and to represent themselves in a new way in the letters they wrote in greater numbers as their studies of the English language advanced. They now proudly called themselves "the Mendi People." That this was a collective decision was made clear in a newspaper article that appeared under the headline "The Mendi People." The first line read, "Thus the Africans, late of the schooner Amistad, call themselves."[53]

The new name represented an apotheosis of their long-standing fictive kinship. Drawing on the additive nature of Mende and other surrounding cultures, they achieved a new level of social bonding through a two-sided process that took place inside the jail: the linguistic and cultural assimilation of the non-Mende people to the ways of the numerically dominant Mende among them, and the creation of a new "we," a collective identity, against a newly perceived "they" in the external world. In a real sense, a language community became a political community. The collective would use its new name to make claims—about who the group was and what its future should be.

The "Mendi People" was an unusual social formation, a complex compound for which there was no precise equivalent in West Africa, not even in Mendeland. Indeed, Professor Gibbs seemed to discover that Mende stood for all Africa. When he asked the captives to translate "I go to Africa," they answered *"gna gi-ya Men-di."* The "Mendi People" was thus a multiethnic entity, which included Mende, Temne, Kono, Gbandi, Loma, and Gola people. It was American in its genesis: it arose in relation to, and antagonism with, the learning of the English language and the ways of Christianity. In other words, as the abolitionists insisted that the *Amistad* Africans become new people, they in turn insisted on an African identity. This process of ethnogenesis was driven by specific struggles in jail: the Africans invented themselves as the "Mendi People" as they faced hardships that required a collective response. They used the new collective name to make three fundamental political demands: to shape their legal defense, to protect themselves against violence, and to insist upon their own rights to self-emancipation and ultimately repatriation.[54]

The earliest recorded reference to the "Mendi People" as a chosen form of identity and belonging appeared in a famous letter said to have been written by the young boy Kale to John Quincy Adams on January 4, 1841. In truth, the letter was a collective composition, explained teacher Sherman Booth: Kale was "assisted by some of the other Africans," especially, it would seem, by Cinqué and Kinna, both of whom were leaders within the group and advanced in their own studies. They composed the letter after Adams visited the New Haven jail in November and "in view of his having been engaged as one of their counsel" for the Supreme Court hearing. In other words, the *Amistad* Africans wanted to communicate to Adams who they were and what he should say on their behalf. The letter, which oddly has never been treated by scholars with the careful attention it deserves, is the single best surviving expression of collective goals and identity the *Amistad* Africans produced.[55]

The letter begins in the idiom of love and friendship: Kale addresses Adams as his friend at the outset, mentions the former president's "love" for the "Mendi People," emphasizes friendship as a primary human value, and closes with "your friend." This is an African language of alliance, applied to the relationship that has developed between abolitionists and insurrectionists during the jail encounter. Kale wants Adams to know that he and his comrades have ideas about what to do: "Mendi people think, think, think," but most Americans do not know what they think. Booth knew some of their thoughts: "We tell him some." The eleven-year-old Kale therefore told the seventy-three-year-old Adams what to say on their behalf to the "Great Court," the Supreme Court: "Dear friend, we want you to know how we feel." The letter expresses both indignation and confidence in their cause: "We want you to ask the court what we have done wrong. What for Americans keep us in prison." Their rebellion was a just act, warranting no incarceration.

Kale also states, and comments on, what he considers to be the most important legal facts of the case: first and foremost, the "Mendi People" were indeed "Mendi People." They were born in Mende country. They had not been born, or had lived long, in Havana; they had been in the city only ten days before being taken on board the *Amistad*.

They had not learned the Spanish language, Kale explained, and had not, therefore, become legal "ladino" slaves. José Ruiz had lied about these issues in his testimony to the court. Kale insisted, "We want you to tell court that Mendi people no want to go back to Havanna. We no want to be killed." The goal was unequivocal: "All we want is make us free not send us to Havanna." Freedom meant going home.

Kale also rehearsed basic historical facts about the rebellion. He stressed the threatened cannibalism of Celestino and the reaction of his shipmates: "Cook say he kill he eat Mendi people. We afraid. We kill cook." He also stated that the plan for the uprising did not originally include killing Captain Ferrer: "Then captain kill one man with knife and cut Mendi people plenty. We never kill captain if he no kill us." He made a case for armed self-defense.

Kale recalled the powerful emotional moment at Culloden Point, Long Island, when the *Amistad* Africans learned from white men on shore that they had managed to work their way to a "free country." The white men had said, "We make you free," and indeed the promise had been reiterated endlessly by abolitionists during the time in jail. Even Judge Andrew Judson declared them free and commanded the government to take them home. Was it all a lie, Kale now wondered aloud in his letter to Adams, and does not the Christian God punish liars?

Most of the letter discussed what happened during the "17 moons" the "Mendi People" had spent in jail. Kale detailed the progress they had made in their studies: they had learned to read and write; they had studied the Bible. "We love books very much." He objected to the implication that the "Mendi People" were somehow stupid, just because they spoke a different language. He asked, pointedly, "Americans no talk Mendi. Americans crazy dolt?" He answered those who had criticized the *Amistad* Africans as having been too happy, too sad, or too angry while in jail. He applied the Golden Rule from the book of Matthew, 7:12: "Therefore all things whatsoever ye would that men should do to you, do ye even so to them." He puts the shoe of African experience on the American foot: "Dear friend Mr. Adams, you have children and friends. You love them. You feel very sorry if Mendi people come and take all to Africa."

The letter concludes with a strong assertion of collective agency: "If court ask who bring Mendi people to America," you say "We bring ourselves. Ceci hold the rudder." Throughout the letter, Kale maintains a parity between "the Mendi People" and "the America people." Indeed, it seems that the idea of the "Mende People" was a creative adaptation of political language the *Amistad* Africans heard during their time in jail about the powerful, sovereign "American people." But Kale went further, commenting specifically on the relationship between the abolitionists and the insurrectionists, saying, in essence, we have held up our end of the deal. We have learned your language and your religion. Now you must hold up your end of the deal: you must win the court case here in your country and you must help us to get home to ours. In making these overt and subtle demands, Kale uses the phrase "Mendi People" nineteen times. The letter—and its sovereign subject—made quite an impression on Adams and others around the country.[56]

A second important moment in the use of the "Mende People" occurred soon after the letter was written, in the aftermath of jailer Pendleton's visit to Farmington in early February 1841, when he threatened reenslavement, vilified the abolitionists, and tried to cut off access to food and water. Fuli referred to the "Mendi People" in a letter he wrote to Lewis Tappan about the attack, and Cinqué did the same, sixteen times, in a letter to Roger S. Baldwin about the tense, angry encounter. The closing of the ranks at a time of danger was inscribed in the "Mendi People."[57]

The biggest danger was now at hand. The United States Supreme Court was scheduled to hear the *Amistad* case January 25, 1841. The Van Buren administration had appealed the lower court ruling in favor of the Africans, with clear intent. Now the fate of the "Mendi People" lay in the hands of nine justices, a majority of whom, including Chief Justice Roger B. Taney, had southern backgrounds. As the legal debate resumed and intensified, numerous newspapers reported a spate of rumors, all saying in one way or another that "these poor fellows are, after all, to be given up to the Spanish authorities."[58]

CHAPTER SIX

Freedom

By February 1841, the *Amistad* Africans had appeared in American court five times. The first was on the deck of the U.S. brig *Washington* at the docks of New London, Connecticut, where Judge Andrew Judson of the United States District Court held a hearing on August 29, 1839, soon after they came ashore, to consider charges of piracy and murder. A second set of hearings was held in Hartford between September 19 and 23, presided over by Judson and Smith Thompson of the U.S. Circuit Court. In October Lewis Tappan brought charges of violent assault and false imprisonment against José Ruiz and Pedro Montes on behalf of four of the *Amistad* Africans, which resulted in a new set of hearings before judges Inglis and Jones in New York. The original case resumed in Hartford November 19, but James Covey's sickness required postponement to January 7–13, 1840, in New Haven. When the United States Supreme Court convened in Washington on February 22, 1841, to make a definitive ruling about whether the *Amistad* Africans would be returned to their "owners" under the provisions of the Pinckney Treaty of 1795, the Africans were not present in the courtroom. They awaited the verdict in jail in Westville, Connecticut.

Anxiety about the big palaver had settled over the Africans about two months earlier, reported their teacher Sherman Booth. The case was originally scheduled for January. Cinqué was losing weight because of "mental disquiet." By the time the court began its deliberations, nerves were on edge in the jailhouse. Every day the leader of the

Africans came to Booth to ask, "What the Grand Court say? Tell me." The "Mendi People" knew that this would be the final judgment. Their fates, and their necks, hung in the balance of pro- and antislavery forces that met in Washington, DC.[1]

By this time the adult *Amistad* Africans had enough experience with the law to be wary. Indeed, four of them were in Connecticut because they had fallen afoul of it in their homelands and were sold into slavery for "criminal conduct." All were accustomed to palavers held in the *bari*, the communal meeting house where disputes about law and custom were argued and settled, often with eloquent speeches given by parties on both sides of the dispute to a king, chief, or head man, a group of elders, and the interested part of the community in attendance. The local leader usually consulted with the elders in reaching a judgment, which all parties would be obliged to accept. Occasionally a verdict might be appealed to the jurisdiction of a more powerful regional leader, but issues of justice were usually decided locally. Behind the palavers stood the Poro Society, which to a large extent determined the rules and practices that would be followed in the legal procedure. This would have been the framework in which the *Amistad* Africans interpreted their legal experience in the United States. They knew courtroom argument and drama, but not the larger American system of law, especially its federal jurisdictional structure and lengthy process of appeal. Amos Townsend Jr. noted that the Africans were accustomed to a "summary process" of trial "in their own country," and that the delay caused by appeal was hard for them to understand and endure.[2]

In Washington, interest in the case quickened as the court date approached. Visitors surged into the capital from out of town, including abolitionists such as Joshua Leavitt, a member of the Amistad Committee, from New York, to report on the hearings. As excitement mounted, abolitionists circulated for sale John Sartain's mezzotint portrait of Cinqué. The Spanish-language newspaper *Noticioso de Ambos Mundos*, published in New York, asked, provocatively, whether the United States government would consider "uprising, mutiny, and murder the best recommendation in order not to comply with the provisions of a treaty." Once again the court chambers would fill with spectators, including recent presidential candidate Henry Clay and Senator John J. Crittenden, both of Kentucky, among others. Everyone understood that the court would decide issues of national and international significance.[3]

Another interested party was the British government, which, at the urging of the British and Foreign Anti-Slavery Society, mobilized its diplomatic corps to apply pressure to Spain and the United States. Statesman G. S. Jerningham wrote to Spanish minister Don Evaristo Pérez de Castro in Madrid at the end of December 1840, reminding him of the treaty that made it illegal "to import negroes from Africa into the Spanish dominions" after 1820. He recommended that the *Amistad* Africans "be put in possession of the liberty of which they were deprived." Britain had, after all, paid Spain £400,000 (almost $37 million in 2012 dollars) to agree to eliminate the evil trade. On January 20, 1841, Ambassador Henry Stephen Fox wrote Secretary of State John Forsyth that "a powerful and humane interest" in the case existed in the United States and Britain, reminding him of the treaty with Spain and the Treaty of Ghent (1814), negotiated by John Quincy Adams, in which Great Britain and the United States mutually pledged "to use their best endeavors for the entire abolition of the African slave trade." Fox urged that the president of the United States act to secure the liberty to which the *Amistad* Africans were clearly entitled. Above these suggestions to Spain and the United States loomed Britain's military capacity to seize the island of Cuba if it so desired.[4]

Attorney General Henry D. Gilpin explained in his opening statement why the Supreme Court should overturn the ruling of the lower court. He sought the straightforward restoration of private property based on the Pinckney Treaty of 1795, in which the United States and Spain agreed to mutual assistance for ships in distress. Article 8 stipulated that if a ship "be forced through stress of weather, pursuit of pirates or enemies, or any other urgent necessity" to seek shelter, it "shall be received and treated with all humanity" and properly assisted. Article 9 added: all ships "rescued out of the hands of any pirates or robbers on the high seas, shall be brought into some port" and returned to those who originally owned them. The Spanish slave-holders Ruiz and Montes made claims based on these articles of the treaty, as had the government of Spain through their ambassadors, Angel Calderón de la Barca and Pedro Alcántara de Argaiz. The vessel, cargo, and slaves, argued Gilpin, should be "restored to the Spanish owners." These black pirates—"enemies of all mankind"—had committed a crime against property by seizing themselves. They should be returned to Cuba.[5]

Roger S. Baldwin, who had worked with the Amistad Committee throughout the ordeal, spoke on behalf of the thirty-six Africans, contending "for freedom and for life, with two powerful governments arrayed against them." Baldwin cleverly turned the tables on Gilpin. Drawing on an American federal law of 1820 that any citizen of the United States who engaged in the slave trade "shall be adjudged a pirate" and if convicted "shall suffer death," he asked, who are the pirates here? Not the *Amistad* rebels but rather Ruiz, Montes, and by implication the deceased Captain Ramón Ferrer, all of whom were, in this rhetorical flourish (if not in law, for they were not American citizens), illegal slave-trading pirates. Baldwin insisted that the *Amistad* rebels were *not pirates*, were *not slaves*, and that the United States government must not turn them over to Ruiz, Montes, Cuba, Spain, or anyone else. They should go free. Baldwin stated that his clients "were not pirates, nor in any sense hostes humani generis" (enemies of all mankind). They had no goal of enrichment in seizing the vessel and they attacked no other ships. Their sole objective was to free themselves from unlawful bondage. They were in fact the "victims of piracy."[6]

Twelve times in his fluent address Baldwin acknowledged the *Amistad* rebels as the agents of their own emancipation. By their own "successful revolt," they had "achieved their deliverance from slavery, on the high seas." They had arrived "in a condition of freedom within the territorial limits of a FREE AND SOVEREIGN STATE"—that is, what the Africans called "a free country." This was an important legal point because it meant a return to Cuba or Spain would require the United States government to "re-enslave them, for the benefit of Spanish negro-dealers," which was clearly unconstitutional. Baldwin railed against the "executive interference" that sought to place them back in bondage. He also noted the "intense interest [in the case] throughout the country;—I may almost say throughout the civilized world." An observer noted that Baldwin's speech was "one of the most complete, finished, conclusive legal arguments ever made before that court."[7]

When John Quincy Adams rose to address the court, he noted that his "learned friend and colleague" had defended the *Amistad* Africans "in so able and complete a manner as leaves me scarcely anything to say." His address would therefore last a mere seven and a half hours, over two court sessions. In the first, the wily master of rhetoric had some fun with the contradictions of the argument about piracy. Both the American and Spanish governments had insisted on treating the *Amistad* Africans as both "merchandise"—as passive property, that is to say, as slaves—and at the same time as "pirates and robbers," who were active, aggressive human agents. Referring to the treaty of 1795, Adams remarked, "My clients are claimed under the treaty as merchandise, rescued from pirates and robbers." But who were the merchandise and who were the robbers? "According to the construction of the Spanish minister, the merchandise were the robbers, and the robbers were the merchandise. The merchandise was rescued out of its own hands, and the robbers were rescued out of the hands of the robbers." Adams then turned to the justices and asked, no doubt with a glint of mischief in his eyes, "Is this the meaning of the treaty?" Adams also assailed Lt. Thomas Gedney and the other officers of the navy, who had no legal right to attack the rebels, drive them belowdecks, seize them, or forcibly carry them to New London. Their "sympathy" for the white slaveholders was all too apparent. Adams expanded upon Baldwin's argument that the Africans arrived in the United States in full, rightful possession of both the vessel and their freedom.[8]

After the court adjourned for the day, its proceedings were "interrupted by the solemn voice of death." Justice Philip Barbour of Virginia was found dead in his bed the following morning, causing a postponement of the case until March 1. Other dramatic news came soon after, from Liberia, by way of an American shipmaster: the British antislavery patrol, led by Captain Joseph Denman, had destroyed the slave-trading factories of Pedro Blanco on the Gallinas Coast, the very place from which the *Amistad* Africans had been shipped to Cuba aboard the *Teçora* in April 1839. Eleven boats with one hundred twenty armed sailors had pushed off from the *Wanderer*, the *Saracen*, and the *Rolla* on the evening of November 19, 1840, arrived undetected, and forced the overseers to grab their papers and fly into the bush in fright and consternation. The sailors liberated more than eight hundred enslaved Africans and torched the barracoons, destroying property worth an estimated £200,000 ($9 million in 2012 dollars). Lord Palmerston, British secretary of state for foreign affairs, commended the action: "Taking a wasp's nest . . . is more effective than catching the wasps one by one." At roughly the same time, Captain H. F. Seagram had negotiated the surrender of Blanco's former partner, Theophilus Conneau, now the second biggest slave trader on the coast. Suddenly a "mammoth market for human flesh" had been destroyed and "a thousand miles of coastline cleared" of the horrid trade.[9]

Back in Connecticut, abolitionists were once again debating what to do in the event of a verdict against the *Amistad* Africans. The discussion was complicated this time because Wilcox the marshal and Pendleton the jailer expected a jailbreak. Abolitionists therefore worried that they might take preemptive action to move the Africans to another location. Amos Townsend Jr. met with Cinqué to alert him to the possibility, telling him to keep everyone together and to "make all the resistance in their power & not suffer themselves to be carried off by stealth." Cinqué and his fellow warriors had demonstrated "all the resistance in their power" aboard the *Amistad*, but he understood that a different, lesser kind of resistance was called for on this occasion. He promised that "if they come we will all halloo loud & make plenty noise" to alert sympathetic neighbors. In any case, many local abolitionists remained "ready forcibly to interfere," if necessary. Wilcox and Pendleton added guards and extra locks to the prison doors.[10]

When Adams resumed on Monday, March 1, in a "well filled Court room" as a snowstorm raged outside, he waged a blistering attack on

Martin Van Buren for "executive interference" in the case. He pointed repeatedly to the courtroom copy of the Declaration of Independence, emphasizing the principle of equality as crucial to the case. As he concluded, he was gripped by emotion, his voice almost failing, his face lined with tears. A correspondent, profoundly moved, wrote, "The closing part of his speech was the most touching and affecting of anything of the kind to which I ever listened." "Old Man Eloquent," as Adams was called, had given his all to the defense.[11]

Acknowledging the public engagement in this "interesting and important controversy," the eight sitting justices reviewed all of the evidence, arguments, and previous rulings of the *Amistad* case and decided, 7–1, that "these negroes never were the lawful slaves of Ruiz or Montes or of any other Spanish subjects." Writing for the majority, Justice Joseph Story affirmed the narrative the Africans had given in September and repeated endlessly ever since: "They are natives of Africa, and were kidnapped there, and were unlawfully transported to Cuba, in violation of the law and treaties of Spain, and the most solemn edict and declarations of that Government." The Court lamented the "dreadful acts" by which they "asserted their liberty" during the rebellion, but implicitly acknowledged them as legitimate. The Africans were not "robbers or pirates" and the treaty of 1795 therefore "cannot be obligatory upon them." The court, however, rejected Adams's argument that the ship and cargo lawfully belonged to the Africans, ruling that they were the property of Spanish subjects and that Gedney and the other officers were entitled to salvage, as the lower court had ruled. The court also ruled that the United States government bore no obligation of repatriation.[12]

As the decision was being rendered in Washington, the *Amistad* Africans were nervously calling out the windows of the Westville jail to passersby, asking if they had heard any news. Everyone was waiting on the arrival of the New York newspapers. Soon Wilcox and Pendleton showed up at the jail to deliver the verdict. They gathered into one room all of the captives, who, on Cinqué's signal, sat down to receive the fateful news. Their faces expressed "the deepest anxiety." Marshal Wilcox then said, "The big Court has come to a decision—

they say that you—one and all—are free." He then showed them the newspaper and said, "Read it." Cinqué turned to Kale, the best reader in the group, and told him to read it aloud for all. The leader remained skeptical, adding, "Paper lie sometimes." Soon abolitionists Henry G. Ludlow and Amos Townsend Jr. arrived at the jail to give the Africans the news from more trustworthy sources. The Africans demonstrated "great joy," although not "the tumultuous outbreak of feeling which the first decision of the lower court produced." They were wary and subdued in their response as they remembered their previous disappointment more than a year earlier, when they thought they had won their freedom, only to have the United States district attorney appeal the case and extend their incarceration.[13]

The visitors wanted to know what the Africans would do now that they were truly free. Would they return to Africa or would they remain in America? Townsend thought many of them might prefer to stay, especially when they said, "America country good country—America people good people—set we free." Cinqué then answered the question directly, saying "We talk together and think—then I tell." They would hold a communal meeting to make a decision, "one and all." Kinna added that he would follow Cinqué's advice: "He great man—he get us all free—he President." "Yes," added Grabeau with his impish sense of humor, "he President of the poor."[14]

As the word of the verdict spread, so did the ecstasy of the abolition-ist community. Many, including John Quincy Adams, used the Bible to interpret the joyful moment, turning to Isaiah 61:1 and the biblical Jubi-lee: God had sent his people "to proclaim liberty to the captives" and to open "the prison to them that are bound." As soon as he heard the ver-dict Adams wrote to the Amistad Committee, "The Captives are free!" Townsend commanded, with Old Testament gravity, "Bless the Lord, for his right hand hath gotten him the victory. The oppressor is con-founded, and the oppressed delivered." The *Youth's Cabinet* praised the faith that had brought "deliverance to the captive," and "the opening of the prison doors to them that were bound." The abolitionist movement in Philadelphia announced a "public Thanksgiving" involving the ministers of six congregations to celebrate "liberty to the captive," while the New York Anti-Slavery Society suggested that "thanks be given in all the churches of the land, in view of the decision." The *Colored American* joyously announced that "our long-imprisoned brethren . . . ARE FREE on this soil, without condition or restraint." The "people of color" of Columbus, Ohio, "deeply touched with the result of the trial of the Amistad captives," wrote expressions of gratitude to Baldwin and Adams.[15]

Knowing that the public would, after the verdict, once again hunger for reading material about the Africans, the *American and Foreign Anti-Slavery Reporter* brought out a special edition "extra" on March 15, 1841, featuring several of John Warner Barber's engravings (although not the one of the rebellion), news of the destruction of Pedro Blanco's slave factories, and excerpts of the speeches by Baldwin and Adams before the Supreme Court. The Amistad Committee advertised the availability of Sartain's portrait of *Cinque, Chief of the Amistad Captives* for purchase. The image was now a symbol of victory: "It is hoped that every friend of human rights throughout the country will secure one of these engravings, and preserve it in memory of Cinque not only, but of the righteous triumph of justice and humanity over cruelty and oppression in the decision that has set the arrested captives free."[16]

Knowing too that the *Amistad* Africans would be in ever greater demand by the admiring public, the abolitionists moved them immediately out of the New Haven region, twenty-eight miles away, to Farmington, under the watchful eyes of an "abolition town" in general, and gentleman farmer John Treadwell Norton, who had founded the local Anti-Slavery Society in 1836, in particular. When his son, John Pitkin Norton, found out on March 16, 1841, that the Africans were "coming here en masse to morrow to stay for a time & continue their education," he explained why: "The circus & menagerie proprietors & managers of theatres are gathering around them in New Haven like so many sharks & it is on that & other accounts thought best to remove them hither."[17]

What role had the Africans played in their own legal defense? They had met with both Baldwin and Adams, and Kale had written a long letter to Adams on behalf of the entire group to explain what he should say to the "Great Court." Through interpreters John Ferry, Charles Pratt, and especially James Covey, and through their own advancing facility in the English language, the "Mendi People" had told their individual and collective stories and made claims for freedom that were honestly reflected in the attorneys' remarks. Of course Baldwin and Adams brought their own perspective, skills, and stature to bear on the case, but they did say, by and large, what the "Mendi People" had wanted them to say: they were free natives of Africa; they had suffered greatly in their enslavement and shipment; they had won their own freedom in battle; they had brought themselves to a "free country." Ruiz and Montes had lied about their history. With this critical information at hand, Baldwin and Adams did their essential part in the freedom palaver. They had "accompanied" the Africans in a successful struggle.[18]

New Conflicts

The Supreme Court ruling raised an important question about the younger people involved in the case: what would be done with the three little girls, Kagne, Teme, and Margru, and the Afro-Cuban teenager Antonio? Soon after the ruling, Lewis Tappan and Amos Townsend Jr. brought a lawsuit on behalf of the "Mendi People" to remove the girls from the household of Stanton Pendleton. The jailer had employed them as servants in his kitchen and had provided neither domestic training nor education. Mrs. Pendleton had said it would be pointless to teach them to sew "as they were so soon to go back to Africa where they went naked." Because the girls had fallen so far behind their male counterpart, Kale, in speaking and reading English, the abolitionists lobbied Pendleton to allow the girls to study at the "Sabbath School of the Colored Church" in New Haven. This mistreatment was compounded by the rising tensions between Pendleton and the rest of the *Amistad* Africans.[19]

While the court was in session deciding the fate of the little girls, Pendleton returned to the Westville jail with his wife, his brother

William, a ship captain, and Thomas Mook ("not good man" according to Kinna) who worked for him and proceeded to inflame tensions further. The group threatened the *Amistad* Africans with reenslavement and death, promising again, as Fuli explained, to send a "hundred men to kill Mendi people." He continued to vilify Tappan, who would buy the entire lot of them, whip them "plenty," then sell them again. Pendleton had told the same things to the little girls: "a white man told them that Mr. Tappan wanted to sell them as slaves." The *Amistad* Africans had apparently encountered Pendleton's brother earlier in the New Haven jail, when he had said, "This is great business—teaching these *niggers*—might as well teach monkeys—I suppose they will establish a college, when they get back to Africa." Now the men sought out Cinqué, cursing and threatening him with deportation to Cuba, as Kinna reported: "They want fight and Cinque did not like fight." The men then tried to confine all of the *Amistad* Africans in a small room and take away their food and water. When Tappan and other abolitionists found out about the threats, they immediately went to Westville to lend support. They found the prisoners "in a great state of alarm, expecting to be sold again, and supposing they had been deceived as formerly."[20]

The conflict with Pendleton concluded in court, when a judge ruled to remove the girls from the jailer's household and to make abolitionist Townsend their legal guardian. The judgment was reached after Cinqué had been allowed to address the girls in Mende in a New Haven courtroom: "His eyes blazed and his voice was elevated in its tone—and his action passionate." In "one of the *finest* specimens of Mendee eloquence," he explained that the Pendletons were not to be trusted. They would do as they had many times threatened to do: they would "send them away and sell them." Tensions boiled over again as the sheriff removed William Pendleton from the courtroom, "by order of the Judge, for striking one of the Africans in court." The struggle to keep the collective together had been won. Kinna wrote Tappan to say how "very glad" and "joyful" the "Mendi People" were now that the little girls had been freed from the clutches of the wicked Pendleton.[21]

As soon as the *Amistad* Africans moved to their new free home among abolitionists in Farmington, Connecticut, they resumed the hard work of maintaining the collective. This was made clear by Charlotte Cowles, in whose home lived Kagne, one of the three little girls liberated from Pendleton after the Supreme Court ruling. The other *Amistad* Africans visited Kagne constantly and in large numbers: "Every day we have troops of them calling," wrote Charlotte to her brother. The callers were no doubt making sure that young Kagne was being treated properly, but they were at the same time reminding her that she was one of them, binding her to the collective through an endless series of gifts and personal connections.[22]

The Supreme Court upheld the lower-court ruling that Antonio should be returned to Cuba and the heirs of the deceased Captain Ferrer. The boy himself had requested as much, to the delight of proslavery journalists, soon after the *Amistad* came ashore. Marshal Wilcox assigned Antonio to the care of Pendleton, who received $2.50 per week from the government for his room and board and who nonetheless forced the teenager to work "without wages," all the while forbidding him to be educated with his shipmates. By the time the district court ordered his delivery to Ferrer's widow as her rightful property in late March 1841, Antonio had begun to think differently about his future.[23]

A writer for the *Colored American* noted that when the Supreme Court ruled that the *Amistad* Africans were free, Antonio "thought it better to be free also." As "a species of property which thinks, reasons, and wills," he decided to "*walk off*" from the marshal and the jailer. In New Haven he stole aboard a steamboat appropriately named the *Bunker Hill* and made his way to New York, where he stayed at the home of an African American friend of Lewis Tappan. The New York Vigilance Committee then "took charge of Antonio & have conveyed him away." It was noted that he "rejoiced to be at liberty, and is desirous of laboring for wages."[24]

Antonio traveled by night "to Canada, by the usual route" of safe houses on the Underground Railroad. One of the stops was Enosburgh, Vermont, about fifteen miles from the Canadian border, where Elias S. Sherman housed the "jolly and good natured" young man, who gratefully helped his host family with the cooking. Antonio told Sherman's seven-year-old son the dramatic stories of the "capture of the Amistad, and his escape through the kindness of friends." A night or two later, Antonio disappeared as mysteriously as he had appeared. He soon arrived in Montreal, where, a local abolitionist announced proudly, he is "now beyond the reach of all the slaveholders in the world." Captain Ferrer had branded Antonio's shoulder with a hot iron so that he might be known as his slave, but he was a slave no more. Thy prey, abolitionists told the slaveholders, "hath escaped thee."[25]

The "Mendian Exhibitions"

Without resources of their own, and hoping to capitalize on their fame, the *Amistad* Africans went on what might be called a "victory tour" in May 1841, to raise funds for their lodging and education. In November they went on a second tour to raise money for their repatriation. The Amistad Committee organized all events and drew heavily on abolitionist networks of cooperation and publicity. The "Mendi People" performed eight times on the first tour, in New York and Philadelphia, and at least sixteen times on the second, primarily in New England, with five meetings in Boston and usually single meetings in smaller towns such as Andover, Hampton, Haverhill, Northampton, Lowell, and Springfield, Massachusetts, and Nashua, New Hampshire. They also held farewell meetings in Hartford and Farmington, Connecticut, and two final meetings in New York just before they boarded the *Gentleman* to return to Sierra Leone on November 27, 1841. Dozens of newspapers around the nation covered one or more of these events.[26]

The venues varied from the Broadway Tabernacle, a hive of antislavery activity located at the corner of Houston and Thompson streets in New York, where four of the meetings were held to overflow crowds of as many as twenty-five hundred people, with many turned away, to the African Methodist Episcopal Zion Church on Church Street in New York and the large Melodeon Concert Hall in Boston, which hosted two meetings each. Organizers scheduled most of the events in churches. Turnout was extraordinary everywhere. Observers described the buzzing scenes as "crowded," "overflowing," and "immensely large." The crowds were made up of "blacks and whites, and every intermediate hue and color," by provocative design. In the disapproving words of the *New York Morning Herald*, "On one seat was a negro fellow, as black as the ace of spades, with a mulatto wife, and a couple of children, a shade whiter than the mother, and next to them, well dressed white ladies and gentlemen, all mingling together, regardless of the oder [sic] exhaled by their neighbours, and happy to receive their colored brethren and sisters on terms of perfect equality." Ticket prices were usually twenty-five cents. The funds raised would have amounted to roughly $4,000—a little more than $100,000 in 2012 dollars.[27]

A large part of the draw was the sheer celebrity of the people who had been in the news and in the larger circuits of American popular culture since late August 1839 and who had recently won their case before the highest tribunal in the land. Gallons of ink and paint and wax had been spent on the African freedom fighters. Not surprisingly, people wanted to see them in the flesh. When the *Amistad* Africans entered the Broadway Tabernacle on the very first exhibition, an excited tumult ensued: "So eager were the audience to see them, that they rose in great numbers, and many rushed towards the desk to get a nearer look of the blacks." Those people blocked the view of everyone else, who cried out, "Sit down there in front . . . we can't see through you."[28]

Cinqué in particular, the "hero of the *revolution*" as he was called by the *New Hampshire Sentinel*, was a special attraction. At the Marlboro Chapel in Boston, a youthful audience greeted him with "a tremendous shout of applause." When Lewis Tappan tried to translate what the hero had said in the Mende language, the young people "made so much noise that he could not succeed." At the Broadway Tabernacle, every time Cinqué rose to address the crowd, "great bursts of applause resounded from all parts of the house." The *Colored American* urged all to turn out to shake hands with the great man; "hundreds on hundreds" seized the opportunity.[29]

Early events, such as the first one at the Broadway Tabernacle, featured sixteen of the *Amistad* Africans, but the number slowly dropped over time, to twelve, then ten in later performances. Cinqué led the group into the hall, each person clutching an octavo Bible given them by the American Bible Society. They appeared happy and healthy, well dressed in American clothing, and they had a physical presence: they were "finely built, and possess great physical strength." A reporter for the abolitionist *Pennsylvania Freeman* noted that they had "intelligent countenances and dignified and manly bearing—showing that they never had their spirits broken by the yoke." They had survived their many incarcerations with their self-respect and political will intact.[30]

All events followed a basic pattern. A local minister led the assembled in prayer, then a member of the Amistad Committee, usually Lewis Tappan, provided a brief introduction, with a statement about the three main purposes of the event: "to show to the public the improvement which the Africans had made;—to excite an interest in a religious mission to Mendi, their country;—to raise money to defray the expense of supporting and educating them here, and of returning them to their country." The meetings lasted about two hours.[31]

Tappan introduced Sherman Booth, the main teacher of the *Amistad* Africans in jail and during their residence in Farmington following their liberation. Booth served as a sort of master of ceremonies for the event, providing "interesting facts relative to the improvement and conduct of his pupils" and making observations about Mende culture. He assisted as several of the *Amistad* Africans recounted their own personal histories—where they were from and how they were forced into Atlantic circuits of slavery. Booth then gave his charges Bible verses to recite as well as words and sentences to spell, in order to demonstrate their knowledge, and invited the audience to ask questions of Kale, Kinna, and Fuli, the best English-speakers. The queries usually concerned their understanding of Christianity and how they would use it when they returned to Africa. The Africans then sang a Christian hymn and a couple of "native songs." Kinna recounted for the audience, in English, their recent history as a prelude to the grand finale: Cinqué told, or perhaps it would be more accurate to say, *acted out* the story of the *Amistad* rebellion. He always spoke *in Mende*. The meeting concluded with another hymn, the audience joining the *Amistad* Africans in song.[32]

The heart of the program had emerged from an antislavery meeting in Bloomfield, Connecticut, attended by Kinna and Cinqué, in April 1841. They listened to the speakers with great interest, and at the end of the meeting were asked if they would like to address the group. Kinna "arose in a very dignified manner" and told their story. Abolitionist A. F. Williams noted that "before he sat down I saw many around me in tears." Cinqué then spoke for fifteen minutes in Mende, Kinna translating. The audience was dazzled by a talk that was "truly grand and sublime." After this meeting Sherman Booth advised Lewis Tappan that Kinna and Cinqué should speak in precisely these ways during the exhibitions. The rest of the program was likely the result of negotiation between the abolitionist organizers and the "Mendi People," some of whom did not originally embrace the idea of performing their "progress" before large audiences. Cinqué in particular could be a tough negotiator. Abolitionist George Day recalled him as a "turbulent fellow, hard to manage." Eventually the leader and his comrades agreed to do the tour, in large part because it was presented to them as a requirement for going home—they had to help raise the money for their return voyage. They said they would do it gladly.[33]

The content of the program on the tour reflected the nature of the alliance between the Africans and the American reformers as it had developed in jail prior to the Supreme Court ruling. The abolitionists wanted the freedmen to show the American public that they had become "civilized" Christians, which the hardworking students were willing to do as long as they could simultaneously enact and explain their own independent African identity. They sang their own songs and recited their own history in their own language, even if the audience could not always understand precisely what was being sung or said to them. Those attending the events would, in fact, understand something more important than specific words: they would see a sovereign political entity called the "Mendi People" in action.

Booth emphasized to the audience that the Africans came from an inland area of the continent where "a higher degree of civilization prevails . . . than was generally supposed." The condescension contained within it important facts. The Africans lived in towns and cities and engaged in manufacture, weaving in particular, examples of which he displayed, holding up a "number of specimens of cloth, in the shape of napkins . . . which the Africans had cut out and fringed after the African style." Members of the audience purchased these after the performance "at liberal prices." Booth added that the *Amistad* Africans were multiethnic and multilingual: they consisted of six different culture groups; one individual (probably Burna the younger) spoke Temne, Kono, Bullom, and Mende. Booth also commented on the moral characteristics of his students, who had worked hard and distinguished themselves by a "remarkable honesty." Booth then introduced the *Amistad* Africans, a few of whom spoke about their personal histories—where they were from, how they were enslaved, how they reached Lomboko—reciting the narratives they had told in court, in the newspapers, and through popular publications for many months now. Their individual life stories dramatized the human ordeal of slavery. Woven into these accounts were comments by the "Mendi People" that they wanted, more than anything else, to go home.[34]

Booth assigned individuals passages to read from the Bible, usually from the books of Matthew and John, and words to spell. Some of the performers were nervous and had mixed success. The engaged audience offered encouragement, cheering the readers and spellers no matter how they performed. Young Kale, already known as the correspondent of John Quincy Adams, was the star of this portion of the program, reading the longest passages and spelling the most difficult words and sentences. The people who had come ashore in the United States unable to "say a word for themselves," now read, spelled, spoke, and conversed in what they called the "Merika language."[35]

Booth then invited members of the audience to ask questions. Many concerned Christianity: How will you explain God to your countrymen in Africa? How do you know the Bible is God's truth? The Africans gave thoughtful, dutiful answers. Someone asked Kinna if he could "love his enemies" as a good Christian should. Kinna replied that he would pray to God to forgive his enemies their transgressions. Asked if the slaveholder José Ruiz "should come to Mendi, and should you meet him alone in the bushes, what would you do?" Kinna replied, "I let him *go*, I no touch *him*." But knowing the ways of slavers, he added, quickly and spontaneously, "But if him catch our children— him see what he catch!" This answer brought a "loud shout of laughter and applause from the crowded audience," who shared his perhaps unchristian "instinct of retaliation."[36]

The *Amistad* Africans then sang "If I Could Read My Title Clear," an old hymn that was a staple in the abolitionist musical pantheon. Based on lines of a poem by the antislavery poet William Cowper, the song combined the ideal of self-improvement by learning to read with the promise of a homestead in heaven, hinting that God's poor might eventually find justice and even the land they had lost to expropriation and enslavement—which is one reason why the song passed into the African American musical tradition. The *Amistad* Africans sang it well, "in perfect time," with their "sweet voices."[37]

If the singing of a Christian hymn brought forth universal approbation from the audience, the singing of African songs earned a mixed reaction. Led by Sessi, who sang in a "high pitch," the others joined in as a chorus, modulating their voices "from loud to soft expression" and from "rapid to slow movement," growing quiet at the end of one verse, then bursting forth in sound with the next. It was done "in wild and peculiar measure," said one listener. "It was wild and irregular, but not unpleasant," added another. Booth had advised Tappan not to list the native song on the program. In the actual performance he translated the first verse of the African song, an appeal to a deity, as "Help me today, and I will serve you to-morrow." This seemed to illustrate Kinna's claim that the Mende acknowledge a "Great Spirit," but they do not worship him. A second song was "an African welcome to newly arrived guests." It asked, in a soft, friendly, and melodious way, "Will you stay? Will you stay?" The chorus answered, "I love you, and will stay with you."[38]

The next part of the program featured the eighteen-year-old Kinna, an excellent student. The feminist abolitionist Lydia Maria Child, who attended the final meeting at the Broadway Tabernacle, thought Kinna "the most intelligent and interesting" of the entire group. He sometimes explained how education worked among his comrades, but more commonly he concentrated on the history of the "Mendi People" as he had done in the abolitionist meeting—"their condition in their own country, their being kidnapped, the sufferings of the middle passage, their stay at Havana, the transactions on board the Amistad, &c." This was a prelude to the event's dramatic climax.[39]

Cinqué was the "great man of the evening." When his comrades whispered to him, "he replied with a dignified bend of the head, not even turning his eyes." When he rose to speak, the crowd greeted him with stormy applause. He was the undoubted leader of the *Amistad* Africans, the symbol of their cause. He had played the leading role in the revolt, and he was the keeper of the common story about it, around which the *Amistad* Africans had built a new collective identity as the "Mendi People." Like Kinna, he recounted "a history of their capture" and the "various stages of their history" up to the present, but, as Lewis Tappan noted, he "related more minutely and graphically the occurrences on board the Amistad." The battle was the centerpiece of the warrior's story, as it would have been back in Mende country. He always addressed the audience in his native tongue.[40]

Knowing that Cinqué would give an active and energetic performance at one of the churches in Philadelphia, the organizers "thought prudent to remove the pitchers and tumblers that were on a table before him, lest he should sweep them off." He began his speech slowly, speaking with a "deep and powerful voice" and using "a restrained action of the right arm, which moved from his elbow downwards, and increased in frequency and rapidly as he progressed, till at length his whole frame was excited; he moved quickly from side to side—now addressing the audience, and now appealing to his countrymen, who would answer his appeals with a low guttural exclamation." Child wrote that his eloquence was "perfectly electrifying." He moved rapidly around the pulpit, "his eyes flashed, his tones were vehement, his motions graceful, and his gestures, though taught by nature, were in the highest style of dramatic art. He seemed to hold the hearts of his companions chained to the magic of his voice. During his narrative they ever and anon broke forth into spontaneous responses, with the greatest animation." He recalled the fateful moonless night aboard the *Amistad*.[41]

Precisely what Cinqué said about the rebellion is unknown, for no one in the numerous audiences translated his words for publication. Perhaps no one but James Covey could have done so. Yet Lewis Tappan, who saw and heard him deliver his speech numerous times and knew the story he told, provided a detailed summary. Cinqué described his origins in Mende country, how he was enslaved and sent to Fort Lomboko. He narrated the horrors of the Middle Passage aboard the *Teçora* and the dismal time he and his comrades spent in the barracoons of Havana. He recounted the harsh conditions of life on the *Amistad*, especially the struggle over water. He gave special emphasis to Celestino's threat and the collective decision to rise up in revolt.[42]

In one of the most dramatic moments of his speech, Cinqué reenacted how, with the help of Grabeau, "he freed himself from the irons on his wrists and ancles [*sic*], and from the chain on his neck. He then, with his own hands, wrested the irons from the limbs and necks of his countrymen." Like Child and everyone else who saw and heard Cinqué's account, Tappan was tremendously moved by the drama that unfolded before him: "It is not in my power to give an adequate description of Cinque when he showed how he did this and led his comrades to the conflict and achieved their freedom. In my younger years I saw [the great British actresses] Kemble and Siddons, and the representation of Othello, at Covent Garden, but no acting that I ever witnessed came near that to which I allude." What Cinqué had learned in the *bari* and its palavers outshone the brightest lights of the English stage.[43]

Other reviews of Cinqué's performance were equally glowing. One observer noted, no one "can hear him, and resist the conclusion that he is a master-spirit, and a great natural pastor." Another added, "so far as we could judge, without understanding his language, we should think him a natural and powerful orator. Indeed we could not resist the impression, that no ordinary mind was addressing us, though we were unable to sympathize fully with the sentiments expressed." Even the correspondent for the hostile *New York Morning Herald* was forced to admit that the speech represented "a high order of oratorical display." When Cinqué expressed gratitude for the solidarity of the abolitionists, he "shewed himself able also, to touch with a master's hand the finer chords of the human heart." He moved many to tears.[44]

After Cinqué finished his stirring speech, the organizers seized the moment to appeal to the audience for additional donations. They resumed, and concluded, the program with a singing of "Greenland's Icy Mountains," known as the "Missionary Hymn," written in 1819 by Reginald Heber, who would soon become the Anglican Bishop of Calcutta. The song reflected the missionary desire to spread the Gospel to the "earth's remotest nation," to India, Ceylon, and Africa, where "the heathen in his blindness bows down to wood and stone" rather than to the Christian "Redeemer, King, Creator." The *Amistad* Africans sang the hymn with "great propriety" and were joined in the final verse by the congregation. The song pointed the way to a Mende Mission in Africa. Once again "weeping eyes" looked on from the audience.[45]

Amid its many successes, the tour aroused controversy. Joseph Tracy, a Congregational minister from Vermont, complained that the tour events looked too much like a "show"—that is to say, a cheap popular entertainment unbecoming the lofty ideals of the Christian-based abolition movement. This may have been the issue in Springfield, Massachusetts, where an event was held in Town Hall rather than a local church as "as some of the Parish committee objected . . . fearing it would desecrate the place." The *New York Morning Herald* had snorted early on: "if the performances had been diversified with a few summersets, in which the negroes are very skillful, the entertainments would have been more complete, and more agreeable to the audience." A writer from Boston added, "if these men are carried about the country as *shows*, as they have been in one or two instances, they will be thoroughly spoiled for all missionary purposes, so that the necessity of being encumbered with them will be reason enough for not attempting a mission in Mendi." Even abolitionists complained that after the first tour Kinna was "puffed up," as "proud as Lucifer," Cinqué was demanding and difficult, and three people refused to work.[46]

Someone at the *Emancipator,* probably editor Joshua Leavitt, a member of the Amistad Committee, insisted that these critics had given an incorrect impression of the meetings, which "were calculated to remove prejudice—awaken sympathy—excite prayer, and stimulate Christian enterprise." He explained, "It was no part of the design to *show off* these Mendians for the purpose of indulging mere curiosity. Those who attended the examinations or exhibitions did not have such an impression, and it is *carping* to insinuate to the contrary." No matter what their intentions, the organizers continued to attract criticism.[47]

Around the same time, an unnamed "Native African" joined the fray and took it to a higher level. He published a scathing critique of the "Mendian Exhibitions" in the Hartford *Observer*. He maintained that the *Amistad* Africans "enter very reluctantly into the exercises of the meetings at which they are exhibited, and are evidently disgusted at the idea of being made puppet shows." Again, the point of reference was the "low" entertainment of popular culture. It is not clear whether the writer had actually talked to the *Amistad* Africans about the shows, but he had, he claimed, heard Cinqué say, in Hartford, "that he did not like to be carried to and from New York." The critic added that the rehearsal of the traumatic events aboard the *Amistad* "must have an unhappy effect upon the minds of these his brethren, &c." His harshest criticism was that the *Amistad* Africans did not appreciate being carried about "as a giraffe of their native plains." Clearly the writer thought the exhibitions were in poor taste. They had crossed the line from humanitarian event to a crass commercial effort to make money, degrading the *Amistad* Africans in the process.[48]

The Amistad Committee, who had organized the tour, was stung by the critique and felt compelled to respond. One of its members, in all likelihood Lewis Tappan, answered that the committee had considered all of the issues the critic had raised. He admitted that the

Amistad Africans initially resisted the idea of performing "before the public to exhibit their improvements," but once it was explained to them that the events were necessary "not only to raise funds for their support and education, but to raise a fund to aid in their return to their native land," they agreed to do them, and did them cheerfully, the organizer maintained. Yet Tappan's answer did not entirely satisfy even himself, for he continued to feel uneasy about the matter. At an exhibition in November, he apologized to the crowd "for having the duties of 'showman' devolve upon him."[49]

The social composition of the *Amistad* campaign and the larger abolitionist movement of which it was a central component was reflected in the decision to hold six meetings in fundamentally proletarian locations: one was held in a factory and another five were held in African American churches made up mostly of poor but extremely interested people. The *Amistad* Africans visited the cotton mills of the Boott Corporation in Lowell, Massachusetts, where they inspected the machinery and fabrics and met their fellow textile workers, who spontaneously and collectively gave $58.50 to the "Mendi Fund." Other venues included the Reverend Amos Beman's African Methodist Episcopal Church in Boston, where it was "impossible for all to get in" to see the program; the Reverend James Pennington's Talcott Street Church in Hartford, Connecticut; and the Reverend C. W. Gardner's "Colored" Presbyterian Church in Philadelphia. Pennington's flock contributed a hard-earned $8 to the *Amistad* cause, which may have been a greater portion of their collective income than any other church visited on the tours.[50]

The two meetings held at the African Methodist Episcopal Zion Church at Church and Leonard streets in New York seem to have had special qualities and meanings, for both the abolitionist organizers of the events, who were, for the most part, African American, and the "Mendi People." The church was a large one, into which a massive crowd consisting mostly of black people jammed themselves. A correspondent for the *New York Journal of Commerce* noted, "A more compact mass of human beings was perhaps never seen in a church," while another, for the *Colored American*, added, "We do not recollect of ever having seen a larger assemblage of our people upon any occasion."[51]

In the black churches, the content of the program changed. Tappan and Booth made briefer comments as the leaders of the black community—the Reverend Christopher Rush; the Reverend Timothy Eato (a founder of the New York African Society for Mutual Relief); and William P. Johnson—made the meeting their own. Dr. James McCune Smith, the first professionally trained African American physician in the United States, offered a series of resolutions, which were seconded by Charles B. Ray, publisher of the *Colored American* and a founder of the New York Vigilance Committee. Other leading black activists who took part in the resolutions were Philip A. Bell, George Downing, Junius C. Morel, the Reverend Theodore S. Wright, and John J. Zuille, all of whom were active in one way or another in the Underground Railroad.[52]

The resolutions affirmed the revolutionary implications of the *Amistad* rebellion and the larger struggle against slavery. The assembled resolved that in "their resistance against the captain and crew of the Amistad, . . . the Mendi people did no more than exercise that natural resistance against tyrannical oppression, which the consent of all ages of mankind, and the example of the American Revolution has sanctioned as both right and lawful." They also resolved that the *Amistad* case, based on a "just and righteous decision" by the Supreme Court, "has a powerful influence on the question of human rights, not only in this country, but throughout the world." It represented "the faint glimmering of a more auspicious morn, which will usher in that bright and glorious day, when the judges of our land, and men high in power, will be compelled by the force of reason and truth, to throw aside the bigotry and prejudice which too often soils the ermine of justice, and boldly declare that property in man cannot be held, wither by inheritance, purchase, or theft." The "Mendi People" embodied the revolutionary force of reason and truth.[53]

When it came time for the Africans to speak, James Covey joined the program. Having studied with missionaries in Freetown after his liberation from a slave ship in 1834, he "made an admirable address, which drew tears from nearly every eye, and the manner in which he quoted and illustrated Scripture was amazing, and would serve as quite a lesson to a learned divine." Covey also described his relationship with the *Amistad* Africans, especially their joy on meeting him and discovering that he was a Mende speaker. He and the other "Mende People" were, in the Zion Church, more expansive and "more interesting, we [the *Colored American*] thought, than at any of the previous meetings." Kinna greeted the audience with "you are my brethren, the same color as myself." He "seemed to feel himself at home, and his address was exceedingly concise, distinct and happy." A joyous pan-African mood animated the occasion.[54]

Mission to Africa

At the May 17 meeting at the African Methodist Episcopal Zion Church, the Reverend Theodore S. Wright resolved that "in connection with the ardent desire of these people to return to their own country to communicate the truths of the gospel, a favorable opportunity is providentially presented to the friends of missions, to unite for the evangelization of Africa." According to Lydia Maria Child, who attended the event, this resolution "rejoiced the hearts" of the African Americans who heard it, for it promised a "pure mission," in contrast to that of the detested American Colonization Society, which had "joined hands with the slaveholder" and accepted his money for the racist removal of black people to Africa. "Not a cent from those who bought or sold human beings would ever be allowed to pollute" the funds of what would become the Mende Mission. The project to establish a mission in southern Sierra Leone was gaining strength and momentum.[55]

The origins of the idea lay in conversations that took place in the New Haven jail. An anonymous visitor described an interaction between teacher Benjamin Griswold and the *Amistad* Africans in late November 1839. When Griswold suggested that the captives might go home to Mende country, they responded with joy. The teacher then pointed to himself and then to them, saying, "I, you, you, Mendi!"

They did not understand his meaning. Then he said, "You, me, Mendi, go!"—or, "I will go with you to Mende country." The Africans all agreed, yes, yes, but Griswold apparently thought the response tepid. He put on a stern look, rose from his seat, folded his arms, and walked away, indicating "neglect and ill-will." They in turn extended their arms "as if embracing some object of affection, clasping it to their bosom," insisting that they did want him to go. One man made a gesture of eating, promising that they would feed him in Africa, adding "you Merica man, *yandinguo, yandinguo*" (good, good). Griswold's students then gathered around him, warmly grasping and shaking his hand, to emphasize the truth of their pledge.[56]

Griswold reported this conversation to Lewis Tappan, who construed it as an African request for the teacher to go home with them, as he wrote in a letter to abolitionist John Scoble on January 20, 1840: "Mr. Benjamin Griswold of the Theological Seminary was . . . strongly solicited by the Africans to accompany them home." Tappan visited the captives in jail and asked "if they wished to have teachers go with them to Mendi." They answered yes. Tappan then asked, more specifically, if they wanted Griswold to go with them. The teacher then interjected his own question: "I asked them what they would do to me, if I should go?" Cinqué, Griswold reported, expressed "a willingness to do whatever I should wish & all assured me that they would take care of me & not let any one injure me." As the leader, Cinqué vowed to take responsibility for any missionaries who might accompany them to Mende country. Griswold trusted the response: "I think I have the certain confidence of these men & I believe they would defend & protect me at all hazards." In a war-torn land he would certainly need protection.[57]

It is not clear how the *Amistad* Africans thought about this proposition. Did they understand the difference between a teacher and a missionary, especially in a time when communications remained difficult? The two roles were in many respects inseparable to the Christian abolitionists as they ministered to pagans, but the Africans probably held a different view. Did they support the idea for instrumental and strategic reasons, because they thought the arrangement would increase the likelihood of their eventually returning home? Is this why Cinqué declared his willingness to do whatever Griswold wanted? If so, his judgment was sure, for in the coming months the prospect of establishing a mission in Sierra Leone would become a leading motivation of many associated with the *Amistad* case, including a significant number of African American Christians. The mission idea became part of the working misunderstanding in the alliance between the *Amistad* Africans and the abolitionist movement.

As Tappan and others continued to think about a mission, a new initiative came from another quarter of the abolitionist movement. As Farmington attorney and abolitionist John Hooker later recalled,

> The first public movement made with reference to doing something to carry the Gospel to Africa, and for the aid of colored people in America, was by the Rev. James W. C. Pennington, the colored pastor of the First Colored Congregational Church, Hartford, Conn., who called a meeting in his own church, May 5, 1841, at which a committee was appointed to call a general meeting of the friends of missions, which was held in Hartford, August 18, 1841, to consider the subject of missions to Africa. This was the origin of associated society work for Africa, and some of the antecedents of the American Missionary Association, which has done so great and good a work for the freedmen, Chinese, and Indians.[58]

At a large public meeting held at the Talcott Street Church ("1st Colored Congregational Church") in Hartford on May 5, 1841, Pennington expressed "his sense of the obligations of Christians, colored Christians, to do something in relation to carrying the gospel to Africa." Pennington challenged the members of his congregation, saying that unless "our whole people, and this church particularly" should do something, "I don't know but that I shall have to go myself." Many of the world's greatest enterprises had "small beginnings" like their own. Deacon James Mars spoke about the "providential arrival, defence and deliverance of the Mendi people of the Amistad," and hoped that young missionaries would accompany them home. The African Augustus W. Hanson, who had briefly served as a translator for the *Amistad* Africans, added that "the destiny of a portion of his brethren in the country, was ultimately connected with the regeneration of Africa." Those attending the meeting resolved that because "Divine Providence has now, in the case of the citizens of Mendi, (late Amistad captives,) most evidently opened a wide door for access to the heart of that country" and that "a mission should be established in the interior [of Africa]." They decided to hold a larger meeting in August 1841 to unite all evangelical groups in the cause.[59]

The call for the missionary convention was reiterated and publicized in the *Colored American* in July 1841. Although directed primarily at the African American community, the message was come one, come all: "Let the artist forsake his studio, and the merchant his counting-room; let the student forego the fascinations of literature, let the mechanic quit his workshop, and the husbandman his rural domicil and healthful occupation." It was of special importance that "something should be done by us for the land which our fathers loved as the land of their nativity." The call quoted Mark 16:15 as its mandate from God: "Go into all the world and preach the Gospel to every creature."[60]

Crisis

As the plans for a mission developed, the "Mendi People" were living in Farmington, under the care of abolitionist John Treadwell Norton, studying hard, cultivating fifteen acres of land, and hoping to go home. They still had no idea when, how, or if their ultimate goal would be achieved. The Amistad Committee had petitioned the administration of President John Tyler for the funds to pay their way back to their native lands, but the request had been unceremoniously denied as being without legal precedent. Getting thirty-six people across the Atlantic and back to their homelands was a complex and expensive proposition still under discussion in abolitionist circles. As the debate dragged on, several of the *Amistad* Africans began to despair.[61]

One of these was the normally bright and cheerful Foone, a rather short man at five feet two inches, with a "Herculean frame" and athleticism: he was an excellent swimmer. When news arrived from people knowledgeable about the Gallinas Coast that warfare might make it difficult for the "Mendi People" to find their way to their inland homes, the effect was demoralizing: "Nearly all of the Mendians became sad & became indifferent as to work or study," recalled A. F. Williams, who was helping to oversee their time in Farmington.

Foone in particular was hit hard by the news. He "lost all activity of body & mind," he became gloomy, and on several occasions he was seen weeping profusely. When asked what was the matter, he answered, *"He was thinking about his Mother."* He felt he would never see her again. When Foone said he was going to swim (and bathe) in the Farmington River on Thursday, August 7, several of his comrades tried to talk him out of it, saying it was the same day of the week on which Mr. Chamberlain had drowned and was therefore unlucky. Foone was determined to go and was finally joined by two teenage members of the group. Soon after he went in, he sank in ten to twelve feet of water. His smaller mates, panic-stricken, tried to save him but could not. They climbed out of the river and cried for help. Grabeau and Burna came running and dove into the water to search for Foone. After Burna surfaced with his friend's limp, muscular body in tow, a local doctor tried to revive him, without success.

The "Mendi People" were devastated by the death. Along with "a col'd man one of their best friends," Williams spent two full days with them and came to a sad conclusion: "I have no doubt Foone drowned himself." He had been seen weeping the morning of his death. He had expressed to Burna his fear of not living long enough to get home. Burna, ever the good shipmate, promised to "take care of his child" if he himself should return.

Williams discovered that most of the group no longer trusted the Americans to help them get home. They believed that they "should never see their Fathers & Mothers, Brothers & Sisters or their Children & that they will all die in America." Williams also came to understand a traditional West African spiritual belief: "They believe that when they die they will go immediately to Mendi & some of them think the sooner the better." It so happened that Foone was not the only person entertaining the thought. Sessi, who was something of an elder among the group, had considered jumping out of a tall tree, cutting his throat, or taking his life as Foone had done, in the Farmington River. Kinna, meantime, was keeping track of the deaths of his shipmates. He told Williams, "8 men die on board schooner, 6 die in New Haven, & now one die in Farmington." He added, "I don't know, I think all die pretty soon & we never see Mendi."

Williams did his best to explain the meaning of the correspondence about the Gallinas Coast, and reiterated, as sincerely as he could, the abolitionist commitment to have them "restored to the bosom of their families" as soon as possible. The news of Foone's death rippled through the antislavery community. Arrangements to go to Mende had to be made soon, lest others go back there by their own means, joining Foone and their own revered ancestors in spirit if not in flesh.

As the late summer gave way to their third fall in America, the remaining thirty-five *Amistad* Africans recovered their spirits, taking renewed interest in work and study. Williams was especially encouraged when several of the advanced students stepped up to teach while their regular instructor was away. But now a new problem approached—the chill of a New England winter. Cinqué complained, "Cold catch us all the time." He and his comrades had had enough: "We want to see no more snow. We no say this place no good, but we afraid of cold." This added greater urgency to the quest for both money and a plan to go home.[62]

A Mission Plan

Reverend Pennington opened the Hartford meeting of August 18–19, 1841, with a sermon to forty-three delegates from six states, including many of the leading black abolitionists of the day, some of them, like Pennington himself, formerly enslaved. They decided to form the Union

Missionary Society and to undertake work in Africa. They elected officers, most of them African American. (The absent Tappan was made an "auditor" but declined the post.) The entire proceedings were concluded with "delightful harmony." A special feature of the meeting was noted in the report of the *Colored American*: "Joseph Cinque and four of his countrymen were present, and enrolled their names as members of the Convention, which added much interest to the meeting." Once again the *Amistad* Africans actively shaped their own fate.[63]

Moved by the initiative, less than a week later the Amistad Committee decided officially that "when these Mendians return to their native land, it is desirable that a mission should be formed in that country, and that an appeal be made to the Christian public for funds for that object." The committee consciously separated itself from the American Colonization Society and its donations received of slaveholders, for such an association would be "contrary to the feelings and principles of a large majority of the donors to the Amistad fund, and of the friends of the liberated Africans." The committee issued a new appeal for funds, highlighting the "evangelization of Africa." What was presented to the public as an "Appeal on behalf of the Amistad Africans" was subtly mistitled: it was not an appeal for them alone, but rather a request to finance a new Christian abolitionist project, the Mende Mission.[64]

Cinqué and the "Mendi People" had their own idea about how this would work. "Their plan," wrote one of their teachers, William Raymond, in October 1841, was "for all to help together & somewhere in the vicinity of Cinque's town to settle down and commune a new town & persuade their friends to come & join them." This was the traditional way a Mende warrior settled a town, but this one would have a cultural twist: they "would adopt American dress & manners so far as may be." Out of gratitude for those who had worked so hard on their behalf, they would build a house for the teachers and a new community on an African model.[65]

Abolitionists had their own notion of a proper mission and it did not include leadership by a Mende warrior. They began to search for missionaries to carry the word of God to the heathens in Africa. Benjamin Griswold was the first and perhaps most likely choice, and indeed from January 1840 until November 1841 he seriously considered the prospect, but in the end he declined to go. Other candidates included the Quaker Joshua Coffin, who seemed a certain choice in September 1841: Tappan wrote that he had "been selected as the proper individual to go to Sierra Leone on this important mission." His abolitionist credentials consisted of "his noble daring, skill and perseverance in visiting Mississippi, and bringing off Isaac Wright, a New York colored young man, who had been sold into slavery by a Yankee Captain." This history, "together with his general intelligence, eminently qualify him for such an undertaking." Coffin would later write *An Account of some of the Principal Slave Insurrections, and others, which have occurred, or been attempted, in the United States and elsewhere, during the last two centuries*, published by the American Anti-Slavery Society, 1860, in which he included the *Amistad* rebellion. Yet in the end he would not accompany the *Amistad* insurrectionists to their homelands.[66]

The committee finally chose five missionaries. William Raymond and James Steele, both former students of Oberlin College and committed abolitionists, led the way. Raymond, who was twenty-six years old, had worked among self-emancipated Africans in Canada, taught the *Amistad* Africans in Farmington, and assisted on the final fundraising tour. The thirty-three-year-old Steele had studied at the Lane Theological Seminary in Cincinnati. The "Lane Rebel" came to Oberlin, where he edited and printed the *Oberlin Evangelist*. In 1840 he married the beautiful Frances Cochran, but she died, suddenly and unexpectedly, prompting the young widower, who was suffering a "deep depression," to sign on for the Mende Mission on short notice. The other three missionaries were Raymond's wife, Elizabeth, and Henry and Tamar Wilson, free people of color from Barbados now living in Hartford and members of Pennington's church. The Amistad Committee was now making preparations for the return of thirty-five Africans, with these five missionaries, to their native land.[67]

Reversing the Middle Passage

On Friday, November 26, the *Amistad* Africans boarded the barque *Gentleman*, commanded by a Captain Morris, in New York. They would spend the night on board, under conditions very different from the last time they had been on a deep-sea vessel. Lewis Tappan had arranged for the missionaries and the female passengers to be accommodated in the captain's cabin, the African men in steerage. An observer noted, "Nothing could exceed the delight manifested by the Mendians as they found themselves started on their way." The "Mendi People" continued to contribute to their own freedom struggle. Having raised through their tours more than enough money to pay for the voyage they were beginning, they now brought aboard food they themselves had produced, in their large truck patch in Farmington, for the voyage. The dream of going home was at hand.[68]

The day of departure brimmed with emotion. Lewis Tappan spoke on behalf of the Amistad Committee, Cinqué on behalf of the "Mendi People." The former wished Godspeed to the mission. He was pleased that the *Gentleman* was "a thorough temperance vessel, and takes neither rum nor powder to the Coast of Africa." Instead it brought free people and the word of God. The latter was his usual eloquent self, thanking his friends who had helped to make this historic day possible. He "pledged himself to take good care of them [the missionaries] in Mendi." When the time came for parting everyone embraced. As abolitionist A. F. Williams noted, "the young ladies wept, the young men wept, the old ladies wept, & the old men wept, & all right together." Some of the *Amistad* men sobbed aloud as tears streamed down their faces. Speaking "was out of the question, they could only express their deep regret at parting in a flood of tears." Tappan later wrote "The vessel sailed this morning with a fine breeze." His fondest hope was, "May the smiles of the Lord Jesus be upon it." Now began a second freedom voyage, this time with proper navigational knowledge and equipment on board.[69]

The Atlantic recrossing was uneventful. No one was hungry or thirsty, no one was whipped, no one raised arms, and no one died.

Everyone was in good health as the *Gentleman* neared the harbor of Freetown, Sierra Leone. While still at sea, Cinqué wrote to Lewis Tappan: "captain good—no touch Mendi People." To people who had had traumatic experiences under three violent ship captains—on the *Teçora* and the *Amistad*, and in the person of William Pendleton, brother of jailer Stanton—this was in itself excellent news. Kinna also wrote to Tappan, although with difficulty because of the rolling of the ship: "We have been on great water. Not any danger fell upon us."[70]

Yet all was not well aboard the *Gentleman*. The issue was, who was actually in charge of this repatriation. Was it the missionaries, William Raymond and James Steele? Or was it Cinqué and the "Mendi People"? Cinqué had no doubt about the matter. They were sailing to his country, where his local knowledge and connections would guide the mission. He wrote to Tappan, "big man" to "big man": "You give Cinque two white men and one colored man to go with Cinque." He would take them, first to Freetown, then to "my country." Once there, he would "make house and take care of white man." He still planned to create his own settlement in the way of the Mende warrior. Tappan, Raymond, and Steele, however, had other plans. The working misunderstanding that had been forged between the *Amistad* Africans and the American abolitionists was beginning to break down.

Return

The arrival of the *Gentleman*, full of people who had reversed the Middle Passage, was a big event and a rare one, in Freetown or anywhere else in West Africa. Those aboard the vessel understood just how unusual such returns were. Cinqué had written to President Tyler in October 1841: "When we are in Mendi we never hear such a thing as men taken away and carried to Cuba, and then return home again." Mende people made up the largest share of those shipped out of the Gallinas Coast in the 1830s, and one of the largest groups brought to Cuba on slavers and to Freetown on captured slavers. Kinna agreed, during the "Mendian Exhibition" tour in November: "I ask Mendi people, 'You ever know Mendi to come back to father and mother, when darkness-white man catch him?' They say, 'No, never come back. We never no more see him.'" Their comments revealed how widely known was the experience of enslavement and transatlantic shipment, and how unusual they knew their own return to be. They had waged a titanic struggle against the "darkness white men" for more than two years now, since they arrived at Pedro Blanco's factory in early 1839.[71]

The *Gentleman* was not the only vessel to arrive in Freetown harbor on January 13, 1842. It so happened that a British naval vessel was bringing to port a captured slave ship, to be anchored alongside several others already awaiting condemnation in the Court of Mixed Commission. It must have been an eerie sight, and smell, as the soon-to-be-repatriated *Amistad* Africans encountered at close quarters the kind of vessel on which their Atlantic saga of slavery and freedom began. The memory of their own earlier experience must have increased their elation at the prospects of freedom that now lay before them.[72]

Homecoming excitement was not theirs alone. Previous communications with political and religious officials in Freetown had prepared the way, and many port city residents had been alerted to the imminent return of the wayward sons. Among Freetown's forty thousand inhabitants, most of them Liberated Africans taken from captured slave ships, were thousands of "Kossa" or Mende people. "There are multitudes in this colony who speak their language—some of them being recaptured persons, and some having come here voluntarily," observed missionary James Steele. Cinqué's own brother Kindi fit both descriptions: liberated from a slave ship, he had returned home to Mende country, then chose to come back to work in Freetown. He and other relatives and friends of the *Amistad* Africans were among the hundred or so Mende people who greeted the arriving vessel.[73]

The arrival itself was a moment of truth for all of the transatlantic passengers, African and missionary alike. What would the *Amistad* Africans do when they were back among their own people, on African soil? The missionaries had hoped the Africans would go ashore singing a hymn, to show Christian discipline and announce new identities. The Africans had other ideas. They rushed ashore in an almost ecstatic state, encountering and embracing friends and family. Cinqué found his brother, Bartu found his "countrymen," and Grabeau, who apparently knew more people than most because of his wide travels as a merchant, found his kin and "old acquaintances." James Steele wrote that soon after going ashore, "The Mendians have found many of their friends and relatives." For some, joy swelled to delirium.[74]

Especially striking, upon their arrival, was the Africans' change in attitude to the Western clothing they wore. According to Raymond and Steele, "Some of them indicate a strong desire to lay aside their clothing and return to their former savage life of nakedness." As they stripped off the most outwardly visible aspects of their newly acquired "civilization," the missionaries saw a regression to heathenism and "licentiousness." They solemnly denounced it at the time and in their correspondence to abolitionists in America after their arrival. The desire of the Africans to revert to "country fashion" was a continual source of friction.[75]

The shedding of clothes was not simply a repudiation of the hard work the abolitionists had done in the New Haven jail to educate the Africans and to make them Christians. It laid bare the cultural conflict that had been there all along, which the abolitionists now began, for the first time, to understand. Snatched from Africa without a trace and now returning to Freetown, home to more than fifty displaced African nations and ethnicities, the *Amistad* Africans had to show everyone who they were. The easiest and most convincing way to do this was to show one's "country marks," the ritual scarifications by which the peoples of Freetown recognized and understood, cooperated and fought with, each other. Raymond and Steele saw that the Africans were eager to show "the *gree-gree* marks as they call them, which are found upon their bodies." The missionaries even came to see that these marks had deep cultural significance: "These are marks of honor, diplomas which have great meaning with them." Because the Africans kept the secrets of the Poro Society while they were in America, no one had understood that they received these marks "when they pass through certain branches of learning, or acquit themselves of feats of agility or danger, and are then entitled to change their names or adopt an addition to them, and not before." The cicatrices variously signified the young man's initiation, the warrior's conquest of fear and mastery of acrobatic maneuver, and the man's quest for ultimate spiritual knowledge. These people were Africans, and indeed they had acted as such throughout their ordeal—no matter that the white men could not understand them. Now they were Africans *back in Africa*. The configuration of historical forces had once again been changed by an oceanic voyage.[76]

This set of truths, and the geopolitical situation in which they emerged, shocked the missionaries. They were taken aback not only by their own "brethren," but by the Mende people they encountered in Freetown. They considered them "warlike" and "troublesome," noting that some had been involved in the slave trade. Indeed a large group of them had recently caused a whole new set of problems for the Sierra Leone colony when they armed themselves, moved into a region of Temne territory called "Aquia," and squatted on the fertile, unoccupied land to grow rice. They fought the Temne and they also fought each other.[77]

During the first few months in Sierra Leone, as the missionaries searched for land on which to build the mission, about two-thirds of the *Amistad* Africans deserted the project, a sure sign that the parties' ideas about the future had diverged. Some found work as wage laborers in Freetown or other towns nearby. Several of the men worked with Cinqué on a trading expedition by canoe to Bullom country, while several others labored, together, in a nearby town called Waterloo. In new material circumstances the "Mendi People" transformed themselves into work teams. Yet probably a majority of the *Amistad* Africans managed, in one way or another, to get home to the fathers and mothers, brothers and sisters, wives and children for whom they had longed. There is no way to be sure, for after leaving the mission most of them disappear from the historical record.[78]

For a few, there was no going home again. This was especially true for the children, who simply could not fend for themselves in an insecure world of warfare and continuing enslavement. Kagne, Teme, Margru, and Kale all stayed with the missionaries. They and several of the men signaled the seriousness of their cultural transformation by taking English/American names: Kagne became Charlotte; Teme, Maria; Margru, Sarah Kinson; and Kale, George Lewis. Steele wrote, "Those who remain are the very best of the company (except Cinque) and they had at their own request assumed English names, and thoroughly adopted civilized habits." Yet even several of those who stayed, oscillated into and out of the mission over time. Ba, who took the name David Brown, stayed at the mission for more than two years, although some of the time he lived apart, much to the disapproval of William Raymond, who eventually excommunicated him for living "in adultery" and for having "taken some of the articles belonging to the mission and put them into the hands of his paramour." Raymond had "required him to leave the woman or to leave me, and he chose the latter." He was, the missionary solemnly intoned, "no longer one of my people." The men who stayed basically became wage laborers at the mission, performing a variety of tasks in the crafts, agriculture, or manufacturing. They were "hard to manage" and they had fitful relationships to Christianity. Raymond himself believed that only Margru was a "true Christian."[79]

In April 1842, Fuli wrote to Lewis Tappan that he, Cinqué, Burna, and James Covey had gone to Bullom country to look for land for the mission, and added that "all the rest gone away to Mendi to see their parents." He thought many of them "will come again," but he was not certain, and he assured Tappan that God would punish them if they did not. Most apparently did not return, for within four months, by April 1842, the number of the "Mendi People" at the mission had dropped to ten men and the three little girls. The number remained the same twenty months later, after the mission had moved in 1843 to Kaw Mende, about halfway between Freetown and Monrovia. A few, like Kinna and Cinqué, came and went according to the vicissitudes of their lives, coming when they had fallen on hard times and needed assistance, going when familial or working commitments called.[80]

222 | The *Amistad* Rebellion

In the end, perhaps the single most important thing those free people called the *Amistad* Africans did upon returning to Sierra Leone was to strengthen the struggle against slavery, the pervasiveness of which was obvious to one and all. The missionaries and the Africans not only saw hundreds of slaves, some domestic, some meant for Atlantic markets, they also encountered people such as Thomas Caulker of the infamous mulatto slave-trading family that had originally "sold two of our company" into slavery, noted Steele. To make matters worse, some of the *Amistad* Africans got caught up in the wars that surrounded the slave trade. Three of them were caught in Fuli's hometown, Mperri, when it was attacked by the army of King Kissicummah. Fuli and Tsukama escaped, but Sa was killed.[81]

Homecoming

The human meaning of the return was perhaps most poignantly expressed when Burna encountered his mother after a long and mysterious absence of more than three years. Leaving early to catch the flood tide, Burna and James Steele arrived by canoe at the woman's small home of wattle and thatch while she was gathering wood in the bush. The men took a seat in the shade of orange trees to await her return. They soon heard a deep sigh and then a crash as the large bundle of wood the woman had carried upon her head fell to the ground. They caught sight of her as she came around the house, walking toward them slowly, with her hands raised to the level of her face, her "open palms presented." Tears streamed down her "furrowed face" and soon she began to moan "most piteously." The look on her face suggested that she had "seen one returned from the land of spirits." The son she had long thought dead now "sat in full view before her."[82]

She did not approach him directly. She walked around him, to the side from which she had first come, "continually weeping and moaning" and uttering exclamations in Gbandi. Burna himself did not move, but rather sat "like one petrified with the intensity of his feelings." He placed his elbow on his knee, his head in his hand, and he too began to weep.

Eventually his mother came to stand directly in front of him, whereupon her "maternal feelings" rushed upon her "at once like a torrent." She threw herself at his feet in the sand and embraced one of them, rolling from side to side, "still uttering her mournful cries," in seeming "perfect agony." The intensity of the moment was so great the missionary had to turn his face away. He wrote, "I had never before seen such an expression of nature's own feelings, unrestrained by art or refinement." After a considerable time, the mother began to sing the *seno*, a song of welcome, as she and her long-lost son joyously rubbed the palms of their right hands in the traditional way. The cold, ruthless hand of slavery had been replaced by the tender warmth of the mother's palm. Burna, known for his strong feeling for his shipmates, probably thought of Foone, who on the other side of the Atlantic had so dearly longed to see his own mother.[83]

Reverberations

During the fall of 1841, Madison Washington, a self-emancipated former slave from Virginia, knocked on the door of Robert Purvis in Philadelphia as he was on his way back south to assist his wife's escape from bondage. Washington had certainly come to the right place. Purvis had been active for several years in the Vigilance Committee and the Underground Railroad. He remembered, years later, "I was at that time in charge of the work of assisting fugitive slaves to escape." Purvis already knew Washington because he had helped him gain his freedom by getting to Canada two years earlier. Washington had since "opened correspondence with a young white man in the South," who had promised to ferry his wife away from her plantation and to bring her to an appointed place so that the two of them could then escape northward. Purvis did not like the plan. He had witnessed others undertake such dangerous labors of love and fail. He was sure that his visitor would be captured and reenslaved. Washington, however, was determined to carry on.[1]

By coincidence Washington arrived at the abolitionist's home on the very same day a painting was delivered: Nathaniel Jocelyn's portrait, "Sinque, the Hero of the Amistad," as Purvis called it. It so happened that Cinqué and twenty-one other *Amistad* Africans had also been in Purvis's large, majestic home on the northwest corner of Sixteenth and Mount Vernon streets, when they visited Philadelphia on their fund-raising tour of May 1841. (Cinqué later sent a message, *"Tell Mr. Purvis to send me my hat."*) Purvis had long been inspired by the *Amistad* struggle and in late 1840–early 1841, as the Supreme Court prepared to rule on the case, he commissioned Jocelyn to paint the portrait.[2]

Washington took a keen interest in the painting and the story behind it. When Purvis told him about Cinqué and his comrades, Washington "drank in every word and greatly admired the hero's courage and intelligence." Washington soon departed, headed southward in search of his wife, but he never returned, as he had hoped to do in retracing his steps toward Canada. Someone betrayed him, as Purvis had predicted (and only learned some years later). Washington was "captured while escaping with his wife." He was clapped into chains again and placed on board a domestic slave ship called the *Creole*, bound from Virginia to New Orleans in November 1841.[3]

As the *Creole* set sail, Washington remembered Cinqué's story—the courage and the intelligence, the plan and the victory. Working as a cook aboard the vessel, which allowed him easy communication with his shipmates, Washington began to organize. With eighteen others he rose up, killed a slave-trading agent, wounded the captain severely, seized control of the ship, and liberated a hundred and thirty fellow Africans and African Americans. Wary of trickery, Washington forced the mate to navigate the vessel to Nassau in the Bahama Islands, where the British had abolished slavery three years earlier. In Nassau harbor they met black boatmen and soldiers, who sympathized with the emancipation from below and took charge of the *Creole*, supporting the rebels and insuring their victory.[4]

Representatives of the federal government literally screamed bloody murder, just as those of Spain had done two years earlier, following the rebellion aboard the *Amistad*. They demanded the return of the slaves, who must, they insisted, be tried in the United States for rising up to kill their oppressors. U.S. officials self-righteously defended the institution of slavery and called for all property to be restored to its rightful owners. The British government, however, refused to comply with the order. Madison Washington and many of his comrades gained their freedom, boarded vessels bound hither and yon around the Atlantic, and left no further traces in the historical record.[5]

The reverberations of the *Amistad* rebellion were beginning to be felt in the wider world of Atlantic slavery, as predicted by abolitionist Henry C. Wright, an associate of William Lloyd Garrison. He foresaw that Purvis's painting, properly displayed, would confront slaveholders and their apologists with a powerful message about successful rebellion against bondage. To have it in a gallery would lead to discussions about slavery and the "inalienable" rights of man, and convert every set of visitors into an antislavery meeting.

Wright did not imagine a meeting of only two people, one of them a rebellious fugitive, nor could he have known that the painting would inspire radical action on another slave ship, which would result in both a collective self-emancipation and an international diplomatic row between the United States and Great Britain. The combination of the *Amistad* and *Creole* rebellions had a major impact on the antislavery struggle, pushing activists toward more militant rhetoric and practices. As Purvis concluded many years later, "And all this grew out of the inspiration caused by Madison Washington's sight of this little picture."[6]

To Africa

Three weeks after the *Creole* emancipation, the *Amistad* Africans made their way to Freetown and other parts of West Africa, including Vai, Temne, and Mende country. They carried a potent history with them, as revealed when William Raymond, James Steele, and several of the rebels met with local kings, chiefs, and big men, hoping to secure land for the Mende Mission and support for the spread of Christianity. The missionaries apparently had not considered that the makers of a successful revolt against slavery would not be welcomed by African rulers who owned and traded slaves. "Who are the friends of these men!" Steele asked of the repatriated African rebels. He answered, not the rulers of West African societies with whom they were meeting, but "principally the poor, the oppressed, and the slaves." They and their like were commoners, always in danger of being enslaved in war-torn Sierra Leone. Steele then used a telling comparison to explain his dilemma in using the *Amistad* Africans in his ministry: "Let me ask what reception the mutineers of the Creole would meet with if they should return with missionaries to Virginia?" It was a good question. The veterans of armed struggle against slavery on one side of the Atlantic did not advance his cause among slaveholders and slave-traders on the other. He would have been better off without them, he explained.[7]

The original action of the Africans aboard the *Amistad* and their hard work of cooperation with abolitionists while in jail in New Haven propelled the American antislavery struggle back to Africa, where it took its place alongside indigenous struggles—the escapes, marron-age, and revolts, including the Zawo War, in which enslaved people fought King Siaka and, after him, his son Crown Prince Mana, over many years beginning in the late 1820s. The Mende Mission, accord-ing to historian Joseph L. Yannielli, became "a transatlantic extension of the Underground Railroad," a new place of cooperation between (missionary) abolitionists and those seeking to escape or overthrow slavery. William Raymond and, later, George Thompson turned the mission into something of a "liberated zone," to which those fearing or escaping enslavement might flee.

Raymond himself liberated war captives, buying them from slave traders and settling them at the mission. Those who studied there gained protection as "no slave-trader will buy a man who speaks the English language." Thompson wrote that "the Mission was a 'City of Refuge' to the surrounding inhabitants, when fleeing from their burn-ing towns and deadly pursuers." As the news of the Mende Mission spread up and down the coast of Sierra Leone, and as far as two hun-dred miles inland through the travels of Cinqué and others, along with it spread the dramatic news of successful rebellion against slav-ery in America. The *Amistad* Africans had become transoceanic sym-bols of insurrection against bondage.[8]

In America

The *Amistad* rebellion also reverberated powerfully throughout the United States, primarily along two tracks: the first was American popular culture; the second was the American abolitionist movement. The result was to expand and radicalize the movement against slavery, to strengthen what we might call "abolitionism from below," involving the enslaved, the African American community more broadly, and those who wanted to take militant action to bring bondage to an end.

One of the remarkable features of the images of the *Amistad* rebellion in American popular culture was their anti-slavery message. *The Long, Low Black Schooner* made Cinqué its hero, recounting his personal history early in the drama in order to create sympathy in the audience. The play also highlighted the horrific Middle Passage, already made infamous by the abolitionist movement, by going below-decks to the hidden space where the "wretched slaves" lay jumbled together and where they would begin their conspiracy. The title page of the pamphlet, *A True History of the African Chief Jingua and his Comrades*, explained that

Liberty is Heaven born,
'Twas man that made the slave.

The author referred to the "unfortunate victims" of the slave trade, offered a sympathetic (if largely invented) biography of Cinqué, and chronicled the horrors of his enslavement, march to the coast, and Middle Passage. The popular *Book of Pirates* did likewise, using the testimony of Grabeau and Bau and other abolitionist sources, arguments, and sentiments to render a compassionate portrait of the *Amistad* Africans.[9]

The images of Cinqué produced by the *New York Sun* likewise played up the drama of the rebellion, gave voice to its leader, conveyed strong antislavery messages, and actively sought to enlist public sympathy for the rebels and their cause. The text that accompanied the images of Cinqué repeatedly expressed his insistence on "Death or

Liberty," echoing the revolutionary cry of Patrick Henry. Here was a bold, romantic, even swashbuckling hero who "dared for freedom" and justice. Significantly, the antislavery images and text produced by the *Sun* appeared, like *The Long, Low Black Schooner*, within a week of the arrival of the *Amistad* Africans in New London, *before* Lewis Tappan, Roger S. Baldwin, and other abolitionists had worked out the legal strategy to represent them as freedom fighters. Perhaps the elite abolitionists learned from the penny press, which in turn had learned from the rebels themselves.[10]

John Warner Barber, Sidney Moulthrop, and Amasa Hewins lent their artistic hands to the cause, dramatizing the insurrection as a struggle for freedom. Hewins likened Cinqué to George Washington. These artists moved beyond the individual portraits of Cinqué produced by the commercial artists of the *New York Sun* to depict, by popular engraving, wax figures, and monumental painting, images of collective armed struggle. Nathaniel Jocelyn returned to the individual hero in his serene, noble portrait. "This little picture" produced radical results in the *Creole* rebellion.

The popular images of the *Amistad* rebellion stood in sharp contrast not only to the racist antiabolitionist images of the day, but to longstanding paternalist depictions by abolitionists that suggested either grateful deference among supplicant slaves—"Am I Not a Man and a Brother?"—or their status as sentimentalized victims of atrocity. Sarah Grimké wrote that such images expressed the "speechless agony of the fettered slave." By contrast, the rebels of the *Amistad* appeared as powerful, independent actors, not as individuals acted upon by others. They inspired admiration, not condescension, benevolence, or pity. They certainly were not "helpless victims," as attorney Baldwin described them in court.[11]

Institutions of a rapidly commercializing popular culture transformed resistance into a commodity, to be consumed in playhouses, pamphlets, newspapers, galleries, and museums. The images humanized the rebels and evoked popular sympathy. Literary and visual evidence—Zemba Cinques the mutineer, Cinquez the leader of a "Piratical Gang of Negroes," Jingua the Barbary corsair, Cinqué as freedom fighter and revolutionary—whether on stage, in print, in wax, or in paint demonstrate the process at work. It did not go unnoticed, or uncriticized, at the time. Nathaniel Rogers, leader of the New Hampshire Anti-Slavery Society, noted in the *Herald of Freedom* the aggressive entry of the market into the *Amistad* case and remarked, "Our shameless people have made merchandise of the likeness of Cinque" and his comrades. Rogers resented the "wood-cut representation of the royal fellow," even though he thought it a good likeness. He considered it "effrontery" that artists had studied the "lion-like" face of the "African hero" to draw the image that was now for sale. He detested the intrusion of money and profits into the realm of high principle, but he may have underestimated how much "making merchandise" of resistance helped his cause.[12]

The popular images, and the celebrity that resulted from them, may help to account for a curious feature of the *Amistad* case. In a decade notorious for urban riots against African Americans and abolitionists—one of which, in 1834, resulted in an attack that moved from the Bowery Theatre to the home of Lewis Tappan—there was a signal lack of violence, or even the threat thereof, directed against the rebels or their supporters. Certainly the opportunities for such violence were many, whether in jail as the thousands filed through, or on New Haven Green, where the *Amistad* Africans routinely went for fresh air and acrobatics. Even more likely moments were May and November 1841, when the Africans went on their fund-raising tours, especially to New York and Philadelphia, where antiabolitionist mobs had been most violent. It is hard to be sure why something *did not happen*, but it may be that the positive images and the larger publicity surrounding the case protected the *Amistad* rebels and their supporters against the racist violence frequently used in this period by rampaging white mobs. A New York woman commented on the change: "some years ago," she explained to the British abolitionist Joseph Sturge, large public meetings like those featuring the *Amistad* Africans "would have excited the malignant passions of the multitude, and probably caused a popular outbreak." Now the gatherings caused "a display of benevolent interest among all classes."[13]

The antislavery movement in 1839 consisted of a rebellious and sometimes insurrectionary wing of enslaved people, a reform wing of various, quarreling, mostly white middle-class abolitionists, and a growing antislavery public that crossed many social and economic lines. The popular representations of the *Amistad* rebellion helped to connect the first two and to expand the third by circulating antislavery images and ideas into new social domains—into the streets, where boys hawked the images and newspapers to urban workers, and where the stories of the revolt would circulate to free and enslaved laborers alike; on the waterfront, where Vigilance Committees in New York and Philadelphia were already undertaking direct action in the struggle against slavery; into factories, where workers contributed to the defense campaign; and into African American churches, where interest in the case ran high. The *Amistad* rebellion helped to change the social composition of the antislavery movement.[14]

The popular nature of the movement to free the *Amistad* Africans is revealed by its funding. It has long been assumed that the wealthy Lewis Tappan bankrolled the entire operation, but his own punctilious accounts as treasurer of the Amistad Committee tell a different story. The committee itself made several public appeals for funds. A broad-based response from people of all classes sustained the long and uncertain struggle, and in the end made possible the free return to Africa.[15]

The *Amistad* Africans played the single largest role in raising money for their own education, lodging, and repatriation, earning $4,000 or more through the "Mendian Exhibitions" described in chapter 6. Antislavery groups, civic organizations, and churches made a range of smaller, still significant contributions. The Montpelier, Vermont, Female Anti-Slavery Society, for example, gave $10, while the "Color'd Citizens of Cincinnati" sent $90 to the Amistad Committee. Members of the Congregational Church of Farmington, Connecticut, where the Africans lived from the time of the Supreme Court ruling in March 1841 until their departure in late November, pledged an extraordinary $1,337.21 (more than $32,000 in 2012 dollars).[16]

A huge portion of the money came from thousands of private

citizens, most of them from the Northeast, who made modest contributions. Many of the donations were of twenty-five and fifty cents, sometimes combined into gifts of a dollar or two. Mary Ann Parker, "a mute," gave twenty-five cents. Former seaman and African American abolitionist J. B. Vashon of Pittsburgh sent $1. A nine-year-old boy in Oswego County, N.Y., gathered $2 from his Sunday School classmates and sent it in support of the cause. An anonymous "Anti-Abolitionist" gave $5. Henry Post and thirteen others who worked at an iron foundry on Elm Street in New York added $9.87. When the mother of missionary William Raymond heard the story of the *Amistad* Africans, she "out of a full heart exclaimed, 'I have no money to give, but I will give my son.'" In the same spirit Raymond himself added, "I go,— I have not money to give, but I give *myself*." To be sure, Tappan gave generously of his own fortune and time, but so did many others of limited means. After the federal government appealed the favorable ruling of January 1840 and extended the long jail sentence of the *Amistad* Africans, the *Emancipator* wondered, "Will the public sustain the defense?" Many voices, including those of the *Amistad* Africans themselves, answered with a determined yes.[17]

Another sign of the growth of the antislavery movement was the number and variety of people who supported the *Amistad* campaign while insisting that they were not abolitionists. The effects of the images in popular culture can be seen in a note accompanying a contribution to the Amistad Committee in early September 1839: "A friend of 'human rights,' but no Abolitionist, desires your acceptance of the enclosed *Five Dollars*, for the benefit of '*Joseph Cinquez*' and his African comrades, who nobly and righteously liberated themselves from illegal and involuntary bondage." The editor of the *New London Gazette* likewise announced, "We are no abolitionist, though we are an enemy to slavery in all its shapes." Soon thereafter a writer named "Humanitas," a "true friend" to the Africans, worried that abolitionists would "prejudice the public mind against them" and in the end get them all hanged. The movement in support of the *Amistad* Africans and the abolitionist movement were never identical.[18]

In an article of 1842 entitled "What the Mechanics of the Country

Think," Samuel Thompson of Poughkeepsie, New York, reported to Joshua Leavitt, editor of the *Emancipator*, that the *Amistad* and *Creole* rebellions had gained "general approval" among his fellow workers. He noted that "one gentleman of influence" expressed his hope at a public meeting that "every time they attempted to ship slaves to the south they would kill every individual concerned in the deed." The speaker then swore to God that "he was no abolitionist." The room full of mechanics "all endorsed his sentiment." As they made their resolution, merchants in Virginia worried that the murder of their employees was growing, and disrupting the domestic slave trade.[19]

Abolitionism itself evolved in the wake of the *Amistad* rebellion. As the mechanics suggested, the combination of the *Amistad* and *Creole* rebellions strengthened "abolitionism from below," especially its most militant parts. As historian Stanley Harrold has written, "The slave revolts aboard the *Amistad* in 1839 and the *Creole* in 1841 were central to the sense of crisis among abolitionists," to the growth of a more militant and confrontational approach, especially among African American activists, and to abolitionist "Addresses to the Slaves," which now acknowledged the agency of the enslaved and the great significance of resistance from below. The advance of this tendency from the time of the *Amistad* to the Civil War can be followed through the growing power and popularity of a phrase that originated with Lord Byron in *Childe Harold's Pilgrimage* (canto II, stanza 76) in 1818:

> *Hereditary Bondsmen! know ye not,*
> *Who would be free themselves must strike the first blow?*

In the stirring climax of a speech to the National Convention of Colored Citizens in Buffalo, New York, on August 16, 1843, the once-enslaved black abolitionist Henry Highland Garnet remembered "the immortal Joseph Cinque, the hero of the Amistad" and Madison Washington, "that bright star of freedom." They were "Noble men!" Their very names, "surrounded by a halo of glory," were an inspiration as Garnet proclaimed a coming jubilee that could be brought about only by resistance from below. "No oppressed people have ever secured their liberty without resistance," he thundered. Garnet repeated Cinqué's claim that it was better to "die freemen than live to be slaves." His message was clear: "Brethren, the time has come when you must act for yourselves. It is an old and true saying that, 'if hereditary bondmen would be free, they must themselves strike the blow.'"[20]

The phrase was popular among the most radical abolitionists. The street fighter David Ruggles had urged striking the first blow in 1841 in an open letter announcing a black antislavery convention, which itself had been partially inspired by the *Amistad* rebellion, and the militant Martin R. Delany would place it on the masthead of his journal *The Mystery*, which began publication in Pittsburgh in 1843. The phrase would achieve its classic expressions when John Brown and his fellow insurrectionists "struck the first blow" at Harper's Ferry in 1859, to inspire slave revolts throughout the South, and when Frederick Douglass's broadside *Men of Color, to Arms* used the phrase to encourage enlistment in the Union army in 1863. Advocated primarily by African American abolitionists in the aftermath of the *Amistad* and *Creole* rebellions, collective armed struggle against slavery had become the order of the day.[21]

The militant effects of the *Amistad* rebels were not simply a matter of rhetoric. In January 1840, in defiance of the law, abolitionists planned a jailbreak and escape for the Africans had the court ruling gone against them and the Van Buren administration tried to load the prisoners onto the *Grampus* for a quick return to Cuba before an appeal could be made. More significantly still, abolitionist John Treadwell Norton wrote to Lewis Tappan in February 1841 that "many here," around Farmington, were "ready forcibly to interfere" on behalf of these "brethren" should the Supreme Court rule against them. He added, "If such a step could ever be justified it would be in this case, where injustice is apparent at every step"—and where there existed broad popular support for the cause. As tensions rose, so did local militancy, wrote Norton two weeks later: "Many of the good friends here are very desirous to get the Africans out of the hands of the oppressors at once; and some are willing to go so far as to shoulder a Musket, or to turn *Mohawks* for this purpose." One armed struggle inspired another: rank-and-file abolitionists now wanted to free the very people who themselves had risen under arms to escape their oppressors. Norton and his "good friends" invoked the memory of the Boston Tea Party, in which people took the law into their own hands as "Mohawks" and tomahawked casks of tea, and thereby wrapped the *Amistad* struggle in the glorious mantle of the American Revolution.[22]

In an effort to restore the *Amistad* Africans to their rightful place in their own story, this history has returned to Henry Highland Garnet's observation about the relationship between white abolitionists and his own people of color, enslaved and free, in the nineteenth century: "They are our allies—Ours is the battle." But what extraordinary allies they were! Lewis Tappan may have been a condescending Christian paternalist, but his devotion to the Africans was exceptional, his commitment of time, energy, and money to the cause exemplary. Roger S. Baldwin and John Quincy Adams made singular contributions to the struggle, winning a tense and dramatic battle against the United States government before the Supreme Court. The role played by rank-and-file abolitionists such as Dwight Janes and the unnamed militants in Farmington who were prepared to pick up the gun must also be acknowledged. The alliance of the African insurrectionists and the American abolitionists was essential to the victory.

The reverberations of the *Amistad* rebellion in American popular culture made a difference to the outcome. The peculiarities of the case made it easier for Americans of all walks of life to embrace: the rebels of the *Amistad* were African, not African American, and the slaveholders were Cuban, not American. Yet here was a group of black men who had killed a white figure of authority during a fearful time of widespread slave revolt, and Americans showed a level of interest and support that was extraordinary by the standards of the day. The newspaper coverage, the play, the prints, the engravings, the paintings, the wax figures, the pamphlets, the long lines leading to the doors of the jail and the courtroom—all created a charged atmosphere in which district, circuit, and Supreme Court judges made what were, at the time and in retrospect, surprising decisions favorable to the *Amistad*

Africans and their claims of freedom. District court judge Andrew Judson was known to be hostile to people of color; one abolitionist called him "Andrew Sharka Judson" after the Vai king who ruled a slave-trading empire. A majority of the Supreme Court justices had southern backgrounds. All of the judges who issued written rulings on the case acknowledged the extraordinary degree of popular interest in the case.[23]

An unnamed abolitionist rightly gave credit for the *Amistad* victory to the antislavery movement, with "no thanks to the Supreme Court" and "No thanks to American law." Without the resolute efforts of the rebels, and without the translators, legal assistance, publicity, and fundraising provided by the abolitionists, the Supreme Court surely would have done the bidding of President Martin Van Buren and American slaveholders, delivering "these people up to the anacondas whose throats were stretched for them." The author concluded, "Thanks to God only, and to the anti-slavery movement, His instrumentality." Many regarded the *Amistad* victory as the movement's greatest achievement, as the *Anti-Slavery Standard* and the *Emancipator* announced: "Let those who ask what we have done, look at the generous excitement, the universal public sentiment, in behalf of the Amistad captives." Never had an American antislavery campaign been so popular—or so victorious. Winning, first on the deck of the *Amistad*, then in the chambers of the Supreme Court, changed everything.[24]

The victory in the *Amistad* case contributed to a broad set of changes in the complex and evolving struggle against slavery. It strengthened the "political" abolitionists, led by Arthur and Lewis Tappan, as well as African American and other increasingly militant activists, led by the likes of Henry Highland Garnet, Frederick Douglass, and Thomas Wentworth Higginson. John Brown noted that he was inspired by the "personal bravery" of "Cinques, of ever lasting memory." The victory also helped to broaden and integrate the movement, which became increasingly interracial after 1840. It answered the call for a "Black Warrior" or a "Black Spartacus" who could wage war against slavery and win, thereby expanding the pantheon of liberators, adding Cinqué and, by his example, Madison Washington, to the names of David

Walker, Toussaint Louverture, Denmark Vesey, and Nat Turner. It helped to establish and popularize the theme of legitimate armed self-defense by those seeking freedom. Although it would take years for these changes, and others, to create a revolutionary overthrow of the entire slave system, it may be said that in their own day and after, the *Amistad* rebels contributed to a shift in thinking about what might be possible in the war against slavery.[25]

A small band of multiethnic Africans aboard the *Amistad* succeeded against all odds. Enslaved in their homelands and shipped to Cuba, they planned and executed a revolt, worked their way to a "free country," cooperated and allied themselves with a small, much-despised group of antislavery activists, then overcame the opposition of two powerful governments, Spain and the United States, to gain their freedom and go home, accomplishing precisely what they had always wanted to do. They carried out the entire epic cycle of loss, quest, and recovery. From beginning to end, their odyssey was unprecedented in the annals of New World slavery.

Cinqué's revolution in miniature aboard the *Amistad* reverberated around the Atlantic. Abolitionist Henry C. Wright noted in April 1841 that "his name and his deeds have been heralded in every paper in this nation and in England—have stirred every heart and been the theme of every tongue." Even when confined in a prison for nineteen months, he and his comrades commanded debate and discussion in the United States, Spain, England, and France. Cinqué's name "will be the watchword of freedom to Africa and her enslaved sons throughout the world." Through a long, heroic struggle in which insurrectionists and reformers cooperated to create an interracial movement of great power, he had come to symbolize a revolutionary future, that "bright and glorious day" on which slavery would be overthrown.[26]

Mystery has long surrounded Lomboko, the slave-trading factory where the *Amistad* Africans were incarcerated and forced aboard the slave ship *Teçora* in mid-April 1839 for a death-filled middle passage to Cuba. This was partly a matter of design by its owner, Pedro Blanco. His trade was illegal and therefore the location was kept secret, for fear that the British anti-slave trade patrols would find and destroy the factory, as indeed they eventually did, in December 1840 and, upon its rebuilding, several times thereafter. Gruesome stories of floggings, starvation, and mass death circulated along the coast about what happened at the complex of buildings, mostly barracoons, at the mouth of the ever-shifting swampy and estuarial waters of the Kerefe River on the Gallinas Coast. In 1983, the leading historian of the region, Adam Jones, stated that Lomboko was now lost under water, its connection to the slave trade almost entirely forgotten, and the efforts of subsequent researchers to find the place failed. The mystery deepened when nearby Vai-Mende village elders, who knew about Lomboko, insisted that it has not withstood the ravages of nature and time and could no longer be found.

In May 2013 I traveled to Sierra Leone to look for Lomboko and other connections to the *Amistad* rebellion, especially living local memory of the uprising and the people who made it. The trip was originally suggested by Konrad Tuchscherer, a specialist in Sierra Leone's history who teaches at St. John's University. We recruited our mutual friend Philip Misevich, also a historian of Sierra Leone at St. John's, and Taziff Koroma, lecturer in linguistics at Fourah Bay College in Freetown, who would be our translator and cultural broker. We were accompanied by the documentary filmmaker Tony Buba and his crew: Jan McMannis, John Rice, and Idriss Kpange (Concept Multimedia, Freetown). As we embarked I realized I was finally answering a question posed to me a couple years earlier by Geri Augusto of Brown University, who studies the transit of knowledge systems in the African diaspora: "When are you going to Sierra Leone to learn the part of the story only the elders there know?"

We left Freetown for the far southern Kerefe/Gallinas region, one of the poorest and most remote parts of one of the world's most poverty-stricken countries. Underdeveloped in the eighteenth and nineteenth centuries by the European slave trade and a subsequent British imperialism that sucked vast quantities of laboring bodies and glittering diamonds out of the country, Sierra Leone has been weakened further in the late twentieth century by a long, bloody civil war that left more than fifty thousand dead and hundreds of thousands with amputated limbs. Much of the fighting took place in the southern and eastern parts of the country. We traveled on roads cratered by bombs meant to hinder the deployment of troops more than a decade earlier.

We stopped in several villages near the historic location of Lomboko to ask about the history and whereabouts of the mysterious place. In Gendema—once the Vai King Siaka's thriving, opulent seat of empire, now a tiny village of abject poverty—Town Chief Mamadou Massaquoi told us in no uncertain terms that Lomboko no longer existed. (A descendent of King Siaka's royal line, Mamadou, when questioned, answered that he knew nothing of the *Amistad* captives and added, why should he? They were "just slaves" and therefore of no concern.) Several other chiefs and elders likewise told us Lomboko was lost and that we would not find it. Each time we heard these words Konrad's face expressed ever greater determination to find the place.

After two long, hot days of interviewing we were weary and discouraged. We began to head north out of the region. Yet Taziff—a small, energetic Mende man always in motion and always talking—was not willing to admit defeat. He instructed our driver to pull over as we entered the village of Funehun. He jumped out and strolled around a local market to ask if anyone there knew anything of Lomboko. A young man stepped forward to say that the people of a remote fishing village called Toko, about seven miles downriver, would know. There was no Toko on our detailed map, but off we went, on a "road" that would more aptly be described as a bush path. The Funehun man rode with us to make sure we found it.

With thick verdant growth scratching our windows and our heads bobbing as we negotiated one deep, water-filled rut after another, we finally emerged into a clearing with seven or eight small huts made of mud, wattle, and thatch, more or less identical to the homes the *Amistad* Africans would have inhabited in the 1830s. Taziff approached a stout, older man, Vandi Massaquoi, and asked if he had ever heard of Lomboko. The man answered clearly and decisively: "Yes, and I know where it is." He then gestured at his two teenage sons standing nearby and said, "These boys are fishermen on the river. They know where Lomboko is. They have seen the remains of old buildings there." An electrical current shot through our group, instantly transforming disappointment into hope. Can you take us there, asked Taziff, adding for emphasis, the old Malcolm X phrase, in English, "by any means necessary." The man smiled and said he could. We walked with him and his sons down a two-mile path through the bush that led to the Kerefe River. Along the way we met Toko's town chief, a young, thin, wiry-strong man who was returning to the village from work on the river. He joined our group and reversed course.

Three old dugout canoes awaited us at the end of the path, two of which did not appear up to the task. One had been used as a container for the distillation of palm oil; the oil itself had been skimmed off, leaving a canoe full of strangely sweet-smelling orange water. The second canoe was missing part of its bow. The fishermen flew into action, bailing and cleaning, and in fifteen minutes we were ready to board. The three largest members of our group (Phil, Konrad, and me) lost their heads in the enthusiasm of the moment and we all got into the same canoe. We soon pushed off into the lazy green river, beginning what was, without a doubt, the eeriest, most surreal journey of my life. The town chief and the two young fishermen propelled us along with hand-carved paddles, expertly navigating an endless maze of mangrove swamps, dodging the wild profusion of tall, white, grainy, ropy roots that stand high out of the water. Lush vegetation bloomed around us as fish skittered in the water here and there. Crocodiles and even the more dangerous hippopotamus inhabited the swampy river, but we were too full of purpose to consider them. Fifteen minutes into an hour's ride our overburdened canoe began to take on water, but the canoe man was undaunted. He stopped, bailed out the water with a wooden bowl, and in no time had us back on our way. He zigzagged among the mangrove roots and finally steered us through an eighteen-inch opening between two dense, tangled thickets. Ahead of us lay a sandy beach at what seemed to be the very end of the earth. Here was Lomboko, or at least part of it. No wonder no one else had ever found it.

We had arrived on an island called Kabuti, which in Vai means "Beyond the bush strawberry tree." The island was shown on a British admiralty chart of 1839 as "Kambating" (see the map on page four of the illustration insert). The island was one part of the Lomboko complex, perhaps the only surviving part. On the chart are drawn dark rectangles to represent "buildings," barracoons, slave holding pens. Pedro Blanco held the enslaved in this isolated place, surrounded by crocodiles, pending transfer by canoe to the main port across the river, where he and his mostly Kru workers loaded the slave ships with thousands of people, including those who would end up on the *Amistad*.

When we disembarked and went ashore, we quickly discovered that Vandi not only knew the location of the place, he knew a tremendous amount about it. His family had lived in Toko for generations, and he had heard stories about Lomboko from his forebears. Their source of knowledge was local lore and the printed word. Vandi's grandfather had read a missionary's account of the *Amistad* case, perhaps written by the American abolitionist George Thompson, who lived in Mende country for several years in the nineteenth century.

Vandi's first point to us was that the beach had been built by slave labor: no other island in the area—and there are many—has a beach. Pedro Blanco had it built as a landing place for the canoes of local traders who brought to the island the slaves he would purchase. We had unwittingly reenacted the very process of arrival on the island by which the enslaved of southern Sierra Leone moved from their native continent into Atlantic orbits, toward Brazil, Cuba, and the United States, mediated by this liminal place called Lomboko. I imagined the manacled captives of "slavery times," as people here call it, stepping out of the canoes and trudging ashore amid the taunts and shoves of slavers and soldiers. Wherever they had come from must have seemed far away once they had arrived in this desolate, forbidding place.

Toko's town chief, who had so deftly paddled one of the canoes, now wielded his machete with equal grace, slashing a path that enabled us to walk inland from the beach, through overgrown vines, brush, and thin, scruffy trees. Immediately we saw the chilling sight of raised soil and rotted organic material that would have been the wooden foundations of the barracoons. Twenty or thirty feet farther along Vandi announced that this was the place where Pedro Blanco had set up a canopy, as protection against the sun, beneath which he conducted business with King Siaka, guns for slaves. (He added that rum, wine, tobacco, and salt were also traded from this spot.) Blanco's European employees trained Siaka's soldiers in the use of "the white man's gun," which became the basis of the king's rapidly growing power throughout the region. Vandi emphasized that Blanco did not stay on the island but rather at another part of the Lomboko complex, near what is today the village of Mina. He also noted that the Spanish slave trader at some point left Lomboko and had not died there.

Taziff asked Vandi if he had heard any stories about the people of the *Amistad* at Lomboko. He said he had and that they had all been held in this place. He added that Sengbe (as Cinqué is called in Sierra Leone) was known as a great warrior and upon capture had begged to be put to death, as befit an elite fighter. For some unknown reason, perhaps gratuitous insult and degradation, his captors refused and brought him to the island as a slave. Vandi explained that he wasted no time in organizing an uprising, which was suppressed but prompted the slavers to separate him from all of the other bondsmen to limit resistance. They took him to another island and held him in solitary confinement until it was time to load him and the others on a slave ship.

We were stunned by Vandi's knowledge, which was confirmed by or consistent with primary and archival evidence to which he had no access. He knew much about Pedro Blanco and King Siaka and he knew well the practices of the slave trade. His portrait of Cinqué as warrior and fomenter of rebellion on the island was consistent with what we know of his role in revolts aboard the *Teçora* and on the *Amistad*. Even the response of the Lomboko slavers paralleled what navy officers and jailers in Connecticut did when they held the *Amistad* Africans captive: both groups separated the leader from his comrades in fear of his power to inspire revolt. Of course we will not know for sure that the island was part of Lomboko until archaeologists analyze its material culture, but Vandi's detailed account of place and time past was impressive and convincing.

Vandi also solved a nagging problem for us: why no one else we talked to had known the whereabouts of Lomboko—and why other researchers had failed to find it. Several people in nearby villages, even King Siaka's own Gendema, said Lomboko was either destroyed or underwater; no one knew where any part of it could be found. Vandi explained that a redrawing of the lines of the chiefdoms in the Pujehun District of southern Sierra Leone had resulted in the placement of Lomboko outside the Gallinas-Peri Chiefdom, where it had long resided, into the Kpaka-Mende Chiefdom, whose people were now its official overseers. This is why no one else we visited knew about Lomboko while Vandi and the people of Toko did; the link to Lomboko had vanished when a government map was redrawn. We too might have missed it entirely, had not Taziff discovered the strategic connection.

As we returned by canoe to Toko at twilight, the mysterious Magritte-like time of evening when the landscape is darker than the luminous deep blue sky above, it seemed entirely fitting that our successful search for Lomboko and its history from below should have depended on the knowledge of fishermen who worked on the Kerefe River. Lomboko was now part of their commons, which they knew intimately, like no one else, because their survival depended on it. They had carried us to a dark part of the past, a small, isolated place that had historic implications for the peoples of the four continents that surround the Atlantic.

———

Our other main goal, in addition to finding Lomboko, was to visit villages in southern and eastern Sierra Leone and to talk with elders about the memory and meaning of the *Amistad* rebellion and the people who made it. Setting out from Freetown we visited ten villages and towns: Bangorma, Blama, Bumbe, two villages with the name Dzhopoahun, Folu, Gendema, Kandowalu, Jojoima, and Mano. Several of these places had been the homes of various *Amistad* veterans before their enslavement. This we knew because they had given their village or town of origin and named their local chief or king when asked by Americans about their lives back in Africa. Were any of these people who played historic roles in the struggle against slavery remembered back home, and if so, how?

The eastern Mende village Folu was promising from the outset. Not one but two of the *Amistad* Africans, Grabeau and Fabanna, came from there, and both apparently returned, Fabanna briefly, before he went back to live at the Mende Mission, and Grabeau permanently as far as we know. Both had been men of significance in the village before their enslavement: Grabeau was a member of a rich and powerful family (although poor himself), and he was also apparently a high-ranking member of the Poro Society. Fabanna was a self-described "big man." These facts increased the likelihood that one or the other might be remembered in Folu.

But were we in the right place? There are several villages in Sierra Leone called Folu. We chose the one south and more or less equidistant from the towns Segbwema and Daru, north of the Gola Hills, about twenty miles from the Liberian border. It seemed to be an appropriate distance from the Gallinas Coast, as both Grabeau and

Fabanna had traveled a long way to Pedro Blanco's factory. Yet such information about travel could be deceiving: an enslaved person might be sold from one trader to another, then work for a time before being sold to someone closer to the coast and the dreaded Lomboko. This Folu seemed our best bet.

When we arrived we noticed right away that the village had an unusual, and quite beautiful, physical configuration. It was surrounded by tall cottonwood trees that would have served lookouts and self-defense well. It was, we later confirmed, founded as a palisaded war village to protect against the slaving expeditions of hostile warriors. In contrast to Gendema, the small, impoverished village that had once been King Siaka's rich imperial headquarters, the once-raided Folu was now prosperous, boasting about six hundred people divided into four sections, each with its own head man, rice fields, and a lively cultural life.

After Taziff spoke to the town chief, Asumana Samai, requesting that he summon the elders with the longest and best memories, we assembled at the home of the man who was said to be the wisest and most learned in town: Pa Brima Kallon. The building was made of old mud bricks but the roof was new, zinc rather than thatch, a sign of village prosperity. Pa Brima was "the father" of the settlement, and had long been a leader; his son was now the paramount chief of the entire region. Dressed in a loose-fitting long brown robe, he greeted us with a kindly regal smile from his hammock as his chickens clucked underfoot. Cataracts could not dim the sparkle of his eyes. Another five elders and several important younger people joined us on the long porch. Dozens of villagers—especially older men and women, and younger women with their children, those not working in the rice fields on this hot, fly-filled late afternoon—gathered around, keenly interested in whatever was going to happen.

After Muslim prayers blessed our undertaking, we introduced ourselves. John C. Kallon spoke for the village, saying that he was a teacher and that "he was born here, and this was his home." He then indicated the presence of important people beginning with Chief Samai. He noted the presence of elders Sheku Kallon and Mama

Fodie Haloa Kallon, "the oldest lady in this town; they call her 'the mother.'" John then pointed to Imam Fofie O. Konneh, head man Bockarie Kargoma, and Imam and teacher Yankuba I. Konneh. We gave a brief explanation of our purpose in visiting Folu, but rather than pose leading questions, we decided to ask about the history of the village. Pa Brima's first words were "The one who founded this town is . . . Chief Bohbohwa."

I knew immediately that we were in the right place. Grabeau and Fabanna had both mentioned that their king was a man named "Bawbaw," noting that he lived in the village. (Taziff later explained that "Bohbohwa" means "Big Bohboh" or "Bohbohwa the Great," as the founder is now remembered.) Pa Brima continued, detailing the settlement of the village amid the slaving wars. The early village warriors, he explained, did not capture slaves to sell to the likes of Pedro Blanco, but rather kept them as laborers, domestic slaves, to expand the population and strengthen the village against attack. By the time Pa Brima finished his history of Folu, the crowd of villagers surrounding us had grown deep, everyone listening with quiet, intense concentration.

At this point, with Taziff's assistance, I told the assembled the basic story of the *Amistad* rebellion—that forty-nine men and four children, all from southern and eastern Sierra Leone, had been enslaved and shipped from Lomboko to Havana, where they were sold and reshipped aboard the *Amistad*. They rose up, killed the captain of the vessel, and sailed to the United States, where, in a struggle of great international importance, they won their freedom and eventual repatriation to Sierra Leone. Two of those men came from this very village, I said to a hushed crowd. These men had explained in America that they were from "Fulu" and that their king was named "Bawbaw." This information created a rush of excited murmurs. I will never forget the beaming pride on Pa Brima's face.

Amid the excitement, we encountered the same dilemma we faced in every village we visited: the names the *Amistad* Africans were known by in the United States were poor approximations of their actual names. The names had been written down by Americans who had no knowledge of Mende or any other West African language; most of them found West African words strange, incomprehensible, and unpronounceable. Names were therefore usually mangled when rendered in English. So in Folu, as elsewhere, we had to play a communal game: what could have been the real names of these people the Americans called "Grabeau" and "Fabanna"?

The collective wisdom (confirmed by Taziff, who is an expert on these matters) was that "Grabeau" was actually Gilabau, which means "let this one be saved," poignantly suggesting death among the family's previously born children. This conclusion came close to a phonetic spelling of the name (Gi-la-ba-ru) offered by a man who visited the *Amistad* Africans in jail. "Fabanna" was apparently Faba, with emphasis on the second syllable. Yet we could not seem to get any further in the discussion of either man, even though their proper Mende names had been deduced; they stirred no memories. The elders repeated the names and shook their heads, no. Nothing was coming back to them. We were in the right place but we had hit a dead end.

I began to tell the villagers what I knew of each man in the hope of unlocking the memory of a story. As I talked about Gilabau I saw John tap his temple with his finger, indicating that he remembered something relevant to the discussion. He said that his father had narrated much history to him so that he would preserve it. This included a story of a man named "Johnny," who during "slavery times" was sent far away, he did not know where, but when he returned to the village he spoke "broken English." The community therefore gave him a new English name, Johnny. He did not know the man's previous name. As soon as John spoke the new name, several others on the porch blurted out "Johnny!" more or less simultaneously, indicating they too had heard stories about the man. Suddenly we had something to work with.

Johnny was a traveling merchant who knew many languages, explained John. According to the documentary record, Gilabau was indeed a mobile trader who sold camwood and ivory over a broad expanse that included Gola country and Liberia, both near the village of Folu. We know from other sources that Gilabau spoke Mende, Vai,

Kono, and Kissi. Johnny was known for his courage as a warrior and for his ability to bring people together, said Yankuba Konneh. Gilabau was a warrior, second in command after Cinqué while the group was in America. He would have been deeply involved in keeping the "Mende people" together during their long and trying ordeal. Johnny was a weaver, added Pa Brima. Gilabau, like several of the *Amistad* men, had also been a weaver.

As the villagers drew their portrait of Johnny, I announced that I had a picture of Gilabau, who may have been the man remembered in the village. I opened the book (page eight of the illustration insert) and pointed to a reproduction of the pencil sketch done in New Haven jail by the American artist William H. Townsend. People rushed to gather 'round, a few (in this village without regular electricity or running water) holding cell phones aloft to take photos of the image. I circulated the illustration, asking if anyone in the village resembled this man. Several did, I was told. Somehow the image made the history real in ways that words could not.

Soon afterward Fodie Haloa Kallon, who sat on the porch in a colorful print dress and a white turban, dropped a stunning new fact into the conversation: "Johnny was my grandfather," she announced quietly. Pa Brima smiled; he had known all along. Could it be true? Gilabau had probably been in his twenties around 1840, which means that he may have lived another fifty years or more after his return. If he fathered a child later in life, that child may have had a child of his or her own in the early twentieth century. Had we found a descendant of one of the *Amistad* Africans? It was impossible to be sure, but it certainly seems possible. As soon as the village mother declared her kinship, the ritual adoption was complete. Gilabau was Johnny and he was now their "ancestor," part of their village history. He was theirs; they were convinced. The mood was happy, animated, exultant.

I suddenly realized why the discussion meant so much to these Folu villagers. Ancestors—whose spirits are called *ndebla*—are crucial to the cosmology of Mende people: they are revered living presences who inhabit the landscape, who must be approached and appealed to by rituals, and who must be kept happy if one is to prosper in the present and future. We had, without fully realizing it, brought an ancestor home to Folu—or at the very least we had brought home his story, which gave new life to his memory. Gilabau was being received and welcomed with joy.

Soon a man stood up and sounded a discordant note: "Did you say our ancestor killed a white man?" Yes, he helped to kill the Cuban slave trader Ramón Ferrer, captain of the *Amistad*. The man wondered, with a grave look on his face amid a sudden and heavy collective silence, "Will we get in trouble for that?" In that instant the ghost of slavery, race, and colonialism hovered above the village. I assured the man, and everyone else, that no one in the village would get in trouble. The information they had given us would be used only for the purposes of research and teaching. The man smiled as relieved laughter broke out all around and the festive mood returned. Another man was a bit embarrassed by the expression of worry and reminded everyone that they were descended from brave warriors.

As the formal meeting broke up, we talked with the elders and villagers who were eager to follow up on points discussed earlier. Imam Fofie Konneh emphasized the local Gola influence on the development of gymnastics in Poro training, the likes of which Gilabau/ Johnny had mastered. John asked if I could send photographs of the portrait of their ancestor, as well as a copy of my book for the school. Pa Brima wanted us to see the nearby grave of Bohbohwa, the great warrior-founder, the very man Gilabau and Faba acknowledged as their king. In a final show of hospitality, the town chief assembled a group of bright-eyed children in purple school uniforms to sing for us. Soon we departed Folu for the next village, in search of more local history of the *Amistad* rebels.

———

I came home from Sierra Leone with a deepened understanding of my own book. Our group had talked to fishermen, elders, chiefs, and teachers, and to professors, truck drivers, playwrights, and students, and learned from all of them. I learned anew an old truth: a book is never finished. I tested my ideas among people who knew vastly more about the cultures of Sierra Leone than I ever could, and I gained new understandings in the process—of the physical environment, the ecologies, and the life ways of an ancient land. Fishermen on the Kerefe River and commoners from the village of Folu not only contributed their own knowledge to my project, they reaffirmed one of the guiding principles of history from below: anyone who would understand how working people make history must use all available means of research, including fieldwork, and explore all possible sources, some of which are living and far from the traditional archive.

Perhaps most important of all, my conversations with the people of contemporary Sierra Leone suggested how much we still have to learn about the *Amistad* rebellion and indeed about the entire African background to the history of the Americas. The sometimes painful but always deeply human links of Atlantic history live on, showing how an isolated island and a small village thousands of miles away were, and remain today, part of American history.

ACKNOWLEDGMENTS

The origins of this book lay in the work I did on *The Slave Ship: A Human History*, published by Viking Penguin in 2007. That book, about a malevolent machine central to an entire phase of modern history, was hard to write. I studied how enslaved Africans made many a heroic revolt under extreme circumstances, only to fail repeatedly and to suffer, in the aftermath, almost unimaginable torture, terror, and death at the hands of the slaver's captain. In such a grisly context, the *Amistad* Rebellion stood out as one of the very few successful uprisings ever to take place aboard a slaving vessel. I wanted to know how it happened, this hopeful counterpoint to a gruesome history.

Because this book is a companion to *The Slave Ship*, I wish to acknowledge once again the many people and institutions that helped me in the earlier work. To their names I gratefully add many others. I thank the staffs at the Stanley-Whitman House in Farmington, Connecticut (especially Lisa Johnson); the New London County Historical Society (Tricia Royston and Edward Baker); the New Haven Colony Historical Society (James Campbell); the Beneicke Rare Book and Manuscripts Library, Yale University (George Miles); the Department of Manuscripts and Archives, Sterling Memorial Library, Yale University; the G. W. Blunt White Library, Mystic Seaport, Mystic, Connecticut (Paul O'Pecko); the Canton Historical Museum, Collinsville, Connecticut (Gordon Harmon); the Connecticut Historical Society, Hartford, Connecticut (Barbara Austen and Rich Malley); Manuscript Division, Library of Congress, Washington, DC (Margaret McAleer); National Archives at Boston, Frederick C. Murphy Federal Center, Waltham, Massachusetts; the Boston Athenaeum, Boston, Massachusetts; the

Amistad Research Center, New Orleans; the Huntington Library, San Marino, California; the National Archives of the United Kingdom (Guy Grannum); the Department of Manuscripts, National Library of Ireland (Gerry Long); the British Library; and Rhodes House Library, Oxford. Special thanks to the staff at my own Hillman Library at the University of Pittsburgh, especially Pat Colbert and Philip Wilkin.

I thank Tim Murray and the Fellows of the Society for the Humanities at Cornell University, where I spent a happy, productive term in the spring of 2009 and where I made the first presentation on this project. Conversations with Edward Baptist, Margaret Washington, Barry Maxwell, and Eric Cheyfitz were especially useful, as were meetings with Cornell graduate and undergraduate students who took a course I offered on the *Amistad* Rebellion.

Warm thanks to the following colleagues who gave me opportunities to discuss the ideas of this book through invited lectures: Tony Bogues and Tricia Rose at Brown University; Mary Lindemann and Michael Miller at the University of Miami; Vincent Brown at the Charles Warren Center for Studies in American History, Harvard University; Eric Roorda and Glenn Gordinier at Mystic Seaport; Graham Hodges at Colgate University; Paul Youngquist at the University of Colorado; Christina Heatherton and Heather Ashby at the University of Southern California; Jennifer Gaynor at the University at Buffalo; Alan Gallay at the Ohio State University; Antoinette Burton at the University of Illinois; Michael Zeuske at the University of Cologne; Leos Müller at the Vasa Museum and the University of Stockholm; Marco Sioli and Giovanni Venegoni at the University of Milan; and Raffaele Laudani at the University of Bologna.

It was my good fortune to deliver the Lawrence A. Brewster Lecture in the Department of History, East Carolina University (2009); the Gilbert Osofsky Lecture in the Department of History, University of Illinois-Chicago (2010), and the John Kemble Lecture, Huntington Library, San Marino, California (2010). Special thanks to John Tucker and Mona Russell, James F. Searing, and Robert C. Ritchie for these exceptional occasions. I also wish to thank the many people who attended all of the events above and participated in the discussions, from which I learned much.

Four outstanding historians—Ira Berlin, Steven Hahn, Douglas Egerton, and Jeremy Brecher—read the entire manuscript and gave me the benefit of probing, tough-minded responses. All made signal contributions to these pages, to context, narrative, and conclusion. James Brewer Stewart and Stanley Harrold shared their enormous knowledge of the American abolitionist movement with me, and I am much the better for it.

A host of talented historians of West Africa have helped me with that crucial part of the story. My friend and colleague Patrick Manning has been stalwart in his support since the very beginning of the project. James F. Searing provided useful commentary early in the work and again late, for which I am most grateful. Joseph Opala, who knows the history of Sierra Leone like few others, gave friendly encouragement that I was on the right track. Philip Misevich and Konrad Tuchscherer have helped me tremendously, and in numerous ways, by sharing their research and expertise about Sierra Leone and the Mende people in particular, and by helping me to think through important interpretive issues. Thanks to both for reading the manuscript and offering many valuable suggestions.

Other helpful people have included the sailor-writer William Gilkerson, who offered his deep knowledge of early-nineteenth-century schooners, and Sean Bercaw, captain of the reconstructed *Amistad* based at Mystic Seaport, who gave me a fascinating tour of the vessel in 2010. Emma Christopher, Joseph L. Yannielli, and Michael Zeuske kindly shared their research on related topics, and many fine scholars answered questions of various kinds: thanks to Roquinaldo A. Ferreira, Manolo Florentino, Walter Hawthorne, Mary Karasch, Henry Lovejoy, Paul Lovejoy, Beatriz Mamagonian, Leonardo Marquez, Joseph C. Miller, Peter A. Reed, João José Reis, and Jaime Rodrigues. My friends Forrest Hylton, Peter Linebaugh, and Ken Morgan also helped out in various ways.

It was my great good fortune to work with a group of talented research assistants. Isaac Curtis, Veronica Szabo, and Levi Raymond Pettler not only found important materials, they posed discerning questions about what they found, thereby shaping the nature of the research itself. Likewise did Melissah Pawlikowski, a superb researcher who did yeowomen's work on the *Pennyslvania Freeman*.

I have received much help, of many kinds, from friends and colleagues at the University of Pittsburgh. Kirk Savage kindly invited me to speak on the images of the *Amistad* Rebellion in the History of Art and Architecture Department, then gave me valuable advice about their genesis and meaning. Other colleagues at Pitt and Carnegie Mellon University provided valuable fora for presentation and discussion: Kathleen DeWalt and the members of the Perlman Roundtable; Jonathan Arac and the Humanities Center; Holger Hoock and the Eighteenth Century Studies Group; and Edda Fields-Black and the African Studies Research Consortium. Five different talks on the same project must have tried everyone's patience, but good manners, critical engagement, and genuine encouragement prevailed, for which I am grateful. Bruce McConachie helped me to understand the play *The Long, Low Black Schooner*, treated in chapter 3. Jim Burke once again applied his photographer's art to various materials that appear in the book. Thanks to an enthusiastic group of undergraduates who studied the *Amistad* case with me in the spring of 2010 and to a gang of lively Atlantic history graduate students who gave both the manuscript and its author a vigorous workout in the spring of 2012. I owe special gratitude to N. John Cooper, Bettye J. and Ralph E. Bailey Dean of the Kenneth P. Dietrich School of Arts and Sciences at the University of Pittsburgh. His support of my work and, indeed, of my entire department, has been foundational.

Some people have workplaces that offer civility but little intellectual engagement; others have engagement but little civility; many, unfortunately, have neither. In the department of history at the University of Pittsburgh I have both, for which I feel lucky indeed. I thank the members of our "collective" for the things they do, large and small, that make ours a good place to study and to teach, to think and to act. Thanks to Alejandro de la Fuente for discussion of the Cuban dimensions of the *Amistad* case and to the other members of the Atlantic group for stimulation and support: Reid Andrews, Seymour Drescher, Van Beck Hall, Holger Hoock, Patrick Manning, Lara Putnam, and Rebecca Shumway. I must add, Grace Tomcho, Molly Estes, Patty Landon, and Kathy Gibson have helped me a hundred different ways.

My dear friend and colleague Rob Ruck not only engaged the ideas of the book, he recognized my occasional need to escape them. He'd always say, "Time to get serious. What are the match-ups?" and off we went to a land of joy called Pitt basketball. Thanks too to Coach Jamie Dixon, my former student Assistant Coach Brandin Knight, the rest of the staff, and the players, who by their character, hard work, and achievement continue season after season to make the University of Pittsburgh a better place to live and work.

Thanks to the Sandra Dijkstra Literary Agency—Elise Capron, Andrea Cavallaro, Elisabeth James, and Sandy herself, who helped me to figure out that this was the book to write and then encouraged me at every step thereafter. It has been a pleasure to work again with the creative gang at Viking. Ted Gilley and Noirin Lucas did an expert job copyediting the manuscript; Carla Bolte brought a sensitive intelligence to bear on the design of the book; Paul Buckley and his staff in the art department designed an arresting cover; Maggie Riggs did all kinds of helpful things; and my editor, Wendy Wolf, proved once again that she is an unrivaled master of her craft. She gives lie to the adage that the relationship between editor and author is the relationship between knife and throat. Her wise judgment has shaped the project from idea to book.

———

Finally, thanks to my son, Zeke, and daughter, Eva, for their forbearance and good humor about a father who stays up late into the night reading strange documents and putting black marks on paper. My wife, Wendy Goldman, discussed every bit of this book with me over days, weeks, months, and years. Like no one else I know, she has an ability to go straight to the heart of the matter at hand. I dedicate the book to her, with love.

NOTES

Abbreviations

AFASR	*American and Foreign Anti-Slavery Reporter*
ARC	Sierra Leone Papers, American Missionary Association, Amistad Research Center, New Orleans, Louisiana
ARCJ	*African Repository and Colonial Journal*
Baldwin Family Papers	Baldwin Family Papers, Manuscripts and Archives, Sterling Memorial Library, Yale University
Barber	John Warner Barber, *A History of the Amistad Captives: Being a Circumstantial Account of the Capture of the Spanish Schooner Amistad, by the Africans on Board; Their Voyage, and Capture Near Long Island, New York; with Biographical Sketches of Each of the Surviving Africans; Also, an Account of the Trials had on Their case, Before the District and Circuit Courts of the United States, for the District of Connecticut* (New Haven, CT: E. L. and J. W. Barber, 1840)
CA	*Colored American*
CHS	Connecticut Historical Society, Hartford, Connecticut
Forbes	Frederick E. Forbes, *Six Months' Service in the African Blockade, from April to October, 1848, in Command of H.M.S. Bonetta, by Lieutenant Forbes* (Originally published London, 1848, reprinted London, Dawsons, 1969)
Jones	Adam Jones, *From Slaves to Palm Kernels: A History of the Galinhas Country (West Africa), 1730–1890* (Wiesbaden, Germany: F. Steiner, 1983)
Laing	Major Alexander Gordon Laing, *Travels in the Timmannee, Kooranko, and Soolima Countries in Western Africa* (London: John Murray, 1825)
LC	Library of Congress, Washington, DC
NA	National Archives, Kew Gardens, United Kingdom
NAB	National Archives at Boston, Frederick C. Murphy Federal Center, Waltham, Massachusetts

NHCHS   New Haven Colony Historical Society, New Haven, Connecticut

Norton Papers   John Pitkin Norton Papers, MS 367, Manuscript and Archives, Sterling Memorial Library, Yale University

NLG   *New London Gazette*

NYCA   *New York Commercial Advertiser*

NYJC   *New York Journal of Commerce*

NYMH   *New York Morning Herald*

NYS   *New York Sun*

The Palm Land   George Thompson, *The Palm Land; or, West Africa, Illustrated. Being a History of Missionary Labors and Travels, with Descriptions of Men and Things in Western Africa. Also, a Synopsis of All the Missionary Work on that Continent* (Cincinnati: Moore, Wilstach, Keys & Co., 1859)

PF   *Pennsylvania Freeman*

Rankin   F. Harrison Rankin, *The White Man's Grave: A Visit to Sierra Leone in 1834* (London: Richard Bentley, 1836), two volumes

Tappan Papers   Lewis Tappan Papers, Manuscript Division, Library of Congress

TAST   Transatlantic Slave Trade Database, available at www.slavevoyages.org

Thompson in Africa   *Thompson in Africa; or, an Account of the Missionary Labors, Sufferings, Travels, and Observations of George Thompson in Western Africa, at the Mendi Mission,* ninth ed. (Dayton, OH: Printed for the author, 1857; originally printed 1852)

Introduction: Voices

1. This work owes much to Levi Raymond Pettler, "Education and *The Amistad*: Black Agency, the American Left, and Spielberg's *Amistad*," unpublished paper; and Jesse Lemisch, "Black Agency in the *Amistad* Uprising, or, You've Taken Our Cinque and Gone," in *Souls: A Critical Journal of Black Politics, Culture, and Society* 1 (1999): 57–70. I have chosen to use the name "Cinqué," which grew from the freedom struggle in America, rather than the Mende name Sengbe. My decision was based on the fact that Cinqué himself embraced the name and used it in daily life, signing his letters that way, for example, no doubt because the name, the person, and the cause had become famous in the course of the struggle.

2. Julie Roy Jeffrey, "*Amistad* (1997): Steven Spielberg's 'True Story,'" *Historical Journal of Film, Radio and Television* 21 (2001): 77–96; Marouf Hasian Jr. and A. Cheree Carlson, "Revisionism and Collective Memory: The Struggle for Meaning in the *Amistad* Affair," *Communications Monographs* 67 (2000): 42–62. Novels include Barbara Chase-Riboud, *Echo of Lions* (New York: William Morrow & Co., 1989); Alexs D. Pate, *Amistad* (New York: Signet, 1997); and David Pesci, *Amistad* (Marlowe and Co., 1997). A poetic reflection on the history and meaning of the case is Kevin Young, *Ardency: A Chronicle of the Amistad Rebels* (New York: Alfred A. Knopf, 2011).

3. The *Amistad* Rebellion has attracted many fine writers and scholars over the years. The first major work was a historical novel, based on extensive research and therefore sometimes mistaken for history: William A. Owens, *Black Mutiny: The Revolt on the Schooner Amistad* (New York: John Day Co., 1953). Mary Cable's *Black Odyssey: The Case of the Slave Ship "Amistad"* (New York: Viking Press, 1971) is a brief, lucid account of the mutiny and its aftermath. Two studies by literary scholars are Maggie Montesinos Sale, *The Slumbering*

Volcano: American Slave Ship Revolts and the Production of Rebellious Masculinity (Durham, NC: Duke University Press, 1997) and Iyunolu Folayan Osagie, *The Amistad Revolt: Memory, Slavery, and the Politics of Identity in the United States and Sierra Leone* (Athens: University of Georgia Press, 2000). The latter stresses the meanings of the *Amistad* case in American popular culture and in recent West African history, especially in the author's own war-torn Sierra Leone during the 1990s. The pinnacle of scholarship, to which I am much indebted, is Howard Jones's *Mutiny on the Amistad: The Saga of a Slave Revolt and Its Impact on American Abolition, Law, and Diplomacy* (New York: Oxford University Press, 1987). Jones used extensive research to offer a thorough and insightful exploration of the legal, diplomatic, and political aspects of the case. Other important scholarship includes James A. Miller, ed., "The Amistad Incident: Four Perspectives," *Occasional Papers of the Connecticut Humanities Council* 10 (1992); Arthur Abraham, *The Amistad Revolt: An Historical Legacy of Sierra Leone and the United States* (Washington, DC : U.S. Department of State International Information Programs, 1998); and David Brion Davis, "The Amistad Test of Law and Justice," in his *Inhuman Bondage: The Rise and Fall of Slavery in the New World* (Oxford, UK: Oxford University Press, 2006), chap. 1.

4. Henry Highland Garnet's *An Address to the Slaves of the United States of America* was delivered before the National Convention of Colored Citizens, Buffalo, New York, August 16, 1843, then published in Henry Highland Garnet, *Walker's Appeal, with a Brief Sketch of His Life, and also Garnet's Address to the Slaves of the United States of America* (New York: J. H. Tobitt, 1848); Peter Hinks, *To Awaken My Afflicted Brethren: David Walker and the Problem of Antebellum Slave Resistance* (College Park: Pennsylvania State University Press, 1997); C.L.R. James, *The Black Jacobins: Toussaint L'Ouverture and the San Domingo Revolution* (New York: Vintage Books, 1989; orig. publ. 1938); Kenneth S. Greenberg, *Nat Turner: A Slave Rebellion in History and Memory* (New York: Oxford University Press, 2003); Michael Craton, *Testing the Chains: Resistance to Slavery in the British West Indies* (Ithaca, NY: Cornell University Press, 1982); Joaô José Reis, *Slave Rebellion in Brazil: The Muslim Uprising of 1835 in Bahia* (Baltimore: Johns Hopkins University Press, 1993); Robert L. Paquette, *Sugar Is Made with Blood: The Conspiracy of La Escalera and the Conflict Between Empires over Slavery in Cuba* (Middletown, CT: Wesleyan University Press, 1988); James Brewer Stewart, *Holy Warriors: The Abolitionists and American Slavery* (New York: Hill and Wang, 1996).

5. "Motín en alta mar, piratería, y asesinatos," *Noticioso de Ambos Mundos*, August 31, 1839.

6. The best, and most poetic, account of the struggle against slavery and its long aftermath remains Vincent Harding, *There Is a River: The Black Struggle for Freedom in America* (New York: Vintage Books, 1981).

7. Peter Linebaugh and Marcus Rediker, *The Many-Headed Hydra: Sailors, Slaves, Commoners, and the Hidden History of the Revolutionary Atlantic* (Boston: Beacon Press, 2000), chap. 9. Other scholars whose work has been especially valuable in including enslaved rebels in the abolitionist movement include Merton L. Dillon, *Slavery Attacked: Southern Slaves and Their Allies, 1619–1865* (Baton Rouge: Louisiana State University Press, 1990); Stanley Harrold, *American Abolitionists* (Harlow, UK: Longman, 2001); and Douglas R. Egerton, "The Scenes Which are Enacted in St. Domingo: The Legacy of Revolutionary Violence in Early National Virginia," in Jack R. McKivigan and Stanley Harrold, *Antislavery Violence: Sectional, Racial, and Cultural Conflict in Antebellum America* (Knoxville: University of Tennessee Press, 1999), 41–64.

8. I would also like to acknowledge the recent and forthcoming work of five talented scholars on one or another dimension of the *Amistad* rebellion: Orlando García Martínez, Benjamin N. Lawrance, Robert S. Wolff, Joseph L. Yannielli, and Michael Zeuske.

9. Quoted in Jones, *Mutiny on the Amistad*, 210. On the radicalism of the waterfront, see Linebaugh and Rediker, *The Many-Headed Hydra*, chaps. 7 and 8.

10. "Incarcerated Captives," *NYCA*, September 6, 1839.

Chapter One: Origins

1. "The Amistad Africans," *Pennsylvania Inquirer and Daily Courier*, May 29, 1841; Forbes, 75–76.

2. "Fuli," William H. Townsend (1822–1851), Sketches of the Amistad captives, [ca.

1839–1840], box 1, folder 4, GEN MSS 335, Beneicke Rare Book and Manuscript Collection, Yale University; "Captives of the Amistad," *Emancipator*, December 19, 1839.

3. Barber, 11.

4. Barber, 15; "Marqu," Townsend Sketches, box 1, folder 7. See Paul E. Lovejoy and David Richardson, "Trust, Pawnship, and Atlantic History: The Institutional Foundation of the Calabar Slave Trade," *American Historical Review* 104 (1999): 332–55, and "The Business of Slaving: Pawnship in Western Africa," *Journal of African History* 42 (2001): 67–89. On the experience of Margru and the other children aboard the *Amistad*, see Benjamin N. Lawrance, "'All We Want Is Make Us Free': The Voyage of *La Amistad's* Children Through the Worlds of the Illegal Slave Trade," in Gwyn Campbell, Suzanne Miers, and Joseph C. Miller, eds., *Child Slaves in the Modern World* (Athens: Ohio University Press, 2011), 13–36.

5. Barber, 12; "Malhue," Townsend Sketches, box 2, folder 18. Moru played a leading role in the rebellion, suggesting that he was an experienced warrior. Thanks to Konrad Tuchscherer for the identification of the Margona family name, which is often given as Magona.

6. *No Rum!—No Sugar! Or, The Voice of Blood, being Half an Hour's Conversation between a Negro and an English Gentleman, shewing the Horrible Nature of the Slave-Trade, and Pointing Out an Easy and Effective Method of Terminating It, by an Act of the People* (London, 1792). In case readers were disinclined to believe Cushoo, the author of the pamphlet provided footnotes, with eyewitness accounts of Africa, the slave trade, and New World slavery itself to support the argument.

7. Robert Paquette, *Sugar Is Made with Blood: The Conspiracy of La Escalera and the Conflict Between Empires over Slavery in Cuba* (Middletown, CT: Wesleyan University Press, 1988).

8. The articulation of slavery and industrialism has been called the "second slavery." See Dale Tomich, "The Wealth of Empire: Francisco Arrangoy Parreno, Political Economy, and the Second Slavery in Cuba," *Comparative Studies in Society and History* 45 (2003): 4–28.

9. Raphael Samuel, "Workshop of the World: Steam Power and Hand Technology in Mid-Victorian Britain," *History Workshop* 3 (1977): 6–72; Christopher Lloyd, *The Navy and the Slave Trade: The Suppression of the African Slave Trade in the Nineteenth Century* (London: Routledge, 1968).

10. Alexander Jones, *Cuba in 1851; Containing Authentic Statistics of the Population, Agriculture, and Commerce of the Island . . .* (New York: Stringer and Townsend, 1851); Dale Tomich, "Sugar and Slavery in an Age of Global Transformation," in his *Slavery in the Circuit of Sugar: Martinique and the World Economy, 1830–1848* (Baltimore: Johns Hopkins University Press, 1990), 14–32.

11. Daniel Walker Howe, *What Hath God Wrought: The Transformation of America, 1815–1848* (New York: Oxford University Press, 2007), chap. 20.

12. Bronislaw Novak, "The Slave Rebellion in Sierra Leone, 1785–1796," *Hemispheres* 3 (1986): 151–69; Ismail Rashid, "'A Devotion to the Idea of Liberty at any Price': Rebellion and Antislavery in the Upper Guinea Coast in the Eighteenth and Nineteenth Centuries," in Sylviane A. Diouf, ed., *Fighting the Slave Trade: West African Strategies* (Athens: Ohio University Press, 2003), 132–51; Ismail Rashid, "Escape, Revolt, and Marronage in the Eighteenth and Nineteenth Century Sierra Leone Hinterland," *Canadian Journal of African Studies/Revue Canadienne des Études Africaines* 34 (2000): 656–83.

13. Much valuable biographical evidence was gathered by Connecticut engraver John Warner Barber, who visited the *Amistad* Africans in the New Haven jail numerous times in early 1840, and through Mende sailor and interpreter James Covey talked with them at length about their lives in Africa.

14. "The Captive Africans," *Emancipator*, October 17, 1839. Teacher Sherman Booth noted in August 1841 that four were Temne, four were Kono, one was Gola, and that four were "from the Bullom country," although three of the final group, Kinna, Fuli, and Kwong, were Mende who had lived in Bullom country. The Mende, by Booth's calculation, would have been approximately twenty-six in number. See "The Liberated Mendians," *PF*, August 18, 1841. Since there were two *Amistad* Africans by the name of Burna, subsequent references to the elder will be simply "Burna," the other as "Burna the younger."

15. *The Palm Land*, 429. See also the astute remarks on the Mende and other peoples of Sierra Leone in Michael A. Gomez, *Exchanging Our Country Marks: The Transformation of African Identities in the Colonial and Antebellum South* (Chapel Hill: University of North Carolina Press, 1998), chap. 5.

16. Jones, 177; Barber, 8. Two abolitionists who later worked closely with the *Amistad* Africans agreed that the "Mohammedan influence" among them had not been great. See A. F. Williams to Lewis Tappan, Farmington, March 25, 1841, and Notes by Professor [Josiah] Gibbs, July 1841, ARC.

17. "The Mendi People," *Emancipator*, September 23, 1841; Governor William Fergusson to Lewis Tappan, 1842, published in *North American and Daily Advertiser*, June 15, 1842. Adam Jones remarks that information about Mende country before 1870 is "very limited"; Jones, 18, 85. The Temne were known because the British had bought land from one of their kings for the settlement at Freetown. The Bullom were closer to the coast and hence had more contact with European and American traders. Little was known of the Gbandi, Kono, Loma, and Gola peoples. Richard Robert Madden included "Menda Country" on the map that accompanied his "Report on Sierra Leone, 1841," Colonial Office (CO) 267/172, NA. Based on his conversations, Barber added "Mendi" to the map he engraved for *A History of the Amistad Captives* (1840). Philip Misevich has found a reference to the "Cursa" (Kossa) dating from 1713 (personal communication to the author, Janary 12, 2012).

18. *The Palm Land*, 415; A. Menzies, "Exploratory Expedition to the Mende Country," *Church Missionary Intelligencer: A Monthly Journal of Missionary Information* (London: Seeley, Jackson, and Halliday, 1864), vol. XV, 115; "The Liberated Mendians," *PF*, August 18, 1841.

19. *Thompson in Africa*, 414–15; Robert Clarke, *Sierra Leone: A Description of the Manners and Customs of the Liberated Africans; with Observations upon the Natural History of the Colony, and a Notice of the Native Tribes* (London: James Ridgway, 1843), 163.

20. Forbes, 62–63; *The Palm Land*, 246; Clarke, *Sierra Leone*, 44; "Liberated Mendians," *PF*, August 18, 1841. According to Jones, a "king" was a regional overlord, a "chief" was the political head of a town or larger unit, and a "big man" was one who possessed prestige, wealth, allies, and relatives/dependents, often on the village level. See Jones, 13.

21. *The Palm Land*, 202–14; "Liberated Mendians," *PF*, August 18, 1841.

22. Barber, 8–14.

23. Anthony J. Gittins, *Mende Religion: Aspects of Belief and Thought in Sierra Leone* (Nettetal: Steyler Verlag, 1987), 166; *Thompson in Africa*, 300; *The Palm Land*, 197; Kenneth Little, *The Mende of Sierra Leone: A West African People in Transition* (London: Routledge & Kegan Paul, 1951, rev. ed. 1967), 70–80; Jones, 62. The relationship between the slave trade and rice production is explored well by James F. Searing, *West African Slavery and Atlantic Commerce: The Senegal River Valley, 1700–1860* (Cambridge, UK: Cambridge University Press, 2003).

24. Rankin, vol. II, 241–43.

25. *The Palm Land*, 129; *Thompson in Africa*, 212; Forbes, 58; Laing, 201–04.

26. The information about urban origins was provided in May 1841 by Sherman Booth, who had worked for many months as the primary teacher of the *Amistad* Africans and who had therefore spent more time in conversation with them than anyone: "They lived in cities, most of which were of about the size of New Haven; adjacent to their cities, they cultivated farms, grew cotton, manufactured cloth, &c." See the *Pennsylvania Inquirer and Daily Courier*, May 29, 1841. The size of many Mende towns and cities is unknown because of the lack of surviving evidence, but travelers frequently mention concentrations of several thousand people. George Thompson was convinced, based on local conversations, that much larger cities, with tens of thousands of people, existed further east, distant from the reach of the slave trade, which had depopulated coastal areas (*The Palm Land*, 428–29). Yet the cities were probably not as large as suggested here. This may have been because the *Amistad* Africans did not realize how large New Haven was, or they may have exaggerated the size of their own cities. It should also be noted that abolitionists wanted to present the *Amistad* Africans as denizens of advanced, "civilized" societies in Africa.

27. Testimony of Francis Bacon, *New Haven Palladium*, n.d. (January 1840), copy in the Baldwin Family Papers. See also "The Liberated Mendians," *PF*, August 18, 1841.

28. *Pennsylvania Inquirer and Daily Courier*, May 29, 1841; *ARCJ*, June 1, 1841.

29. Richard Robert Madden estimated the ages of eight of the Amistad Africans, but seems to have suggested that they were younger than they actually were. For comparative ages of a sample of Liberated Africans in Sierra Leone, see P.E.H. Hair, "The Enslavement of Koelle's Informants," *Journal of African History* 6 (1965): 194–95. Kale was described as being eleven years old in 1841, after he had learned to speak English well, hence the estimate of nine in 1839.

30. Norton Papers, Diaries, vol. III: entry for Thursday, March 18, 1841, box no. 3, folder 18, MS 367.

31. *The Palm Land*, 282; *Emancipator*, September 23, 1841. On the connections among the Mende, Loma, and Gbandi languages within the "South-Western Mande" language group, see Valentin Vydrine, "Note on Current Use of Manding and Mande Ethnonyms and Linguonyms," available at http://mandelang.kunstkamera.ru/. On the localized nature of political power in the region surrounding Freetown, see Philip Misevich, "The Sierra Leone Hinterland and the Provisioning of Early Freetown, 1792–1803," *Journal of Colonialism and Colonial History* 9 (2008).

32. The centrality of the Poro Society to the self-organization of multiethnic warriors from Sierra Leone was confirmed by Dr. Ernest T. Ndomahina, the senior ranking member of the Wundu, the Mende secret military society (Interview, Fourah Bay College, Freetown, May 6, 2103). See also Kenneth L. Little, "The Role of the Secret Society in Cultural Specialization," *American Anthropologist*, n.s., 51 (1949): 202; F.W.H. Migeod, "The Poro Society: The Building of the Poro House and Making of the Image," *Man* 16 (1916): 102. An important study of how secret societies moved from the Cross River region of present-day Nigeria to Cuba is Ivor L. Miller, *Voice of the Leopard: African Secret Societies and Cuba* (Jackson: University of Mississippi Press, 2009).

33. Jones, 19; Little, *The Mende of Sierra Leone*, 8–9, 97–99, Forbes, 60; Barber, 13; Hannah Moore to William Harned, October 12, 1852, ARC. On the relationship between the degree of scarification and Poro standing, see Kenneth. L. Little, "The Political Function of the Poro, part I," *Africa: Journal of the International Africa Institute* 35 (1965): 359, 360.

34. Jones, 179; Laing, 99. For a valuable exploration of the Atlantic migration of cultures, including spiritual beliefs, see Walter Hawthorne, *From Africa to Brazil: Culture, Identity, and an Atlantic Slave Trade, 1600–1830* (Cambridge, UK: Cambridge University Press, 2010).

35. W. T. Harris and Harry Sawyerr, *The Springs of Mende Belief: A Discussion of the Influence of the Belief in the Supernatural Among the Mende* (Freetown: University of Sierra Leone Press, 1968), 111; Little, *The Mende of Sierra Leone*, 184.

36. *The Palm Land*, 418; Laing, 93–95; Jones, 48, 187. It should be noted that some Poro Societies were also known to have been involved in slave trading.

37. Jones, 179; Forbes, 61; *Thompson in Africa*, 418–19.

38. Forbes, 60; Rankin, vol. II, 82; Arthur Abraham, *Mende Government and Politics under Colonial Rule: A Historical Study of Political Change in Sierra Leone, 1890–1937* (Freetown: Sierra Leone University Press, 1978), 159–60.

39. Rankin, vol. I, 259–60; Sigismund Wilhelm Koelle, *African Native Literature* (Graz, Austria: Akademische Druck–U. Verlagsantalt, 1968. First published 1854 by Church Missionary Society, London), vii; *The Palm Land*, 38; Laing, 206–7.

40. Little, *The Mende of Sierra Leone*, 197; Donald Cosentino, *Defiant Maids and Stubborn Farmers: Tradition and Invention in Mende Story Performance* (Cambridge, UK: Cambridge University Press, 1982); Marion Kilson, *Royal Antelope and Spider: West African Mende Tales* (Cambridge, MA: Press of the Langdon Associates, 1976).

41. *Thompson in Africa*, 61; Koelle, *African Native Literature*, xiii.

42. *Thompson in Africa*, 169, 194, 244; *The Palm Land*, 237; Forbes, 66; Barber, 8.

43. Abraham, *Mende Government and Politics*, 15–16; *Thompson in Africa*, 127.

44. *Thompson in Africa*, 105, 108.

45. Clarke, *Sierra Leone*, 163; *Thompson in Africa*, 225–26, 237; Christopher Fyfe, *A History of Sierra Leone* (Oxford, UK: Oxford University Press, 1962), 246.

46. Abraham, *Mende Government and Politics*, 7; S. W. Koelle, *Outlines of a Grammar of the Vei Language, Together with a Vei–English Vocabulary and an Account of the Discovery and Nature of the Vei Mode of Syllabic Writing* (Westmead, UK: Gregg International Publishers, 1968. First published 1854 by Church Missionary House, London), iii; *The Palm Land*, 293; Adam Jones, "Who Were the Vai?" *Journal of African History* 22 (1981): 159.

47. Abraham, *Mende Government and Politics*, 3; Jones, 65; Little, *The Mende of Sierra Leone*, 84, 176.

48. "The Mendians," *Vermont Chronicle*, June 8, 1842; Barber, 10. See also "Goterah, African Warrior," *ARCJ* 15 (1839): 290–94. On the geopolitical context of Goterah's mercenary war making, see Svend Holsoe, "A Study of Relations Between Settlers and Indigenous Peoples in Western Liberia, 1821–1847," *African Historical Studies* 4 (1971): 331–62.

49. *ARCJ*, 18 (1842): 300; *Thompson in Africa*, 308. Harris and Sawyerr wrote: "Ambuscades were naturally only successful in dark nights, as moonlight would always expose attackers to the view of the defenders" (*The Springs of Mende Belief*, 119), while Forbes added, Africans "never fight in the day time, and seldom in the night unless the opposite party is asleep in a town" (102). See also Rankin, vol. II, 237. On the traditions of warfare in the region, including fighting at night, see A. P. Kup, *A History of Sierra Leone, 1400–1787* (Cambridge, UK: Cambridge University Press, 1961), 167–70, and John Thornton, *Warfare in Atlantic Africa, 1500–1800* (London: Routledge, 2000), chap. 2.

50. Abraham, *Mende Government and Politics*, 20; Jones, 19; Rankin, vol. II, 76; Barber, 10.

51. Walter Rodney, *How Europe Underdeveloped Africa* (Washington, DC: Howard University Press, 1972), 141–43; Rankin, vol. II, 74, 224; Laing, 217. For subsequent history, see John J. Grace, "Slavery and Emancipation Among the Mende in Sierra Leone, 1896–1928," in Suzanne Miers and Igor Kopytoff, eds., *Slavery in Africa: Historical and Anthropological Perspectives* (Madison: University of Wisconsin Press, 1977), 415–31.

52. The world market sprouted other local roots when Susu traders, armed with bows and arrows poisoned with snake venom, manned their fearsome war canoes in the 1850s to capture slaves along the Boom and Kittam rivers. They carried them north to work on their own plantations, where they grew peanuts for export to England, France, and the United States; *The Palm Land*, 186, 187. The presence of tobacco in the region may have predated the slave trade.

53. Jones, 89–91. See also Laing, 127, and the articles by Rashid in note 12 above. On the early history of the slave trade see Toby Green, *The Rise of the Trans-Atlantic Slave Trade in Western Africa, 1300–1589* (Cambridge, UK: Cambridge University Press, 2011).

54. Jones, 21, 24–25, 37, 43–44; Testimony of Bacon, *New Haven Palladium*; Rankin, vol. II, 74; Adam Jones, "White Roots: Written and Oral Testimony on the 'First' Mr. Rogers," *History in Africa* 10 (1983): 151–62. Other important slave-trading families in the region included the Caulkers, Clevelands, Coles, and Tuckers. It is difficult to square the figures available through the Transatlantic Slave Trade Database about slave shipments from Sierra Leone during the 1830s with the evidence provided by people who visited the region at the time, including the British naval officers whose job it was to gauge the nefarious commerce. The former suggests exports of about 2,000 slaves per year, while the latter almost all agreed that the number was closer to 10,000. Sierra Leone's governor, Sir John Jeremie, reported that the slave traders on the Gallinas Coast had shipped "upwards of thirteen thousand" during the year 1840 ("Destruction of African Slave Factories," *Bury and Norwich Post*, April 14, 1841). Much of the discrepancy can no doubt be accounted for by the illegal nature of the trade: the slavers, such as the *Teçora*, made it their business to create no records, hence there is no documentation about many of them to include in the database.

55. Madden, Report on Sierra Leone, 25; Forbes, v–vi; Theophilus Conneau, *A Slaver's Logbook, or 20 Years' Residence in Africa*, ed. Mabel M. Smythe (Englewood Cliffs, NJ: Prentice Hall, 1976), chap. 15. On Conneau, see Svend E. Holsoe, "Theodore Canot at Cape Mount, 1841–1847," *Liberian Studies Journal* 4 (1972): 163–81; Bruce L. Mouser, "Théophilus Conneau: The Saga of a Tale," *History in Africa* 6 (1979): 97–107; and Adam Jones, "Théophile Conneau at Galinhas and New Sestos, 1836–1841: A Comparison of the Sources," *History in Africa* 8 (1981): 89–105. On the anti-slave-trade squadron, see Marika Sherwood, *After Abolition: Britain and the Slave Trade After 1807* (London: I. B. Taurus, 2007), 114–20 and Allen M. Howard, "Nineteenth-century Coastal Slave Trading and the British Campaign in Sierra Leone," *Slavery and Abolition* 27 (2006): 23–49.

56. Rankin, vol. II, 78, 80; *The Palm Land*, 245; Barber, 12–15; Moore to Harned, October 12, 1852, ARC. The experiences of enslavement among the *Amistad* Africans were in many ways similar to those of 179 Africans interviewed by linguist Sigismund Koelle in Sierra Leone around 1850, 34 percent of whom had been captured in war, 30 percent kidnapped, and the remaining 36 percent enslaved for crime, debt, or other reasons. See Hair, "The Enslavement of Koelle's Informants," 193–203.

57. A. F. Williams to Lewis Tappan, Farmington, September 23, 1841, and S. W. Booth to Lewis Tappan, Farmington, October 4, 1841, ARC.

58. Barber, 10.

59. Cinqué "had never seen a white man until he was sold a slave into their hands." See Amos Townsend Jr. to Lewis Tappan, New Haven, November 13, 1839, ARC.

60. Jones, 1, 5–6; Rankin, vol. II, 206; Clarke, *Sierra Leone*, 7–8, 18, 20; *The Palm Land*, 122, 188–89, 266; Forbes, 124–25; Laing, 78; "Sketches of the Colony of Sierra Leone and Its Inhabitants, by Robert Clarke, Surgeon, late of Her Majesty's Colonial Service; formerly Member of the Executive and Legislative Councils of the Gold Coast; Acting Judicial Assessor; Corresponding Member of the Ethnological Society, etc. With pictorial Illustrations, from original drawings by Mrs. Clarke," *Transactions of the Ethnological Society of London* 2 (1863): 322–23.

61. Forbes, 13–15; Clarke, "Sketches of the Colony of Sierra Leone," 329; Madden, Report on Sierra Leone, 4, 8. Important work on the Liberated Africans includes Rosanne Adderley, *"New Negroes from Africa": Slave Trade Abolition and Free African Settlement in the Nineteenth-Century Caribbean* (Bloomington and Indianapolis: Indiana University Press, 2007); Philip R. Misevich, "On the Frontier of 'Freedom': Abolition and the Transformation of Atlantic Commerce in Southern Sierra Leone, 1790s to 1860s," Ph.D. dissertation, Emory University, 2009; Sharla M. Fett, "Middle Passages and Forced Migrations: Liberated Africans in Nineteenth-Century U.S. Camps and Ships," *Slavery and Abolition* 31 (2010): 75–98; and Robert Burroughs, "Eyes on the Prize: Journeys in Slave Ships Taken as Prizes by the Royal Navy," *Slavery and Abolition* 31 (2010): 99–115.

62. Conneau described the examination process as he learned it from John Ormond, alias "Mongo John," at Bangalang, in 1826. See Conneau, *A Slaver's Logbook*, 71–72.

63. Moore to Harned, October 12, 1852, ARC.

64. *Ports on the Western Coast of Africa by Captain Alexander T. E. Vidal, R.N., 1837, 38, 39* [Admiralty Chart], British Library, Map Collections; Maps SEC.11 (1690).

65. Testimony of Bacon, *New Haven Palladium*; Sherwood, *After Abolition*, 186–87. Much can be learned about Blanco's slaving operation through documents generated in a legal case against a London merchant who was part of his network: *Trial of Pedro de Zulueta, Jun., on a Charge of Slave Trading* (London, 1844).

66. "Slave Holding and Trading," *Hull Packet*, February 14, 1840; James Hall, "Dr. Hall's Report as Trustee of the Ship M. C. Stevens," *ARCJ* 33 (1857): 338–40. An American sailor aboard the anti-slave-trade vessel *Dolphin* patrolling the Gallinas Coast in early 1840 heard that Blanco had recently retired from slaving "with a capital of four millions of dollars." Quoted in Donald L. Canney, *Africa Squadron: The U.S. Navy and the Slave Trade, 1842–1861* (Washington, DC: Potomac Books, 2006), 27.

67. "Dr. Hall's Report," 338–40; James Hall, M.D., "Abolition of the Slave Trade of Gallinas," *Annual Report of the American Colonization Society*, 33 (1850): 33–36.

68. Forbes, 105–06.

69. Hall, "Abolition of the Slave Trade," 33–36.

70. Clarke, "Sketches of the Colony of Sierra Leone," 329, 355; Rankin, vol. I, 143–48; *The Palm Land*, 190. George E. Brooks, Jr., *The Kru Mariner in the Nineteenth Century: A Historical Compendium* (Newark, DE: Liberian Studies Monograph Series, 1972).

71. Testimony of Bacon, *New Haven Palladium*. See Richard Robert Madden's poem, "The Slave Trade Merchant," which he wrote during his visit to the United States to give testimony on the *Amistad* case, dedicated to Trist, and published in *The Philanthropist*, December 10, 1839.

72. "Abolitionists going to the Devil—False Affidavits—Arming of the Africans," *NYMH*, October 23, 1839; Forbes, 82–83.

73. Richard Robert Madden to the Rt. Honorable Lord John Russell, Secretary of State, December 20, 1839; Correspondence from Dr. R.R. Madden, Mr. D.R. Clarke, and the Foreign Office relating to the removal of the "Liberated Africans" from Cuba, 1839, Colonial Office (CO) 318/146, NA.

74. Charlotte Cowles to Samuel Cowles, Farmington, April 12, 1841, Charlotte and Samuel Cowles Correspondence, MS 101754, CHS. It should be noted that children were easier to capture once palisades had been breached. Thanks to Philip Misevich for this point. The prominence of children in the slave trade of the region is also noted by Major H. I. Ricketts, *Narrative of the Ashantee War; with a View of the Present State of the Colony of Sierra Leone* (London: Simkin and Marshall, 1831), 218.

75. Hall, "Abolition of the Slave Trade," 33–36; *Hull Packet*, February 14, 1840.

76. Forbes, 82–84.

77. Forbes, 77–78; *The Palm Land*, 399–400.

78. *Thompson in Africa*, 18–19. The origin of the slave ship images used by Thompson was Rev. Robert Walsh, *Notices of Brazil in 1828 and 1829* (London: Frederick Westley and A. H. Davis, 1830), Vol. II, facing 479. The part of the image showing the lower deck ("3 feet 3 in. high") circulated from Walsh to Lydia Maria Child, *An Appeal in Favor of That Class of Americans Called Africans* (Boston: Allen and Ticknor, 1833), 16, to Barber, 20, to Thompson. Barber redrew the faces of the Africans to reflect his acquaintance with the *Amistad* Africans in jail.

79. See chapter 5 below. Cinqué's face is the fifth from the right.

80. It appears that the four children—Margru, Teme, Kagne, and Kali—all came over on a different slave ship, but that the 49 men came over together on the *Teçora*. See "Case of the Captured Africans," *NYMH*, October 1, 1839. For background, see Marcus Rediker, *The Slave Ship: A Human History* (New York: Viking-Penguin, 2007), especially chap. 9.

81. The Dolben Act stipulated that five slaves could be loaded for every three tons of carrying capacity, or 1.6/1 slave/ton ratio. If we estimate the *Teçora* at 175 tons, its ratio would have been 2.86/1.

82. Forbes, 86–87; "Case," *NYMH*, October 1, 1839.

83. Forbes, 86–87.

84. Grabeau estimated that the *Amistad* Africans had about 48 inches headroom.

85. Rankin, vol. I, 120–23.

86. Forbes, 95–96.

87. TAST. Based on data collected in Freetown about captured slave ships, Madden reported in 1841 that the slave/ton ratio there was 2.6/1, which is close to the estimate for the *Teçora* and to the findings of the TAST. Based on his own knowledge of the slave trade to Havana he thought the ratio was higher, the crowding worse, as high as 5/1 in some cases. See Madden, Report on Sierra Leone, 32.

88. Clarke, "Sketches of the Colony of Sierra Leone," 331; Moore to Harned, October 12, 1852, ARC; Stephanie E. Smallwood, "African Guardians, European Slave Ships, and the Changing Dynamics of Power in the Early Modern Atlantic," *William & Mary Quarterly* 64 (2007): 679–716; Joseph Sturge, *A Visit to the United States in 1841* (London, 1842), Appendix E, xliv; [Captain Joseph Denman], *Instructions for the Guidance of Her Majesty's Naval Officers Employed in the Suppression of the Slave Trade* (London: T. R. Harrison, 1844), 9.

89. Entry for Wednesday, September 8, 1841, Norton Papers, MS 367, series II, Writings, Diaries, volume III: June 29, 1840–September 15, 1841, box no. 3, folder 18; Kale to Lewis Tappan, Westville, October 30, 1840. Rankin, vol. II, 119–20; Forbes, 100.

90. Moore to Harned, October 12, 1852, ARC.

91. "The Negroes of the Amistad," *New Hampshire Sentinel*, October 2, 1839; "The Captive Africans," *Emancipator*, October 17, 1839; originally published in the *New Haven Record*; "Case," *NYMH*, October 1, 1839; Forbes, 99–100.

92. Testimony of Cinqué, January 8, 1840, U.S. District Court, Connecticut, NAB.

93. Rankin, vol. II, 129; Abraham, *Mende Government and Politics*, 23–25; Clarke, "Sketches," 330; Little, *The Mende of Sierra Leone*, 108, 131.

94. Moore to Harned, October 12, 1852, ARC; Testimony of Founi and Kimbo, State of Connecticut, County of New Haven, New Haven, Oct. 7, 1839, Lewis Tappan Papers, Miscellany: "Amistad Case"; "Private Examination of Cinquez," *NYCA*, September 13, 1839; "Slavery in Cuba," *PF*, November 21, 1839; "Case of the Amistad," *New-York Spectator*, November 28, 1839. The Transatlantic Slave Trade Database lists 55 voyages with Cuba as the primary endpoint in 1839: 22,242 slaves were embarked and 19,241 were delivered alive. The significant number of undocumented (and unlisted) voyages, such as the one made by the *Teçora*, suggest that Madden's estimate was reasonably accurate.

95. *Case of the Amistad. Deposition of Dr. Madden, 7th November 1839*, West India Miscellaneous, 1839; vol: Removal of the Liberated Africans from Cuba, Superintendent Dr. Madden and Superintendent Mr. Clarke, Foreign Office, NA; Sturge, *Visit*, Appendix E, xliv; Correspondence from Dr. R.R. Madden, Mr. D.R. Clarke, and the Foreign Office CO 318/146, NA. For an account of Madden's tense relationship with the government of Cuba during his tenure as superintendent of Liberated Africans, see David R. Murray, *Odious Commerce: Britain, Spain, and the Abolition of the Cuban Slave Trade* (Cambridge, UK: Cambridge University Press, 1980), chap. 7.

96. Testimony of Cinqué, January 8, 1840, U.S. District Court, Connecticut, NAB; "Narrative," NYJC, October 10, 1839.

97. Ibid.

98. "The Case of the Captured Negroes," NYMH, September 9, 1839, and "Case of the Captured Africans," NYMH, September 22, 1839.

99. These ports of origin appear in the records of 91 slave ships that arrived in Havana between 1835 and 1845, as recorded in the Transatlantic Slave Trade Database.

100. "Fate in Cuba," NYJC, November 30, 1839; Emancipator, March 24, 1842. Thanks to Michael Zeuske for information about El Horcón.

Chapter Two: Rebellion

1. This chapter is based on dozens of eyewitness accounts of the rebellion provided by eleven people who were on the vessel: Ruiz, Montes, Antonio, the two sailors, and six of the Africans (Cinqué, Grabeau, Fuli, Kale, Kimbo, and Kinna). It also draws on a letter written by abolitionist missionary Hannah Moore in 1852, in which she summarizes the oral history of the Amistad rebellion as preserved and recalled by a handful of veterans who were still living at the Mende Mission thirteen years after the event. These included Fabanna (Alexander Posey), Kinna (George Lewis), Margru (Sarah Kinson), Teme (Maria Brown), and perhaps one or two others. See Hannah Moore to William Harned, October 12, 1852, ARC.

2. "Case of the Captured Africans," NYMH, September 22, 1839. The time of day when the captives boarded was disputed throughout the legal battle over the Amistad, the Africans and abolitionists claiming it took place, secretly and illegally, at night, the Cuban slaveholders Ruiz and Montes saying the opposite: boarding took place in the full light of day. Once the slaveholders had left the Connecticut courts to return home to Cuba, Antonio also admitted that the loading occurred in the evening, which is consistent with the forged papers and other aspects of illegality.

3. "The Africans," NYMH, October 21, 1839.

4. See Quentin Snediker's excellent article on the history of the vessel: "Searching for the Historic Amistad," Log of Mystic Seaport (1998): 86–95, in which he cites Captain George Howland, "An Autobiography or Journal of his Life, Voyages, and Travels with an Appendix of his Ancestry," 1866, typescript 295, Rhode Island Historical Society, Providence, Rhode Island and Temporary Registry #15, for the Schooner Ion, ex-Amistad, New London Customs Records, RG36, NAB. Howland bought the Amistad at auction on October 15, 1840.

5. Testimony of Antonio, January 9, 1840, U.S. District Court, Connecticut, NAB.

6. For detailed accounts of the cargo, see NLG, August 28, 1839; "Superior Court," NYMH, October 24, 1839; Intelligencer, October 27, 1839; and the Libel of José Ruiz, September 18, 1839, U.S. District Court for the District of Connecticut, NAB. On the scarcity of casks see Captain J. Scholborg to R.R. Madden, Havana, June 28, 1839, West India Miscellaneous, 1839; vol: Removal of the Liberated Africans from Cuba, Superintendent Dr. Madden and Superintendent Mr. Clarke, Foreign Office; Correspondence from Dr. R.R. Madden, Mr. D.R. Clarke, and the Foreign Office relating to the removal of the "Liberated Africans" from Cuba, 1839, Colonial Office (CO) 318/146, NA. The letter carried the same date as the Amistad's loading and departure from port.

7. Dwight P. Janes to Lewis Tappan, New London, September 6, 1839, ARC.

8. NLG, September 4, 1839. Thanks to William Gilkerson for sharing his knowledge of this type of vessel.

9. Testimony of Bahoo (Bau), "Case," NYMH, September 22, 1839. Ruiz testified, "Principe is about two days sail from Havana, or 100 leagues, reckoning 3 miles to a league. Sometimes the winds are adverse, the passage occupies 15 days." See "The Long, Low Black Schooner," NYS, August 31, 1839; Michael Zeuske and Orlando García Martínez, "La Amistad de Cuba: Ramón Ferrer, Contrabando de Esclavos, Captividad y Modernidad Atlántica," Caribbean Studies 37 (2009): 97–170.

10. "The Amistad," NLG, October 16, 1839.

11. "Narrative of the Africans," NYJC, October 10, 1839.

12. "Private Examination of Cinquez," NYCA, September 13, 1839.

13. "Mendis Perform," NYMH, May 13, 1841. In collective memory the amount of food had shrunk by 1852 to half a plantain per meal; see Moore to Harned, October 12, 1852, ARC.

14. "Mendis Perform," *NYMH*, May 13, 1841.

15. Testimony of Cinqué, January 8, 1840, United States District Court, Connecticut, NAB; "Narrative," *NYJC*, January 10, 1840.

16. "Ruiz and Montez," *NYCA*, October 18, 1839; "Mendis Perform," *NYMH*, May 13, 1841; "Plans to Educate the Amistad Africans in English," *NYJC*, October 9, 1839; "To the Committee on Behalf of the African Prisoners," *NYJC*, September 10, 1839. Ruiz denied these allegations about poor conditions: "It is untrue that the negroes were taken on board by night, . . . the negroes all went on board willingly, and required no force or violence to induce them to go on board the schooner—that the negroes were not in irons; that they were never tied on board, but perfectly loose, and went about the deck as they pleased. That there were no irons or fetters on board. That it is not true that they were kept on an insufficient allowance of food neither before nor after the mutiny and the murder of the whites by the negroes." See "Superior Court," *NYMH*, October 24, 1839.

17. "Ruiz and Montez," *NYCA*, October 18, 1839. The phrase in pidgin English used by Liberated Africans in Freetown to describe a proud person such as Cinqué is recorded in Robert Clarke, *Sierra Leone: A Description of the Manners and Customs of the Liberated Africans; with Observations upon the Natural History of the Colony, and a Notice of the Native Tribes* (London: James Ridgway, 1843), 11.

18. *Farmer's Cabinet*, November 19, 1841; Joseph Sturge, *A Visit To The United States In 1841* (London, 1842), Appendix E, xliv; Moore to Harned, October 12, 1852, ARC. Cinqué later remarked, "The cook could not speak the Mendi language but used some words that they could understand." See "African Testimony," *NYJC*, January 10, 1840.

19. Marcus Rediker, *The Slave Ship: A Human History* (New York: Viking-Penguin, 2007), 266–69.

20. W. T. Harris and Harry Sawyerr, *The Springs of Mende Belief: A Discussion of the Influence of the Belief in the Supernatural Among the Mende* (Freetown: University of Sierra Leone Press, 1968), 83; Jones, 185; Anthony J. Gittins, *Mende Religion: Aspects of Belief and Thought in Sierra Leone* (Nettetal: Steyler Verlag, 1987), 122.

21. "Mendis Perform," *NYMH*, May 13, 1841; "The Long, Low Black Schooner," *NYS*, August 31, 1839; "The Amistad," *NLG*, October 16, 1839.

22. "Narrative," *NYJC*, October 10, 1839; "Mendis Perform," *NYMH*, May 13, 1841; *Youth's Cabinet*, May 20, 1841.

23. "Private Examination of Cinquez," *NYCA*, September 13, 1839; Barber, 13; "The Mendians," *Vermont Chronicle*, June 8, 1842.

24. "Correspondence of the Journal of Commerce," *NYJC*, July 25, 1839. This evidence was provided by the two sailors, Manuel Padilla and Jacinto Verdaque, after they jumped overboard and managed to get back to Havana. There is no evidence that the abolitionists knew of the revolt aboard the *Teçora*, and it is not hard to imagine why the Africans would not have mentioned it to them. It is possible that the revolt led to executions of their fellow rebels and shipmates in Havana, and that this was why they feared the place ever after. For background on slave ship revolts, see Eric Robert Taylor, *If We Must Die: Shipboard Insurrections in the Era of the Atlantic Slave Trade* (Baton Rouge: Louisiana State University Press, 2006).

25. Barber, 11; Moore to Harned, October 12, 1852, ARC. Faquorna is an especially important figure, as is clear in the narrative of the rebellion above. Unfortunately he died soon after the *Amistad* was towed into New London. Therefore much less is known about him than about many of the others. On Grabeau's background, see *Vermont Chronicle*, June 8, 1842; Testimony of Antonio, United States District Court, January 9, 1840, NAB. It seems likely that the plot was planned by the prisoners kept belowdecks, for those on the main deck, near the crew, would have been more limited in their ability to talk among themselves.

26. "Narrative," *NYJC*, October 10, 1839. Kinna also claimed, "We break chain." See "Mendis Perform," *NYMH*, May 13, 1841; "Anniversaries—Amistad Freemen," *Youth's Cabinet*, May 20, 1841; Barber, 11; "The Amistad Negroes," *Farmer's Cabinet*, November 19, 1841; "The Amistad Captives," *Liberator*, November 19, 1841.

27. "African Testimony," *NYJC*, January 10, 1840; "The Case of the Africans Decided for the Present—Habeas Corpus not Sustained," *NYMH*, September 25, 1839. The oral history of the event maintained that Celestino screamed, waking the rest of the crew. It seems that Antonio's account is more credible on this point as he witnessed the event while those who gave the oral history may not have.

28. "The Long, Low Black Schooner," *NYS*, August 31, 1839; "Case," *NYMH*, September 22, 1839; "The Amistad," *NLG*, October 16, 1839; "The Case of the Captured Negroes," *NYMH*, September 9, 1839. Richard Robert Madden wrote in October 1839: "There was much merchandize also on board, and amongst the rest a package of swords or machetes as they are called, which are used for cutting down canes. The female negroes of the party, true to their sex, indulged their curiosity in examining the contents of various packages around them whenever there was an opportunity, and faithful also to the communicative character of the fair part of humanity, they imparted the information they had acquired to their male friends, and the latter true to themselves, and faithful to one bold man among them who became their chief, they acted on it." The so-called female negroes were the three little girls—Margru, Kagne, and Teme—who used their intelligence, their ability to range freely, and their ability to communicate to find the cane knives and inform their male shipmates of the location, thereby making the successful rebellion possible. See Madden to A. Blackwood, Esq., October 3, 1839, Correspondence from Dr. R.R. Madden, Mr. D.R. Clarke, and the Foreign Office relating to the removal of the Liberated Africans from Cuba, 1839, Colonial Office (CO) 318/146, NA. The oral history suggested that the knives were found before the rebellion began, but this seems unlikely, for it also noted that Cinqué killed Celestino with a "billet of wood." It is inconceivable that a Mende warrior would have used a club if a cane knife had been available.

29. Interview of Antonio, "The Long, Low Black Schooner," *NYS*, August 31, 1839.

30. Kale to John Quincy Adams, January 4, 1841, John Quincy Adams Papers, Massachusetts Historical Society. Fuli stated, "Capt. Ferrer killed one of the Africans, Duevi by name, before the Africans killed him." See "African Testimony," *NYJC*, January 10, 1840. Kinna later alleged that Captain Ferrer had killed two of the Africans. One of them, unnamed, seems to have died later of wounds inflicted by Captain Ferrer.

31. "Mendis Perform," *NYMH*, May 13, 1841. Ruiz: "The cabin boy said they had killed only the captain and cook. The other two he said had escaped in the canoe—a small boat." See "The Captured Slaves," *NYMH*, September 2, 1839.

32. "Mendis Perform," *NYMH*, May 13, 1841.

33. Testimony of Antonio, January 9, 1840, United States District Court, NAB.

34. "The Long, Low Black Schooner," *NYS*, August 31, 1839; "The Negroes of the Amistad," *New Hampshire Sentinel*, October 2, 1839. According to the oral history as mediated by Hannah Moore, "the ocean reverberated with the yells and frantic dances of a savage clan." See Moore to Harned, October 12, 1852, ARC.

35. "The Long, Low Black Schooner," *NYS*, August 31, 1839; "Case," *NYMH*, September 22, 1839.

36. Testimony of Antonio, United States District Court, NAB; "The Long, Low Black Schooner," *NYS*, August 31, 1839; Barber, 11; "Superior Court," *NYMH*, October 24, 1839.

37. "The Case of the Africans Decided," *NYMH*, September 25, 1839. Antonio also wanted Burna to hold his money; he gave it to him "tied up in a stocking." See "Herald on Amistad Trial," *NYMH*, November 21, 1839.

38. Antonio, "Case," *NYMH*, September 22, 1839; "The Long, Low Black Schooner," *NYS*, August 31, 1839.

39. Testimony of Antonio; Testimony of Kinna, November 19, 1839, U.S. District Court, NAB.

40. Antonio, "Case," *NYMH*, September 22, 1839; "The Amistad," *NLG*, October 16, 1839. The body of Celestino had apparently been thrown overboard soon after the rebellion ended.

41. Much of the evidence in this section comes from the extraordinarily long and detailed account of the post-rebellion voyage written by José Ruiz and Pedro Montes, especially the latter, who was navigating the vessel the entire time. This 6,600-word account originally appeared on the Spanish-language newspaper *Noticioso de Ambos Mundos*. It was translated into English and republished in the *NLG* on October 16, 1839. I have relied on the latter version, supplementing it with other evidence where possible. The *Amistad* Africans said little about the voyage.

42. "Case," *NYMH*, September 22, 1839.

43. "The Amistad," *NLG*, October 16, 1839. The long account provided by Montes and Ruiz described extensive communication between the two Spaniards and the Africans, made possible by Antonio's ability to translate and interpret.

44. "The Long, Low Black Schooner," *NYS*, August 31, 1839.

45. Lewis Tappan to Joseph Sturge, November 15, 1841, reprinted in Sturge, *Visit*, Appendix E, xlvi.

46. "The Amistad African Appearance," *NYCA*, September 4, 1839. The story was repeated in *A True History of the African Chief Jingua and his Comrades. With a Description of the Kingdom of Mandingo, and of the Manners and Customs of the Inhabitants.—An Account of King Sharka, of Gallinas. A Sketch of the Slave Trade and Horrors of the Middle Passage; with the Proceedings on Board the "Long, Low, Black Schooner," Amistad.* (Hartford, New York, and Boston, 1839), 11.

47. "The Amistad," *NLG*, October 16, 1839; Moore to Harned, October 12, 1852, ARC.

48. Ibid.

49. "The Amistad," *NLG*, October 16, 1839.

50. For a survey of the history and arts of Mami Wata, see Henry John Drewal, *Mami Wata: Arts for Water Spirits in Africa and Its Diaspora* (Los Angeles: Fowler Museum at UCLA, 2008). On Mende water spirits, see M. C. Jędrej, "An Analytical Note on the Land and Spirits of the Sewa Mende," *Africa: Journal of the International Africa Institute* 44 (1974): 40–41. The suggestion that irons and chains were thrown overboard is based on the fact that none of the several post-rebellion inventories of the *Amistad* disclosed their presence on the vessel.

51. "The Amistad," *NLG*, October 16, 1839.

52. Testimony of Henry Green, November 19, 1839, U.S. District Court, Connecticut, NAB.

53. "The Amistad," *NLG*, October 16, 1839.

54. *NLG*, August 28, 1839; Moore to Harned, October 12, 1852, ARC.

55. "Case," *NYMH*, September 22, 1839; J. M. Harris, "Some Remarks on the Origin, Manners, Customs, and Superstitions of the Gallinas People of Sierra Leone." *Memoirs Read Before the Anthropological Society of London, 1865–1866* (London: Published for the Anthropological Society, by Trubner and Co., 1866), vol. II, 26.

56. Moore to Harned, October 12, 1852, ARC. At this point the oral history maintained that the Africans "approach[ed] New Haven and anchor[ed]." They probably thought of New Haven as the entire region rather than a city per se.

57. "The Amistad," *NLG*, October 16, 1839.

58. Ibid.

59. Testimony of Green. Lewis Tappan reported on another interview with Henry Green in "To the Committee," *NYJC*, September 10, 1839.

60. Testimony of Green.

61. The white men had probably seen the article, "A Suspicious Sail—a Pirate," *NYMH*, August 24, 1839.

62. Testimony of Green; Testimony of Cinqué, January 8, 1840, Records of the U.S. District and Circuit Courts, NAB.

63. "Case of the Amistad," *Charleston Courier*, November 26, 1839; Testimony of Captain Fordham; Testimony of Green, Records of the U.S. District and Circuit Courts, NAB; "The Long, Low Black Schooner," *NYS*, August 31, 1839.

64. Testimony of Cinqué, January 8, 1840, U.S. District Court, Connecticut, NAB; Moore to Harned, October 12, 1852, ARC.

65. Rough transcript of the first day's testimony in district court at Hartford, Conn., Coll. 247—box 1, folder 6, Andrew T. Judson Papers, Coll. 247, f. 4, Manuscripts Collection, G. W. Blunt White Library, Mystic Seaport Museum, Mystic, Connecticut.

66. Testimony of Dr. Sharp, n.d., Records of the U.S. District and Circuit Courts for the District of Connecticut: Documents Relating to the Various Cases Involving the Spanish Schooner Armistad, NAB.

67. Libel of Thomas R. Gedney, Records of the U.S. District and Circuit Courts, NAB. There was disagreement about the number of men on shore when the brig Washington arrived on the scene. The lowest estimate was 8–9, the highest 30. Most of the eyewitnesses, three of the white men and Antonio, put the number around 20.

68. Depositions of James Ray and George W. Pierce, December 1839, Records of the U.S. District and Circuit Courts, NAB.

69. Testimony of Lt. Richard Meade, November 19, 1839, Records of the U.S. District and

Circuit Courts, NAB; "The Low Black Schooner Captured," *NYJC*, August 28, 1839; "The Long, Low Black Schooner," *NYS*, August 31, 1839.

70. "The Long, Low Black Schooner," *NYS*, August 31, 1839; Moore to Harned, October 12, 1852. The *Sun* printed these speeches separately, with images of Cinqué, and sold them in the streets as broadsides and handbills.

71. *NLG*, September 4, 1839.

72. *NLG*, August 28, 1839.

73. "The Long, Low Black Schooner," *NYS*, August 31, 1839.

Chapter Three: Movement

1. *NLG*, August 28, 1839; "The Spanish Piratical Schooner Amistad," *NYMH*, August 30, 1839.

2. *NLG*, August 28, 1839.

3. On the life and legal career of Judson, see Douglas L. Stein, "The *Amistad* Judge: The Life and Trials of Andrew T. Judson, 1784–1853," *Log of Mystic Seaport* 49 (1998): 98–106.

4. "The Long, Low Black Schooner," *NYS*, August 31, 1839. It is impossible to know what was inside Cinqué's greegree bag, but it is possible to know what *kinds of things* might have been there, because missionary George Thompson, who was in many ways the first ethnographer among the Mende peoples of southern Sierra Leone, inspected and wrote about such containers and their contents. When a "benighted heathen" converted to Christianity, he or she sometimes surrendered a "greegree bag" to Thompson. That of an "old conjurer" included an "old, dirty, greasy cloth, containing live bug-a-bugs (white ants), and some of their dirt from the large hillocks; also one piece of iron, and one very small antelope's horn." A "big-war medicine" contained "some old dirt, an iron rod about one foot long, a nail and two screws." A third was "a goat's horn, containing three or four pieces of leopard skin, and a piece of paper written on both sides with Arabic writing." The inclusion of what appear to have been Quranic inscriptions, offered by "Muslim strangers" in times of war, illustrates the advance of Islam in Cinqué's region. Thompson wrote that small bags "were tied to a string and worn about the neck!" To the missionary, these were "the delusions of Satan." See *Thompson in Africa*, 152, 194, and *The Palm Land*, 178–79, 390. See also Jones, 77, 184; M. C. Jędrej, "Medicine, Fetish, and Secret Society in a West African Culture," *Africa: Journal of the International Africa Institute* 46 (1976): 247–57; and Mariane Ferme, *The Underneath of Things: Violence, History, and the Everyday in Sierra Leone* (Berkeley: University of California Press, 2001), 3, 4, 5, 67.

5. For more on the legal history of the case, see R. Earl McClendon, "The *Amistad* Claims: Inconsistencies of Policy," *Political Science Quarterly* 48 (1933): 386–412; Bruce A. Ragsdale, "'Incited by the Love of Liberty': The *Amistad* Captives and the Federal Courts," *Prologue: Quarterly of the National Archives and Records Administration* 35 (2003): 12–24.

6. "Joseph Cinquez, Leader of the Piratical Gang of Negroes, who killed Captain Ramon Ferris and the Cook, on board the Spanish Schooner Amistad, taken by Lieut. Gedney, commanding the U.S. Brig Washington at Culloden Point, Long Island, 24th Augt 1839, Drawn from Life by J. Sketchley, Aug. 30, 1839," lithograph by John Childs, NHCHS. The speech: "My brothers, I am once more among you, having deceived the enemy of our race by saying I had doubloons. I came to tell you that you have only one chance for death, and none for Liberty. I am sure you prefer death, as I do. You can by killing the white man now on board, and I will help you, make the people here kill you. It is better for you to do this, and then you will not only avert bondage yourselves, but prevent the entailment of unnumbered wrongs on your children. Come—come with me then–." The same quotation appears in "The Long, Low Black Schooner," *NYS*, August 31, 1839. See also Gwendolyn DuBois Shaw, in *Portraits of the People: Picturing African Americans in the Nineteenth Century* (Seattle: University of Washington Press, 2006), 130.

7. "Joseph Cinquez, Leader of the Gang of Negroes, . . . Captured by Lieutenant Gedney of the U.S. Brig Washington at Culloden Point, Long Island, August 24th 1839," hand-colored lithograph, Stanley Whitman House, Farmington, Connecticut. Shaw dates the lithograph October 1, 1839, but the basis for this is not clear; see *Portraits of the People*, 130–31.

8. "Joseph Cinquez, The brave Congolese Chief, who prefers death to Slavery, and who now lies in Jail at New Haven Conn. awaiting his trial for daring for freedom," LC.

A second, smaller version of the image—perhaps a handbill—is in the Frances Manwaring Caulkins Scrapbook, reference 029.3 Scr 15, Misc. American, 1830–1850, New London County Historical Society, New London, Connecticut. Below the caption was the "Speech to his Comrade Slaves after Murdering the Captain &c and Getting Possession of the Vessel and Cargo": "Brothers we have done that which we purposed, our hands are now clean as we have Striven to regain the precious heritage we received from our fathers. We have only to persevere. Where the sun rises, there is our home, our brethren, our fathers. Do not seek to defeat my orders, if so I shall sacrifice any one who would endanger the rest. When at home we will kill the old Man, the young one shall be saved. He is kind and gave you bread. We must not kill those who give us water. Brothers, I am resolved that it is better to die than be a white man's slave, and I will not complain if by dying I save you. Let us be careful what we eat that we may not be sick. The deed is done and I need say no more." The *New York Sun* of August 31, 1839, identified "James Sheffield of New London" as the artist, but it appears the main maritime artist of New London in this period was Isaac Sheffield (1798–1845). See H. W. French, *Art and Artists in Connecticut* (Boston, 1879), 60.

9. "Joseph Cinquez Addressing his Compatriots on board the Spanish Schooner AMISTAD 26th Augt 1839," lithograph by John Childs, Chicago Historical Society (ICHi 22004).

10. This broadside was, like the others, apparently commissioned by the *New York Sun*. The text, though not the image, was republished in the newspaper on August 31, 1839: "Friends and brothers—We would have returned but the sun was against us. I would not see you serve the white man, so I induced you to help me kill the Captain. I thought I should be killed—I expected it. It would have been better. You had better be killed than live many moons in misery. I shall be hanged, I think, every day. But this does not pain me. I could die happy, if by dying I could save so many of my brothers from the bondage of the white man." The speech was republished in the *NYJC* on September 2, 1839, and in the *Charleston Courier* on September 5, 1839. The speech was said to have been translated by Antonio. The print and speech provide a good example of the "print-performance culture" described by Peter Reed, *Rogue Performances: Staging the Underclasses in Early American Theatre Culture* (London: Palgrave Macmillan, 2009), 4.

11. "Portrait of Cinquez" from the Monday, September 2, 1839 edition, reprinted in the *NYS*, September 7, 1839, Country Edition, Weekly—no. 147. The reach of the *New York Sun* extended all the way to Havana, where Richard Robert Madden read the paper and learned of the *Amistad* case. He later went to New Haven to visit the captives and subsequently gave crucial testimony. See Gera Burton, "Liberty's Call: Richard Robert Madden's Voice in the Anti-Slavery Movement," *Irish Migration Studies in Latin America* 5 (2007): 202–03. On the rise of the penny press see James L. Crouthamel, *Bennett's New York Herald and the Rise of the Popular Press* (Syracuse, NY: Syracuse University Press, 1989) and Dan Schiller's classic account, *Objectivity and the News: The Public and the Rise of Commercial Journalism* (Philadelphia: University of Pennsylvania Press, 1981).

12. Interest in the case was also great in Boston, where 4,000 copies of a September 1 "Extra" of the *NYMH* sold out by noon; "Boston," *NYMH*, September 4, 1839.

13. "The Long, Low Black Schooner," *NYS*, August 31, 1839. The correspondent even threw in a glowing phrenological analysis of Cinqué's head, suggesting among other things that he possessed "unshaken courage, and intense love of home and kindred."

14. Dwight P. Janes to Rev. Joshua Leavitt, New London, August 30, 1839; Dwight P. Janes to R. S. Baldwin, New London, August 31, 1839; Dwight P. Janes to R. S. Baldwin, New London, September 2, 1839; Dwight P. Janes to Joshua Leavitt, New London, September 2, 1839, ARC. See also two articles by Maria Hileman, "The Amistad's Unsung Hero" and "Dwight Janes: Conscience of the Amistad," both published in *The Day*, October 5, 1997.

15. For biographies of Tappan and Leavitt see Bertram Wyatt-Brown, *Lewis Tappan and the Evangelical War Against Slavery* (Cleveland: Case Western University Press, 1969, reprinted Baton Rouge: Louisiana State University Press, 1997) and Hugh Davis, *Joshua Leavitt, Evangelical Abolitionist* (Baton Rouge: Louisiana State University Press, 1990).

16. "The Captured Slaves," *NYMH*, September 2, 1839.

17. South Carolina Senator John C. Calhoun had declared slavery to be a "positive good" in 1837. See Jones, *Mutiny on the Amistad*, 10.

18. Stanley Harrold, *American Abolitionists* (Harlow, UK: Longman, 2001), 34; James

Brewer Stewart, "From Moral Suasion to Political Confrontation: American Abolitionists and the Problem of Resistance, 1831–1861," in his *Abolitionist Politics and the Coming of the Civil War* (Amherst: University of Massachusetts Press, 2008), 3–31.

19. For the background to the abolitionist movement, see Richard S. Newman, *The Transformation of American Abolitionism: Fighting Slavery in the Early Republic* (Chapel Hill: University of North Carolina Press, 2001).

20. James Pennington, *The Fugitive Blacksmith; or, Events in the History of James W. C. Pennington, Pastor of a Presbyterian Church, New York, Formerly a Slave in the State of Maryland, United States* (London: Charles Gilpin, 1849); Margaret Washington, *Sojourner Truth's America* (Champaign-Urbana: University of Illinois Press, 2009), 138.

21. "Incendiaries," *New Orleans Bee*, October 11, 1839; "Mobile," *Richmond Enquirer*, November 1, 1839; "Another Exciting Rumor," *NYS*, September 3, 1840; "A Negro Revolt in Louisiana," *NYS*, September 12, 1840; "A Negro Plot," *NYS*, November 10, 1840; "A Revolt," *PF*, September 22, 1840; "Slave Insurrection," *PF*, September 24, 1840; "An Attempted Slave Insurrection in South Carolina," *PF*, October 20, 1841; *NYS*, August 31, 1839; Kenneth W. Porter, *The Black Seminoles: History of a Freedom-Seeking People* (Gainesville: University Press of Florida, 1996).

22. Fergus Bordewich, *Bound for Canaan: The Underground Railroad and the War for the Soul of America* (New York: Amistad, 2005).

23. Philip M. Hamel, "Great Britain, the United States, and the Negro Seamen Acts, 1822–1848," *Journal of Southern History* 1 (1935): 3–28; Peter Hinks, *To Awaken My Afflicted Brethren: David Walker and the Problem of Antebellum Slave Resistance* (State College: Pennsylvania State University Press, 1996).

24. "Incarcerated Captives," *NYCA*, September 6, 1839; "Conditions for Amistad Captives," *NYCA*, September 9, 1839; "Case of the Captured Africans," *NYMH*, September 22, 1839; "Visit to Hartford, Connecticut," *NYMH*, September 24, 1839; and "Removal of the Africans to Hartford—Crim. Con. among the Savages—Exposure of the Abolition Falsehood, &c.," *NYMH*, November 19, 1839; *NYS*, September 20, 1839; "Calvin Edson, The Living Skeleton," *Daily Chronicle*, January 18, 1832.

25. "To the Committee on Behalf of the African Prisoners," *NYJC*, September 10, 1839; "Removal of the Africans," *NYMH*, November 19, 1839; "Incarcerated Captives," *NYCA*, September 6, 1839; "The Captives of the Amistad," *Emancipator*, October 3, 1839.

26. "The Captives of the Amistad," *Emancipator*, October 3, 1839.

27. Anonymous, "Treatment of the Captured Africans," November 1, 1839, ARC. This appears to have been an unpublished article written for the *Emancipator*.

28. Ibid. See also *Emancipator*, September 9, 1839.

29. "The Captured Africans of the Amistad," *NYMH*, October 4, 1839. This comment referred to the Hartford jail; see below, 129–32.

30. "Private Examination of Cinquez," *NYCA*, September 13, 1839; "The Negroes of the Amistad," *New Hampshire Sentinel*, October 2, 1839.

31. "Captured Africans," *NYMH*, October 4, 1839; "The Negroes Lately Captured," *NYMH*, September 5, 1839; "The Africans," *Patriot and Democrat*, September 21, 1839; "The Africans," *NYMH*, October 5, 1839. Abolitionist A. F. Williams wrote that "1,000 $ was recd in Hartford & more than 1,000 $ (as I am informed) in N. Haven at 12 ½ cts admission" from visitors to the jails. The figure for Hartford, where the *Amistad* Africans spent only two weeks in September 1839 and a few days in November, is credible, but the figure for New Haven is far too low. See A. F. Williams to Lewis Tappan, Farmington, March 13, 1841, ARC.

32. "Captured Africans," *NYMH*, October 4, 1839; "The Africans," *NYMH*, September 13, 1839.

33. "Captured Africans," *NYMH*, October 4, 1839; *NYS*, September 20, 1839.

34. William H. Townsend, Sketches of the Amistad captives, [ca. 1839–1840]. GEN MSS 335, Beneicke Rare Book and Manuscript Collection, Yale University.

35. Family tradition had it that Townsend produced his pencil sketches around the time of one of the several trials of the *Amistad* captives: September 1839, November 1839, January 1840, or March 1841. The sketch of Faquorna suggests an earlier date. See Charles Allen Dinsmore, "Interesting Sketches of the Amistad Captives," *Yale University Library Gazette* 9 (1935): 51–55.

36. David Grimsted, *Melodrama Unveiled: American Theater and Culture, 1800–1850* (Chicago: University of Chicago Press, 1968), 149; Rosemarie K. Bank, *Theatre Culture in America, 1825–1860* (Cambridge, UK: Cambridge University Press, 1997), 159. Phillips was apparently employed by the Bowery Theatre in May 1838, when he wrote a statement to be read to "an overflowing house" when the theatre reopened after a fire. Another suggestive fact is that Inez, the only female character in the play, was played by a "Mrs. Phillips."

37. The playbill is in the Harvard Theatre Collection. See also "Bowery Theatre," *NYCA*, September 4, 1839; "The Long, Low Black Schooner," *NYS*, August 31, 1839. I am especially indebted in this section to Bruce A. McConachie, "'The Theatre of the Mob': Apocalyptic Melodrama and Preindustrial Riots in Antebellum New York," in McConachie and Daniel Friedman, eds., *Theatre for Working-class Audiences in the United States, 1830–1980* (Westport, CT: Greenwood Press, 1985), 17–46; the same author's *Melodramatic Formations: American Theatre and Society, 1820–1870* (Iowa City: University of Iowa Press, 1992); and Reed, *Rogue Performances*. See also Shane White, *Stories of Freedom in Black New York* (Cambridge, MA: Harvard University Press, 2007).

38. Christine Stansell, *City of Women: Sex and Class in New York, 1789–1860* (New York: Knopf, 1986), 89, 90, 93–95; McConachie, *Melodramatic Formations*, 122; Reed, *Rogue Performances*, 9, 11, 15; Bank, *Theatre Culture in America*, 84; Peter George Buckley, "To the Opera House: Society and Culture in New York City, 1820–1860," Ph.D. dissertation, State University of New York at Stony Brook, 1984, 181–82.

39. *Philadelphia Inquirer*, September, 2, 1839. The *New York Mirror* ("The Theatre," September 14, 1839) listed the play as one of the successes of the season. The Bowery Theatre was known for pioneering longer runs. See McConachie, *Melodramatic Formations*, 120. The estimated revenue comes from a well-researched but unfootnoted article by Perry Walton, "The Mysterious Case of the Long, Low Black Schooner," *New England Quarterly* 6 (1933): 360. Walton also notes that the play was performed at the Park Theatre, the National Theatre, and Niblo's Garden as well as the Bowery. I have not been able to confirm the revenue or the other venues in primary sources. The last newspaper mention of the play was in the *New Orleans Bee*, September 17, 1839.

40. "Bowery Theatre," *NYCA*, September 4, 1839; "Theatricals—The Seven Ages," *NYMH*, February 28, 1840; Bank, *Theatre Culture*, 72.

41. The name Zemba apparently came from a story, "Tales of the Niger: Zemba and Zorayde," published in *The Court Magazine, containing Original papers by Distinguished Writers* (London: Bull and Churton, 1833) 3 (July–December 1833): 71–74, republished in the *Philadelphia Inquirer* on January 2, 1838. Zemba is Muslim guide to a British traveler, who kindly saves him from a despotic African king, allowing him to marry his beloved Zorayde.

42. The use of the hold of the schooner as a setting made the play unusual. Heather Nathans has noted that the Middle Passage "virtually disappeared" from the American stage at midcentury as the slave trade was rethought as something internal to the nation's borders. See her *Slavery and Sentiment on the American Stage, 1787–1861: Lifting the Veil of Black* (New York: Cambridge University Press, 2009), 129–30.

43. Peter Reed writes that a staged execution was not likely and that a more common plot outcome at the time would have been a reprieve for the hero. Personal communication to the author, December 14, 2010.

44. Rosemarie K. Bank notes that *The Gladiator* was "considered too rebellious for black ears," hence free people of color were banned from the audience, but the ban may not have been enforced. See her *Theatre Culture*, 96. Three-fingered Jack was called a "daring freebooter" in the *Supplement to the Royal Gazette*, January 27–Feb 3, 1781, 79, cited in Diana Paton, "The Afterlives of Three-Fingered Jack," in Brycchan Carey and Peter J. Kitson, eds., *Slavery and the Cultures of Abolition: Essays Marking the Bicentennial of the Abolition Act of 1807* (London: Cambridge: D. S. Brewer, 2007), 44. See also McConachie, *Melodramatic Formations*, 70–71, 142, 143, and Reed, *Rogue Performances*, 21, 37, 100, 122, 159–160. For the pirate plays of the era, see George C. D. Odell, *Annals of the New York Stage* (New York: Columbia University Press, 1928), vol. IV (1834–1843), 30, 144, 149, 151, 163, 313, 315, 373, 390, 481, 488. Other plays included *Pirates of the Panda, or the Plunder of the Mexican* (1834–1835), based on current events); *The Pirate Boy* (1837); *Pirates of the Hurlgate* (1839); and *The Pirates Signal, or the Bridge of Death* (1840).

45. Reed, *Rogue Performances*, 5, 13 (quotation), 43; McConachie, *Melodramatic Formations*, 97–100.

46. "Private Examination," *NYCA*, September 13, 1839; "The Long, Low Black Schooner," *NYS*, August 31, 1839.

47. Reed, *Rogue Performances*, 10, 175–85; Jonas B. Phillips, *Jack Sheppard, or the Life of a Robber! Melodrama in Three Acts founded on Ainsworth's Novel* (written and performed in 1839). On Sheppard, see Peter Linebaugh, *The London Hanged: Crime and Civil Society in the Eighteenth Century* (London: Allen Lane, 1991), chap. 1.

48. "Incarcerated Captives," *NYCA*, September 6, 1839.

49. Dwight P. Janes to Rev. Joshua Leavitt, New London, August 30, 1839, ARC; "Incarcerated Captives," *NYCA*, September 6, 1839. For other efforts to find interpreters, see Seth Staples to Roger Baldwin, September 4, 1839, and Ellis Gray Loring to Roger Baldwin, September 19, 1839, Baldwin Family Papers.

50. "To the Committee" *NYJC*, September 10, 1839; "Captured Africans," *NYMH*, October 4, 1839.

51. "To the Committee," *NYJC*, September 10, 1839. A controversy surrounded the issue of whether Antonio could translate for the *Amistad* Africans, although in practical terms the question was moot as he was segregated from them after September 10, 1839. Around this time, Ruiz insisted that "the cabin boy knows nothing of the language" of the Africans and could not translate. Yet there is abundant evidence to contradict that claim, some of it provided by Ruiz himself. In an earlier account of the rebellion he had explained that the Africans would have killed Antonio, but for the fact that "he acted as interpreter between us, as he understood both languages." The pro-Ruiz *Morning Herald* also reported that "no one but Antonio can understand" the *Amistad* Africans. During his court testimony in November 1839, Burna looked to Antonio every time he did not understand a question. The *New Bedford Mercury* also reported that "Antonio is the only one able to communicate with them," although "very imperfectly." On top of all this is the practical evidence of his abilities to translate provided by Ruiz and Montes in their account of the *Amistad*'s voyage after the rebellion. See "The Case of the Captured Negroes," *NYMH*, September 9, 1839; "Important from Washington—The Captured Africans," *NYMH*, September 10, 1839: and "Herald on Amistad Trial," *NYMH*, November 21, 1839; "The Long, Low Black Schooner," *NYS*, August 31, 1839; "The African Captives," *New Bedford Mercury*, September 13, 1839; *NLG*, October 16, 1839.

52. "Funds Appeal," *NYCA*, September 5, 1839.

Chapter Four: Jail

1. "The Long, Low Black Schooner," *NYS*, August 31, 1839; Charles Dickens, "The Italian Prisoner," no. XVII in *The Uncommercial Traveller* from *All the Year Round* (October 13, 1860): 13–17. The definition of "political prisoner" used here is someone incarcerated for a technically illegal act that a substantial part of the population considered ethically justified.

2. "Education of the Africans—Doubtful whether they are Negroes Personal History—Sketch of their Country, &c.," *NYMH*, November 12, 1839. This chapter builds on the work of James L. Huston, "The Experiential Basis of the Northern Antislavery Impulse," *Journal of Southern History* 56 (1990): 609–40. See also the excellent essay by Susan Eva O'Donovan, "Universities of Social and Political Change: Slaves in Jail in Antebellum America," in Michele Lise Tartar and Richard Bell, eds., *Buried Lives: Incarcerated in Early America* (Athens, GA : University of Georgia Press , 2012), 124–46.

3. Henry Mayer, *All on Fire: William Lloyd Garrison and the Abolition of Slavery* (New York: W. W. Norton & Company, 2008), chap. 5.

4. Tappan had written the day before that attorney Seth Staples was to attend the September 10 interview along with Baldwin and the others, but he was not listed among those who did. See Tappan's letter, "To the Committee on Behalf of the African Prisoners," *NYJC*, September 10, 1839. Bau (or Bahoo) was incorrectly identified as "Bowle" in the first accounts of the interview, according to a correspondent of the *NYS*. See "The Amistad Case," *NYS*, September 23, 1839.

5. "The Captured Africans of the Amistad," *NYMH*, October 4, 1839. Antonio also gave testimony in the hearing conducted by Judge Andrew Judson aboard the U.S. brig *Washington*. His remarks were published in "The Long, Low Black Schooner," *NYS*, August 31, 1839.

6. "Private Examination of Cinquez," *NYCA*, September 13, 1839. This paragraph and the seven following are based on this article and another, published as "To the Committee," in the *NYJC*, September 10, 1839, both by Lewis Tappan. Shorter summaries of the interviews also appeared in the *NLG*, September 11, 1839, and the *NYS*, September 12, 1839.

7. Arthur Abraham, "Sengbe Pieh: A Neglected Hero?" *Journal of the Historical Society of Sierra Leone* 2 (1978): 22–30.

8. "To the Committee," *NYJC*, September 10, 1839; "The Slaves," *NLG*, September 11, 1839; "Private Examination," *NYCA*, September 13, 1839.

9. John Warner Barber later recorded that Bau had lived "near a large river named Wo-wa," probably the Moa. See Barber, 11. Based on evidence gathered from Liberated Africans by linguist Sigismund Koelle in Freetown, Sierra Leone, around 1850, P.E.H. Hair suggests that the peoples of the region began to form families around the age of 25. See "The Enslavement of Koelle's Informants," *Journal of African History* 6 (1965): 193–203. Cinqué's age would have increased his authority within the relatively young group.

10. "To the Committee," *NYJC*, September 10, 1839; Lewis Tappan to Roger Baldwin, November 21, 1840, Baldwin Family Papers; Deposition of Dr. Richard R. Madden, November 20, 1839, U.S. District Court, Connecticut, NAB; "Adams Letter on Amistad Africans," *NYJC*, December 25, 1839; "Plans to Educate the Amistad Africans in English," *NYJC*, October 9, 1839; "Amistad Trial—Termination," *Emancipator*, January 16, 1840; L. N. Fowler, "Phrenological Developments of Joseph Cinquez, Alias Ginqua," *American Phrenological Journal and Miscellany* 2 (1840): 136–38; *New England Weekly Record*, May 23, 1840; "Peale's Museum and Portrait Gallery," *NYCA*, June 16, 1840; "Visit to Hartford, Connecticut," *NYMH*, September 24, 1839.

11. "The Captured Africans," *NYMH*, September 17, 1839; "The Amistad Africans in Prison," *NYMH*, October 9, 1839.

12. Phillip Lapsansky, "Graphic Discord: Abolitionists and Antiabolitionist Images," in Jean Fagan Yellin and John C. Van Horne, eds., *The Abolitionist Sisterhood: Women's Political Culture in Antebellum America* (Ithaca, NY: Cornell University Press, 1994), 218–21; Marcus Wood, *Blind Memory: Visual Representations of Slavery in England and America, 1780–1865* (Manchester, UK: Manchester University Press, 2000), 172–76; Richard Powell, "Cinqué: Antislavery Portraiture and Patronage in Jacksonian America," *American Art* 11 (1997): 56–57.

13. *Haverhill Gazette*, September 27, 1839; "Removal of the African Prisoners," *NYCA*, September 16, 1839.

14. Roderick Stanley, "Journal of Farmington Farmer," 1837–1843. (Ms 74260), CHS; *Emancipator*, September 19, 1839.

15. "The Amistad," *NYCA*, September 19, 1839; "Amistad," *NYCA* September 20, 1839; "Visit to Hartford, Connecticut," *NYMH*, September 24, 1839.

16. "Teaching Philosophy to Lewis Tappen & Co. in the Prison at Hartford," *NYMH*, October 4, 1839.

17. Ibid.; Lapsansky, "Graphic Discord," 222–30. On "amalgamation," see James Brewer Stewart, "The Emergence of Racial Modernity and the Rise of the White North, 1790–1840" and Leslie M. Harris, "From Abolitionist Amalgamators to 'Rulers of the Five Points': The Discourse of Interracial Sex and Reform in Antebellum New York City," both in Patrick Rael, *African-American Activism Before the Civil War: The Freedom Struggle in the Antebellum North* (New York and London: Routledge, 2008), 220–49 and 250–71.

18. "Case of the Captured Africans," *NYMH*, September 22, 1839; "The Amistad," *Richmond Enquirer*, September 27, 1839.

19. "Details of the Slow Hartford Trial," *NYCA*, September 21, 1839. See Jones, *Mutiny on the Amistad*, chap. 4.

20. "Case of the Captured Africans," *NYMH*, September 22, 1839; [Lewis Tappan], "The Amistad Circuit Court Trial," *NYCA*, September 23, 1839.

21. "The Amistad," *NYCA*, September 24, 1839.

22. "The Captured Africans," *NYCA*, October 4, 1839.

23. Reverend Alonzo N. Lewis, M.A., "Recollections of the Amistad Slave Case: First Revelation of a Plot to Force the Slavery Question to an Issue more than twenty Years before its Final Outbreak in the Civil War—Several Hitherto Unknown Aspects of the Case Told," *Connecticut Magazine* 11 (1907): 127.

24. "Important from Washington—The Captured Africans," *NYMH*, September 10, 1839; "Captured Africans," *NYCA*, October 8, 1839; "Teaching Philosophy to Lewis Tappen [*sic*]," *NYMH*, October 4, 1839; "The Africans," *NYMH*, September 26, 1839.

25. "The Africans," *NYMH*, October 5, 1839; "The Captives of the Amistad," *Emancipator*, October 3, 1839. For a broader history of warrior moves, see T. J. Desch Obi, *Fighting for Honor: The History of African Martial Art Traditions in the Atlantic World* (Columbia: University of South Carolina Press, 2008).

26. "The Negroes of the Amistad," *New Hampshire Sentinel*, October 2, 1839. On Poro training in acrobatics, see F.W.H. Migeod, "The Poro Society: The Building of the Poro House and Making of the Image," *Man* 16 (1916): 102; Kenneth L. Little, "The Role of the Secret Society in Cultural Specialization," *American Anthropologist*, n.s., 51 (1949): 202; Little, *The Mende of Sierra Leone: A West African People in Transition* (London: Routledge & Kegan Paul, 1951, rev. ed. 1967), 121.

27. "An Incident," *NYCA*, September 26, 1839.

28. "Plans to Educate," *NYJC*, October 9, 1839; Barber, 9; Muriel Rukeyser, *Willard Gibbs* (Garden City, NY: Doubleday, Doran & Co., 1942), 16–46.

29. "Conditions for Amistad Captives," *NYCA*, September 9, 1839. Gibbs would later testify that he acquired his knowledge of the Mende language from James Covey, but here too the dependence on the African sailor would become clear: when Covey grew sick in November 1839 and could not attend the legal hearing in Hartford, Gibbs tried to replace him as interpreter and failed. See Testimony of Professor Josiah W. Gibbs, January 8, 1840, Records of the U.S. District and Circuit Courts for the District of Connecticut, NAB; "Trial," *NYMH*, November 22, 1839.

30. Deposition of Charles Pratt, October 1839, Records of the U.S. District and Circuit Courts for the District of Connecticut, NAB. For an account of the anti-slave-trade activity of the *Buzzard*, including the capture of the *Emprendedor* with 470 enslaved people aboard, see "Cruise of the H.B.M. Brig Buzzard," *Emancipator*, November 21, 1839.

31. Deposition of James Covey, January 7, 1840, Records of the U.S. District and Circuit Courts for the District of Connecticut, NAB.

32. "The Captured Africans," *NYCA*, October 4, 1839; "The Africans," *NYCA*, October 8, 1839. See also "The Captured Blacks," *NYS*, October 7, 1839.

33. "Narrative of the Africans," *NYJC*, October 10, 1839.

34. Entry for October 17, 1839, Second Journal/Notebook, August 31, 1838–June 10, 1840, Journals and Notebooks, 1814–1869 Lewis Tappan Papers; "Extraordinary Arrest," *NYMH*, October 18, 1839; "Case of the Spaniards," *NYCA*, October 24, 1839; "From the New York Evening Star," *PF*, February 13, 1840.

35. "Case of Montez and Ruiz," *NYCA*, October 23, 1839; "Don Montez Absconded," *PF*, November 14, 1839. For the full text of the first ruling by Inglis, see "Case of Montez and Ruiz," *PF*, November 14, 1839.

36. "Ruiz and Montez," *NYCA*, October 18, 1839; "Another Abolition Arrest," *Richmond Enquirer*, November 5, 1839; Testimony of Founi and Testimony of Kimbo, State of Connecticut, County of New Haven, New Haven, Oct. 7, 1839, Miscellany: "Amistad Case," Lewis Tappan Papers.

37. "The Abolitionists," *Richmond Enquirer*, November 5, 1839; "Signor Ruiz," *Southern Patriot*, February 14, 1840; Lewis Tappan to Joseph Sturge, October 19, 1839, in Annie Heloise Abel and Frank J. Klingberg, eds., *A Side-Light on Anglo-American Relations, 1839–1858, Furnished by the Correspondence of Lewis Tappan and Others with the British and Foreign Anti-Slavery Society* (Lancaster, PA: Association for the Study of Negro Life and History, 1927), 60; "Great Point Gained," *PF*, November 14, 1839. The first two articles were originally published in the *New York Express* and the *New York Star*, demonstrating proslavery attitudes in the North. See Tappan's account of his actions in the *PF*, February 13, 1840.

38. "Plans to Educate," *NYJC*, October 9, 1839. On the parallel enthusiasm among Liberated Africans for schooling in Sierra Leone in the same time period, see David Northrup, "Becoming African: Identity Formation Among Liberated Slaves in Nineteenth-Century Sierra Leone," *Slavery and Abolition* 27 (2006): 7–8.

39. "Case of Ruiz and Montez—Atrocious Developments at New Haven," *NYMH*, October 23, 1839; "Another African Death," *NYMH*, November 9, 1839.

40. "Abolitionists going to the Devil—False Affidavits—Arming of the Africans,"

NYMH, October 23, 1839; "Abolitionists a Disgrace," *NYMH* October 26, 1839; "Another African Death," *NYMH,* November 9, 1839; "Private Examination of Cinquez," *NYCA,* September 13, 1839.

41. George Day to Lewis Tappan, October 23, 1839, and Amos Townsend Jr. to Lewis Tappan, October 29, 1839, ARC; "The Africans," *NYJC,* November 6, 1839. The same article appeared in the *Emancipator* the following day. It was unsigned but likely written by Lewis Tappan.

42. "The Long, Low Black Schooner," *NYS,* August 31, 1839; "To the Committee," *NYJC,* September 10, 1839; "Private Examination," *NYCA,* September 13, 1839; "The Negroes of the Amistad," *New Hampshire Sentinel,* October 2, 1839; *CA,* October 5, 1839.

43. "Removal of the Africans to Hartford—Crim. Con. among the Savages—Exposure of the Abolition Falsehood, &c.," *NYMH,* November 19, 1839; "Herald on Amistad Trial," *NYMH,* November 21, 1839. Among the works quoted and, more commonly, plagiarized are Mungo Park, *Travels in the Interior Districts of Africa: Performed in the Years 1795, 1796, and 1797* (London, 1799); Richard Lander, *Journal of an Expedition to Explore the Course and Termination of the Niger* (London, 1832); Joseph Hawkins, *A History of a Voyage to the Coast of Africa, and Travels into the Interior of that Country* (Troy, NY, 1797); Captain J. K. Tuckey, *Narrative of an Expedition to Explore the River Zaire* (London, 1818); and Sir Thomas Fowell Buxton, *The African Slave Trade, and its Remedy* (London, 1839). On the visitors to Hartford, see "Amistad," *NYCA,* September 20, 1839.

44. The identification of the *Amistad* Africans as "Mandingoes" appeared in "Incarcerated Captives," *NYCA,* September 6, 1839. See also the *NYS,* September 10, 1839. A couple of months later, a correspondent of the *NYMH* (November 12, 1839) also surveyed Mandingo culture as a way of describing the captives, even though James Covey had made it clear by then that they were Mende.

45. The 1820s and 1830s witnessed a popular fascination with "Moorish culture," not least because of Lord Byron's influence. See the reference to the romantic "Moorish knights" above and the comments by Nathans in *Slavery and Sentiment* 12: 120–22. The final paragraph of *A True History* is taken from the *ARCJ* 8 (1832): 121 (quotation).

46. "Herald on Amistad Trial," *NYMH,* November 21, 1839; "Trial," *NYMH,* November 22, 1839.

47. "Lynch Law among the Amistad Africans," *Farmer's Cabinet,* December, 6, 1839. One of the first to recognize the importance of African secret societies to American history was Sterling Stuckey, chapter 1, "Introduction: Slavery and the Circle of Culture," 3–97.

48. *Pennsylvania Inquirer and Daily Courier,* December 28, 1839; "The Amistad Africans," *Boston Courier,* December 13, 1841.

49. "Extract of a letter from Rev. H. G. Ludlow, to one of the Editors, dated New Haven, Jan. 13, 1840," *NYJC,* January 15, 1840; "The Amistad Negroes," *Barre Gazette,* December 6, 1839.

50. "Captives of the Amistad," *Emancipator,* December 19, 1839.

51. "The Negroes of the Amistad," *New Hampshire Sentinel,* October 2, 1839; Lewis, "Recollections of the Amistad Slave Case," 126. For additional evidence of the fear of execution among the *Amistad* Africans, see "Trial of the Africans," *NYMH,* November 20, 1839; "Captives of the Amistad," *Emancipator,* December 19, 1839; "Anecdotes of the Captured Africans," *PF,* February 27, 1840.

52. "Trial of the Amistad Africans," *Liberator,* January 17, 1840; "The Amistad Case," *NYS,* January 14, 1840; Lewis Tappan to John Scoble, January 20, 1840, and Lewis Tappan to Richard R. Madden, n.d. (probably January 20, 1840), Lewis Tappan Letterbook, vol. III, October 5, 1839–September 7, 1840, Correspondence, 1809–1872, Tappan Papers; John W. Barber Diary, Jan. 1813–Dec. 1883, unpaginated, folder A, J. W. Barber Collection (1813–1883), NHCHS; "Letter from Rev. H. G. Ludlow," *NYJC,* January 15, 1840.

53. "Trial of the Amistad Africans," *Liberator,* January 17, 1840.

54. "The Africans of the Amistad," *Rhode Island Republican,* January 15, 1840.

55. Deposition of Charles Pratt, U.S. District Court, October 1839, NAB.

56. Testimony of Cinqué, Testimony of Grabeau, Testimony of Fuliwa, all January 8, 1840, U.S. District Court, Connecticut, NAB.

57. "African Testimony," *NYJC,* January 10, 1840.

58. "Trial of the Amistad Africans," *Liberator,* January 17, 1840.

59. [Lewis Tappan], *The African Captives: Trial of the Prisoners of the Amistad on the Writ of Habeas Corpus, before the Circuit Court of the United States, for the District of Connecticut, at Hartford; Judges Thompson and Judson, September Term, 1839* (New York, 1839).

60. "A Decision at Last in the Amistad Case," *NYMH*, January 15, 1840; "Ruling of the Court," Records of the U.S. District and Circuit Courts for the District of Connecticut, NAB.

61. Tappan to Madden, 1840; "Amistad Trial—Termination," *Emancipator*, January 16, 1840.

62. *Argument of John Quincy Adams Before the Supreme Court of the United States in the case of the United States, Appellants, vs. Cinque, and others, Africans, captured in the schooner Amistad, by Lieut. Gedney, Delivered on the 24th of February and 1st of March 1841* (New York: S. W. Benedict, 1841), 84; "Amistad Trial—Termination," *Emancipator*, January 16, 1840; "U.S. Schr. Grampus," *NYJC*, January 17, 1840; "The Grampus to New Haven," *Charleston Courier*, January 27, 1840; "Executive Interference," *New-Bedford Mercury*, February 21, 1840; "Strange Disclosure," *New Hampshire Sentinel*, June 3, 1840; "The Secretary of State to the Secretary of the Navy," *Connecticut Courant*, June 6, 1840; "Amistad Captives," *Oberlin Evangelist*, July 1, 1840.

63. "Amistad Trial—Termination," *Emancipator*, January 16, 1840. After its voyage to New Haven the *Grampus* was dispatched to Africa as one of two vessels in an American anti-slave-trade patrol. See Donald L. Canney, *Africa Squadron: The U.S. Navy and the Slave Trade, 1842–1861* (Washington, DC: Potomac Books, 2006), 26–27.

64. "The Late Deacon Nathaniel Jocelyn," *New Haven Journal and Courier*, January 15, 1881; Simeon E. Baldwin, "The Captives of the Amistad," *Papers of the New Haven Colony Historical Society* 4 (1888), 349; Lewis, "Recollections of the Amistad Slave Case," 125–28. Thanks to Joseph Yannielli for supplying a copy of Jocelyn's obituary. It should be noted that Tappan disavowed "physical resistance" in the event of an unfavorable legal decision. See Lewis Tappan to Roger Baldwin, January 20, 1841, Baldwin Family Papers.

65. "Common Sense," *Portsmouth Journal of Literature and Politics* (October 5, 1839).

Chapter Five: "Mendi"

1. "The Africans of the Amistad," *North American and Daily Advertiser*, February 5, 1840; Benjamin Griswold to Lewis Tappan, January 28, 1840, ARC.

2. *Emancipator*, January 30, 1841; "Amistad Captives," *Oberlin Evangelist*, July 1, 1841.

3. L. N. Fowler, "Phrenological Developments of Joseph Cinquez, Alias Ginqua." *American Phrenological Journal and Miscellany* 2 (1840): 136–38; "The Amistad Painting," *New England Weekly Record*, May 23, 1840; "Amistad Exhibit at Peale's Museum and Portrait Gallery," *NYCA*, June 16, 1840; "Visit to Hartford, Connecticut," *NYMH*, September 24, 1839.

4. "Another of the Amistad Africans is Dead," *Farmer's Cabinet*, November 8, 1839; "Trial of the Amistad Africans," *Liberator*, January 17, 1840; *New Hampshire Sentinel*, September 9, 1840.

5. "Letter from New York," *PF*, December 29, 1841; *Thompson in Africa*, 285–86.

6. "Plans to Educate the Amistad Africans in English," *NYJC*, October 9, 1839; "Amistad Captives," *Oberlin Evangelist*, July 1, 1840.

7. "Letter from Rev. S.W. Magill," *AFASR*, October 1, 1840; *AFASR*, January 1, 1841; "James B. Covey, the Interpreter, in the Case of the Africans Taken in the Amistad," *Protestant Vindicator*, February 3, 1841; "Letter from the Teacher of the Africans," *PF*, March 31, 1841.

8. "Trial," *Liberator*, January 17, 1840; "The Africans of the Amistad," *North American and Daily Advertiser*, February 5, 1840.

9. J. W. Gibbs, "A Mendi Vocabulary," *American Journal of Science and Arts* 38 (1840): 41–48; Lewis Tappan to Messrs Bartlett and Cary, October 21, 1839, New York, Lewis Tappan Letterbook, vol. III, October 5, 1839–September 7, 1840, Correspondence, 1809–1872, Tappan Papers, f. 41.

10. "The Amistad Africans," *Farmer's Cabinet*, October 9, 1840; "Letter from the Teacher," *PF*, March 31, 1841. One of the textbooks was likely John Pierpont, *The American First Class book, or, Exercises in Reading and Recitation selected principally from Modern Authors of Great Britain and America, and Designed for the Use of the Highest Class in Public and Private Schools* (Boston, 1836).

11. Lewis Tappan to Richard R. Madden, n.d., but probably Jan. 20, 1840, Tappan Papers;

"Africans Taken in the Amistad," *AFASR*, July 1, 1840; Gibbs, "A Mendi Vocabulary," 48; "Plans to Educate," *NYJC*, October 9, 1839.

12. Kale to Miss Chamberlain, Westville, Feb. 9, 1841, Afro-American Collection (1688–1896), "Amistad Case, 1839," box I, folder R-2, NHCHS.

13. *Boston Courier*, September 3, 1840 (capture of birds); "Mendis Depart," *NYJC*, November 27, 1841.

14. Charlotte Cowles to Samuel Cowles, Farmington, April 12, 1841, Cowles Correspondence, MS 101754, CHS; Barber, 13; "Removal of the African Prisoners," *NYCA*, September 16, 1839; "New Haven," *Daily National Intelligencer*, September 19, 1839; "The Liberated Mendians," *PF*, August 18, 1841.

15. Charlotte Cowles to Samuel Cowles, Farmington, April 8, 1841, Cowles Correspondence, MS 101754, CHS.

16. "Letter from the Teacher," *PF*, March 31, 1841.

17. Barber, 2.

18. Barber, 2; John W. Barber Diary, Jan. 1813–Dec. 1883, unpaginated, folder A, J. W. Barber Collection (1813–1883), NHCHS.

19. Barber, 2.

20. Barber, 9, 20, 24. Abolitionists later discussed the pamphlet in ways that suggested no role in its creation. See Amos Townsend to Lewis Tappan, November 22, 1841, ARC.

21. Barber's own views of the event may be seen in the caption he wrote to accompany the "Death of Capt. Ferrer": "Don Jose Ruis and Don Pedro Montez of the Island of Cuba, having purchased fifty-three slaves at Havana, recently imported from Africa, put them on board the Amistad, Capt. Ferrer, in order to transport them to Principe, another port on the Island of Cuba. After being out from Havana about four days, *the African captives on board, in order to obtain their freedom, and return to Africa*, armed themselves with cane knives, and rose upon the Captain and crew of the vessel. Capt. Ferrer and the cook of the vessel were killed; two of the crew escaped; Ruiz and Montez were made prisoners" (emphasis added). Barber thus repeated the central abolitionist argument about the case.

22. John Vanderlyn, *The Murder of Jane McCrea*, 1804, Wadsworth Atheneum, Hartford, Connecticut. Thanks to Kirk Savage for pointing out the influence of this painting/lithograph. Barber had written about and illustrated the "Murder of Miss McCrea" in his book for young readers: *Historical Scenes in the United States: A Selection of Important and Interesting Events in the History of the United States* (New Haven, CT: Monson and Co., 1827), image facing 40, text 42–43.

23. Samuel Warner [comp.], *Authentic and impartial narrative of the tragical scene which was witnessed in Southampton County (Virginia) on Monday the 22d of August last when fifty-five of its inhabitants (mostly women and children) were inhumanly massacred by the blacks! Communicated by those who were eye witnesses of the bloody scene, and confirmed by the confessions of several of the blacks while under Sentence of Death* (Printed for Warner & West, New York, 1831).

24. "Amistad Exhibit," *NYCA*, June 16, 1840, and June 23, 1840. Less is known of Moulthrop than the other artists who engaged with the *Amistad* case. He seems not to have been well-known or financially successful in his work; indeed he was bankrupt shortly after his dramatization of the rebellion. See "Bankrupts in Connecticut," *Law Reporter* 5 (1842): 139.

25. "Barnum's American Museum," *NYMH*, October 3, 1847; "Gavitt's Original Ethiopian Serenaders," *The North Star*, June 29, 1849.

26. "Amistad Captives," *Norwich Aurora*, September 2, 1840.

27. "Peale's Museum and Portrait Gallery," *New York Evening Post*, June 23, 1840.

28. "Wax Figures," *CA*, June 27, 1840; "The Exhibition," *Workingman's Friend*, July 11, 1840; "Amistad Captives," *Norwich Aurora*, September 2, 1840.

29. Broadside advertisement of "The Magnificent Painting of the Massacre on board the schooner Amistad," 1839, Afro-American Collection (1688–1896), "Amistad Case, 1839," box I, folder R-6, NHCHS. Hewins wrote that in Italy, "the lower orders as it is said, are more subject to transports of rage and in that state to commit desperate actions, especially the romans. Still I think few strangers have done them even handed justice, and for myself I like them better than any other Europeans of whom I have knowledge." Papers of Amasa Hewins, 1795–1855, Mss. L450, fo. 64, Boston Athenaeum. The published edition of the journal is Francis H. Allen, ed., *Hewins's Journal: A Boston Portrait-Painter Visits Italy; the Journal of Amasa Hewins, 1830–1833* (Boston: The Boston Athenaeum, 1931).

30. Simeon E. Baldwin, "The Captives of the Amistad," *Papers of the New Haven Colony Historical Society* 4 (1888): 331–70. The paper was read at the Society on May 17, 1886. Baldwin notes Hewins's "large picture of the scene, which is now deposited in this building, the property of our associate, Mr. Wm B. Goodyear" (333).

31. Broadside advertisement, "The Magnificent Painting."

32. Benjamin Griswold to Lewis Tappan, New Haven, April 25, 1840, ARC. This and the next seven paragraphs quote from this letter.

33. Griswold, who knew the *Amistad* Africans well, considered the artist's representation of several of them to be not only unrealistic, but unfair. Fuli was not malicious but rather "noble-spirited," while Konoma was nothing of the cannibal. Griswold had "noticed a scar of a wound on his [Ndamma's] head received in that affray, from which it is probable, he had a part to act somewhat different from that which the artist has ascribed to him." He thought that only the images of Grabeau and Konoma bore any resemblance to the people he knew so well.

34. "Letter from Magill," *AFASR*, October 1, 1840.

35. Dwight P. Janes to Rev. Joshua Leavitt, New London, August 30, 1839, ARC.

36. For an early example of the recurring claim that the captives had the right to resist, see "Amistad Issues," *NYCA*, September 4, 1839.

37. Peter Linebaugh and Marcus Rediker, *The Many-Headed Hydra: Sailors, Slaves, Commoners, and the Hidden History of the Revolutionary Atlantic* (Boston: Beacon Press, 2000), 223.

38. "Amistad Case as Revolution," *CA*, October 5, 1839. On the African American appropriation of the American Revolution in this era, see Patrick Rael, *Black Identity & Black Protest in the Antebellum North* (Chapel Hill: University of North Carolina Press, 2002), 262–66. Washington was not the only military hero to which Cinqué was compared. For an account of how his heroic feats exceeded those of Napoleon, see "The Amistad Captives," *Liberator*, November 19, 1841.

39. William Lloyd Garrison to Harriet Minot, May 1, 1833, in Walter M. Merrill, ed., *The Letters of William Lloyd Garrison*, vol. I (Cambridge, MA: Belknap Press of Harvard University, 1971), 226; Foster Wild Rice, "Nathaniel Jocelyn, 1796–1881," *Connecticut Historical Society Bulletin* 31 (1966): 97–145.

40. *Joseph Cinque*, by Nathaniel Jocelyn (1796–1881), oil on canvas, 1840, 1971.205, Gift of Robert Purvis, 1898, NHCHS. See also Eleanor Alexander, "A Portrait of Cinque," *Connecticut Historical Society Bulletin*, 49 (1984): 30–51; Richard J. Powell, "Cinqué: Antislavery Portraiture and Patronage in Jacksonian America," *American Art* 11 (1997): 49–73.

41. Charlotte Cowles to Samuel Cowles, Farmington, April 12, 1841, Cowles Correspondence, MS 101754, CHS. For advertisements of Sartain's engraving see *PF*, February 24, 1841; "Portrait of Cinque," *CA*, February 27, 1841; "Portrait of Cinque, Chief of the Amistad Captives," *AFASR*, March 15, 1841.

42. "Conditions for Amistad Captives," *NYCA*, September 9, 1839; Dwight P. Janes to R. S. Baldwin, New London, August 31, 1839, ARC. See also *New Hampshire Sentinel*, September 4, 1839; *NYCA*, September 10, 1839; "The Prisoners of the Amistad," *Haverhill Gazette*, September 27, 1839.

43. "The Negroes of the Amistad," *New Hampshire Sentinel*, October 2, 1839; Letter from A. F. Williams to Bro. Tappan, published in the *Emancipator*, August 19, 1841.

44. Charlotte Cowles to Samuel Cowles, Farmington, March 24, 1841, Cowles Correspondence, MS 101754, CHS; Steele quoted in Helen Pratt, "My Grandfather's Story," MSS HM 58067, Huntington Library.

45. "Trial of the Africans," *NYMH*, November 20, 1839.

46. Testimony of Antonio, January 9, 1840, U.S. District Court, Connecticut, NAB.

47. "The Case of the Africans Decided for the Present—Habeas Corpus not Sustained," *NYMH*, Sept. 25, 1839. It is possible that Burna learned English by contact with Liberated Africans in and around Freetown, but no such evidence emerged, even though the planners of the return to Africa solicited this kind of information.

48. *Boston Courier*, September 3, 1840.

49. "Mendis in Jail," *Hartford Daily Courant*, March 27, 1841.

50. Amos Townsend Jr. to Lewis Tappan, October 29, 1839, ARC.

51. Cinqué to Roger Baldwin, February 9, 1841, Baldwin Family Papers.

52. Africans to Lewis Tappan, Westville, February 9, 1841, ARC.

53. "The Mendi People," *Emancipator*, September 23, 1841; see also "Africans of the Amistad—Love of Home," *ARCJ* 17 (1841).

54. On the way in which creolization and Africanization went together within a process of ethnogenesis, see David Northrup, "Becoming African: Identity Formation among Liberated Slaves in Nineteenth-Century Sierra Leone," *Slavery and Abolition* 27 (2006): 16–17. An important study of the genesis of Igbo society and culture in the African diaspora is Alexander X. Byrd, *Captives and Voyagers: Black Migrants Across the Eighteenth-Century British Atlantic World* (Baton Rouge: Louisiana State University Press, 2008), pt. I. For a broad survey of the process of ethnogenesis, see James Sidbury and Jorge Cañizares-Esguerra, "Mapping Ethnogenesis in the Atlantic World," *William and Mary Quarterly*, 3rd ser., (2011): 181–208, and the comments by James H. Sweet, Claudio Saunt, Pekka Hämäläinen, Laurent Dubois, Christopher Hodson, Karen B. Graubart, and Patrick Griffin, with a response by Sidbury and Cañizares-Esguerra, 209–46.

55. Kale to John Quincy Adams, January 4, 1841, John Quincy Adams Papers, Massachusetts Historical Society. The letter was edited slightly and published as "Ka-le's Letter to Mr. Adams," *NYJC*, March 20, 1841. Josiah Gibbs mentioned "Mendi People" in an article of November 28, 1839, but he simply meant people who were from Mende, not a self-conscious collectivity. See "On the Names of the Captured Africans," *Emancipator*, November 28, 1839.

56. Kale to Adams, MHS.

57. *Oberlin Evangelist*, April 28, 1841; Cinqué to Roger Baldwin, February 9, 1841, Baldwin Family Papers. Kale also used the phrase in a letter to Juliana Chamberlain, thanking her on behalf of the "Mendi People" for a monetary contribution to the cause. See Kale to Miss Chamberlain, NHCHS.

58. "The Amistad Africans," *NYCA*, January 14, 1841; "Case of the Amistad," *Farmer's Cabinet*, January 22, 1841; *Newport Mercury*, January 23, 1841; "The Amistad Africans," *NLG*, January 27, 1841.

Chapter Six: Freedom

1. Amos Townsend Jr. to Lewis Tappan, January 18, 1841, ARC; "Mendis in Jail," *Hartford Daily Courant*, March 27, 1841; "Ka-le's Letter to Mr. Adams," *NYJC*, March 20, 1841.

2. Amos Townsend Jr. to Lewis Tappan, February 22, 1841, ARC; "Washington," *Hudson River Chronicle*, January 26, 1841.

3. "Goleta Española 'Amistad,'" *Noticioso de Ambos Mundos*, January 30, 1841, 34; "Portrait of Cinque," *PF*, February 24, 1841; "Portrait of Cinque," *CA*, February 27, 1841.

4. Minute Books of the British and Foreign Anti-Slavery Society, 1839–1868, E2/6, vol. I, February 27, 1839–October 7, 1842, Material Relating to America from the Anti-Slavery Collection in Rhodes House, Oxford, edited by Howard R. Temperley; "The Amistad Africans," *Liberator*, December 25, 1840; "Mr. Fox and Mr. Forsyth re. Amistad Case," *NYJC*, February 18, 1841. Forsyth responded to Fox, reminding him of the separation of executive and judicial powers under the U.S. Constitution.

5. *The United States, Appellants, v. the Libellants and Claimants of the Schooner Amistad, her Tackle, Apparel, and Furniture, Together with her Cargo, and the Africans Mentioned and Described in the several Libels and Claims, Appellees, January 1841 term*, United States Supreme Court (Washington, DC, 1841), 40 U.S. 518; 10 L. Ed. 826; Jones, *Mutiny on the Amistad*, 50–53.

6. "The Africans of the Amistad," *NYJC*, September 5, 1839; "Spanish View of the Amistad Case," *NYJC*, September 14, 1839. See also Jones, *Mutiny on the Amistad*, 138–44, and Douglas R. Egerton, *Charles Fenton Mercer and the Trial of National Conservatism* (Jackson: University of Mississippi Press, 1989), 179–81.

7. *Argument of Roger S. Baldwin, of New Haven, before the Supreme Court of the United States, in the Case of the United States, Apellants, vs. Cinque, and Others, Africans of the Amistad* (New York: S. W. Benedict, 1841), 3, 23, 20, 4, 10, 32; "The Captives of The Amistad," *NYJC*, February 23, 1841; "Washington," *Connecticut Courant*, March 6, 1841.

8. *Argument of John Quincy Adams Before the Supreme Court of the United States in the Case of the United States, Appellants, vs. Cinque, and others, Africans, captured in the schooner Amistad, by Lieut. Gedney, Delivered on the 24th of February and 1st of March 1841* (New York: S. W. Benedict, 1841), 23; "The Captives of the Amistad," *NYJC*, February 26, 1841.

9. "Death of Judge Barbour," *Portsmouth Journal of Literature and Politics,* March 6, 1841; "Late from Liberia," *NYJC,* March 2, 1841; "Cheering from Liberia," *NYJC,* March 3, 1841; "Aiding the Slave Trade,"*NYJC,* March 6, 1841. Palmerston quoted in Leslie Bethell, *The Abolition of the Brazilian Slave Trade* (Cambridge, UK: Cambridge University Press, 1970), 183. The *Amistad* Africans who were still at the Mende Mission in 1852 remembered Justice Barbour as the judge who, before his death, "was about to condemn them." See Hannah Moore to William Harned, October 12, 1852, ARC.

10. Amos Townsend Jr. to Lewis Tappan, January 22, 1841, and John Treadwell Norton to Lewis Tappan, February 10, 1841, ARC.

11. "From Our Washington Correspondent," *CA,* March 6, 1841.

12. Original trial record as published in the *National Intelligencer,* republished as "The Case of the Amistad, Supreme Court of the United States," *NYJC,* March 17, 1841.

13. "Amistad Africans," *PF,* March 24, 1841.

14. "Amistad Negroes," *Hartford Daily Courant,* March 18, 1841.

15. "Letter from Mr. Adams," *NYJC,* March 12, 1841; "Amistad Africans," *PF,* March 24, 1841; "The Mendians," *Youth's Cabinet,* October 14, 1841; "Public Thanksgiving," *PF,* March 17, 1841; *New Hampshire Sentinel,* March 24, 1841; *CA,* March 13, 1841; D. Jinkins, W. Johnson, J. Bennett and others to Roger Baldwin, March 30, 1841, Baldwin Family Papers; "Correspondence relative to the Amistad case," *Daily Ohio Statesman,* May 5, 1841.

16. "The Africans Taken aboard the Amistad" and "Portrait of Cinque, Chief of the Amistad Captives," *AFASR,* March 15, 1841.

17. Norton Papers, Diaries, vol. III, June 29, 1840–September 15, 1841, box no. 3, folder 18, MS 367.

18. One issue on which Adams did not do what Kale and the rest had instructed him to do was to tell the court that the Africans had ended up on Long Island by their own labor. Nonetheless the *Amistad* Africans held the memory of Adams in their hearts. See Moore to Harned, October 12, 1852, ARC. "Accompaniment" is an idea developed by Staughton Lynd about how solidarity can assist struggles from below. See Staughton Lynd, *Accompanying: Pathways to Social Change* (Oakland, CA: PM Press, 2012).

19. James Birney to Lewis Tappan, New Haven, October 2, 1840, and Amos Townsend Jr. to Lewis Tappan, New Haven, October 3, 1840, ARC.

20. "The Amistad," *New-York Spectator,* March 24, 1841; "Anecdotes of the Captured Africans," *PF,* February 27, 1840; Kinna to Roger Baldwin, March 12, 1841; Fuli to Lewis Tappan, Westville, March, 1841, ARC. Fuli's letter was reprinted in the *Oberlin Evangelist,* April 28, 1841.

21. "The Amistad," *New-York Spectator,* March 24, 1841; "Letter from the Teacher of the Africans," *PF,* March 31, 1841; Kinna to Lewis Tappan, Westville, March 20, 1841, ARC.

22. Charlotte Cowles to Samuel Cowles, Farmington, March 30, 1841, and April 8, 1841, Cowles Correspondence, MS 101754, CHS.

23. "Antonio Ferrer," *PF,* April 14, 1841.

24. "The Boy Antonio," *CA,* April 10, 1841; Lewis Tappan to Roger Baldwin, April 1, 1841, Baldwin Family Papers; "Antonio Ferrer," *PF,* April 14, 1841. On Ruggles and the Vigilance Society see the excellent study by Graham Russell Gao Hodges, *David Ruggles: A Radical Black Abolitionist and the Underground Railroad in New York City* (Chapel Hill: University of North Carolina Press, 2010).

25. John Dougall to Rev. Joshua Leavitt, Montreal, April 26, 1841, ARC; Lewis Tappan to Joseph Sturge, November 15, 1841, reprinted in Joseph Sturge, *A Visit To The United States In 1841* (London, 1842), Appendix E, xliv.

26. Among the newspapers that covered the tour were *ARCJ, AFASR, Boston Courier, CA, Connecticut Courant, Daily Atlas, Daily Evangelist, Emancipator, Farmer's Cabinet, Liberator, Log Cabin, Lynn Record, Mercantile Journal, New England Weekly Review, New Hampshire Sentinel, NYJC, NYMH, New York Observer, New York Tribune, Newport Mercury, Oberlin Evangelist, PF, Philadelphia Inquirer and Daily Courier, Vermont Chronicle,* and *Youth's Cabinet.*

27. "Amistad Africans at the Tabernacle," *CA,* May 8, 1841; "Mendis Perform," *NYMH,* May 13, 1841. It was reported that the tour of Massachusetts towns netted $1,000 after expenses, and that $1,350 had been raised at the Farmington meeting alone. See "The Mendians," *NYMH,* November 19, 1841, and "The Mendians," *Vermont Chronicle,* November

24, 1841. The first meeting at the Broadway Tabernacle was attended by an estimated 2,500 people who paid fifty cents each admission. Another 2,500 attended a meeting in Hartford, probably at twenty-five cents each.

28. "Mendis Perform," *NYMH*, May 13, 1841.

29. "Meeting of Freed Africans," *CA*, May 1, 1841; "Mendis Perform," *NYMH*, May 13, 1841; "The Amistad Negroes," *Farmer's Cabinet*, November 19, 1841; *New Hampshire Sentinel*, May 19, 1841; "Meetings of the Liberated Africans," *CA*, May 22, 1841; "Departure of the Mendians—Farewell Meeting," *CA*, December 4, 1841.

30. "The Amistad Africans' Meeting," *Philadelphia Inquirer and Daily Courier*, May 25, 1841; *New Hampshire Sentinel*, May 19, 1841; "Amistad Captives," *PF*, May 26, 1841.

31. "Freed Africans," *NYJC*, May 13, 1841; "Meeting of Freed Africans," *CA*, May 1, 1841.

32. "Mendi Meeting," *NYJC*, May 13, 1841.

33. A. F. Williams to Lewis Tappan, Farmington, April 29, 1841 and S. W. Booth to Lewis Tappan, May 3, 1841, ARC; Reverend Alonzo N. Lewis, M.A., "Recollections of the Amistad Slave Case: First Revelation of a Plot to Force the Slavery Question to an Issue more than twenty Years before its Final Outbreak in the Civil War—Several Hitherto Unknown Aspects of the Case Told," *Connecticut Magazine* 11 (1907): 126. Williams originally suggested the idea of a fund-raising tour, predicting that the fame of the *Amistad* Africans might help to raise as much as $100,000 ($2.5 billion in 2012 dollars) for the mission over a year of performances. See A. F. Williams to Lewis Tappan, March 13, 1841, ARC.

34. "Freed Africans," *NYJC*, May 13, 1841; "The Amistad Africans, An Interesting Meeting," *Philadelphia Inquirer and Daily Courant*, May 29, 1841; "Interesting Meeting of the Liberated Africans," *PF*, May 19, 1841.

35. "Mendis Perform," *NYMH*, May 13, 1841.

36. "Letters from New York," *PF*, December 29, 1841.

37. "Mendis Perform," *NYMH*, May 13, 1841; "Interesting Meeting of the Liberated Africans," *PF*, May 19, 1841.

38. "Mendis Perform," *NYMH*, May 13, 1841; "The Amistad Africans," *Philadelphia Inquirer and Daily Courant*, May 29, 1841; "Letters from New York," *PF*, December 29, 1841.

39. Ibid.; "The Amistad Africans," *Philadelphia Inquirer and Daily Courant*, May 25, 1841; Tappan to Sturge, November 15, 1841, reprinted in Sturge, *Visit*, Appendix E, xlii.

40. Ibid., xliii.

41. "Letters from New York," *PF*, December 29, 1841.

42. Tappan noted that "The transactions of this meeting [at the Marlboro Chapel in Boston] have thus been stated at length, and the account will serve to show how the subsequent meetings were conducted, as the services in other places were similar." See Tappan to Sturge, November 15, 1841, *Visit*, Appendix E, xlvi.

43. Seeing that Cinqué was "a powerful natural orator, and one born to sway the minds of his fellow men," Tappan grew excited at the prospect of his converting to Christianity, and becoming "a preacher of the cross in Africa." See Sturge, *Visit*, xliii.

44. "Letters from New York," December 29, 1841; "Mendis Depart," *NYJC*, November 27, 1841; "The Amistad Africans," *Philadelphia Inquirer and Daily Courant*, May 29, 1841; "Mendis Perform," *NYMH*, May 13, 1841, and "Philadelphia," *NYMH*, May 29, 1841.

45. "Letters from New York," *PF*, December 29, 1841; "Mendis Depart," *NYJC*, November 27, 1841.

46. A. F. Williams to Lewis Tappan, June 3, 1841, and S. W. Booth to Lewis Tappan, June 4, 1841, ARC.

47. "The Mendian Mission," *Emancipator*, July 1, 1841; "Mendis Perform," *NYMH*, May 13, 1841.

48. "The Mendian Exhibition," *AFASR*, July 1, 1840.

49. "The Amistad Africans—Speeches of Lewis Tappan, and Cinquez," *New-England Weekly Review*, November 20, 1841.

50. Tappan to Sturge, November 15, 1841, reprinted in Sturge, *Visit*, Appendix E, xlviii.

51. "Meetings of the Liberated Africans," *CA*, May 22, 1841.

52. "Public Meeting in New York," *CA*, May 22, 1841. For more on many of those involved in the Zion Church meeting, see David E. Swift, *Black Prophets of Justice: Activist Black Clergy*

Before the Civil War (Baton Rouge: Louisiana State University Press, 1989), especially his observations on the *Amistad* case, 129–31. For a survey of the political role of black abolitionists in the era of the *Amistad* case, see Richard Newman, "Not the Only Story in 'Amistad': The Fictional Joadson and the Real James Forten," *Pennsylvania History* 67 (2000): 218–39.

53. The African American leaders also thanked the members of the Amistad Committee, who "came forward, spontaneously and unsought, to protect God's poor from the hands of the oppressor"; Sherman Booth for his good work as teacher; and the "Hon. John Q. Adams, and Roger B. Baldwin, Esq." for their legal labors. Other resolutions called the arrival of the "citizens of Mendi" in America providential and suggested that their actions proved the "common humanity" of Africans and Americans. A final resolution criticized the executive branch of government for its efforts to undermine the judicial process.

54. "Public Meeting in New York," *CA*, May 22, 1841; "The Amistad Africans, Farewell Meetings and Embarkation," *Connecticut Courant*, December 25, 1841; "Letters from New York," *PF*, December 29, 1841.

55. "Public Meeting in New York," *CA*, May 22, 1841; "Letters from New York," *PF*, December 29, 1841. Important work on the Mende Mission includes Clifton Herman Johnson, "The American Missionary Association, 1846–1861: A Study of Christian Abolitionism," Ph.D. dissertation, University of North Carolina, Chapel Hill, 1958; Clara Merritt DeBoer, *Be Jubilant My Feet: African American Abolitionists and the American Missionary Association* (New York and London: Garland, 1994); and the forthcoming dissertation by Joseph L. Yannielli, "Dark Continents: Africa and the American Abolition of Slavery," Ph.D. dissertation, Yale University, forthcoming 2013.

56. "Captives of the Amistad," *Emancipator*, December 19, 1839. The letter from "Beta" was written on November 24, 1839, and reprinted from the *New Haven Record*.

57. Lewis Tappan to John Scoble, January 20, 1840, New York, Correspondence, 1809–1872, Tappan Papers; Benjamin Griswold to Thomas Hopkins Gallaudet, January 13, 1840, Baldwin Family Papers.

58. John Hooker, *Some Reminiscences of a Long Life, With a Few Articles on Moral And Social Subjects of Present Interest* (Hartford, CT: Belknap and Warfield, 1899), 25; Christopher Webber, *American to the Backbone: The Life of James W. C. Pennington, the Fugitive Slave Who Became One of the First Black Abolitionists* (New York: Pegasus Books, 2011).

59. Lewis Tappan, *History of the American Missionary Association* (New York, 1855); "Meeting of the Mendians," *CA*, May 15, 1841.

60. "Call for a Missionary Convention," *CA*, July 3, 1841.

61. This and the following four paragraphs are constructed from these sources: John Treadwell Norton to Lewis Tappan, Farmington, August 9, 1841, and A. F. Williams to Lewis Tappan, Farmington, August 18, 1841, ARC; Austin F. Williams Account Book, 1845–1881, CHS, 12. Williams also thought the *Amistad* Africans were concerned that their primary teacher, Sherman Booth, "care no more for Mendi People" and that he was contemplating leaving them, as indeed he was.

62. "The Mendian Negroes," *ARCJ*, December 1, 1841. For the practice and meaning of suicide among people of the African diaspora in America, see Walter C. Rucker, *The River Flows On: Black Resistance, Culture, and Identity Formation in Early America* (Baton Rouge: Louisiana State University Press, 2006), 52–55.

63. "Missionary Convention," *CA*, September 4, 1841.

64. "Return of the Mendians," *Emancipator*, August 26, 1841; "Appeal on Behalf of the Amistad Africans," *Emancipator*, September 30, 1841.

65. William Raymond to Lewis Tappan, October 11, 1841, ARC.

66. "Amistad Trial—Termination," *Emancipator*, January 16, 1840; "The Mendi People," *Emancipator*, September 23, 1841; Joshua Coffin, *An Account of some of the Principal Slave Insurrections, and others, which have occurred, or been attempted, in the United States and elsewhere, during the last two centuries, With Various Remarks* (New York: American Anti-Slavery Society, 1860), 33–34.

67. "Africans of the Amistad," *Emancipator*, November 4, 1841; "The Mendians—Amistad Freemen," *Oberlin Evangelist*, December 8, 1841; Helen Pratt, "My Grandfather's Story," mss HM 58067, fo. 18a, Huntington Library.

68. Voyage contract between P. J. Farnham & Co. and Lewis Tappan, New York,

November 1, 1841, ARC; "The Amistad Africans," *Connecticut Courant*, December 25, 1841; Tappan to Sturge, November 15, 1841, reprinted in Sturge, *Visit*, Appendix E, xlvi.

69. "The Mendians—Amistad Freemen," *Oberlin Evangelist*, December 8, 1841; "The Amistad Africans," *Connecticut Courant*, December 25, 1841; "Farewell Meeting of the Mendians at Farmington," November 30, 1841, ARC.

70. Mary Cable, *Black Odyssey: The Case of the Slave Ship "Amistad"* (New York: Viking Penguin, 1971), 138–39; Iyunolu Folayan Osagie, *The Amistad Revolt: Memory, Slavery, and the Politics of Identity in the United States and Sierra Leone* (Athens: University of Georgia Press, 2000), 59; Letter from Captain Morris dated February 13, 1842, published in the *Daily Atlas*, March 10, 1842.

71. "The Mendian Negroes," *ARCJ*, 23 (1841); "Letters from New York," *PF*, December 29, 1841.

72. James Steele to Lewis Tappan, Freetown, February 1, 1842, ARC.

73. "The Mendians," *Vermont Chronicle*, June 8, 1842. The Mende in Freetown tended to live in a multiethnic town called Gloucester or in "Kosso Town" (where Cinqué's brother Kindi lived). See Samuel W. Booth to Lewis Tappan, October 4, 1841, ARC; Lamin Sanneh, *Abolitionists Abroad: American Blacks and the Making of Modern West Africa* (Cambridge, MA: Harvard University Press, 1999), 122–23.

74. Steele letter quoted in the *Vermont Chronicle*, June 8, 1842; "The Amistad Africans," *ARCJ* 28 (1842).

75. James Steele to Simeon Jocelyn, Freetown, April 19, 1842, published in the *AFASR*, June 20, 1842.

76. *Emancipator*, April 28, 1842.

77. C.L.F. Harnsel to Lewis Tappan, Quebec, November 22, 1841, ARC; Dr. Madden's Report on Sierra Leone, 1841, Colonial Office (CO) 267/172, 22-24, NA.

78. "Late Intelligence from the Mendians," *New-York Spectator*, October 5, 1842. This is not the place to rehearse the subsequent history of the Mende Mission. It has been explored well by Osagie in *The Amistad Revolt*, chap. 3. Joseph L. Yannielli's "Dark Continents" will take scholarship on the subject to a new level. A preview of his work appeared in an award-winning article, "George Thompson among the Africans: Empathy, Authority, and Insanity in the Age of Abolition," *Journal of American History* 96 (2010): 979–1,000, and in *Cinqué the Slave Trader: New Evidence on an Old Controversy* (New Haven: The Amistad Committee, 2010). See also De Boers, *Be Jubilant My Feet*.

79. "The Mendi Mission," *Cleveland Daily Herald*, July 11, 1842; William Raymond to Lewis Tappan, York, Sierra Leone, February 19, 1844, published in the *Union Missionary*, May 1844. See also *North American and Daily Advertiser*, June 15, 1842, and Marlene D. Merrill, *Sarah Margru Kinson: The Two Worlds of an Amistad Captive* (Oberlin, Ohio: Oberlin Historical and Improvement Organization, 2003).

80. Fuli to Lewis Tappan, April 15, 1842, reproduced in Helen Pratt, "My Grandfather's Story," mss HM 58067, Huntington Library. The ten who remained loyal longest were Fuli (George Brown), Kinna (Lewis Johnson), Beri (Thomas Johnson), Ndamma (John Smith), Kali (George Lewis), Tsukama (Henry Cowles), Fabana (Alexander Posey), Sa (James Pratt), Ba (David Brown), and Moru (John Williams). The three little girls were Margru (Sarah Kinson), Teme (Maria Brown), and Kagne (Charlotte, last name unknown). See DeBoer, *Be Jubilant My Feet*, 106.

81. "The Mendians," *Vermont Chronicle*, June 8, 1842.

82. "Letters from New York," *PF*, December 29, 1841. After his enslavement Burna spent six weeks in transit to Lomboko, "three and a half moons" (months) at the fortress itself, eight weeks in the Middle Passage, two weeks in Cuba, and eight weeks at sea in the *Amistad* before he came ashore in New London on August 27, 1839. He met his mother in February 1842 after a period of roughly three years, three months. The encounter is described in letters written by missionary James Steele, published in the *Ohio Observer*, August 4, 1842, and the *Liberator*, August 5, 1842, from which the quotations are taken. I assume that "Banna" here was Burna the elder, who was frequently called on by that name, while Burna the Younger was called "Little Banna" or "Banna wulu." The mother of Burna the younger was deceased. See Barber, 9.

83. *Thompson in Africa*, 201.

Conclusion: Reverberations

1. Purvis gave this account to a journalist in 1889, a half century after the *Amistad* rebellion. See "A Priceless Picture," *Philadelphia Inquirer*, December 26, 1889. Frederick Douglass mentioned the meeting of Purvis and Washington in "Great Anti-Colonization Mass Meeting of the Colored Citizens of New York," *National Anti-Slavery Standard*, May 3, 1849. Later Douglass wrote a novella about Washington and the *Creole* rebellion entitled *The Heroic Slave, a Thrilling Narrative of the Adventures of Madison Washington, in Pursuit of Liberty* (Boston: John P. Jewitt & Co, 1852).

2. "The 'Hanging Committee' of the 'Artists' Fund Society' Doing Homage to Slavery," *PF*, April 21, 1841. See also the excellent article by Richard J. Powell, "Cinqué: Antislavery Portraiture and Patronage in Jacksonian America," *American Art* 11 (1997): 49–73.

3. "A Priceless Picture," *Philadelphia Inquirer*.

4. Stanley Harrold, "Romanticizing Slave Revolt: Madison Washington, the *Creole* Mutiny, and Abolitionist Celebration of Violent Means," in John R. McKivigan and Stanley Harrold, eds., *Antislavery Violence: Sectional, Racial, and Cultural Conflict in Antebellum America* (Knoxville: University of Tennessee Press, 1999), 89–107; Howard Jones, "The Peculiar Institution and National Honor: The Case of the *Creole* Slave Revolt," *Civil War History* 21 (1975): 28–50; Walter Johnson, "White Lies: Human Property and Domestic Slavery Aboard the Slave Ship *Creole*," *Atlantic Studies* 5 (2008): 237–63.

5. George Hendrick and Willene Hendrick, *The Creole Mutiny: A Tale of Revolt Aboard a Slave Ship* (Chicago: Ivan R. Dee, 2003).

6. "The 'Hanging Committee,'" *PF*, April 21, 1841. Wright spoke of the controversy that surrounded the refusal of the Artists' Fund Society to include the portrait of Cinqué in an exhibition, out of their fear of violence from an antiabolition mob. Their fears may have been unfounded, as discussed below. See also Roy E. Finkenbine, "The Symbolism of Slave Mutiny: Black Abolitionist Responses to the *Amistad* and *Creole* Incidents," in Jane Hathaway, ed., *Rebellion, Repression, Reinvention: Mutiny in Comparative Perspective* (Westport, CT: Greenwood Press, 2001), 233–52.

7. Steele letter quoted in "The Amistad Africans," *Ohio Observer*, August 4, 1842.

8. Joseph L. Yannielli, "Dark Continents: Africa and the American Abolition of Slavery," Ph.D. dissertation, Yale University, forthcoming, 2013, chap. 1, 14; "The Mendi Mission," *ARCJ*, May, 1843; *Thompson in Africa*, 335; William Raymond to Lewis Tappan, Woburn, Mass., June 15, 1843, ARC. After it became clear that the missionaries had their own agenda and that he would not be the leader he expected to be, Cinqué left the mission and struck out on his own. He soon remarried and became a merchant, trading locally in and around Freetown. He did not abandon the mission entirely, although his relationship with the missionaries remained vexed for years. He nonetheless kept up intermittent contact, and indeed he played a crucial role in acquiring land at Kaw Mende, to which the mission would relocate in 1844. George Thompson noted that Cinqué traveled for a time to Jamaica in 1844 or 1845, perhaps as part of a British initiative to transport Liberated Africans to the colony as workers. He disappears from the historical record for years at a stretch, but finally returned to the Mende Mission when he was near death in 1879. He died there and was buried in the mission graveyard. Like Howard Jones and Joseph L. Yannielli, I have found no evidence to suggest that Cinqué became a slave trader upon return to Sierra Leone, as has long been alleged. See Jones, "Cinqué of the *Amistad* a Slave Trader? Perpetuating a Myth," *Journal of American History* 87 (2000): 923–39, and Joseph L. Yannielli, *Cinqué the Slave Trader: Some New Evidence on an Old Controversy* (New Haven, CT: The Amistad Committee, 2010). The proslavery *NYMH* had reported on September 13, 1839, that Cinqué had been a slave trader before he himself was enslaved. This claim was often repeated in the proslavery press, but is unsubstantiated.

9. Peter Reed, *Rogue Performances: Staging the Underclasses in Early American Theatre Culture* (London: Palgrave Macmillan, 2009), 11; Bruce A. McConachie, *Melodramatic Formations: American Theatre and Society, 1820–1870* (Iowa City: University of Iowa Press, 1992), 97–100. *The Long, Low Black Schooner* was one of five plays found by Melinda Lawson to represent slave insurrection on the American stage in the early national and antebellum eras. See her "Imagining Slavery: Representations of the Peculiar Institution on the Northern Stage, 1776–1860," *Journal of the Civil War Era* 1 (2011): 34. It was the only one to deal with a current

event. The couplet would later appear in the *Chartist Circular*, published in Glasgow, May 1, 1841, in a poem entitled "Liberty! Universal Liberty!" by "Argus." See *The True History of the African Prince Jingua and his Comrades*, frontispiece.

10. Stanley Harrold, "Romanticizing Slave Revolt," 90, 96; Douglas R. Egerton, *Gabriel's Rebellion: The Virginia Slave Conspiracies of 1800 and 1802* (Chapel Hill: University of North Carolina Press, 1993), 40, 51, 109; Egerton, *Death or Liberty: African Americans and Revolutionary America* (New York: Oxford University Press, 2009).

11. *Arguments of Roger S. Baldwin, of New Haven, before the Supreme Court of the United States, in the Case of the United States, Apellants, vs. Cinque, and Others, Africans of the Amistad* (New York: S. W. Benedict, 1841), 3. Phillip Lapsansky has written: "As part of their effort to defuse fears of violence, the antislavery movement did not produce representations of black violence, self-assertion, or control." See his "Graphic Discord: Abolitionists and Antiabolitionist Images," in Jean Fagan Yellin and John C. Van Horne, eds., *The Abolitionist Sisterhood: Women's Political Culture in Antebellum America* (Ithaca, NY: Cornell University Press, 1994), 203; Marcus Wood, *Blind Memory: Visual Representations of Slavery in England and America, 1780–1865* (Manchester, UK: Manchester University Press, 2000), chap. 5; 172–76; Heather Nathans, *Slavery and Sentiment on the American Stage, 1787–1861: Lifting the Veil of Black* (New York: Cambridge University Press, 2009), 202. Compare the racist, demeaning "bobalition" images as analyzed by Patrick Rael, *Black Identity & Black Protest in the Antebellum North* (Chapel Hill: University of North Carolina Press, 2002), 72–74.

12. The article from the *Herald of Freedom* was republished in the *CA*, October 19, 1839.

13. One minor instance of violence occurred in Farmington, Connecticut, after the Supreme Court decision, when several of the *Amistad* Africans got into a fight with a gang of local toughs and apparently beat them up. See John Pitkin Norton's account of the fight in Norton Papers, MS 367, Diaries, vol. III: June 29, 1840–September 15, 1841, box no. 3, folder 18, entries for Tuesday, September 7, 1841, and Wednesday, September 8, 1841; A. F. Williams to Lewis Tappan, September 7, 1841, and September 23, 1841, ARC. A minor incident occurred in Springfield, Massachusetts, in November 1841, when some "fellows of a baser sort" insulted Kinna, but used no violence. See Lewis Tappan to Joseph Sturge, November 15, 1841, printed in Joseph Sturge, *A Visit to the United States in 1841* (London, 1842), Appendix E, xlviii–xlix. Tappan himself received a letter threatening tar and feathers; see Mr. Johnsting to Lewis Tappan, April 13, 1841, ARC. In *Gentlemen of Property and Standing: Anti-Abolition Mobs in Jacksonian America* (New York: Oxford University Press, 1971), Leonard L. Richards notes the decline of antiabolition mobs in the late 1830s; see chap. 6. See also David Grimsted, *American Mobbing, 1828–1861: Toward Civil War* (Oxford, UK: Oxford University Press, 1998).

14. Mary Cable, *Black Odyssey: The Case of the Slave Ship "Amistad"* (New York: Viking Penguin, 1971), 121.

15. "Funds Appeal," *NYCA*, September 5, 1839.

16. "Farewell Meeting at Farmington," *Emancipator*, December 2, 1841.

17. "The Mendians," *Youth's Cabinet*, December 9, 1841, and December 16, 1841; "In Iron Foundry, Elm Street," *Emancipator*, October 28, 1841; *Emancipator*, January 30, 1840. For accountings of contributions, see "Monies Received for the Amistad Captives," *Emancipator*, March 26, 1840; "Received for the Africans Taken in the Amistad," *AFASR*, January 1841; "Amistad Fund," *AFASR*, February 1, 1841; "Receipts for the Amistad Captives," *AFASR*, March 15, 1841; "Receipts for the Liberated Africans Received since the Third Appeal," *AFASR*, May 1, 1841; "Receipts for Liberated Africans of Amistad," *AFASR*, October 1, 1841; "Africans of the Amistad: Receipts and Disbursements," *Emancipator*, November 4, 1841. See also the hundreds of notes and letters that accompanied the contributions in the AMA Archive, ARC.

18. S.L.H. to S. S. Jocelyn, Bedford, Mass., September 11, 1839, ARC; *NLG*, September 4, 1839; "Humanitas," *NYCA*, September 13, 1839. "Joseph Cinquez" was how Cinqué was named and depicted in the early images published and circulated by the *New York Sun*.

19. "What the Mechanics of the Country Think," *Emancipator*, March 24, 1842; Steven Deyle, *Carry Me Back: The Domestic Slave Trade in American Life* (New York: Oxford University Press, 2005), 255, and chap. 8 more broadly. Other examples of how the *Amistad* campaign strengthened militance against the slave trade were reported in the *Connecticut Courant*, January 25, 1840, and the *North American and Daily Advertiser*, January 21, 1841.

20. Henry Highland Garnet, *Walker's Appeal, with a Brief Sketch of His Life, and also Garnet's Address to the Slaves of the United States of America* (New York: J. H. Tobitt, 1848). The classic work on Garnet remains Sterling Stuckey, "Henry Highland Garnet: Nationalism, Class Analysis, and Revolution," in his *Slave Culture: Nationalist Theory and the Foundations of Black America* (New York: Oxford University Press, 1987), 138–92.

21. Stanley Harrold, *The Rise of Aggressive Abolitionism: Addresses to the Slaves* (Lexington: University of Kentucky Press, 2004), 37–38, 155; Garnet, *An Address to the Slaves*. On Ruggles, see *Liberator*, August 13, 1841, quoted in Herbert Aptheker, "Militant Abolitionism," *Journal of Negro History* 26 (1941): 438–84; *Douglass' Monthly*, March 21, 1863; Graham Russell Gao Hodges, *David Ruggles: A Radical Black Abolitionist and the Underground Railroad in New York City* (Chapel Hill: University of North Carolina Press, 2010). On Delany, see James T. Campbell, *Middle Passages: African American Journeys to Africa, 1787–2005* (London: Penguin Books, 2006), 64. See also Jane H. Pease and William H. Pease, "Black Power: The Debate in 1840," *Phylon* 29 (1968): 19–26, republished in Patrick Rael, ed., *African-American Activism Before the Civil War* (New York: Routledge, 2008), 50–57.

22. John Treadwell Norton to Lewis Tappan, Farmington, February 10, 1841, and February 27, 1841, ARC.

23. "The African Strangers," *Friend of Man*, September 21, 1839.

24. "The Amistad Captives," *Liberator*, April 9, 1841; "What Have You Done?" *Emancipator*, July 22, 1841.

25. Brown quoted in Harrold, "Romanticizing Slave Revolt," 102. See also Stanley Harrold, *American Abolitionists* (Harlow, UK: Longman, 2001), 27, 58, 59, 63, 73, 76, 82–83, 101; Carol Wilson, "Active Vigilance Is the Price of Liberty: Black Self-Defense Against Fugitive Slave Recaptors and Kidnapping of Free Blacks," in McKivigan and Harrold, *Antislavery Violence*, 108–27. The transformation of the abolition movement into something broader, more inclusive, and more egalitarian began in the early 1830s. See Richard S. Newman, *The Transformation of American Abolitionism: Fighting Slavery in the Early Republic* (Chapel Hill: University of North Carolina Press, 2001), 2, 106, 175.

26. "The 'Hanging Committee,'" *PF*, April 21, 1841.

INDEX

Page numbers in *italics* refer to illustrations.

ILLUSTRATION SOURCES AND CREDITS

Insert

Page 1. "La Amistad," watercolor on paper by unknown artist, c. 1839, courtesy of the New Haven Museum & Historical Society, New Haven.

Page 2. "A Warrior with Poisoned Arrows," from Francis B. Spilsbury, *Account of a Voyage to the Western Coast of Africa; performed by His Majesty's sloop Favourite, in the year 1805* (London, 1807), facing p. 39, detail, courtesy of the Albert and Shirley Small Special Collections Library, University of Virginia.

Page 3. *Top*: Mende "booker" and cutlass, details from "African Farming Utensils," *Thompson in Africa; or, an Account of the Missionary Labors, Sufferings, Travels, and Observations of George Thompson in Western Africa, at the Mendi Mission* (Dayton, Ohio: Printed for the Author, 1857, ninth edition; orig. printed 1852), 208, collection of the author. *Middle*: Cane knife, from *A True History of the African Chief Jingua and his Comrades* (Hartford, 1839), courtesy of the Beneicke Rare Book and Manuscript Collection, Yale University. *Bottom*: Knives found in the New Haven jail, *New York Morning Herald*, November 9, 1839, courtesy of the New-York Historical Society.

Page 4. "Ports on the Western Coast of Africa by Captain Alexander T.E. Vidal, R.N., 1837, 38, 39," Admiralty Chart, Map Collections, detail, © The British Library Board, Maps SEC.11.(1690).

Page 5. *Top*: "Section of an Embarkation Canoe," Gallinas Coast, 1849, *The Illustrated London News*, April 14, 1849, 237, collection of the author. *Bottom*: *Description of a Slave Ship* (London, James Phillips, 1789), detail, courtesy of the Peabody-Essex Museum, Salem, Massachusetts.

Page 6. "The Portuguese slaver *Diligenté* captured by H. M. Sloop Pearl with 600 slaves on board. Taken in charge to Nassau by Lieut. Henry Hawker R.N. 1838," watercolor, courtesy of Michael Graham-Stewart.

Page 7. "Joseph Cinquez, Leader of the Gang of Negroes, who killed Captain Ramon Ferrers and the Cook, on board the Spanish Schooner Amistad, Captured by Lieutenant Gedney of the U.S. Brig Washington at Culloden Point, Long Island, August 24th 1839," detail, courtesy of the Stanley-Whitman House, Farmington, Connecticut.

Page 8. *Top*: "Little Kale," *Middle*: "Grabo" (Grabeau), *Bottom*: "Kimbo," all by William H. Townsend (1822–1851), Sketches of the Amistad captives, [ca. 1839–1840]. GEN MSS 335, courtesy of the Beneicke Rare Book and Manuscript Collection, Yale University.

Page 9. Playbill, "The Black Schooner or the Pirate Slaver Armistad!" Bowery Theatre, New York, 1839, courtesy of Harvard Theatre Collection, Houghton Library, Harvard University.

Page 10. "African Chief Jingua," from *A True History of the African Chief Jingua and his Comrades*, courtesy of the Beneicke Rare Book and Manuscript Collection, Yale University.

Page 11. *Top*: Cinqué, detail from "Death of Capt. Ferrer, the Captain of the Amistad, July, 1839" and portrait, both by John Warner Barber, *A History of the Amistad Captives* (New Haven: E.L. and J.W. Barber, 1839), courtesy of Marietta College Library. *Bottom*: Konoma, silhouette and detail from "Death of Capt. Ferrer, the Captain of the Amistad, July, 1839," both by John Warner Barber, *A History of the Amistad Captives*, courtesy of Marietta College Library.

Page 12. "The Murder of Jane McCrea" by John Vanderlyn, 1804, courtesy of Wadsworth Atheneum Museum of Art, Hartford, Connecticut/Art Resource, New York.

Page 13. "Horrid Massacre in Virginia," from Samuel Warner [compiler], *Authentic and impartial narrative of the tragical scene which was witnessed in Southampton County (Virginia) on Monday the 22d of August last when fifty-five of its inhabitants (mostly women and children) were inhumanly massacred by the blacks! Communicated by those who were eye witnesses of the bloody scene, and confirmed by the confessions of several of the blacks while under Sentence of Death* (New York: Warner & West, 1831), courtesy of the Library of Virginia.

Page 14. *Top*: Lewis Tappan, Manuscripts, Archives and Rare Books Division, Schomburg Center for Research in Black Culture, courtesy of the New York Public Library, Astor, Lenox and Tilden Foundations. *Bottom*: John Quincy Adams, courtesy of the Library of Congress.

Page 15. *Top*: Roger S. Baldwin, Print Collection, Miriam and Ira D. Wallace Division of Art, Prints and Photographs, courtesy of the New York Public Library, Astor, Lenox and Tilden Foundations. *Bottom*: Robert Purvis, daguerreotype, 1839, Rare Books Collection, courtesy of the Boston Public Library, Print Department.

Page 16. "Joseph Cinque" by Nathaniel Jocelyn, courtesy of the New Haven Museum & Historical Society, New Haven.

Title Page

Lower Deck, by John Warner Barber, *A History of the Amistad Captives*, courtesy of Marietta College Library.

In Chapter One

Page 14. "Fuli," Townsend Sketches, courtesy of the Beneicke Rare Book and Manuscript Collection, Yale University.

Page 15. "Marqu" (Margru), Townsend Sketches, courtesy of the Beneicke Rare Book and Manuscript Collection, Yale University.

Page 16. "Malhue" (Moru), Townsend Sketches, courtesy of the Beneicke Rare Book and Manuscript Collection, Yale University.

Page 50. "Slave Barracoon," Gallinas Coast, 1849, *The Illustrated London News*, April 14, 1849, 237, collection of the author.

Page 53. Views of a Slave Ship, *Thompson in Africa*, 19, collection of the author.

Page 54. Lower Deck, *Thompson in Africa*, 19, collection of the author.

In Chapter Three

Page 100. "Joseph Cinquez, Leader of the Piratical Gang of Negroes," by J. Sketchley for the *New York Sun*, 1839, lithograph by John Childs, detail, courtesy of the New Haven Museum & Historical Society, New Haven.

Page 101. "Joseph Cinquez, the brave Congolese Chief," for the *New York Sun*, 1839, detail, courtesy of the Library of Congress.

Page 102. "Joseph Cinquez Cinquez Addressing his Compatriots on board the Spanish Schooner AMISTAD 26th Augt 1839," lithograph by John Childs (likely after James Sketchley) for the *New York Sun*, detail, courtesy of the Chicago History Museum.

In Chapter Four

Page 131. "The Captured Africans of the Amistad: Teaching Philosophy to Lewis Tappen & Co. in the Prison at Hartford," *New York Morning Herald*, October 4, 1839, courtesy of the New York Historical Society.

In Chapter Five

Page 162. "Death of Capt. Ferrer, the Captain of the Amistad, July, 1839" by John Warner Barber, *A History of the Amistad Captives*, detail, courtesy of Marietta College Library.

Page 163. Details, "Death of Capt. Ferrer, the Captain of the Amistad, July, 1839" by John Warner Barber, *A History of the Amistad Captives*, courtesy of Marietta College Library.

Page 173. "Cinque: The Chief of the Amistad Captives," mezzotint by John Sartain, after a painting by Nathaniel Jocelyn, Philadelphia, Pennsylvania, 1840, courtesy of the Yale University Art Gallery.

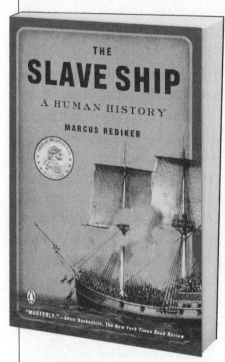